Found ... ion

ONE WEEK

Foundations of Special Education: An Introduction

By

Michael Farrell

WILEY-BLACKWELL

A John Wiley & Sons, Ltd., Publication

This edition first published 2009
© 2009 John Wiley & Sons, Ltd

Wiley-Blackwell is an imprint of John Wiley & Sons, formed by the merger of Wiley's global Scientific, Technical and Medical business with Blackwell Publishing.

Registered office
John Wiley & Sons Ltd, The Atrium, Southern Gate, Chichester, West Sussex, PO19 8SQ, UK

Editorial office
The Atrium, Southern Gate, Chichester, West Sussex, PO19 8SQ, UK
9600 Garsington Road, Oxford, OX4 2DQ, UK
350 Main Street, Malden, MA 02148-5020, USA

For details of our global editorial offices, for customer services and for information about how to apply for permission to reuse the copyright material in this book please see our website at www.wiley.com/wiley-blackwell.

The right of Michael Farrell to be identified as the author of this work has been asserted in accordance with the Copyright, Designs and Patents Act 1988.

Library of Congress Cataloging-in-Publication Data has been applied for

ISBN 978-0-470-75396-5 (hbk) 978-0-470-75397-2 (pbk)

A catalogue record for this book is available from the British Library.
Set in 10/12 pt Minion by Laserwords Private Limited, Chennai, India
Printed and bound in Singapore by Fabulous Printers Pte Ltd

1 2009

Contents

Preface	vii
Acknowledgements	xi
The Author	xiii

1	Components of Special Education	1
2	Legal/Typological	13
3	Terminological	39
4	Social	59
5	Medical	81
6	Neuropsychological	103
7	Psychotherapeutic	127
8	Behavioural/Observational	149
9	Developmental	169
10	Psycholinguistic	191
11	Technological	213
12	Pedagogical	235
13	Conclusion	259

Bibliography	271
Index	303

Preface

I hope this book will help readers seeking an introduction to the underpinning disciplines and perspectives that inform modern-day special education. It seeks to illustrate the wide-ranging contributions of these disciplines and how special education draws on them. This book aims to:

- help understanding special education by identifying its underpinning aspects;
- stimulate a reconsideration of training and support for special educators and others by indicating the complexity of the field of special education;
- encourage multi-disciplinary perspectives and working by indicating the range of disciplines involved in special education and how they contribute.

The first aim of the book is to aid the understanding of special education by identifying a wide range of underpinning aspects (e.g. medical, social, psychotherapeutic and pedagogical) that contribute to the field. These contributions include helping define special education, contributing to understand disability/disorder, informing educational approaches and contributing to provision directly. Legal underpinnings may help define special education. Developmental aspects such as research into typical child development may contribute to ways of understanding the development of children with cognitive impairment. Psycholinguistics can inform the classroom teaching of communication. Psychotherapeutic knowledge and skills are used in cognitive-behavioural therapy for conduct disorder. Consequently, to understand special education and make sense of its approaches and practice, an understanding of the contribution of its foundations is necessary.

The second aim is to encourage a reconsideration of training and support for special educators and others contributing to special education by indicating the complexity of special education. The book, it is hoped, demonstrates that special education is a somewhat complex and broad applied area of study and practice. This in turn suggests that teachers and others involved might benefit from extensive specialist study and training to ensure pupils with disability/disorder receive the best education and care. The book will not explicitly suggest a programme for such training and professional development. However, the contents of the book, it is hoped, will indicate some of the areas of study, knowledge and skills the special educator might need. It should also indicate the understandings of special education that those from different disciplines to education (speech pathologists, medical doctors, psychotherapists and others) might require if they are to have a broad view of special education.

A third purpose of this book, by indicating the contributions of various perspectives in a single volume, is to encourage all those concerned with special education to take a wider perspective than is sometimes the case. This applies to academics and professionals carrying out research as well as professionals connected with schools and clinics working with children with disability/disorder from day to day. It can be difficult for specialists in a single field related to special education such as neuropsychology or psycholinguistics to maintain an awareness of the value and contribution of other areas. Yet this is important. It can help place in context a particular area of specialist professional knowledge and skill so that one can see its contribution to the wider picture. This can indicate the strengths of a particular contribution as well as its limitations. Taking a wider perspective can also highlight the contribution of other disciplines and areas so that the perspectives of others can be better appreciated. Relatedly, it can help those involved with special education to develop more meaningful professional understandings, relationships and ways of working to benefit special children.

Accordingly, the book does the following:

- proposes various underpinning aspects of special education, such as legal, psychological and medical;
- explains how each underpinning aspect relates to special education;
- indicates the scope of each aspect to special education giving brief examples;
- explores fuller examples of the application of each underpinning aspect to special education generally or to a particular disability/disorder.

Intended readers include teachers and other professionals working with children and young people with disorders/disabilities and those who support them including university lecturers and researchers. The book will be suitable for those working in ordinary/mainstream and special schools or in clinics. It is hoped that readers will include those in Australia, New Zealand, the region of Southern Africa, the United States of America, Canada and the United Kingdom as well as those in China (Hong Kong) and Scandinavian countries.

The book could form a course textbook for students studying special education or teachers and other professionals following continuing professional development. School teachers, university lecturers, researchers, social workers, psychotherapists, psychologists, speech and language pathologists, medical and nursing personnel, physical therapists, technicians and related professionals should find the book a useful indication of the breadth of special education.

Specialists will of course be familiar with the content of the chapter that concerns their specialism, although if new to special education, they may not always be completely aware of its application. Also, they may not be as familiar with other areas covered by the book. It is hoped therefore that specialists will consult other chapters as an aid to multi-professional understanding and working.

If even a fraction of the knowledge and understanding to which the book points is required by special educators, it suggests an intensive, probably full time, post graduate training for them. It also brings into question whether it is reasonable to expect teachers in mainstream schools to develop the specialist knowledge and skills necessary for even one or two types of disability/disorder without such training and support.

It is important that special children receive education and support that enables them to progress and develop fully. Educators specializing in particular types of disability/disorder may best provide this education and support. They would also need to work corporately with colleagues with similar specialist understanding. Whether this requires a special school education will ultimately be determined, I believe, not by ideology from either supporters of mainstreaming or believers in some intrinsic value of special schools but by evidence of progress and development in different settings and using different approaches.

My own recent contributions to this debate includes, *Educating Special Children: An Introduction to Provision for Pupils with Disabilities and Disorders* (Routledge, 2008), *Key Issues in Special Education: Raising Pupils' Achievement and Attainment* (Routledge, 2005) and *Celebrating the Special School* (Routldge, 2006) (chapter on 'optimal education') which interested readers may also wish to consult.

Michael Farrell
Consultant in Special Education
United Kingdom
dr.m.j.farrell@btopenworld.com
www.drmjfarrell.co.uk

Acknowledgements

The author is most grateful to the following colleagues who commented on earlier drafts of the various chapters.

Chapter 2: Legal/Typological
Dr Tony Lingard, Director AWLED Consultancy, United Kingdom

Chapter 3: Terminological
Professor Lyndal Bullock, University of North Texas, United States of America

Chapter 4: Social
Professor Simo Vehmas, University of Jyvaskyla, Finland

Chapter 5: Medical
Dr Sally Stucke, Consultant Paediatrician, Herefordshire Primary Care Trust, United Kingdom

Chapter 6: Neuropsychological
Dr Andy Butterfill, Paediatric Consultant, Herefordshire County Hospital NHS Trust, United Kingdom

Chapter 7: Psychotherapeutic
Professor Peter Fonagy, University College London, United Kingdom

Chapter 8: Behavioural/Observational
Dr Michael Arthur-Kelly, University of Newcastle, New South Wales, Australia

Chapter 9: Developmental
Dr Kerry Dally, University of Newcastle, New South Wales, Australia

Chapter 10: Psycholinguistic
Professor Lisa Schoenbrodt, Department of Speech Pathology and Audiology, Loyola College, Maryland, United States of America

Chapter 11: Technological
Professor Trevor Kerry, Professor of Education and Leadership in the Centre for Educational Research and Development, and Emeritus Professor, University of Lincoln, United Kingdom

While the comments of these colleagues certainly strengthened the book, any shortcomings are entirely the author's responsibility. The author would also like to thank all the team at Wiley for their support.

The Author

Michael Farrell was educated in the United Kingdom. After training as a teacher at Bishop Grosseteste College, Lincoln, and obtaining an honours degree from Nottingham University, he obtained his master's degree in Education and Psychology from the Institute of Education, London University. Subsequently, he carried out research for his master of philosophy degree at the Institute of Psychiatry, Maudsley Hospital, London, and for his doctor of philosophy degree under the auspices of the Medical Research Council Cognitive Development Unit and London University.

Professionally, Michael Farrell worked as a head teacher, a lecturer at London University and as a local authority inspector. He managed a national psychometric project for City University, London, and directed a national project developing course structures and training materials for initial teacher training for the United Kingdom Government Department of Education.

His present work as a special education consultant includes policy development and training with local authorities, work with voluntary organizations and universities, support to schools in the private and maintained sectors and advice to government ministries.

Following are his books that are translated into European and Asian languages:

Standards and Special Educational Needs (Continuum, 2001)
The Special Education Handbook (3rd edition) (David Fulton, 2002)
Understanding Special Educational Needs: A Guide for Student Teachers (Routledge, 2003)
Special Educational Needs: A Resource for Practitioners (Sage, 2004)
Inclusion at the Crossroads: Concepts and Values in Special Education (David Fulton, 2004)
Key Issues in Special Education: Raising Pupils' Achievement and Attainment (Routledge, 2005)
The Effective Teacher's Guide to Dyslexia and Other Specific Learning Difficulties (Routledge, 2005)

The Effective Teacher's Guide to Moderate, Severe and Profound Learning Difficulties (Routledge, 2005)

The Effective Teacher's Guide to Autism and Communication Difficulties (Routledge, 2005)

The Effective Teacher's Guide to Sensory Impairment and Physical Disabilities (Routledge, 2005)

The Effective Teacher's Guide to Behavioural, Emotional and Social Difficulties (Routledge, 2005)

Celebrating the Special School (David Fulton, 2006)

The Special School's Handbook: Key Issues for All (Routledge/NASEN, 2007)

Educating Special Children: An introduction to provision for pupils with disabilities and disorders (Routledge, 2008).

1

Components of Special Education

Foundations of Special Education considers disciplines and perspectives under-pinning special education. This chapter defines special education and elaborates components of the definition.

The contents of subsequent chapters are then explained.

Special Education Defined

The United States Department of Education has defined special education as, 'specially designed instruction . . . to meet the unique needs of a child with a disability' (United States Department of Education, 1999, pp. 124–125). However, it may be argued that special education is broader than instruction, and that the term 'provision' better captures what is offered. Other features of special education may also be included in a broader definition. Accordingly, a proposed definition of special education is suggested in the box below that informs the approach of this book.

Special education refers to distinctive provision, including education, for pupils with disability/disorder. It is informed by a range of foundational disciplines, and encourages academic progress and personal and social development. Special education has identifiable aims and methods.

This requires further elaboration of the following terms:

- education
- disability/disorder

- provision
- distinctive
- foundational disciplines
- academic progress and personal and social development.

It also calls for 'aims and methods' to be identified and explained. The following sections cover these points.

Education

Education is defined as, ' . . . the process of giving or receiving systematic instruction' (Soanes and Stevenson, 2003), and to educate someone is to provide, ' . . . intellectual, moral and social instruction' (ibid.). It can be seen that education concerns not just intellectual progress but also social and personal development. Also, instruction is only one way of teaching, and other aspects of pedagogy include: modelling, questioning, and task structuring (Tharp, 1993, pp. 271–272).

Education implies that ' . . . something worthwhile is being or has been intentionally transmitted in a morally acceptable manner' (Peters, 1966). What is considered worthwhile may change over time and differs in various cultures. A general statement of what might be 'worthwhile' could be that it is the skills, knowledge, attitudes and values that a society endorses (Farrell *et al.*, 1995, p. 70). The 'intentional' aspect of Peters' definition distinguishes education from incidental learning and suggests that education involves structured experiences aimed at facilitating learning. The 'morally acceptable manner' element of education concerns the process by which worthwhile content is transmitted. Education implies freedom to consider differing views and information, and coming to a reasoned conclusion. It differs in this respect from indoctrination although the two are not always as easily separable as might at first appear (ibid., pp. 70–71).

Education leads to change. It has been suggested that to be educated, implies that, the individual, ' . . . has been changed by the experience of education in terms of behaviors towards others, ability to understand the world (or aspects of it) and an ability to do things in the world'. Furthermore, the transformation is, ' . . . integrally related to the concepts of knowledge and understanding' (Barrow and Woods, 1982).

Types of Disability/Disorder

Types of disability/disorder are discussed in the present volume in the chapter 'Legal/Typological' and are considered more extensively elsewhere (Farrell, 2008b). They are as follows:

- profound cognitive impairment
- moderate to severe cognitive impairment
- mild cognitive impairment
- hearing impairment
- visual impairment
- deafblindness
- orthopaedic impairment and motor disorder
- health impairment
- traumatic brain injury
- disruptive behaviour disorders (including conduct disorder)
- anxiety disorders and depressive disorders
- attention deficit hyperactivity disorder
- communication disorders (speech, grammar, comprehension, semantics and pragmatics)
- autism
- developmental coordination disorder
- reading disorder
- disorder of written expression
- mathematics disorder.

Recognising types of disability/disorder implies that they can be justified as a way of slicing up reality. This is debated more with regard to some types of disorder/disability (e.g. attention deficit hyperactivity disorder) than with others (e.g. profound cognitive impairments) (Farrell, 2008b, Chapter 1 and passim). Also recognising different types of disability/disorder implies some means of identification.

This may involve the application of criteria such as those set out for some disorders/disabilities in the *Diagnostic and Statistical Manual of Mental Disorders Fourth Edition Text Revision (DSM-IV-TR)* (American Psychiatric Association, 2000). It may include paediatric screening or reference to some agreed benchmark of typical development. Detailed assessment of the child and of the impact of the disability/disorder enables parents, teachers and others to begin to recognize possible implications for learning and development.

Provision

Provision that promotes the learning and development of special children was the subject of the book, *Educating Special Children* (Farrell, 2008b). Elements of provision discussed in that volume are as follows:

- curriculum
- pedagogy
- school and classroom organization
- resources
- therapy.

Doll (1996, p.15) defines the curriculum as, 'the formal and informal content and process by which learners gain knowledge and understanding, develop skills, and alter attitudes, appreciations and values under the auspices of that school'. The present book sees the curriculum less as 'process' and more as the content of what is taught and learned. This includes the aims and objectives of teaching and learning, and the design and structure of what is taught in relation to areas of learning and programmes within those areas. The curriculum may be envisaged and organized by subjects (e.g. mathematics and art) or areas (e.g. communication and personal education). Relatedly, aspects are sometimes considered as permeating the whole curriculum such as literacy, numeracy, computer skills and problem solving skills. The curriculum may differ in various ways. The levels of all subjects or some may be lower than age typical. The balance of subjects and areas of the curriculum may be atypical. The balance of components of subjects could be atypical. The content of certain areas of the curriculum may be different from those for most children. Finally, assessment may be different perhaps involving small steps to indicate progress in areas of difficulty (Farrell, 2008b, Chapter 1).

'Pedagogy' refers to what the teacher does, in the classroom and elsewhere, to promote and encourage pupils' learning. It may involve individualized learning, group work, discussion, audiovisual approaches, whole class teaching and other approaches (Farrell *et al.*, 1995, p. 4). Pedagogy includes the teacher emphasizing certain sensory modalities in presenting information or the teacher encouraging the pupil to use particular senses. A child who is blind may write in Braille requiring interpretation by touch rather than sight.

Pedagogy may involve approaches distinctive to a particular disability/disorder such as, for children with autism, 'Structured Teaching' (Schopler, 1997). On the other hand, pedagogy may emphasize approaches used also with children who do not have a disorder/disability, for example, slower lesson pace for pupils with mild cognitive impairment. Such teaching may be regarded as representing greater adaptation, but essentially being 'more intensive and explicit' examples of approaches used with all children (Lewis and Norwich, 2005, pp. 5–6). However, it is recognized that teaching intended for pupils with learning difficulties could be 'inappropriate for average or high attaining pupils' (ibid., p. 6).

School organization may involve flexible arrival and departure times for lessons, for example, for some pupils with orthopaedic impairment. Consideration is also given to organizational aspects relating to safety. Flexible arrangements for pupil absences from school can include home tuition and e-mailed work supporting home study. Classroom organization for pupils with disability/disorder may be different from that for most children. For pupils with profound or severe cognitive impairment, it may draw on room management approaches (Lacey, 1991). Regarding a pupil with hearing impairment, the classroom may be organized to optimize his seeing other speakers to help lip reading.

Resources can include aspects of school building design such as those aiding access for pupils with orthopaedic impairment. Classroom design embraces available space, lighting, acoustics, and potential distractions and facilitators to learning. Furniture adaptations include adjustable tables and adapted seating. Among physical/sensory aids, equipment such as alternative keyboards and tracker balls can be adapted. Computer technology can enable links to be made between the child's behaviour and what happens in the environment. Resources also include those for augmentative communication (involving ways to augment partially intelligible speech) and alternative communication (other than speech or writing) (Bigge; Stump *et al.*, 1999, p. 130). Cognitive aids include computer software encouraging responses; symbols used for communication; and computer programmes breaking tasks into very small steps.

'Therapy' may refer to provision intended to help promote skills and abilities or well being. For children and young people with disabilities/disorders, these may include elements that are predominantly physical (e.g. aspects of occupational therapy and physiotherapy); psychological (e.g. psychotherapy); communicative (e.g. speech and language therapy); and medical (e.g. drugs). Therapy and aspects of care are intended to lead to changes in behaviour, attitudes and self-valuing, similar to some of the aspirations of education. They are in this broad sense educational.

Distinctive

What is distinctive about provision, including education, for special children? In seeking to tackle this question, Lewis and Norwich (2005) consider the following:

- needs common to all children
- needs specific to a particular group
- needs unique to individual children.

They focus on the second and third positions listed above, considering a 'general difference position' (concerning the group-specific needs of pupils with different types of disability/disorder) and a 'unique differences position'.

In the *general difference* position, 'group-specific needs' of pupils with disability/disorder are brought to the fore although needs common to all learners and needs unique to individual learners remain important (Lewis and Norwich, 2005, pp. 3–4). The *unique difference* position de-emphasizes the common pedagogic needs of all children, emphasizes unique differences of pupils and rejects group-specific needs. Favouring a unique difference position, Lewis and Norwich (2005) suggest that with regard to 'pedagogic *principles*' (p. 216, italics added) that, 'the traditional special needs categories . . . have limited usefulness in the context of planning, or monitoring, teaching and learning in most areas' (p. 220).

Contrary to this, this book maintains that a 'group difference position' can be maintained for all types of disability/disorder with regard to profiles of provision including pedagogy. That is, it is possible to identify distinctive provision effective with different types of disability/disorder. This is discussed in this book in the chapter 'Pedagogy' and more fully in the book *Educating Special Children* (Farrell, 2008b).

Foundations of Special Education

The foundations of special education as presented in this book are the underpinning aspects of contemporary special education. These contribute to the understanding and practice of special education and to provision for different types of disability/disorder. For example, 'psychotherapeutic' underpinnings have particular relevance for pupils with disorders of conduct. However, they may have relevance for other types of disability/disorder, and provision for pupils with conduct disorder may be informed by other disciplines. This book examines 11 foundational areas:

- legal/typological
- terminological
- social
- medical
- neuropsychological
- psychotherapeutic
- behavioural/observational
- developmental
- psycholinguistic
- technological
- pedagogical.

A chapter is devoted to each foundational discipline, in which examples are given of how it provides insights or practical contributions to special education generally and in relation to particular disabilities and disorders. Aspects of these foundations are selected for their relevance to modern day developments and linked to special educational issues, illuminating both.

Academic Progress and Personal and Social Development

Like education generally, special education implies that what is provided enhances learning and development. Academic progress includes progress in school subjects such as mathematics/numeracy, science or art as well as progress in areas of the curriculum like problem solving skills, computer skills or communication. Personal and social development refers to the wide range of development that education seeks to encourage such as personal and social skills, high self-esteem and concern for others.

Where special education is effective, progress in learning and personal and social development are encouraged. There may be times when pupils do not progress and develop, perhaps because of a debilitating illness. Here the aspiration might be to maintain levels of current functioning or to slow the rate of deterioration. The importance of academic progress and personal and social development is discussed more fully in *Standards and Special Educational Needs* (Farrell, 2001b) and in *Key Issues in Special Education* (Farrell, 2005f).

The Aims and Methods of Special Education

Aims The aims of special education, with regard to pupils with disability/disorder, include the following:

- identifying and assessing pupils with disability/disorder and evaluating whether the disability/disorder is likely to hinder learning and development;
- identifying the distinctive provision that best promotes learning and development;
- identifying foundational disciplines that contribute to promoting learning and development;
- ensuring that elements of provision informed by these foundations promote learning and development.

Methods Many methods already in use aid the learning and development of pupils with disability/disorder, for example, tactile approaches for pupils who are blind and behavioural strategies for children with conduct disorder. Such methods may be kept under review to ensure they are benefiting the pupil as expected.

Where newer promising methods are tried, these may be observed, carefully described and analysed to identify which aspects are important and effective. Attempts are made to explain why the approach works and to generalize from particular examples to wider applications and from a small number of pupils to more pupils. Hypotheses may be formed relating to such findings. These may be tested and evaluated leading to accounts of evidence-based practice. Methodology can therefore range from observation and description used for critical reflection (induction) to hypotheses and theory (deduction).

For example, for *reading disorder*, strategies that are used often relate to purported underlying difficulties such as phonological difficulties or visual difficulties. As well as working on associated difficulties, interventions directly tackle reading. This often involves teaching phonological skills necessary for using a phonemic code, and sound–symbol correspondences (Swanson *et al.*, 2003). Where an intervention involves using a phonemic code and sound–symbol correspondences, the implementation of the approach will be observed and described as accurately as possible. Attempts will be made to explain which elements appear successful, aiming to ensure that the approach will work for other pupils with reading disorder (or at least for some of them).

Based on this information, a hypothesis is framed. This might be, 'for pupils with reading disorder, where the main difficulty appears to be phonological (perhaps a phonological deficit), the use of a specified phonic based intervention will enhance progress'. This might be made even more precise. 'For pupils with reading disorder, where the main difficulty appears to be phonological, the use of a specified phonic based intervention for ten minutes per day for 2 months will lead to a four month gain in measured reading ability'. This could be expressed more accurately by specifying the particular programme and any adaptations to the curriculum and assessment, pedagogy or other aspects of provision.

In the United States, an enactment of the *No Child Left Behind Act 2002* is that all students including those with disabilities will demonstrate annual yearly progress and perform at a proficient level on state academic assessment tests. Identifying scientific methods and evidence-based practices can contribute to this aspiration; but identifying, implementing and evaluating a range of valid, effective practices is challenging. Also, families and professionals have to decide on the suitability of an intervention or approach for a particular child looking at various options.

Simpson (2005), while considering autism, makes observations relevant to disability/disorder more generally. Ideally evidence will involve peer review and the validation of products and materials through research designs using random samples and control and experimental groups (ibid., pp. 141–142, paraphrased). However, other methods may be appropriate in different circumstances because of 'limited student samples, heterogeneous clinical education programmes, and the need for flexibility in matching research designs to specific questions and issues . . . ' (ibid., p. 142). Alternatives might include single-subject design validation or correlational methods.

Parents and professionals will want to know about the efficacy and anticipated outcomes in connection with a particular practice. They will need to know whether anticipated outcomes are in line with student needs; the potential risks (including risks to family cohesion of long term very intensive interventions); and the most effective means of evaluation (ibid., p. 143, paraphrased). Evidence-based practice can inform decisions but these are also influenced by professional judgement and the views of the child and family.

A further method in special education is to consider disciplines and perspectives underpinning it, critically examining their relevance for understanding and practice. This is the subject of this book. For example, the foundational discipline of medicine may be related to special education through consideration of the classifications and procedures for seizures and epilepsy, the implications of traumatic brain injury and the use of medication for attention deficit hyperactivity disorder. Developmental perspectives relating to typically

...veloping infants may inform provision for older pupils with profound cognitive impairment.

Structure of the Book

Beyond this introductory chapter, this book comprises 11 chapters, each concerning an underpinning aspect of contemporary special education; a conclusion chapter, a bibliography and a combined author and subject index. Each chapter indicates the contribution of the underpinning aspect (e.g. 'social', 'developmental') to special education. This might be in terms of understanding or provision. At the end of each chapter, the section 'Thinking Points' gives pointers to continuing reflection and discussion. A list of sources of further information including books and Internet sites provide further signposts.

The contents of each chapter are as follows.

Chapter 2, 'Legal/Typological', briefly looks at social, political and economic factors informing the context of special education legislation. It outlines recent legislation informing special education in the United States and in the United Kingdom. The chapter describes the main types of disability/disorder, drawing on classifications used in systems in the United States, the United Kingdom and other sources.

Following this, Chapter 3, 'Terminological', indicates the importance of terminology in special education, and illustrates its scope. In particular it examines the 'needs', 'discrimination' and 'rights'.

Chapter 4, 'Social', considers a social constructionist perspective, setting the context by first looking at individual models and other approaches. A social view of disability is considered with particular reference to hearing impairment and orthopaedic impairments.

Next, Chapter 5, 'Medical', considers the scope of the application of medical perspectives and the use of drugs in relation to children with disability/disorder. It focuses on epilepsy, attention deficit hyperactivity disorder and traumatic brain injury.

Chapter 6, 'Neuropsychological', describes some of the techniques used in neurological research and some uses of psychological and related tests in neuropsychology. It considers, in particular, reading disorder, mathematics disorder and developmental coordination disorder.

Following this, Chapter 7, 'Psychotherapeutic', outlines the systems, psycho-dynamic and cognitive-behavioural approaches. It discusses, in particular, cognitive-behavioural therapy in relation to disorders of conduct, anxiety disorders and depressive disorders.

Chapter 8, 'Behavioural/Observational', considers behavioural approaches to learning with reference to learning theory and looks at observational learning and modelling through social cognitive theory. Learning theory and observational learning/modelling are considered together in their application to conduct disorder and autism.

In Chapter 9, 'Developmental', the main focus is Piaget's theory of genetic epistemology. It examines elements of Piaget and Inhelder's work relevant to contemporary special education and considers implications of Piaget's sensory-motor period for provision for children with profound cognitive impairment.

After this, Chapter 10, 'Psycholinguistics' explores a framework incorporating input processing, lexical representations and output processing, and interventions. Consideration is given to persisting speech difficulties and to specific language impairment.

Chapter 11, 'Technological', explores how technology constitutes a foundation of special education through its enhancement of teaching and learning. It examines the use of technology for visual impairment; orthopaedic/motor impairments and speech disorder. The use of technology to support pupils with challenging behaviour is also considered.

Chapter 12, 'Pedagogical', examines pedagogy in relation to special education, in particular the issue of distinctive pedagogy for different types of disability/disorder. The focus is mild cognitive impairment and moderate to severe cognitive impairment.

The 'Conclusion' draws threads together and suggests implications for future developments.

Thinking Points

Readers may wish to consider the following:

- the extent to which special education is helpfully defined according to 'provision', 'types of disability/disorder', 'academic progress and personal and social development', and 'foundational disciplines';

- how suitable are the aims and methods of special education that have been suggested.

Key Texts

Farrell, M. (2005) *Key Issues in Special Education: Raising Pupils' Achievement and Attainment*. New York/London: Routledge.

This book argues that raising the standards of educational achievement and encouraging better personal and social development can guide many aspects of special education, from identification and assessment to funding and provision. It uses the England context to illustrate this.

Farrell, M. (2004) *Special Education Handbook* (3rd edn). London: David Fulton.

This book gives the definitions of concepts in special education and related information about the curriculum, resources, pedagogy and other matters.

Farrell, M. (2008) *Educating Special Children: An Introduction to Provision for Pupils with Disabilities and Disorders*. New York/London: Routledge.

This book sets out the provision associated with various disorders/disabilities in terms of curriculum, pedagogy, school and classroom organization, resources and therapy/care.

2

Legal/Typological

Introduction

The legal framework in which special education operates within a particular country shapes the way special education is seen. Within this context, typology of the way types of disorder/difficulty may be understood further informs views of special education.

This chapter touches on the social, political and economic factors that inform the context of special education legislation. It then outlines main threads of special education legislation in the United States and (more briefly to avoid repetition) in the United Kingdom. Next, the chapter describes the main types of disability/disorder, drawing on classifications used in systems in the United States and the United Kingdom. These tend to be shaped by legal requirements and subsequent guidance or are otherwise widely agreed.

Social, Political and Economic Contexts of Legal Structures

As social, political and economic factors that influence special education work together, it is sometimes difficult to separate them from one another. Social values and attitudes towards special education change over time and vary in different places. In the late 1900s and into the early twenty-first century, the term 'social inclusion' was widely used and argued for in some circles. People with disabilities were sometimes represented from a social perspective as 'oppressed' (Abberley, 1987). In the field of education and special education, this idea of oppression was linked with the notion that such oppression and subordination could be met by 'resistance', leading to emancipation (Armstrong, 2003). In some quarters, inclusion was equated with educational mainstreaming. Quite early, however, it was suggested that arguments founded on social views of disability were often related to physical disabilities and that the education and provision for those with cognitive impairments and others were 'marginalized' (MacKay, 2002, p. 161). Subsequently, the perspective that special schools can offer entirely appropriate education for some children began to be articulated again (Warnock, 2006, preface). The case for good special schools where children and young people made better educational progress and developed better personally and socially was also argued (Farrell, 2006, passim).

Political factors include the general political climate, whether liberal or conservative. A tendency for greater accountability, however that might be interpreted, tends to be associated with conservative cycles of government. Lobby groups can also exert political influence for increased funds in redistributive societies, especially where there is a lack of regional or local agreement about what constitutes different disabilities/disorders. This may be a factor in the increasing recognition (and apparent greater prevalence) of conditions such as dyslexia/reading disorder and autistic spectrum disorder in the late twentieth century and after (Farrell, 2004a, pp. 62–65).

Economic influences are reflected in national and local responsibilities. In the United States, one of the programmes administered by the Office of Special Education Programmes (OSEP) in the Department of Education is the Individuals with Disabilities Education Act (IDEA) Part B State Grant Programme for Children with Disabilities. Under this, funds are allocated to states to reflect the total numbers of students with disabilities receiving special education and related services. A minimum of three quarters of the funding that the states receive in this way has to be passed on to local educational agencies and intermediate educational units to help in educating students with disabilities. Accountability procedures for such funding include on-site monitoring reviews by a team from the US Department of Education (Ysseldyke and Algozzine, 2006a, p. 14).

In a more practical sense, economic, social and political decisions of a kind are made in the day-to-day work of a school. The political and social views of staff and parents have a bearing on the way the school is organized. Economic decisions taken at school level reflect different priorities of different schools. More broadly, it is such interrelated social, political and economic factors that form the context in which special education legislation is conceived, shaped and implemented.

Special Education Law in the United States

(a) Main legislation

In the United States, federal laws enacted since the 1970s have shaped the nature of provision for pupils with disabilities and disorders. These, in conjunction with the equal protection clause of the US Constitution and court cases and decisions, have helped shape the face of modern special educational provision (Ysseldyke and Algozzine, 2006a, p. 53). For example, the US Supreme Court has determined that schools must provide straightforward medical procedures that the school nurse can administer (ibid., p. 48). The full citation for the main special education laws in the United States in chronological order is as follows:

- Rehabilitation Act, Public Law No. 93-112, 87 Stat. 357 (1973);
- Education for All Handicapped Children Act, Public Law No. 94-142, 89 Stat. 773 (1975);
- Amendments to the Education for All Handicapped Children Act, Public Law No. 99-457,100 Stat. 1145 (1986);
- Individuals with Disabilities Education Act, Public Law No. 101-476, 104 Stat. 1141 (1990);
- Amendments to the Individuals with Disabilities Education Act, Public Law No. 105-17 (1997);
- Individuals with Disabilities Education Improvement Act, Public Law No. 108-446 (2004);
- No Child Left Behind Act, Public Law No. 107-110, 115 Stat. 1425 (2001).

(b) The Education for All Handicapped Children Act 1975 and amendments

Before the *Education for All Handicapped Children Act 1975*, an important piece of legislation was the *Rehabilitation Act 1973* (section 504). This section, adopted in 1977, made it illegal to discriminate against a person with a disability exclusively because of that disability, for example, by denying participation in activities. This applies to programmes or activities 'receiving federal financial assistance'. Those with disabilities have to be given equal opportunity including architectural accessibility to services and programmes. Also, 'auxiliary aids' (such as readers for pupils who are blind and interpreters for students who are deaf) need to be provided for individuals with impairments in speaking, sensory or manual skills, where they would otherwise be excluded.

A landmark was the *Education for All Handicapped Children Act 1975* (Public Law 94-142). Under this, students aged 3 through 21 years with disabilities have the right to free, appropriate public education (FAPE). Any assessments used to determine the nature of the student's disabilities must be racially and culturally fair. The student has to be educated in the 'least restrictive' educational environment in that students are removed from general education environments only when a disability is so severe that such classes and the use of supplementary aids are not effective. Parents have rights to inspect the school records on their child; to receive prior written notice if changes are made to the student's educational placement or programmes; and to challenge both information held in the records and any changes in placement. Schools have to keep an individualized education programme for the student involving assessment by a multidisciplinary team.

In 1986, amendments (Public Law 99-457) to the *Education for All Handicapped Children Act 1975* extended the rights set out under that act to preschool children with disabilities. Regarding these children, each school district was required to carry out a multidisciplinary assessment and draw up an 'individualized family service plan'.

(c) The Individuals with Disabilities Education Act 1990 and amendments/reauthorization

Among the provisions of the IDEA 1990 (Public Law 101-476) was the addition of the categories of 'traumatic brain injury' and 'autism' to the previously defined categories of disability. The IDEA 1990 replaced references to 'handicapped children' with 'children with disabilities'. The act also states that students with disabilities should have access to assistive technology equipment and related services.

In 1997, amendments (Public Law 105-17) to the IDEA 1990 included requiring the states to report on the progress of all students. It aimed at increasing the participation of parents in the process of re-evaluation, placement decisions and programme planning for students with disabilities. Changes were made to requirements for the composition of the Individual Education Programme team to ensure that people with necessary expertise were included.

Included in the provisions of the *Individuals with Disabilities Education Improvement Act 2004* (House Bill 1350) was that students with disabilities be taught by teachers holding full certification in special education or who have passed a state teacher licensing examination and hold a state licence. Special education teachers teaching towards alternative achievement standards, in particular, core academic subjects, must be certified in both the subject in question and in special education. Transition planning must be focused on results. For students who have disability problems and are homeless or are wards of the court, schools must appoint a parent surrogate.

(d) The No Child Left Behind Act 2001 and developments

In 2001, the earlier Elementary and Secondary Education Act (ESEA) was reauthorized, to be known as the *No Child Left Behind Act* (Public Law 107-110) and enacting that provision in the ESEA applied to all students including those with disabilities. It provided for literacy interventions ('Early Reading First' and 'Reading First') and gave an entitlement to supplementary education services. Greater accountability and a focus on proven educational methods were included. A subsequent rewriting of the Act further strengthened accountability.

Special Education Law in England

(a) Main legislation

In England, there are legislative developments parallel to those in the United States. A few among the main legislation are as follows:

- The Education Act 1981;
- The Education Act 1993;
- Disability Discrimination Act 1995;
- The Special Educational Needs and Discrimination Act 2001.

(b) The Education Act 1981

Under section 1 of the Education Act 1981, the previously used ten statutory categories of handicap were replaced by a generic definition of special educational needs (SEN). Special educational provision was defined as 'additional to or otherwise different from' that generally provided for children of the same age by the local authority concerned. Provided certain conditions were met, children with a 'statement' of SEN were to be educated in ordinary schools.

Parents' views were to be taken into account. Education in ordinary school was to be compatible with

- the child receiving the special educational provision required;
- the provision of efficient education for other children;
- the resources being used efficiently.

Children with SEN must engage in the 'activities of the school together with children who do not have special educational needs' provided the three conditions listed are met and it is 'reasonably practicable'. In assessing the child, the local education authority is required by regulations to seek medical, psychological and educational advice.

(c) The Education Act 1993

The Education Act 1993 sought to improve the system of provision for children with SEN, building on the principles established by the Education Act 1981. Parents of children with a statement of SEN are given rights to have their say in the education of the child and to express a preference for the maintained (publicly funded) school that their child should attend. More emphasis was placed on children who had SEN but who did not require a statement. However, the act also strengthened the system for pupils requiring statements and for their parents. It introduced a 'Code of Practice' (Department for Education and Skills, 2001b) containing guidance and criteria for the identification and assessment of children with SEN, to which schools have to 'have regard' when dealing with such pupils. The act reaffirmed the principle that pupils should be educated in mainstream schools whenever it is possible and sensible to do so.

(d) The Special Educational Needs and Disability Act 2001

The Special Educational Needs and Disability Act 2001 (SENDA) amended some earlier acts (the Disability Discrimination Act 1995, the Education Act 1994 and other acts) and made further provision against discrimination on the grounds of disability in schools and other educational establishments.

Part 1 strengthened the right of a child with SEN to be educated in the mainstream unless this is incompatible with the wishes of his parents or the provision of efficient education for other children. The local education authority has to show that there are no reasonable steps they could take to prevent the incompatibility.

Part 2 imposes a duty on local education authorities not to treat a pupil wi
disabilities less favourably for a reason relating to the person's disability tha
someone to whom that reason does not apply, without justification. A furthei
duty is to make reasonable adjustments to admission arrangements and,
regarding education and related services, to make sure pupils with disabilities
are not put at a disadvantage in comparison with peers with no disabilities
without justification.

Some General Points

The legislation considered in the United States and in the United Kingdom
in recent years has several themes. It has sought to discourage discrimination
against pupils with disability/disorder when compared with other pupils unless
this can be justified. It has tried to increase opportunities for pupils with
disability/disorder to be educated in ordinary schools rather than in special
schools or elsewhere as long as certain conditions are met. It has indicated
where different professionals need to work closely together, for example, in
assessing the child.

Legislation and related regulations and guidance have sought to provide a
structure of identification and assessment for children with disability/disorder
to ensure they receive suitable provision. This last point leads to the question of
identifying types of disability/disorder. In the United States, such types are listed
under 'disability codes'. In England, although it appears at first examination
that legislation has discouraged such classifications, in fact they are extensively
used. For example, classifications are an integral part of the guidance to schools
on data collection (Department for Education and Skills, 2005, passim).

Types of Disability/Disorder

Regarding disability/disorder, classification systems have developed in many
countries. Typologies of any kind are based on certain assumptions about
such matters as common features within the classification and its usefulness.
For a discussion of some of these matters, *Educating Special Children* (Farrell,
2008) can be referred to, which also gives fuller descriptions of the types of
disability/disorder described subsequently and information about associated
provision.

In the United States, pupils considered to need special education covered
by federal law have a defined 'disability' and are considered to need special

education because their disability has an adverse educational impact. Categories of disability under federal law as amended in 1997 (20 United States Code 1402, 1997) reflected in subsequent 'designated disability codes' are as follows:

01. mentally retarded (mild, moderate, severe, profound)
02. hard of hearing
03. deaf
04. speech and language impaired
05. visually handicapped
06. emotionally disturbed
07. orthopaedically impaired
08. other health impaired
09. specific learning disability
10. multi-handicapped
11. child in need of assessment
12. deaf/blind
13. traumatic brain injury
14. autism.

In England, a similar classification (Department for Education and Skills, 2005, passim) comprises the following:

- learning difficulty (moderate, severe and profound)
- hearing impairment
- speech, language and communication needs
- visual impairment
- behavioural, emotional and social difficulty
- physical disability
- specific learning difficulties (e.g. dyslexia, dyscalculia and dyspraxia)
- multisensory impairment
- autistic spectrum disorder.

In the American system, 'mental retardation' is broadly equivalent to the English classification of 'learning difficulties' (moderate, severe or profound) (for further comparisons of US and English classifications, see Farrell, 2001, pp. 1–5).

The terms used in the present book, which draws on terminology in the systems used in the United States and in England and on professional usage, are as follows:

- profound cognitive impairment
- moderate to severe cognitive impairment

- mild cognitive impairment
- hearing impairment
- visual impairment
- deafblindness
- orthopaedic impairment and motor disorder
- health impairment
- traumatic brain injury (TBI)
- disruptive behaviour disorders (including conduct disorder)
- anxiety disorders and depressive disorders
- attention deficit hyperactivity disorder (ADHD)
- communication disorders (speech, grammar, comprehension, semantics and pragmatics)
- autism
- developmental coordination disorder
- reading disorder
- disorder of written expression
- mathematics disorder.

Each of these is described in the remainder of the present chapter.

Profound Cognitive Impairment

Profound cognitive impairment is an equivalent term for 'profound mental retardation'. In the *Diagnostic and Statistical Manual of Mental Disorders Fourth Edition Text Revision* (*DSM-IV-TR*) (American Psychiatric Association, 2000, p. 42) profound mental retardation is defined according to limitations in both intellectual functioning and adaptive behaviour. It is associated with an intelligence quotient (IQ) range of below 20 or 25 although IQ levels are not the sole criterion and are interpreted with care. Most children with profound mental retardation have an 'identified neurological condition' accounting for their present state of health (p. 44). Impairments of sensory neural function are evident in early childhood. The diagnostic criteria for mental retardation also include more broadly 'co current deficits or impairments in present adaptive functioning . . . in at least two of the following areas: communication, self care, home living, social/interpersonal skills, use of community resources, self-direction, functional academic skills, work, leisure, health and safety' (p. 49).

A description of pupils with 'profound and multiple learning difficulties' provided in government guidance in England states that these pupils have

' . . . severe and complex needs' and ' . . . other significant difficulties, such as physical disabilities or a sensory impairment'. Furthermore, 'Pupils require a high level of support, both for their learning needs and for their personal care. They are likely to need sensory stimulation and a curriculum broken down into very small steps. Some pupils communicate by gesture, eye pointing or symbols, others by very simple language . . . '. The guidance adds that, throughout their school careers, the attainments of these students are likely to remain in a range typified by the lowest levels of widely used 'performance scales' ('P-scales') that is below a level expected of a typically developing child at the age of 5 or 6 years (Qualifications and Curriculum Authority, 2001a, 2001b, 2001c and later amendments).

Moderate to Severe Cognitive Impairment

Moderate to severe cognitive impairment equates to moderate to severe mental retardation as described in *DSM-IV-TR* (American Psychiatric Association, 2000, p. 42). *DSM-IV-TR* relates 'moderate retardation' to IQ levels of 35/40 to 50/55. 'Severe retardation' is associated with IQ levels of 20/25 to 35/40. Consequently, the range for moderate to severe cognitive impairment is of IQ levels from 20/25 to 50/55. These ranges are treated with care, IQ not being the sole criterion. The diagnostic criteria for mental retardation also include 'co current deficits or impairments in present adaptive functioning . . . in at least two of the following areas: communication, self care, home living, social/interpersonal skills, use of community resources, self-direction, functional academic skills, work, leisure, health and safety' (p. 49). Most people with *moderate* mental retardation acquire communication skills in early childhood. With some supervision, they 'can attend to their personal care' (p. 43). While benefiting from training in social and occupational skills, they are 'unlikely to progress beyond second-grade level in academic subjects' (p. 43). Individuals with *severe* mental retardation tend to acquire little or no communicative speech in early childhood but during the school age may learn to talk and can learn 'elementary self care skills' (p. 43). They profit to a limited degree from teaching in 'pre-academic subjects' such as 'simple counting' and can master skills such as sight-reading some survival words.

In England, 'severe learning difficulties' broadly correspond in IQ terms to the American 'moderate mental retardation' and 'severe mental retardation', that is, an IQ range of 20/25 to 50/55 (Kushlick and Blunden, 1974). Guidance published by the Department for Education and Skills (DfES, 2005,

p. 6)(www.dfes.gov.uk/sen) states that pupils with severe learning difficulties have 'significant intellectual or cognitive impairments'. It continues thus: 'This has a major effect on their ability to participate in the school curriculum without support. They may also have difficulties with mobility and co-ordination, communication and perception and the acquisition of self help skills'. They ' . . . will need support in all areas of the curriculum. They may also require teaching of self-help, independence and social skills. Some pupils may use sign and symbols but most will be able to hold simple conversations and gain some literacy skills. Their attainments will be within the upper P-scale range for much of their school careers (that is below level 1 of the National Curriculum)' (pp. 3–4). This indicates that pupils with severe learning difficulties will, for most of their schooling, be working below a level (level 1 of the National Curriculum) that is usually entered by a typically developing child at about the age of 5 to 6 years.

Mild Cognitive Impairment

Mild cognitive impairment is the equivalent of 'mild mental retardation' as defined in *DSM-IV-TR* (American Psychiatric Association, 2000, p. 42) and is associated with an IQ range of 50/55 to 70. As with other levels of mental retardation, IQ levels are interpreted with care, as they are not the sole criterion. The diagnostic criteria for mental retardation also include 'co current deficits or impairments in present adaptive functioning . . . in at least two of the following areas: communication, self care, home living, social/interpersonal skills, use of community resources, self-direction, functional academic skills, work, leisure, health and safety' (p. 49). Children with mild mental retardation tend to 'develop social and communication skills during the pre-school years (ages 0 to 5 years)' (p. 43) and have minimal impairment in sensorimotor areas. By the late teens, they can acquire academic skills up to about sixth grade level.

In England, a definition of 'moderate learning difficulties' in government guidance states that these pupils 'will have attainments well below expected levels in all or most areas of the curriculum, despite appropriate interventions. Their needs will *not* be able to be met by normal differentiation and the flexibilities of the National Curriculum' (DfES, 2005, p. 6 italicized for emphasis). They 'have much greater difficulty than their peers in acquiring basic literacy and numeracy skills and in understanding concepts. They may also have associated speech and language delay, low self-esteem, low levels of concentration and underdeveloped social skills' (ibid., p. 6).

Hearing Impairment

Categorizations of hearing impairment relate to *intensity/amplitude*. The intensity of a sound is experienced as loudness and is measured in a decibel (dB) scale on which the quietest audible sound has a value of 0 dB and the loudest 140 dB. Normal conversation is carried out at around 40 to 50 dB (Steinberg and Knightly, 1997). Hearing impairment can be measured in terms of dB loss. Categories of hearing impairment are recognized although different countries have different cut-off points for the bands. The following ranges give a broad indication:

- **slight loss:** 15 to 25 dB
- **mild loss:** 25 to 40 dB
- **moderate loss:** 40 to 65 dB
- **severe loss:** 65 to 95 dB
- **profound loss:** above 95 dB (Westwood, 2003, p. 48).

Regarding severe loss and profound loss, a distinction, important for future communication, may be made between pre-lingual and post-lingual loss.

Another important aspect in defining hearing impairment is *frequency*, which concerns the rate at which sound waves vibrate, and is expressed as cycles per second (cps) or in Hertz (Hz). Sound frequency is perceived as pitch, with rapidly vibrating sound waves perceived as high-pitched sounds and slower vibrating waves as low-pitched sounds. The human ear, although normally responsive to sounds between 60 and 16 000 cps, is most responsive to sounds between 500 and 4000 cps. Speech sounds occupy the most responsive band and particular speech sounds involve several frequencies. Vowels tend to occupy the lowest frequency range whereas fricatives, such as 's', 'f' and 'sh', tend to occupy the higher ones. Hearing loss rarely affects all frequencies equally, so hearing tends to be distorted. With low frequency loss, the ability to hear vowels is impaired, whereas with higher frequency loss, the capacity to hear fricatives and sibilants is reduced. Because consonants make speech intelligible, high frequency hearing loss is usually more serious.

Visual Impairment

'Visual impairment' indicates a continuum of loss of sight, which usually includes blindness. Where the expression 'blindness' is explicitly used, it refers to a level of sight loss of children who depend mainly on tactile methods of learning. The term 'low vision' is used in relation to children whose learning and teaching involves predominantly sighted methods.

Among types of visual impairment are refractive errors (myopia or short-sightedness, hypermetropia or long-sightedness and astigmatism). In myopia, the eyeball is too long and parallel light rays coming from a distance focus not on the retina at the central point of the macula (the fovea), but between the lens and the macula, so distance vision is blurred, requiring corrective concave spectacles/contact lenses. With hypermetropia, the eyeball is too short and light rays focus behind the retina so that vision is blurred or ineffective. In straightforward instances, convex lens spectacles/contact lenses can correct hypermetropia so that light rays are focused on the fovea. In astigmatism, the eye lens (or the cornea) has irregularities in its curvature, leading to variable refractive power and distorting the image on the macula. A cylindrical correction built into the lens of spectacles can correct this in straightforward cases.

Other types of visual impairment include retinitis pigmentosa, cataract and nystagmus. Retinitis pigmentosa is a group of progressive conditions affecting the retina, particularly the peripheral area containing the cells (rods) sensitive to vision in dim light, leading to night blindness and 'tunnel vision'. A cataract is an opaqueness or cloudiness of the cornea preventing some light rays passing to the retina, and suitable intervention depends on factors such as the position of the cataract. Nystagmus is a repetitive, rhythmic involuntary movement of the eyes, leading to considerable difficulty fixing the eyes on a specified point, although some children can be helped to find an eye position that reduces this movement (Mason and McCall, 1997, pp. 38–50). Cortical visual impairment, one of the commoner visual problems affecting children with additional or complex difficulties, relates to a disturbance of the posterior visual pathways or occipital lobes or both (Jan, 1993).

Deafblindness

It has been stated that 'Pupils who are deafblind have both visual and hearing impairments that are not fully corrected by spectacles or hearing aids. They may not be completely deaf and blind. But the combination of these two disabilities on a pupil's ability to learn is greater than the sum of its parts' (Qualifications and Curriculum Authority, 1999, p. 7). A child who is deafblind may or may not have other difficulties or disabilities such as cognitive impairment or physical or motor difficulties.

Some functional definitions emphasize the effects of deafblindness on communication, mobility and gaining information. This is partly because assessment of visual impairment and hearing impairment generally does not lead to suggestions for interventions, which functional assessment is intended to do. The needs of children who are deafblind have been described as those of 'multisensory deprivation' (McInnes and Treffry, 1982, p. 1).

Orthopaedic Impairment and Motor Disorders

Under US federal law (the IDEA), an orthopaedic impairment is deemed a severe impairment adversely affecting the child's educational performance. The Code of Federal Regulations (CFR) defines it as 'impairments caused by congenital anomaly (e.g. club foot, absence of some member, etc.), impairments caused by disease (e.g. poliomyelitis, bone tuberculosis, etc.) and impairments from other causes (e.g. cerebral palsy, amputations, and fractures or burns causing contractures)' (34 CFR, section 300.7 [c] [8], 1999). As per this definition, the term 'orthopaedic' is not used strictly and embraces not only orthopaedic conditions but also neuromotor impairment (involving the central nervous system and affecting the child's ability to use, feel, control, and move certain parts of the body). However, both forms of impairments can limit movement (although the type of limitation differs); a neurological impairment hindering limb movement can lead to orthopaedic impairment; and there are similarities for both kinds of impairment in the provision of education, care and therapy.

Health Impairments

In the United States, the CFR definition of 'other health impairments' (taken to exclude orthopaedic impairment as defined earlier) is ' . . . having limited strength, vitality or alertness, including a heightened alertness to environmental stimuli, that results in limited alertness with respect to the educational environment, that (i) Is due to chronic or acute health problems such as asthma, attention deficit disorder or ADHD, diabetes, epilepsy, a heart condition, haemophilia, lead poisoning, leukaemia, nephritis, rheumatic fever and sickle cell anaemia: and (ii) Adversely affects a child's educational performance' (34 CFR, section 3000 [c] [9] [I] [ii], 1999).

Although as the above definition indicates, in the United States, ADHD is seen as a health impairment, in England, it is considered a type of emotional, behavioural and social disorder in government frameworks (e.g. Department for Education and Skills, 2001b).

Traumatic Brain Injury

Within the context of acquired brain injury (which excludes congenital brain injury) 'atraumatic' brain injury is brought about by illness and infection while 'traumatic' brain injury (TBI) is caused by injuries including accidents (e.g. Walker and Wicks, 2005, pp. 1–2).

The US-CFR defines TBI as follows:

' . . . an injury to the brain caused by an external force, resulting in total or partial functional disability or psychosocial impairment or both, that adversely affects the child's educational performance. The term applies to open or closed head injuries resulting in impairments in one or more areas, such as: cognition, language, memory, attention, reasoning, abstract thinking, judgement, problem solving, sensory, perceptual and motor abilities, psycho-social behaviour, physical functions, information processing, and speech. The term does not apply to brain injuries that are congenital or degenerative, or brain injuries induced by birth trauma' (34 CFR, section 300.7 [c] [12]).

Injuries causing TBI may be closed head injuries or open head (penetrative) injuries (Heller *et al.*, 1996). With a closed head injury, which might be sustained in a road accident or a fall, the dura (the membrane inside the skull and covering the brain) is not penetrated. In a penetrative head injury, there is an opening from outside of the skull and dura. If the damage is 'focal', it affects a relatively small brain area and may be caused, for example, by a penetrative injury to a specific part of the brain. 'Diffuse' brain damage (as well as focal damage) may be caused by closed head injuries as the brain is moved about inside the skull.

Disruptive Behaviour Disorders

The main classifications of disruptive behaviour disorders in *DSM-IV-TR* are conduct disorder and oppositional defiant disorder (ODD). Conduct disorder can include aggression, destroying property, stealing, housebreaking and truanting. It is commonly associated with other disorders including ADHD and substance abuse disorders. In *DSM-IV-TR* (American Psychiatric Association, 2000), conduct disorder centrally involves the violation of the rights of others or the transgression of 'major age-appropriate social norms'

(p. 98 criterion A). The behaviour forms a repetitive and persistent pattern and 15 behaviours are specified in 4 groupings as follows:

- aggression towards people or animals (seven behaviours)
- damage to property (two behaviours)
- deceitfulness or theft (three behaviours)
- 'serious' rule transgression (three behaviours).

Three or more of these 15 behaviours must have been present during the previous 12 months with at least one apparent in the previous 6 months. Criterion B (p. 99) specifies that the behavioural disturbance causes 'significant impairment' in social, occupational or academic functioning. A further criterion C concerns those aged 18 years and more (p. 99). Age of onset is specified as childhood, adolescent, or unspecified (unknown). In childhood onset, of the three or more behaviours that will have been identified, at least one will have started before the age of 10. For adolescent onset, no criterion would have been met before the age of 10. With childhood onset, the individual is usually male, is frequently physically aggressive towards others, has 'disturbed peer relationships' and usually has symptoms meeting the full criteria for conduct disorder before puberty. Many children have ADHD also. They are more likely to have persistent conduct disorder and develop adult anti-social personality disorder than those with adolescent onset. The latter are less likely to show aggressive behaviours, or to have persistent conduct disorder or to develop adult personality disorder and more likely to have normal peer relationships. The male to female ratio is lower than that for childhood onset (p. 95).

In *DSM-IV-TR* (American Psychiatric Association, 2000) the essential feature of ODD is a repeated pattern (lasting at least for 6 months) of 'negativistic, defiant, disobedient, and hostile' behaviour towards people in authority. This leads to significant impairment in 'social, academic or occupational functioning' (p. 100). ODD is usually evident before the age of 8 and usually not later than early adolescence (p. 101) and in a significant proportion of cases, it is a developmental antecedent of conduct disorder. Because all the features of ODD are usually present in conduct disorder, ODD is not diagnosed if the criteria for conduct disorder are met. ADHD is common in children with ODD (p. 101).

Anxiety Disorders

In *DSM-IV-TR* (American Psychiatric Association, 2000) most anxiety disorders are adult syndromes whose criteria can be applied to children too. They include generalized anxiety disorders, obsessive-compulsive disorder, specific phobia and social phobia. *DSM-IV-TR* also includes two disorders, separation anxiety disorder and selective mutism, which are usually diagnosed first in infancy, childhood or adolescence. Around a third of children with one anxiety disorder meet the criteria for at least one other anxiety disorder also (Strauss and Last, 1993) and a similar proportion also experience major depression (Bernstein and Borchardt, 1991).

Depressive Disorders

Depression is comparatively rare in children, tending to be expressed through anxiety, frustration or somatic complaints (Birmaher *et al.*, 1996) while adolescents tend to show more biological complaints and thoughts of suicide or actual suicidal behaviour. For children and adolescents diagnosed as having major depression, 40 to 70% have a second psychiatric disorder and 20% or more have three or more disorders (ibid.).

In major depressive disorder, as characterized in *DSM-IV-TR* (American Psychiatric Association, 2000), there are one or more major depressive episodes (p. 369). The depressed mood must be present for most of the day almost every day for at least 2 weeks. Severity may be mild, moderate or severe and may or may not be accompanied by psychotic features.

Another depressive disorder, dysthymic disorder, in comparison with major depressive disorder, is characterized by less severe symptoms that are present more days than not over at least a 2-year period (p. 376). With children and adolescents, the mood may be irritable rather than depressed and the required minimum duration is a year (p. 377). In children, dysthymic disorder may be associated with other conditions including ADHD, anxiety disorders and conduct disorder. Occurring equally in both sexes, it often leads to impaired school performance and poorer social interaction (p. 378). While the individual is depressed, two or more of other features have to be present to meet the criteria, including poor appetite or overeating, low energy or fatigue, low self-esteem, and poor concentration or difficulty making decisions (ibid., p. 380).

Attention Deficit Hyperactivity Disorder

The *DSM-IV-TR* (American Psychiatric Association, 2000, pp. 85–93) definition of ADHD sets out criteria relating to inattention, hyperactivity and impulsivity. The nine criteria for *inattention* include, 'often fails to give close attention to details or makes careless mistakes in school work, work or other activities' and 'often has difficulty sustaining attention in tasks or play activities'. The six criteria for *hyperactivity* include, 'is often on the go' or 'often acts as though driven by a motor'. One among the three criteria for *impulsivity* is 'often has difficulty waiting a turn' (p. 92). The diagnostic criteria state that six or more of the nine criteria for inattention *or* six or more of the nine criteria for hyperactivity–impulsivity should have persisted for at least 6 months to an extent that is 'maladaptive and inconsistent with developmental level'.

Four further criteria must be met including that, 'some impairment from the symptoms is present in two or more settings . . . ' such as at school and home and 'Some hyperactive-impulsive or inattentive symptoms were present before age 7 years' (p. 92). Clearly, a child can meet the criteria through different combinations of inattention, hyperactivity and impulsiveness. The child may show six or more of the nine criteria for inattention; or all six criteria for hyperactivity; or all three criteria for impulsivity and three or more for hyperactivity. These will influence whether the difficulty is seen as predominantly inattention, hyperactivity or impulsivity with hyperactivity.

Speech

The *DSM-IV-TR* (American Psychiatric Association, 2000, pp. 58–69) classifications of communication disorders are essentially as follows:

- phonological disorder
- stuttering ('stammer' is often used instead of 'stutter' in the United Kingdom)
- expressive language disorder
- mixed expressive–receptive language disorder.

Phonological disorder involves failure to develop speech sounds appropriate for the child's age and dialect and may involve errors in 'sound production, use, representation, or organization . . . ' (p. 65). These impede academic or occupational achievement or social communication. Phonological disorder includes phonological production and cognitively based forms of phonological problems involving a 'deficit in linguistic categorization of speech sounds' (p. 65). It may involve errors in the selection and ordering of sounds within syllables and words. It is more common in boys than in girls. In some systems, these difficulties are considered motor/speech articulation problems rather than phonological disorders.

Stuttering/stammering is a disturbance of 'normal fluency and time patterning of speech' (American Psychiatric Association, 2000, p. 67). Inappropriate for the individual's age and typified by repetitions or prolongations of sounds or syllables, stuttering interferes with academic or occupational achievement or social communication.

In expressive language disorder, where a standardized assessment is made, scores for expressive language are substantially below those for nonverbal intellectual capacity and for receptive language. Where standardized tests are not used, functional assessments are made. Features vary but include a limited amount of speech and range of vocabulary; difficulty acquiring new words and word finding, and limited types of grammatical structures. The most common associated feature of expressive language disorder is phonological disorder (American Psychiatric Association, 2000, pp. 58–61).

With mixed expressive–receptive language disorder, standardized test scores for both expressive and receptive language are substantially below those for intellectual capacity. Features are similar to those for expressive language disorder with the addition of a comprehension deficit. Functional assessments may be made in the absence of any standardized assessments (American Psychiatric Association, 2000, pp. 62–64).

Difficulties with Grammar

Grammatical difficulties may become evident in children at about the age of 3. The child may have difficulties with the order of words and with making sentences of four or more words. There may be a problem with function words, with the child using age-inappropriate telegraphic utterances. Key words are included but function words often omitted. A child, while being able to formulate simple sentences, may have problems making compound ones involving long word sequences, perhaps because of difficulties with auditory sequential memory.

The child may also have difficulties with the grammatical relationships implicated in connecting the ideas that are complicatedly hierarchical, dependent, embedded or causal (Martin and Miller, 2003, p. 73). Lacking linguistic knowledge of the rules necessary, the child may not recognize the grammatical role of words, such as the difference between nouns and verbs, or the appropriate structures for verbs (Van der Lely, 1994). Short-term memory difficulties or difficulties with embedded, hierarchical grammatical structures can lead to problems formulating sentences.

Pervasive memory and organizational problems may hinder a child's general organization. The child tends to be unable to make sentence structures with familiar words or use a two-noun phrase with a verb. This is because the demands of processing these requirements in working memory are too great. He may have problems with auditory memory, auditory sequencing, attention and reading and writing.

Regarding morphology, many children acquire a variety of morphemes such as suffixes and prefixes as early as 2½ years (Wells, 1985), if not expressively, then receptively. But some children require specific teaching and practice to learn these. The child may also have difficulty with more complex aspects of morphology including changes to words that negate their meaning (stable/unstable) and suffixes changing the word's grammatical class (adjective 'kind'/noun 'kindness').

Semantic Difficulties

When examining meaning (semantics) in language, the unit of meaning, or lexeme, can be conveyed in one word or several ('go', 'move on'). For a lexeme to be used meaningfully, the speaker requires some concept knowledge, for example, having seen a car having some notion of the concept of car. Also, to grasp the meaning of lexemes implies that other cognitive factors support the understanding of meaning. The child's memory needs to be able to link with the object and the word so when the object is next seen, the word will be available; or when the child next uses the word, it will be with some memory of the concept and object associated with the word.

The verbal context in which the word is used also indicates that the child has grasped its meaning. A child may use the word 'cat' in an utterance bearing no apparent relationship to the usual meaning of the word and if the context does not support the word, the child may well have not grasped the meaning. Aitchison (1987) suggests that in acquiring meaning, children have three basic, related tasks: labelling, packaging and network building and where there are difficulties with these, semantic problems tend to arise. For example, the child might have difficulty labelling because of problems making sense of and storing auditory information beyond an age when it would be expected.

Pragmatic Difficulties

Several features enable utterances to make social and linguistic sense. *Speaker's intention* relates to speaking for a purpose such as posing a question. *Shared understanding of the context* of an utterance involves understanding of the speaker and listener with whom they are communicating. *Inference and implication* relate to speakers and listeners understanding and being able to respond suitably to conventions such as polite, indirect requests. Where pupils have difficulties with these areas, they may respond inappropriately to utterances and struggle to maintain meaningful exchanges.

Pragmatic difficulties may affect expressive and receptive pragmatic abilities. Children with pragmatic difficulties have primary difficulties with communication and conversation. But they do not necessarily exhibit behaviours associated with autism or have difficulties with other aspects of language such as grammar. There is debate about the positioning of children as having features predominantly of autistic spectrum disorder, specific language disorder or some middle position (e.g. Bishop, 2000, pp. 99–113).

Autistic Disorder and Asperger's Syndrome

Kanner (1943), describing several children attending his psychiatric unit, noting their limited interest in other people, odd language, insistence on routines and repetitive behaviour, used the term 'autism' to convey the children's self-absorption. Later definitions have centred around a 'triad' of impairments (Wing and Gould, 1979), concerning social isolation, communication difficulties and insistence on sameness. Accordingly, *DSM-IV-TR* (American Psychiatric Association, 2000, pp. 51–53) defines autism in relation to social difficulties, communication impairment and restricted behaviours. All three must be present, with the social deficit being particularly marked.

Asperger's syndrome takes its name from Hans Asperger (1944), a paediatrician who described behaviours that have come to define the syndrome. Criteria for identifying Asperger's syndrome, unlike autism, do not require that the child experience a communication deficit in the same way. Because many features of Asperger's syndrome are less marked as those of autism, they may not be noticed as early. It is debated whether Asperger's syndrome is best considered as part of the same continuum as autistic disorder or as a separate entity (Mackintosh and Dissanayake, 2004).

Developmental Coordination Disorder

In *DSM-IV-TR*, developmental coordination disorder (DCD) is considered a 'marked impairment of motor co-ordination', which 'significantly interferes with academic achievement or activities of daily living' and is 'not due to a general medical condition' (American Psychiatric Association, 2000, pp. 56–57). DCD is not associated with any medically evident neurological signs and this helps distinguish it from conditions affecting motor coordination in which overt neurological symptoms are apparent (Cermak *et al.*, 2002 pp. 2–22).

A formerly used expression 'clumsy child syndrome' conveys something of a common feature of DCD or at least a possible subtype (e.g. Cermak and Larkin, 2002). Where the term 'dyspraxia' continues to be used, definitions tend to focus on the organization, planning and organization of movement, and dyspraxia is sometimes seen as a subtype of DCD (e.g. Dixon and Addy, 2004, p. 9).

Reading Disorder

In *DSM-IV-TR* (American Psychiatric Association, 2000, pp. 51–53), reading disorder is essentially identified by reading achievement being 'substantially below' what is expected, given the child's age, measured intelligence and education. Reading achievement is assessed in terms of reading accuracy, speed or comprehension measured by individually administered standardized tests. Reading disorder 'significantly' hinders academic achievement of daily living activities requiring reading skills. Oral reading is characterized by 'distortions, substitutions or omissions' (ibid., p. 52) and both oral and silent reading tend to be slow and involve comprehension errors. Developmental delays in language may occur in association with reading disorder (and other learning disabilities). Reading achievement, being 'substantially below' expectations, is often taken to indicate two or more standard deviations below the expected level, but in special circumstances, one standard deviation may be considered sufficient (e.g. Fonagy *et al.*, 2005, p. 360).

Contrary to the implications of the *DSM-IV-TR* criteria (American Psychiatric Association, 2000, pp. 51–53), there is growing consensus that reading disorder should imply reading achievement being below age expectations (e.g. Beitchman and Young, 1997). There are differences between 'reading disorder' and some uses of the term 'dyslexia'. Some definitions of dyslexia include disorder of written expression, whereas the *DSM-IV-TR* criteria separate reading disorder and disorder of written expression while acknowledging that the two often occur together. Mathematics disorder often co-occurs with reading disorder.

Disorder of Written Expression

DSM-IV-TR (American Psychiatric Association, 2000, pp. 54–56) outlines essential features of disorder of written expression. As measured by individually administered standardized tests of writing skills or functional assessment, writing skills are substantially below measured intelligence and 'age appropriate education' and age expectations. The latter is often taken to mean two standard deviations below average. The disturbance hinders academic achievement or daily living activities requiring the composition of written texts. There is generally a combination of difficulties as indicated by errors in grammar and punctuation in written sentences, many spelling errors, poor paragraph organization and very poor handwriting.

However, disorder in spelling and handwriting alone is not generally considered to constitute disorder of written expression. Should poor handwriting be brought about by impaired motor coordination, a 'diagnosis' of developmental coordination disorder may be considered (American Psychiatric Association, 2000, p. 56). Language deficits and perceptual motor deficits may accompany disorder of written expression (ibid., p. 55). Both disorder of written expression and mathematics disorder are commonly associated with reading disorder, as it is unusual for either to be found in the absence of reading disorder (ibid., p. 52).

Mathematics Disorder

Mathematics disorder is considered to be a difficulty in understanding and learning mathematics, not associated with general cognitive difficulties. A pupil with mathematics disorder may have difficulty performing simple calculations; have problems knowing how to respond to mathematical information; substitute one number for another; reverse numbers (e.g. 2 for 5); misalign symbols; and name, read and write mathematical symbols incorrectly.

DSM-IV-TR (American Psychiatric Association, 2000, p. 53) indicates the essential feature of mathematics disorder is mathematical ability falling substantially below that expected for the child's chronological age, intelligence and age-appropriate education. The disorder 'significantly interferes' with academic achievement and daily living that requires mathematical skills.

In England, 'dyscalculia' has been defined as 'a condition that affects the ability to acquire mathematical skills'. Pupils with dyscalculia ' . . . may have difficulty understanding simple number concepts, lack an intuitive grasp of numbers, and have problems with learning number facts and procedures. Even if they produce the correct answer or use the correct method, they may do so mechanically and without confidence' (Department for Education and Skills, 2001c).

Conclusion

Legal structures and guidance including recognized or implied categories of disability/disorder help define the field of application of special education. But they are boundaries intended to assist identification and provision and may change over time as new understanding develops.

Thinking Points

Readers may wish to consider the following:

- possible reasons for the common trends in special education legislation in the United States and England (and elsewhere);
- the extent to which typologies might inform suitable provision for children with disability/disorder.

Key Texts

American Psychiatric Association (2000) *Diagnostic and Statistical Manual of Mental Disorders Fourth Edition Text revision (DSM-IV-TR)*. Arlington, VA: APA.

Guidance and criteria for classifying and diagnosing various disorders.

Chapman, R. (2008) (2nd edn) *The Everyday Guide to Special Education Law: A Handbook for Parents, Teachers and Other Professionals*. Denver, Colorado: The Legal Center for People with Disabilities and Older People.

An accessible guide for parents that is intended as a resource for teachers too.

Farrell, M. (2002) (4th edn) *Special Education Handbook*. London: David Fulton Publishers.

An A to Z series of entries on special education. An appendix describes the main pieces of UK legislation and guidance from 1975 to 2002.

Legal/Typological

Farrell, M. (2008) *Educating Special Children: An Introduction to Provision for with Disabilities and Disorders.* New York and London: Routledge.

Examines the justifications and limitations of classifications of disability/disorder and describes provision associated with different types. The divisions draw on the classifications associated with the systems in the United States and the United Kingdom.

Mandlawitz, M., Mandlawitz, M. R., Latham, P. H. and Latham, P. S. (2007) *Special Education Law.* Boston, MA: Allyn and Bacon.

Includes IDEA and other federal laws and federal cases.

Osborne, A. G. (2006) (2nd edn) *Special Education and the Law: A Guide for Practitioners.* Thousand Oaks, CA: Corwin Press.

Covers federal mandates, statutes, regulations and case law.

Weber, M. C., Mawdsley, R. and Redfield, S. (2007) (2nd edn) *Special Education Law: Cases and Materials.* Albany, NY: LexisNexis.

Intended for schools of education and law schools.

Yell, M. L. (2006) (2nd edn) *The Law and Special Education*: Upper Saddle River, NJ. Prentice Hall.

Includes information on the IDEA 2004 and the No Child Left Behind Act 2001 as well as statutes, regulations, policy guidance and cases.

Ysseldyke, J. and Algozzine, B. (2006a) *The Legal Foundations of Special Education: A Practical Guide for Every Teacher..* Thousand Oaks, CA: Corwin Press.

Outlines and provides commentary on main legislation in the United States from the Rehabilitation Act 1973 to the 2004 reauthorization of the IDEA.

Ysseldyke, J. and Algozzine, B. (2006b) *Public Policy, School Reform and Special Education: A Practical Guide for Every Teacher.* Thousand Oaks, CA: Corwin Press.

Outlines public policy relating to special education in the United States.

Internet Resources

An example of a local Internet resource is: www.vesid.nysed.gov/specialed/publications/policy/perentguide.htm

This leads to the document, *Special Education in New York State for Children Ages 3–21: A Parent's Guide* (May 2002).

VESID is The Office of Vocational and Educational Services for Individuals with Disabilities.

3

Terminological

Introduction

This chapter explains what is meant by 'terminology' and indicates its importance in special education. The scope of terminology is illustrated in relation to connotation, underextended and overextended terms, and more broadly through conceptual analysis. The consideration of connotation takes the example of 'inclusion'.

Underextended and overextended terms are illustrated with reference to 'fairness' and 'barriers'. Broader conceptual analysis is attempted with the fuller examples of 'needs', 'discrimination' and 'rights'.

Terminology

Terminology refers in the present context to the terms used ' . . . with a particular application in a subject of study' (Soanes and Stevenson, 2003). It is not therefore about the general use of words but about their particular use in a specific field although, of course, general and specific usage may overlap. Terminology helps to shape and delineate an area of study. In special education, as in many areas, a starting point and orientation aid is to familiarize oneself with terms frequently used, for example, through the Internet and published texts.

Internet sites may offer basic dictionary-type definitions, an example is (www.lcisd.org/Administration/Instruction/Specialprograms/images/
DictionaryofSpecialEducationalTerms.pdf.) Published encyclopaedias, dictionaries or handbooks tend to provide more detailed explanations. Recent

examples include A to Z format guides to special education generally (Reynolds and Fletcher-Janzen, 2004) and handbooks relating to particular types of disability/disorder such as 'emotional and behavioural difficulties' (Ayers and Prytys, 2002). Some A to Z guides group information seeking to make it more systematic and manageable. For example, using a thematic index brings together headings under different groupings to enable more systematic reading (Farrell, 2003a).

However, as well as shaping an area of study, terminology may constrain the way issues are expressed and thought about. This is because terminology can be taken for granted and, consequently, may go unquestioned. It may be sometimes assumed that because there is a term such as 'attention deficit hyperactivity disorder' that there exists an unquestioned condition that is securely delineated by the term. In fact, there is debate around attention deficit hyperactivity disorder and questions are raised about the usefulness of the expression (Farrell, 2008b, Chapter 13). There may be a particular difficulty with very brief definitions where there is limited space to signal the debates that may exist around the use and usefulness of the terms concerned.

A richer understanding of particular terms is gathered only when one has considered a wide range of explanations of different terms enabling an interrelated picture to emerge. Mathematics disorder is better understood when compared with reading disorder and disorder of written expression. Notions of fairness may be better grasped when equality of opportunity has been examined. Special pedagogy is difficult to see in the round without also familiarizing oneself with special curricula, therapy, and school and classroom organization.

Terminology in Relation to Special Education

It is important in special education that the meaning and use of terms such as 'needs', 'disability' and 'rights' are understood and if possible agreed. However, there is potential for confusion and misunderstanding owing to many professionals being involved from different disciplines and areas of expertise. The range of professions include the following:

- educators including teachers, specialist teachers of the deaf or blind and classroom aides;
- psychologists who may specialize in clinical, educational, cognitive, neuropsychological, psychometric or other spheres;
- speech and language pathologists;

- physical therapists/physiotherapists;
- occupational therapists;
- audiologists;
- optometrists and opticians;
- medical staff such as physicians, surgeons and nurses;
- social care staff working with the family, in residential care homes or in residential schools.

All these professionals are expected to communicate lucidly with parents, children and with each other about their contribution to the better education, care and development of the child. The terms used by some of these professionals appear similar to those used by colleagues from other disciplines. However, there are differences of perspective or emphasis that can lead to misunderstandings. For example, medical professionals may understand a concept such as 'need' in a goal-directed biological sense as when a person 'needs' air in order to breathe. Educational professionals and some parents may use the term 'need' in a sense that is not goal directed. When used in this way in expressions such as 'meeting needs', the goal of the 'need' is not always made explicit. It may describe merely something that someone wants without any justification. (This is elaborated in later sections.) In brief then, although efforts may be made to develop clear and agreed terminology in special education, there is wide potential for misunderstanding.

The Scope of Terminology

This section indicates some ways in which terminology in special education may be considered with reference to connotation, underextended/overextended terms and, more broadly, conceptual analysis.

(a) Connotation

Inclusion The connotation of a word, distinguished from its literal or primary meaning, refers to the ideas or feelings that the word might suggest (Soanes and Stevenson, 2003). These may be positive or negative and so an awareness of the connotations of a term can help engage with description rather than feeling where it is helpful to distinguish the two.

When debate is held about the extent to which pupils are best educated in mainstream schools or special schools, the term 'inclusion', is sometimes used to refer to preferences for mainstreaming. The expression, 'inclusion' is usually taken as having positive connotations, especially when contrasted with 'exclusion'. Therefore, when 'inclusion' is used as a euphemism for school mainstreaming, the issues of whether education in an ordinary school or a special school is best suited to a child may not receive full consideration. Education in an ordinary school may be simply depicted as 'inclusive' and education in a special school may be implied to be exclusionary. In such instances, the terminology does not help identify the supposed benefits of one venue over the other. If this unjustified assumption of the inevitable superiority of mainstream education is recognized, however, the debate can be clearer. It can engage the issue of whether an ordinary school or a special school is the most suitable venue for the education of some children with disability/disorder. This might involve consideration of the extent to which a pupil is engaged in the education provided by a school as reflected in the progress he makes academically and in personal and social development (Farrell, 2006a).

Negative connotation is sometimes so obvious in the choice of terminology that it is easy to recognize the bias. Someone who may be in favour of pupils with disability/disorder being educated in an ordinary school may use terms such as 'segregation' to refer to education in special schools. This may evoke for some people images of the segregation in schools, hotels, transport and elsewhere of black and white people in parts of the United States in the 1960s and earlier. The term 'segregation' applied to special schools is being used to say something like, 'I note that special schools educate pupils with disability/disorder separately and I disapprove'. Once this is recognized, the debate can move on to the extent to which separate education is a good or a bad thing rather than become locked into whether it is or is not 'segregation'.

When referring to types of schools in discussing mainstreaming, terms can have positive or negative connotations. Where a dichotomy may be assumed between 'mainstream' and 'special' schools, the implication may be that pupils in 'mainstream' are in the important part of the education system, whereas pupils in 'special' schools are in less important tributaries. The alternative use of 'ordinary' school (as sometimes used in the present volume) instead of 'mainstream' could be seen as having the opposite implication that the school is merely typical. On that dichotomy, the term 'special' school might have positive connotations suggesting a school that is distinctive and valued.

(b) Underextended and overextended terms

Fairness Some terms may be applied in a limited way (underextended) and others in a very broad way (overextended), which if unexamined may lead to confusion. A term may be underextended. The concept of 'fairness' may be used to argue for the education of pupils with disability/disorder in ordinary schools. It may be maintained it is not 'fair' to exclude pupils from education in an ordinary school when they are no different from other children in the school. The concept of 'fairness' is applied in this instance with the assumption that there are no relevant differences between pupils with and without disability/disorder. However, the concept of fairness can be extended to apply to the extent to which it is 'fair' to educate pupils in ordinary schools, where there is a relevant difference between pupils with and without disability/disorder.

Recognition that the concept of fairness can be applied to both circumstances may then lead to a clearer consideration of issues that may be at stake. These might include, for example, at what point (if any) it can be agreed that differences between a pupil with a disability/disorder and a pupil without such a disability/disorder are relevant to the place where the child is predominantly educated. Such differences might or might not be agreed to include very wide differences in cognitive abilities or behaviour. It is then possible to progress to issues on which further discussion is possible rather than be deadlocked because a difference in the use of the concept of 'fairness' goes unrecognized.

Barriers A term may be overextended. The expression 'barriers' may be used to convey the need to remove obstacles from the path of pupils with disability/disorder. This may be taken to apply to any type of disorder/disability and any degree of severity. It might be used in such a way in the context of a social view of disability/disorder in which all conditions are seen as socially constructed or socially created. This would imply that the task of teachers and others is to identify and remove barriers that they and other members of society have placed in the way of these pupils.

If it is considered reasonable to suggest that such a wide use of the concepts represents an overextension of it, then it may be thought useful to re-examine the use of the term. This could involve trying to determine the types of disability/disorder to which the concept of barriers and removing barriers might apply and types where it applies less convincingly or not at all. It may be considered that the term barriers is more applicable to some aspects of physical disability such as wheelchair use. In such situations, the environment of a school can be modified to help ensure pupils in wheel chairs have physical access to learning facilities. The notion of barriers might be considered less applicable where a pupil, for example, has profound cognitive impairment owing to brain damage. In such instances, one might still be able to talk in terms of removing barriers so that the child can learn better. However, it might be considered more difficult to identify the barriers that society has placed in front of the pupil and how they should be removed. A more pertinent response might be supporting the pupil and helping him learn (see the chapter titled 'Social' of this volume).

(c) Conceptual analysis

A particular approach to terminology, indeed to language more generally, is conceptual analysis. This may be understood in relation to analytic philosophy (linguistic philosophy) and its developments. An important figure in analytic philosophy, Ludwig Wittgenstein, maintains in his early work *Tractatus Logico-Philosophicus* (Wittgenstein, [1918]/1974) that one of the tasks of philosophy is to assist human knowledge through clarifying the logic of language. He argues that, 'In everyday language it very frequently happens that the same word has different modes of signification and so belongs to different symbols'. That is, a single term may signify different meanings that would be more exactly rendered as different terms. Furthermore, ' . . . two words that have different modes of signification are employed in propositions in what is superficially the same way' (ibid. 3.323). This can produce 'the most fundamental confusions' (ibid. 3.324). Wittgenstein maintains that the true logical content of any proposition is concealed by every day language and can only be revealed by an analysis that pares away the potential distortions of language and lays bare the logical content. Metaphysical questions are, when stripped down in this way, Wittgenstein contends, revealed as confusions and the questions themselves are not merely puzzling but meaningless. Wittgenstein also exerted a significant influence on ordinary language philosophy.

Within the ordinary language debate in philosophy, aspects of J. L. Austin's work (Austin, 1962) suggest that many of the traditional problems of philosophy relate to misunderstandings about the misuse of language. It is maintained that, because ordinary language is far subtler than is often realized, a careful consideration of the range of meanings within it is a precursor to further philosophical thinking. Broadly, a clearer awareness of words is expected to lead to a clearer awareness of phenomena. Similarly, John Searle (1969) maintains that problematic concepts such as 'knowledge' can be analysed and clarified by scrutinizing the way the words are used. An implication is that it is possible to lay the conditions of a logical and truthful language through the study of the meaning of natural language rather than, for example, through having to use mathematical languages.

Gilbert Ryle ([1949]/2000), referring to the body–mind dualism of Descartes, proposes that 'The belief that there is a polar opposition between Mind and Matter is the belief that they are terms of the same logical type' (p. 23). This false belief, Ryle calls the dogma of 'the ghost in the machine' and in attempting to explode this 'myth', Ryle suggests that he is rectifying 'the logic of mental-conduct concepts' (p. 17). Such an error is brought about by applying to mental phenomena the vocabulary used to describe physical phenomena, that is, making a series of 'category mistakes' (p. 20 and passim).

This linguistic view of the tasks of philosophy has not been without its critics. At its worst, opponents have argued, such a view limits the remit of philosophy to petty concerns about language, some of them only specific to the structure and use of the English language.

However, at a more prosaic level, an examination of terminology may involve clarifying terms and exploring the range of meanings of words. The purpose of this is to try to ensure that debates are more focused on issues and not sidetracked by hidden misunderstandings and disagreements about terminology. Such analysis involves the exploration of the range of meanings of key concepts and may include an examination of tensions between the different uses of terms. The following sections attempt this in the context of special education with regard to 'needs', 'discrimination' and 'rights'.

Fuller Example: Needs

The concept of 'need' is central to some understandings of special education. This section distinguishes between 'needs' and 'wants', discriminating between goal-directed needs and unconditional needs. The section suggests that a lack of clarity in the term, 'meeting needs', may lead to the overidentification of supposed special educational needs.

Needs and wants The term 'special educational needs' is part of the legal definition of special education in the United Kingdom, where there is much talk of the 'needs' of pupils with disability/disorder and pupils having their 'needs' met'. In Australia, the expression 'additional needs' may be used as an alternative to special educational needs. Yet, the concept of 'needs' is far from simple.

'Needs' may be contrasted with 'wants' (e.g. Farrell, 2004b, pp. 14–15). In some understandings of 'need', the term is used interchangeably with 'want'. The term 'need' can convey being in want of something as when in relation to poverty or misfortune, one may speak of people being 'in need' or 'in want'. Also, 'want' can be used in a different sense from 'need'. If one wants something, this implies a desire to possess something, usually property. One may want a second television set in the kitchen as well as the existing one in the lounge, but this could not be said to be a 'need' in the sense the word has been used so far. A casual television viewer wanting an extra television set is not the same as a television critic 'needing' one television set in order to earn a living.

Goal-directed needs The expression, 'need', may be used in a way that necessitates a particular goal or in a way that may not do so. There are examples where the word 'need' implies a particular goal. An action may need to be performed in order that a goal is reached, as when one may need to cross the street to deposit money in the bank. Or a situation may require a course of action as when one needs to leave the party before a certain time to be able to get home at a reasonable hour. Similarly, one may need something to be able to perform an action or achieve a certain outcome, for example a ladder to be able to climb safely on to the roof. In such cases, when one says one needs something, there is an implication that it is for a particular purpose.

The purpose may be trivial or serious. To take a relatively trivial example, one may need a spoon to consume soup. So long as the context is understood by the person to whom one is communicating, such usage is quite acceptable. It would be unusual in countries where using a soup spoon is customary for a dining companion to disagree and state that one could very well drink the soup from the bowl, or not have the soup at all. On the other hand, the purpose may be serious as when one says one needs air to be able to breathe, or needs something to drink if extremely thirsty. In both trivial and serious cases, the implication is that one is making a conditional assertion of need. More formulaically, what is being said is, 'I need X if I am to achieve Y'. If the goal is serious, as when one says one needs water to survive, there is an implication that there is a justifiable obligation to provide for the need.

In an education context, parents may say their child 'needs' extra tuition. In a state school (in England) or a public school (in the United States) such education would be paid for from taxes and, therefore, paid for at least in part by others. To understand what is meant by this use of 'need', one may have to seek out the unmentioned clause, 'if he is to be able to gain a place at the best university'. Once the hidden clause is made explicit, one may raise and discuss the questions of whether this is a worthwhile goal and if it is, whether the State has any obligation to help the student achieve it.

Parents may say that certain provision should be made because their child has a special educational 'need'. The assertion is not explicitly made in relation to some goal. It may be that the child has a disability/disorder that has led to educational difficulties so severe that the child is unlikely to progress well unless certain extra provision is made. In this instance, there may be a broad justification that the supposed need is provided for. But the blanket term 'special educational need' can mask the unspecified justification for the requested provision. It is usually clearer if the type of disorder/disability, the purported 'need' and the goal are specified. For example:

- A child with profound cognitive impairment may need a small-steps curriculum and related assessment in order to progress and have the progress recognized.
- A child who is blind may need Braille in order to learn to read.
- A child who is deaf may need help and support with communication in order to be able to communicate effectively.

Unconditional needs So far, the question of goal directed needs has been examined. With these needs there is a sense in which it is clear that there is goal, that reaching that goal requires or is conditional upon something to be provided (the 'need') and that the need is justifiable. A goal-directed need in this sense may be understood as a conditional need. It is clear that the 'need' is a condition of achieving the specified goal. Achieving the goal is conditional upon the need being provided for. The blind child being able to read may be conditional upon recognizing his need to be taught Braille.

However, 'needs' are not always goal directed and conditional. They may be unconditional, as when one says that one needs an amount of money but does not specify why or for what purpose it is to be used. A parent or a school may say a pupil 'needs' speech and language therapy but may not specify what the goal of this is or may specify the supposed goal very generally. For example, it may be said that the child needs speech and language therapy in order to make better progress than he otherwise might, but this could be said of any child. Almost any child given speech and language therapy would be expected to make better progress than he otherwise might. In part, this is because it may involve intensive one-to-one work with an expert specialist. If this is correct, then to say the child 'needs' speech and language therapy must mean more than that he would progress better if he received it.

In practice, what is usually meant is that the child is behind other children in the acquisition of speech and language skills and development and that unless speech and language therapy is provided, he is likely to remain so or fall further behind. For a child with certain physical disabilities, it may be that the condition will so predictably affect the development of speech and language if provision is not made that there is a strong case for provision to be made pre-emptively.

However, unless such conditions are made explicit, there is the possibility of the term 'need' being used misleadingly. This is made more likely by the fact that types of disability/disorder are not always easy to identify and assess. Therefore, unless there is at least local agreement among parents, schools and school boards about what is meant by the various types of disability/disorder, the term 'special need' can be used too loosely. The child may be said to have a 'special educational need' and certain provision requested because the child is said to 'need' it without the link being made as to why. In such instances, unconditional needs can be mistaken for conditional goal-directed needs. Whereas a goal-directed need can be examined in relation to its goal and a debate held about whether the goal is justifiable (and if it is whether others should pay for it to be achieved), the unconditional need slips under this scrutiny.

Meeting needs A further potential confusion with the term 'needs' arises in the use of the expression 'meeting needs'. It is sometimes said that it is necessary to ensure that the needs of pupils with disability/disorder are met. However, it is not always made clear what the particular needs are or how they are to be met or how anyone would know if and when they were met. Typical of this sort of usage of 'needs' and having the 'needs met' is an entry on a UK government web site of 2007 (www.everychildmatters.gov.uk/ete/specialschool). This states:

> The government expects the proportion of children educated in special schools to fall as mainstream schools develop the skills and capacity to meet a wider range of *needs*. A small number of children will have such severe and complex *needs* that they will continue to require special provision, but children with less significant *needs* – including those with moderate learning difficulties – should be able to have their *needs met* in a mainstream environment (italics added).

Such usage creates muddle. A child who is considered to have a disability/disorder is said to require certain provision perhaps including possibly specialist individual tuition. His needs will be met when that tuition is provided. The goal in this instance is about providing the support; but in order to be justifiable, it should specify what is meant to be achieved by providing this support, for example, that the child's reading attainment should increase when he is behind other children of the same age.

Lack of clarity of needs and the overidentification of supposed special educational needs Where special educational needs are seen as a continuum related to a continuum of provision, for example, to try to avoid the perceived negative aspects of labelling children, the notion of needs becomes even fuzzier. With 'non-normative' conditions such as emotional and behavioural difficulties the blurring of needs is increased. On a supposed continuum of poor coordination needs, it is difficult to identify when this becomes identifiable as developmental coordination disorder. On a band of attention and overactivity needs, it is hard to determine when the condition of attention deficit hyperactivity disorder is to be recognized. Given this, the likelihood of more and more children being identified who are considered to have special educational needs may be increased (Farrell, 2003b, pp. 14–18).

Fuller Example: Discrimination

This section considers discrimination, firstly indicating the contested nature of equality of opportunity and contrasting the perspectives of 'justice as fairness', and a 'rights view of social justice'. It then examines 'top-down' and 'bottom-up' views of discrimination and their relation to equality of opportunity. Finally, a different view of discrimination is examined that does not depend on equality of opportunity arguments, but sees discrimination as failing to ensure someone is in a 'good-enough' position.

Equality of opportunity and justice as fairness Although equality of opportunity is sometimes regarded as a self-evident good, it can also be seen as a contested concept. Theories may support an egalitarian society, caution against social inequality and suggest support for equality of opportunity. For example, Rawls' (1971) theory proposes a principle that people would adopt if deprived of knowledge of their own social status and position in a proposed society. A hypothetical position is suggested in which a person is denied any knowledge of his abilities. If that person were to be given the choice of living in an egalitarian society or an inegalitarian one, he would likely choose the former. One reason is that the hope of being rich would be countered by the fear of being poor. This would tend to persuade the person behind a veil of ignorance about his own abilities and social status to choose a society that is 'fair' (ibid., p.148). This theory is known as a 'justice as fairness' theory.

Rawls argues that social inequality, in the sense of different treatment, can only be justified in certain circumstances. These are when inequality has the effect of benefiting the least advantaged by improving incentives and increasing the size of the social pot. People cooperating for mutual advantage are entitled to equal claims for the fruits of their cooperation. They should not be penalized because of factors over which they have no control such as gender, racial identity or genetic inheritance. Redistribution, conforming as it does to a widely held view of what is fair is therefore, it is contended, a just procedure.

Equality of opportunity would be justified in a similar way. For example, those who through no fault of their own do not have the ability to achieve as easily as others would be given the support necessary to help them do better than they otherwise might. The funding for this support would come from people who were more fortunate in the level of ability they possessed. In other words property would be redistributed to try to make opportunities in society more equal.

Equality of opportunity and a rights view of social justice Another view is expressed by Nozick (1974). This is that distributive perspectives such as 'justice as fairness' violate property rights and compromise freedom. His rights view of social justice and equality of opportunity relates to a libertarian conception of the state. A rudimentary form of organization, which Nozick identifies with a state of nature, is a system of 'private protection associations'. From these emerges the 'ultra minimal' state, which has a monopoly of the use of force in a territory. This ultra minimal state is transformed into a 'minimal' state, which involves redistribution for the 'general provision' of protective services (ibid., p. 52). Nozick maintains that the transitions leading from a state of nature to the ultra minimal state to the minimal state are morally legitimate and that the minimal state itself is morally legitimate.

The transition from private protection agencies to the ultra minimal state will occur as it were by an invisible hand process. This process is morally permissible and does not violate anyone's property rights as understood in this version of social justice. Furthermore, the transition from ultra minimal state to minimal state is inevitable. It would be morally inadmissible for individuals to keep the monopoly in the ultra minimal state without providing protective services for everyone, even if this requires specific redistribution (Nozick, 1974, pp. 113–119).

However, no state that is more powerful or extensive than the minimal state is considered to be legitimate or justifiable. Consequently, developments such as 'social justice' or 'redistributive justice' and 'equality of opportunity' going further than the minimal state are neither justifiable nor legitimate. Justice is not about equality but about entitlement in relation to individual property rights. A person acquiring property in accordance with 'the principle of justice in acquisition' is entitled to that property. Also, someone acquiring property in accordance with 'the principle of justice in transfer' from someone else entitled to that property is then entitled to that property (Nozick, 1974, p.150).

'Justice as fairness' views assume that everyone has some entitlement on the totality of natural assets in as a 'pool', with no one having differential claims, the distribution of abilities being seen as a collective asset. Nozick accepts that in a free society, people's talents do not benefit themselves only, but others too. What he questions, however, is extracting even more benefits from others, suggesting that envy underlies this notion of justice (Nozick, 1974, p. 229).

In Nozick's view there are two ways of achieving equal opportunity. The first is to deliberately worsen the circumstance of those who are better favoured with opportunity, the second, to improve the situation of those less favoured. The latter requires resources, and as these have to come from somewhere, the implication is that someone else will have to accept a worse situation. Because others' property cannot be seized, people have to be convinced to give some of their property by choice to help achieve greater equality of opportunity. This may take different forms such as charitable giving, or paying taxes for which the population has voted.

Nevertheless, there is no social obligation to 'rectify' inequalities. The pursuit of equal opportunities violates property rights and compromises freedom. There is key objection to considering everyone as having a right to equal opportunity and enforcing that supposed right. This is that the supposed rights ' . . . require a substructure of things and materials and actions; and other people may have rights and entitlements over these' (Nozick, 1974, p. 238).

Top-down and bottom-up views of discrimination 'Discrimination' can have positive connotations as when someone discriminates between a fine piece of architecture and a shoddily conceived building, or a competently developed dramatic play and a poorly constructed one, or a convincing argument and spurious reasoning. However, in relation to special education and disability/disorder, the term discrimination often bears negative connotations.

Discrimination is sometimes understood in relation to equality of opportunity. There is a negative view of control that people's lives should not be affected by anything that is not under their control. This is sometimes combined with a commitment to equality and equality of opportunity. This tends to lead to the view that it is unfair for a person to have less than another through no fault of his own. Where such unfairness is identified, it may be equated with discrimination. This is perhaps the background to suggestions that the lives of disabled people should not be negatively affected by the disability and that where this is so, the root is discrimination.

However, this position appears to confuse the use of the term discrimination, as it is commonly and legally understood. The usual use of the expression can be characterized as 'bottom-up', taking the position that people's prospects should not depend upon disability. For example, schools should not intentionally discriminate against children on the grounds of their disorder/disability where it is not relevant to the circumstances. Such a view is an aspect of anti-discrimination legislation, for example, in the UK *Special Educational Needs and Disability Act 2001*. For a summary of the Act, please see Farrell, 2004b, pp. 32–34.

The view that people's lives should not be negatively affected by disability appears to be 'top-down' and seems to suggest that no one should be at a disadvantage because of his disability. For example, there should be no kind of correlation between disability and any kind of disadvantage. In such cases, the holder of this view may not have any person's behaviour in mind. He may simply mean that there is a correlation between being disabled and experiencing a certain kind of disadvantage.

However, people with disabilities do experience certain disadvantages, many aspects of life being more difficult for them. This is not necessarily because anyone has deliberately constructed the environment to contain 'barriers' that will purposely make life more difficult for people who have a disability/disorder. Designers of complicated transport routes on subways are not discriminating in the sense that they have knowingly behaved in a discriminatory way to someone who has severe cognitive impairments rendering such routes extremely difficult to understand. Yet people try to articulate the point that life is more difficult for people who have a disorder/disability by saying they suffer 'discrimination'.

A child with autism may find busy social situations difficult and distressing and may react negatively to what most children would accept as everyday background noise. It does not mean, however, that the people who decided to set up and use a busy, noisy public square are discriminating against the child who cannot cope with it. It does not imply that lively and voluble social group activities in school are set up to discriminate against the child with autism who may not participate in them with any enjoyment. This does not suggest that for the child with autism, at least at some point in his development, alternative modes of travel cannot be found or that alternative social activities cannot be considered that are more bearable and perhaps even enjoyable. However, it seems to be a misconception to maintain that the usual tenor of school activity is itself discriminating.

Discrimination and a good enough position Other approaches to discrimination do not associate it with equality of opportunity and treating people unequally. In this alternative view, discrimination is defined as treating people with undeserved contempt (Cavanaugh, 2002). Among difficulties with this view are that it leaves open the question of when contempt might be 'deserved' and what treating people who deserve contempt might involve. Also, it does not capture the useful differential aspect of treating one person in one way and treating another person in another way for reasons that are not justifiable.

Cavanaugh (2002) then maintains that society should ensure people are not treated with unjustifiable contempt. He also argues that an attempt should be made to make sure no one is left without hope. This involves not leaving someone in a position where they can do nothing to change their lives for the better. People's lives should be to some extent within their control. Therefore, others should be concerned whether certain groups of people have bad prospects. But this, he contends, involves asking whether people are in a good enough position, not asking whether they are equal or whether they have supposed equal opportunities.

This in turn raises further questions concerning what 'good enough' might mean and who is to decide. It has the advantage, however, of facing up to the impossibility of everyone being equal. Cavanaugh's position also recognizes the dilemma of offering equal opportunities to someone who finds it difficult to take advantage of them and that it may be offering the opportunity for everyone to be unequal. At the same time it allows for people to move towards a position of better circumstances.

Fuller Example: Rights

This section looks at a view of 'rights' that relates it to duties, placing the term in a social context. It considers whether an alternative view of rights as more individualized rather like a possession can have potential negative consequences such as the proliferation of rights that may reduce their credibility.

The nature of rights Rights may be understood as part of normative discourse. That is, the term is used to describe conduct according to rules and has descriptive power only if one assumes the rule is in force (e.g. Benn and Peters, 1959, p. 88). Therefore, an expression such as, 'A citizen of the United States of America has the right to free speech' can only be understood within the context of rules that allow such speech.

A relationship between rights and duties can be argued such that if a person expresses a right, then this implies a correlative duty on someone else. If a citizen of the United States does have a right to free speech, then other citizens are placed under a duty not to interfere with his right. In this instance, the right implies non-interference where the duty lies in doing nothing that will get in the way of free speech. However, a right may impose an active duty on someone else as when a person's right to claim a debt of another implies the duty of that person to repay it.

Benn and Peters (1959, p. 89) maintain that the correlation between rights and duties is not a moral or legal relation but a logical one. A rule that gives rise to a right does not as a separate entity impose a duty. A right and a duty are different names for 'the same normative relation' with reference to the point of view from which it is seen.

Whenever one speaks of rights and duties of one person, this might suggest reciprocity. If a person asserts a right to have his property respected, it would be usual to expect that same person would accept a duty upon himself to respect the property of others. This link, however, is a moral not a logical one. There is nothing that logically connects asserting a right to having property respected and respecting the property of others in the way that a right of one person to have property respected logically assumes the duty of another person to respect that right.

However, in the case of rules that are considered fundamental, with very wide application, it is considered reasonable to assume that the assertion of a right (such as free speech) implies that the same right applies to others. Relatedly, a commensurate duty to allow the free speech of others is part of the general rule whereby a person would expect to exercise free speech himself.

Rights and special education As in many other spheres, in the field of special education various supposed rights have been claimed. There is the 'right' to have particular provision such as speech and language therapy and the 'right' to one-to-one tuition if the pupil is falling behind. There is the 'right' to be educated in an ordinary school, claimed by those who regard inclusion as synonymous with mainstreaming; there is the 'right' for deaf children to be educated in a special school for those who believe that deaf people form a linguistic minority whose form of communication ought to be encouraged.

There have been attempts to ensure new rights are associated with fundamental matters. Alston (1984) suggested that new international human rights be subject to a kind of quality control by the United Nations General

Assembly rather than being 'conjured up'. A United Nations resolution adopted in 1986 set out compliance criteria for international human rights instruments. These included that they should, 'be of fundamental character and derive from the inherent dignity and worth of the human person'. However, there are very different ideas and practices about what constitutes the value and worth of a person, making such statements so broad as to mean little.

Kundera (1991) suggests that 'the more the fight for human rights gains in popularity the more it loses any concrete content'. Everything has become a right; 'The desire for love the right to love' and so on (ibid., p. 154). Glendon (1991) argues, ' . . . there is very little agreement regarding *which* needs, goods, interests, or values should be characterized as "rights", or concerning what should be done when . . . various rights are in tension or collision with one another' (ibid., p. 16). For Glendon, the rights rhetoric is bound up with ' . . . a near silence concerning responsibility, and a tendency to envision the rights-bearer as a lone autonomous individual' (p. 45). Glendon's (1991) linking of rights and responsibilities shares common ground with Benn and Peters' (1959) perception of the reciprocal nature of rights and duties.

A treatise adopted in 2006, The *International Convention on the Rights of Persons with Disabilities* concerned the right to make decisions, marry, have a family, work and receive education. While many people might like to marry or want to marry, does anyone whether having a disability/disorder or not have a 'right' to marry? Again, although some people might want very much to have a family, does anyone have a 'right' to have a family? The supposed right for anyone to marry seems an example of Glendon's point about the rights-bearer seemingly being a lone autonomous individual. One might reasonably ask if a supposed right to marry no longer depends on someone else wanting to marry the rights-bearer.

Such lists of rights are contrary to Benn and Peters' (1959, pp. 88–89) argument that a right implies a correlative duty on someone else or on several other people or on all other people. They seem to reject the view that a right is rule bound normative phenomenon and seems to perceive it as a quality that an individual somehow carries round as part of himself. Glendon's (1991) point is similar that in rights rhetoric there is ' . . . a near silence concerning responsibility, and a tendency to envision the rights-bearer as a lone autonomous individual' (ibid., p. 45). In such a perspective, a person does not 'bear' rights as a lone individual but they emerge from socially agreed rules.

Glendon (1991) raises the concern that the ever-expanding list of rights may trivialize any core rights that may exist while doing little to advance the numerous further causes that have been claimed to be rights. Yet the language of human rights shows little sign of moderating or abating.

After a judge in Scotland had found that a prisoner had had his 'human rights' breached by having to empty his toilet contents ('slopping out'), prison officers were reported to be considering suing the Scottish executive for having to supervise the practice. The Scottish Prison Officers Association asked solicitors to consider whether its members' 'human rights' had been breached. A spokesman for the association said they were assessing the situation 'under the European Commission on Human Rights' (Cramb, 2004). Charles Fforde, an estate owner in the Scottish island of Arran, is stated to have accused the Scottish executive of 'breaching his human rights' by abolishing the feudal system (Peterkin, 2004). A retired police officer is reported to be prepared to take to the European Court of Human Rights a claim that he should be able to cut down protected trees in his garden that are blocking the satellite signal for his television. The aggrieved man says he considers it a 'basic human right to receive television signals and enjoy watching television' (Sapsted, 2004).

If the education and care of children with disabilities/disorders are considered to be among core rights, the proliferation of more and more peripheral rights may not be beneficial to these children.

Conclusion

The analysis of terms used in special education such as 'inclusion', 'fairness', 'barriers', 'needs', 'discrimination' and 'rights' may help avoid concealed arguments about terminology and enable debates to move on to matters of substance. Given the contentious nature of much of special education, this does not, of course, guarantee agreement on the matters of substance. However, it can help ensure that the differences of opinion are more apparent and open to debate.

Thinking Points

Readers may wish to consider the following:

- the extent to which the analysis of terms can clarify discussion, allowing dissent about issues to be distinguished from disagreement about terminology.

- how the terms 'inclusion', 'fairness', 'barriers', 'needs', discrimination' and 'rights' might be further clarified in discussion on special education.
- what other terms and concepts may need clarification.

Key Texts

Ayers, H. and Prytys, C. (2002) *An A to Z Practical Guide to Emotional and Behavioural Difficulties*. London: David Fulton.

This book is an example of a terminological guide to a particular group of disabilities/disorders and their relationship to special education.

Cavanaugh, M. (2002) *Against Equality of Opportunity*. Oxford. Oxford University Press.

This book is about a treatise questioning one of the shibboleths of social justice. Whether one agrees with everything in the book or not, the clarity of argument is stimulating to further thought.

Farrell, M. (2003a) (3rd edn) *The Special Education Handbook*. London: David Fulton.

Definitions and fuller descriptions of terms used in special education in A to Z format. A thematic index groups together headings under different groupings, enabling more systematic reading.

Farrell, M. (2004b) *Inclusion at the Crossroads: Concepts and Values in Special Education*. London: David Fulton.

This book includes chapters such as 'Defining SEN: Distinguishing Goal-Directed Need and Unconditional Need'; 'School Equal Opportunity Policies: Equality and Discrimination'; and 'Including Pupils with SEN: Rights and Duties'.

Fletcher-Janzen, E. and Reynolds, C. R. (Eds) (2007) (3rd edn) *Encyclopaedia of Special Education: A Reference for the Education of Children, Adolescents and Adults with Disabilities and Other Exceptionalities* **Volumes 1, 2 and 3**. Hoboken, NY: John Wiley and Sons.

A thorough A to Z compilation with cross-referenced articles.

Reynolds, C. R. and Fletcher-Janzen, E. (Eds) (2004) (2nd edn) *Concise Encyclopaedia of Special Education: A Reference for the Education of Handicapped and Other Exceptional Children and Adults*. Hoboken, NY: John Wiley and Sons.

A single-volume A to Z reference including biographies, information on tests, legal matters and overviews of disabilities/disorders.

Shakespeare, T. (2006) *Disability Rights and Wrongs*. London: Routledge.

Although this book does not relate very much to special education but to issues around disability more generally, it takes a critical look at the 'strong social model' approach to disability, which it forthrightly rejects.

Internet Resources

www.lcisd.org/Administration/Instruction/Specialprograms/images/DictionaryofSpe-
    cialEducationalTerms.pdf
Typical of several Internet resources, this offers very brief definitions of terms and gives
    full forms for acronyms in special education.

4

Social

Introduction

This chapter considers a social view of disability and its role in an interactionist perspective of special education. (A systems approach, also having social foundations, is considered in the chapter titled 'Psychotherapeutic' in this book.) The chapter sets the context by outlining an individual view of difficulty/disorder and examining attempts to extend this. It then considers various social views of 'disability'. The relationship of a social perspective to special education is explained with reference to changing the physical environment, modifying the way things are done, and changing attitudes. The scope of a social model is indicated and it is suggested that a social contribution to special education is strongest when such a contribution is part of an interactionist perspective. The chapter then moves to more practical matters and provides fuller examples of the application of a social perspective for hearing impairment and orthopaedic impairments.

The final sections seek to present the contribution of the social perspective at its strongest. They do so by maintaining that social views apply more to some types of disability/disorder than others, despite the implication in some interpretations that social views imply rejecting typologies of disability/disorder. The final sections of the chapter also take the position that a social perspective is stronger when seen as part of a contribution to an interactionist view rather than as a sole explanation of disability/disorder. In other words, this position takes into account individual and social factors. Consequently, the examples are of two types of disability/disorder to which a social view could apply and they involve an interactive view in which a social contribution is important.

Individual Perspectives and Attempts to Move Away from Them

(a) *Individual perspectives*

Where social perspectives are considered in relation to special education, there is sometimes an implied positioning of such a perspective in opposition to or at least in creative tension with an individual view. Therefore, in order to explore a social perspective, it may be helpful to recognize the individual view from which some of those having a more social perspective may seek to distance themselves.

In the field of special education, it has been suggested that an individual model, sometimes described as a 'medical' model, has been predominant for some time and, ' . . . still dominates the conceptualizing of the problems students face in schools' (Booth, 1998, p. 84). In this view, people are considered disabled, ' . . . as a result of their physiological or cognitive impairments' (Drake, 1996, p. 148). The 'medical model' has been depicted as emphasizing defects and personal and functional limitations that are the responsibility of the person concerned. Functional limitations are regarded as bringing about any disadvantage the disabled person experiences and it is held that a medical model considers that these can be rectified only by treatment or cure (Barnes and Mercer, 1996).

Others have sought to distinguish between individual and necessarily medical elements, denying the existence of a 'medical model of disability' and recognizing instead, an individual model of disability, where 'medicalisation' is one significant component (Oliver, 1996, p. 31). However, it is difficult to find sources holding, with any credibility, a completely individual view or, for that matter, a completely social view of disability/disorder. It has also been suggested that 'Few practitioners and no textbooks of any repute subscribe to uni-directional causal models and invariably interventions are seen in medical practice as contingent and multi-factorial' (Kelly and Field, 1994, p. 35).

(b) *Approaches moving away from individual perspectives*

Aspects of the work of Byelorussian psychologist Lev Vygotsky (1896–1934) illuminate current debates on the positioning of individual factors and social/cultural factors in conceptualizing disability/disorder and special education (Minick, 1987; Wertsch, 1985). Vygotsky's view of psychology and of special pedagogy (translated from Russian, perhaps rather jarringly to modern ears, as 'defectology'), highlights cultural influences on development (Knox and Stevens, 1993, p. 5, translator's introduction). Two strands of development concern the biological or natural and the historical–cultural, respectively. The historical–cultural strand is internalized through the use of psychological 'tools' such as concepts, signs and symbols, and language. This strand is superimposed on natural behaviour and substantially transforms it so that the natural behaviour is embedded in the structures of personality. For an indication of neo-Vygotskian approaches to child development, see Karpov (2005).

Where there is a failure of biological function, another line of development, helped by socio-cultural 'tools', can come into effect. This enables other biological functions to get around the weak point and form a psychological superstructure over it, so the disability/disorder does not dominate the whole personality (Knox and Stevens, pp. 12–13, translator's introduction). Vygotsky ([1927]/1993) argues that, a child with a disability/disorder has developed differently from peers (p. 30). He proposes a compensatory and adaptive perspective in which such a child's development represents a creative physical and psychological process. This involves the shaping of the child's personality through restructuring adaptive functions and forming new processes brought about by the disability/disorder. In this way new, circumventing paths for development are created (p. 34 paraphrased). However, atypical development, unlike typical development, cannot be conditioned by culture spontaneously and directly (p. 42 paraphrased). Therefore, in special pedagogy, cultural development in a special child involves a particular line of development, guided by distinctive laws, and with specific difficulties and means of overcoming them (p. 43 paraphrased).

While maintaining blindness and deafness are biological, Vygotsky recognizes that education must cope with their social consequences (Vygotsky, [1925–1926]/1993, p. 66; and [original date unknown]/1993, p. 107). A child should be educated, not as a blind child, but first and foremost as a child. Otherwise, one risks special pedagogy becoming completely focused on the disability/disorder alone (Vygotsky, ([1924]/1993), p. 83). He argues for recognizing a child's strengths, and not just his weaknesses alone (Vygotsky, [1925–1926]/1993, p. 68 and [1927]/1993, p. 56). Constructing the educational process on the basis of compensatory drives involves ensuring the child's strengths and concentrates on compensating for the defect, and selecting in proper sequence tasks that will, over time, shape the entire personality 'from a new standpoint' (p. 57).

Other views have been put forward sometimes with the intention of challenging a more individual standpoint. Skrtic (1995b) develops social views of deviance to suggest that special educational needs are to some degree related to inflexible school organization and ossified professional culture and practice in mainstream teaching. Special education, that is separating children within ordinary schools or educating them in special schools, developed in response to a failure of ordinary schools to educate all children. Special education in Skrtic's view has emerged as an 'adhocracy' associated with problem-solving, innovation, flexibility, and developing new programmes. This contrasts with the 'bureaucracy' of ordinary schools. However, the adhocracy of special education points to the structures and professional awareness that public education should adopt if it is to prepare all future citizens for democracy.

Skrtic draws on the philosophy of the American pragmatist philosopher John Dewey (1859–1952) who influenced education and who, as Russell ([1946]/1996, p. 730) points out, wrote about it almost as much as he wrote about philosophy (e.g. Dewey [1899]/1976). Skrtic employs 'critical pragmatism' drawn from Dewey's philosophy to investigate presumptions that have constrained professional discourse and practice. Skrtic uses this method to construct, 'deconstruct' and reconstruct educational practice and discourses. He argues that certain organizational conditions are necessary to educate diverse pupils and the adhocratic approach makes these conditions possible. Public education can be for all if it adopts adhocratic school organization as the condition of critical practice and critical pragmatism as a mode of professional discourse. However, Skrtic gives little indication of the practicalities of what might be involved in these changes. Neither does he indicate what the content might be of any reflective critical development emerging from critical pragmatism.

Efforts to relate post-modern approaches to special education have included drawing on the ideas of the French writer Michel Foucault (1977, 1982) to emphasize the use of knowledge as power (Allen, 1996) (Farrell, 2004a, pp. 73–74). Other perspectives too provide alternatives to polarizing a predominantly individual or predominantly social view of special children. In the United States, a 'civil rights' approach to disability/disorder tends to emphasize the social and civil position of a person in society rather than solely individual characteristics. Various writers have explored social and cultural dimensions of disability (Rioux and Bach, 1994; Wendell, 1996). Minority group approaches also recognize the importance of the social environments and environmental restrictions (Amundsen, 1992).

Social Perspectives

Having considered briefly a mainly individual view and outlined work that recognizes in varying degrees an interaction between individual and social accounts, it is now necessary to consider predominantly social approaches to special education. The section alludes to past structural-functionalist and conflict perspectives, before outlining the perhaps more current social creationist and social constructionist views (Farrell, 2003a, pp. 152–154).

A structural-functionalist view (Parsons, 1952) focuses on structure and equilibrium in society and structures are considered to interact with each other so that each performs some positive function. In special education, those who value the structures that exist to help identify, assess and provide for pupils with disability/disorder might point to these as examples of structures performing a positive function. On the other hand, those who do not value these structures perhaps even regarding them as oppressive would clearly not consider them essentially positive. Criticisms of a structural-functionalist perspective include that it may underplay the existence of conflict and may be too optimistic about social structures having positive functions. From a different angle, Skrtic (1995a) offers a post-modern criticism of a functionalist position.

If the optimistic structural-functionalist view emphasizes stability and everything working to a constructive purpose, conflict approaches, depending on one's vantage point, take either a more jaundiced slant or a more realistic one. They focus on the struggles in society between different groups with different views and vested interests, thought to centre on access to limited economic resources or power. Weber (1972), for example, explores the conflicts between different groups over resources, power and status. The dominance of one group over another can arise in various ways and authority is an important aspect of dominance in this view. In considering special education from conflict perspectives, one could examine the historical development of special education and related economic, social and political circumstances. One might consider how some group interests can permeate the special education system and how interest groups can shape the structures for their own benefit. For example, potential conflicts may be examined between different lobby groups seeking what they consider appropriate recognition and sufficient resources for a particular type of disability/disorder such as reading disorder or attention deficit hyperactivity disorder. Or the grounds of conflict between different professional groups might be examined. Along similar lines, a 'radical structuralist' view of special education is presented by Tomlinson (1995) and by Sleeter (1995).

Structural-functionalist and conflict views are perhaps less current in recent times, and social creationist and social constructionist perspectives appear to be more favoured. A social creationist perspective regards the perceived problem of the disability/disorder as being a facet of the institutional practices of society. Disability is seen as being created as a form of oppression, which would be reduced if society's perceptions of disability as a problem were changed and if there was greater acceptance of human diversity. Also, it is implied, if disability is an aspect of society's institutional practices, then non-disabled members of society should contribute, including in material ways, in rectifying or reducing its effects. Within this context, the position has been used to argue for more resources from national taxation being used to improve the material conditions of disabled people (Allen *et al.*, 1998, p. 23).

Social constructionist perspectives emphasize the 'world' as socially constructed and social categories and social knowledge as being produced by the communications and interactions between people (Berger and Luckmann, 1971). Such a view tends to attribute disability/disorder to environmental factors such as the negative attitudes of teachers and others and the use of inappropriate teaching methods. Disability/disorder is considered to be largely constructed through the use of labelling (usually seen as negative) and categorization, both of which are consequently discouraged. Related to this view are interpretative approaches, 'bottom-up' views that inform research into small-scale interactions in everyday life. In special education, for example, interactions between a teacher and a child considered to have disability/disorder might be examined in terms of how these influence the child's view of himself and his environment (Ferguson and Ferguson, 1995).

When a social model of disability/disorder is considered in recent debates, it is often the social constructionist perspective or the social creationist view that is assumed. Sometimes the two are suggested to be similar in their differentiation from more 'reductionist' views as when Shakespeare (2006) states, 'The social model is social constructionist or . . . social creationist, rather than reductionist or biologically determinist' (ibid., p.29). Accordingly, in this chapter, the terms 'social perspective' or 'social view' are used in this broad sense. 'Strong' versions of the social view tend to differentiate between 'impairment' and 'disability'. 'Impairment' is seen as the physical, bodily aspect of a condition, and 'disability' is regarded as relating to the perceived barriers that an oppressive society places on the individual with an impairment. 'Disability' is regarded as a socially created or constructed phenomenon additional to the impairment (ibid., pp. 12–13) and can be seen as an interaction between the impairment and social influences.

A Social Perspective and Special Education

If 'disability' in the social perspective sense is seen as predominantly related to social oppression, it follows that an appropriate response is likely to be social, that of removing the oppression. Distinctions between different types of disorder/disability would be problematic in this view including claims for particular disability groups. Indeed, it has been suggested that, ' . . . the social model is incompatible with an impairment specific approach to disabled people' (Oliver, 2004, p. 30).

By contrast, it has also been argued that, ' . . . people with different impairments experience specific issues and problems' (Shakespeare, 2006, p. 32). Also, evidence-based practice suggests that for different types of disability/disorder, different types of provision (curriculum and assessment, pedagogy, school and classroom organization, resources, therapy/care) is effective in encouraging educational progress and personal and social development (Farrell, 2008b, passim). For example, for a pupil with autism, several approaches are considered as scientifically based practice: applied behaviour analysis, discrete trial teaching, pivotal response training and Learning Experiences–Alternative Program for Preschoolers and Parents (Simpson, 2005).

A social view has influenced the language in which special education is discussed in some quarters, for example, where provision for special children is seen in terms of removing perceived barriers. Bowe (1978) identified six kinds of social barriers: architectural, attitudinal, educational, legal, occupational and personal. The implication is that society, through its built environment, social organization, relationships and practices and people's attitudes has placed barriers in the way of a special child. It is argued therefore that society can remove such barriers in various ways, for example, by:

- changing the physical environment
- modifying the way that things are done and the associated social relationships
- changing attitudes.

Changing the physical environment If a physical barrier is the obstacle, this might be removed or action taken to reduce its impact. A building with steps that cannot be negotiated by someone in a wheelchair is seen as a barrier. It may be removed by fitting a ramp or installing an elevator wide enough for wheelchair access. Yet modifications to the physical environment tend to be more applicable to physical or sensory impairment rather than to other types of disability/disorder such as cognitive impairment (MacKay, 2002).

Apart from using learning resources effectively in teaching, which is part of what effective educators do anyway, it seems less convincing to speak in terms of removing physical barriers for cognitive impairment, autism, anxiety or depression.

The notion that certain features of the environment are a predominant part of a disability similarly seems to underemphasize both the impact of impairment and the interaction between impairment and environment. The impairment may make life more difficult for a person. Aspects of the environment may be modified to be more helpful to a special child. However, the idea that removing barriers somehow removes the impact of the impairment (that is in the present context, the disability) because it is predominantly brought about by the creation of the barriers seems to overemphasize the role of social aspects.

Modifying the way things are done If the way things are routinely done acts as a barrier, then other ways of doing them might be attempted. The teacher and others working in special education can be represented within the social constructionist model to be creating barriers when they use inappropriate methods of teaching, for example, teaching a special child in the same way as other children, taking insufficient account of his personal ways of learning. If the teacher uses better teaching methods more attuned to individual differences, this barrier can, it might be suggested, be removed or considerably reduced.

This is one of the themes of inclusive pedagogy. The idea is that if teaching and learning and associated aspects such as the curriculum, the use of resources, assessment, therapy and organization are sufficiently individualized for all pupils, special pupils will be no different from other pupils, who, equally will benefit from individualized or personalized learning. However, this seems to overlook evidence in favour of distinctive aspects of provision that appear to work for pupils with different types of disability/disorder as different groups (Farrell, 2008b; the chapter titled 'Pedagogical' in this book). This is not to suggest that there is one approach to pedagogy for special children and another for children without a disability/disorder and that the two have no relationship to one another. A clearer way of representing the possible range of provision including pedagogy for special children is to distinguish three areas (Lewis and Norwich, 2005, passim). The first is those approaches that apply to all children, for example, that they learn better if teaching captures attention and is engaging. These tend to be emphasized in debates about inclusive education. The second is approaches that may apply to a particular child, for example, drawing on a particular set of personal interests and inclinations. These are likely to be foregrounded in discussions about personalized learning. The third is those approaches that tend to work in the education and support of pupils with particular types of special educational needs such as profound cognitive impairment, autism, developmental coordination disorder or disruptive behaviour disorder. These tend to be highlighted when the debate turns to distinctive provision and evidence-based practice.

It is evident in this third area of approaches that sits uncomfortably with claims that the most effective solutions to provision (including pedagogy) have to be individualized ones. All three approaches can be used and the more productive debates centre on the degree to which any particular one is favoured and emphasized.

Changing attitudes In his attitudes to the pupil, the teacher can be presented in the social model as putting up barriers such as having expectations that are too low or seeing the pupil more in terms of his disability/disorder than as an individual. The worry seems to be that identifying pupils as having particular disability/disorder might lower expectations, perhaps because generalizations that might apply to pupils as a group could be incorrectly applied to a particular pupil. This is summarized to some extent by the term 'negative labelling'. The child becomes viewed in terms of the label originally intended for a condition.

Social perspectives of special education can alert practitioners and parents to the need to ensure that the social setting in which the special pupil is educated encourages academic progress and personal and social development. Any tendency to think of the child mainly in terms of his disability/disorder that might lower expectations is challenged. Where such attitudes are questioned and shown not to reflect the abilities of the pupil in question, they may be modified. Higher aspirations than might otherwise be the case are encouraged. In brief, where attitudes are acting as barriers, they may be challenged and changed.

However, with reference to the possibility of negative labelling contributing to attitudinal barriers, the alternative possibility that labelling might be positive is less often considered. Recognition of a particular type of disability/disorder can enable a pupil to receive suitable provision if educators judiciously draw on aspects of the provision previously found to be effective with other children with the condition. This is essentially the theme of evidence-based practice informed by professional knowledge and judgement.

Some Considerations Relating to Social Perspectives of Disability/Disorder

Among the general reservations about social views of disability/disorder, where they are used as an argument for mainstreaming, is that they tend not to draw on empirical justification for their position. For example, 'oppression' may be cited as the reason children should be educated in ordinary schools. This is taken to imply that greater 'equity' will be found where special pupils are educated in ordinary schools. However, these can become accepted positions from which the analysis begins, relegating any empirical enquiry to a merely illustrative role (Clarke *et al.*, 1998).

Attempts have been made to relate a socially constructed view of 'learning difficulty' to the supposed subordination and oppression of those labelled in this way and to further link this view to an emancipatory perspective of resistance. Armstrong (2003) collected the life stories of 40 people who had been 'labelled' as having learning difficulties. The relevance for modern special school education was limited. Over half these participants had experienced schooling 30 years or more prior to the research. Only 9 were at school after 1985, nearly 20 years before the survey. Armstrong maintains that the participants experienced 'subordination' but showed 'resistance'. However, the supposed evidence of subordination did not imply that participants' experience of special schooling was unhappy, sometimes quite the contrary. One participant in particular 'tells a story of his schooling that is filled with fond and happy memories' (p. 60). To the extent that Armstrong's concern is about possible subordination, as Warnock (2005) has pointed out, mainstream schools can be settings where children with special educational needs can be isolated, unhappy, marginalized and disaffected. However, there are implications that the views of pupils in special schools and ordinary schools, as well as those of adults with learning difficulties could be listened to and taken into account more. Voices that are not always taken into account and are sometimes marginalized are those of the many pupils speak highly of their special schools (Farrell, 2006a, pp. 38–45) and those of the many parents of children educated in a special school value the school greatly (Farrell, 2006a, pp. 27–37).

A social perspective recognizes difference but sees this as being at the level of the individual. It criticizes the construction of categories of pupils (such as pupils with autism) because it is considered that categories may ignore individual complexity and lead to responses that are arbitrary and even oppressive. Responses to individual pupils are therefore ad hoc, hindering the development of an explanatory theory of difference and any formalization of pedagogy. Where there are attempts at socially informed pedagogy, they concentrate on problem-solving, adhocracy and mechanistic curriculum models from which it is expected that the structures and practices that will deliver inclusion and equity will emerge. However, this may miss the point that once a curriculum is determined, some pupils will always learn within it better than others, perpetuating pupil differences whether categories are constructed or not (Clarke *et al.*, 1998, p. 166).

One might recognize the physical aspects of the environment that is a concern of a social view. At the same time, one might wish for a language other than that of barriers that would convey the importance of trying to modify the physical environment to improve access for people with disabilities without the suggestion that the environment has been somehow malignly designed for the purpose of excluding them.

The social perspective is reluctant to label pupils sometimes assuming that this is inevitably negative. However, it has been maintained (Farrell, 2008b) that this may have the disadvantage of de-emphasizing pedagogy and other provision shown to be effective for particular types of disability/disorder. Distinctive and effective provision could be given insufficient emphasis in an attempt to present disability/disorder as an aspect of difference with no consequences for provision.

Also the attempt to distinguish 'impairment' as the physical reality of a condition and 'disability' as the social consequences sometimes diminishes the consequences of the physical impairment. Attempts to deny the reality of cognitive impairment have been made attributing this largely to social factors as if by putting quotation marks around the terms they are exposed as fallacious. Goodley (2001, p. 211) maintains, ' . . . social structures practices and relationships continue to naturalize the subjectivities of people with "learning difficulties", conceptualizing them in terms of some *a priori* notion of "mentally impaired"'.

However, contrary to this view, it has been argued that with reference to emotional and social well-being, it is difficult in practice to separate mental distress caused by biological impairment and 'socially engendered psycho-emotional problems' because 'illness and impairment also undermine psycho-emotional well-being' (Shakespeare, 2006, p. 36). Disability is considered to be 'a complex interaction of biological, psychological, cultural and socio-political factors which cannot be extricated except with imprecision' (ibid., p. 38). In a similar vein, it has been maintained, ' . . . injustices to disabled people can be understood neither as generated by solely cultural mechanisms (cultural reductionism) nor by socio-economic mechanisms (economic reductionism) nor by biological mechanisms (biological reductionism). In sum, only by taking different levels, mechanisms and contexts into account, can disability as a phenomenon be analytically approached' (Danermark and Gellerstedt, 2004, p. 350). From this vantage point, the contribution of a social perspective is likely to be at its strongest when part of an interactionist view of special education and of disability/disorder.

The Scope of a Social Perspective

As already suggested (MacKay, 2002), a social approach seems to apply more convincingly to some types of disability/disorder than others. For a pupil with orthopaedic impairment, motor impairment, some health impairments and sensory impairments, the arrangement of the environment and the mitigation of barriers might be a useful way of approaching provision, although not without its difficulties.

For example, for a pupil with visual impairment, social arrangements may contribute to the impairment. Where the environment takes little or no account of the way the child orientates himself and finds his way around, the impairment can be compounded. So schools where there are tactile maps in the reception area to help the pupil check where he needs to be; where there are tactile and bold visual clues to anticipate different floor levels; and where there is the ability to precisely control ambient and localized lighting for different tasks, is likely to aid the pupil's learning and participation.

Physical aids for visual impairment provide other examples of modifying the environment in the broadest sense to allow the participation, progress and development of a pupil. These aids include magnifying devices, tactile modes of learning such as Braille and Moon, and adapted equipment for food preparation. Developing skills and using resources enabling fuller participation are important in developing social skills and independence (e.g., Sacks and Wolffe, 2005).

However, for some other types of disability/disorder such as cognitive impairment, the social basis of intervention is less clear. Criticisms can be made of anyone describing children and adults in ways other than those compatible with social explanations. For example, it has been said, as mentioned earlier, ' . . . social structures, practices and relationships continue to naturalize the subjectivities of people with "learning difficulties", conceptualizing them in terms of some *a priori* notion of "mentally impaired"' (Goodley, 2001, p. 211). This appears to distinguish between cognitive impairment as a physical reality ('mentally impaired') and a more socially constructed response ('learning difficulty'). Social structures, practices and relationships are identified as contributing to or perhaps constructing the 'learning difficulty'.

This point may have some relevance to some children with mild learning difficulties. Indeed, part of the debate about 'mild cognitive impairment' is the degree to which it might be understood as relating to biological or social factors. Conceptual and other difficulties perhaps related to neurological impairments may contribute. Also, materially poor and educationally impoverished family and community environments may have an impact (Farrell, 2008b, Chapter 4). More likely, the interaction of the two may lead, for example, to a slower pace of learning and to difficulty at the level of Piagetian (Piaget and Inhelder, 1966/1969; Piaget, 1970) 'formal operations'.

Yet a teacher and others may be working with a child with profound cognitive impairment who experienced brain damage at birth and who, at the age of 16, is functioning largely at a level of a child under the age of 1. It is difficult to know what the teacher would make of the apparent criticism that he is conceptualizing the child in terms on an '*a priori* notion'. Also, it is not apparent what barriers of 'social structures, practices and relationships' society (and the teacher and parents as representatives of it) has put in the way of the child that they should now remove. Similarly, for a child with autism, it is difficult to see what the removal of barriers might mean in daily living (Singer, 1999). For a child who finds interaction difficult, it is hard to see how the community could be changed to enable him to be accommodated with other people.

However, to the extent that negative labelling might contribute to educators having lower aspirations for pupils with disability/disorder having lower expectations, a social constructionist perspective might act as a corrective. Furthermore, a social view of disability/disorder might contribute to a multi-level perspective. It is suggested that, 'only by taking different levels, mechanisms and contexts into account, can disability as a phenomenon be analytically approached' (Danermark and Gellerstedt, 2004, p. 350). These levels include cultural, socio-economic and biological ones. Disability has similarly been defined as ' . . . the outcome of the interaction between individual and contextual factors–which includes impairment, personality, individual attitudes, environment, policy and culture' (Shakespeare, 2006, p. 58). A related interactional approach, can allow for ' . . . different levels of experience ranging from the medical, through the psychological, to the environmental, economic and political' (ibid., p. 62).

Fuller Examples

The rest of this chapter examines fuller examples of the application of a social perspective, seeking to apply the earlier discussion to practical considerations. In doing so, particular examples of impairment are considered: orthopaedic impairments and hearing impairment. These are chosen to provide the opportunity to demonstrate the contribution of a social understanding of impairment and disability, which is more difficult to apply with many types of disabilities/disorders such as autism, communication disorders, severe and profound cognitive impairment, traumatic brain injury, anxiety and depression.

It is recalled that strong versions of the social model tend to distinguish 'impairment' as the physical, bodily aspect of a condition and 'disability' as a socially constructed phenomenon additional to the impairment (Shakespeare, 2006, pp. 12–13). Impairment specific approaches have been suggested to be incompatible with such a view (Oliver, 2004, p. 30). Conversely it is argued, ' . . . people with different impairments experience specific issues and problems' (Shakespeare, 2006, p. 32). Also, evidence-based practice suggests that for different types of disability/disorder, different types of provision are effective (Farrell, 2008b, passim).

Yet social perspectives, even if having shortcomings, if argued as a sole position have importance for special education. Therefore, the following sections take an interactive view of disability/disorder placing importance on social perspectives, but recognizing their interaction with other aspects including individual perspectives. From this standpoint, the remaining sections begin with an impairment definition but bring in social factors influencing provision. In particular, the sections seek to apply the notion that an aspect of disability (in the social perspective sense) is the barrier hindering fuller participation in education and daily life and that the removal or modification of such barriers can reduce the disability.

In brief, then, the application of a social perspective is at its strongest when applied to some types of disability/disorder than others. This is despite the implication in some interpretations of social perspectives that it necessarily implies a rejection of typologies of disability/disorder. It is also stronger when seen as part of a contribution to an interactionist view rather than as a sole explanation of disability/disorder when it becomes one of the 'reductionist' approaches as limited and reductionist as the caricature medical model. Consequently, the focus of the rest of this chapter is on examples of two types of disability/disorder to which a social view seems to apply and takes an interactive view in which a social contribution is influential.

Hearing Impairment

This section briefly considers the contribution of a social perspective to understanding and responding to hearing impairment, first defining hearing impairment. Definitions of hearing impairment and deafness relate to 'frequency' and 'intensity/amplitude'. Frequency concerns the rate at which sound waves vibrate and is usually expressed as cycles per second (cps), or as Hertz (Hz). Sound frequency is perceived as pitch, with rapidly vibrating sound waves being perceived as high-pitched sounds and slower vibrating waves as low-pitched sounds. Categorizations of hearing impairment relate to intensity/amplitude, experienced as loudness and measured in a decibel (dB) scale. Normal conversation is carried out at 40 to 50 dB (Steinberg and Knightly, 1997). Hearing impairment can be measured in terms of dB loss. Categories of hearing impairment are recognized, for example, slight, severe, mild, moderate and profound, but different countries may have different cut-off points (Farrell, 2008b; Westwood, 2003, p. 48).

Following the argument of the social model and the impairment/disability distinction, hearing impairment can be considered a biological impairment, which may or may not be coupled with a disability brought about by the attitudes and practices of society. In making a distinction between impairment and disability, the social model suggests that disability is removable by social change, which can minimize the effect of any impairment. However, it has been argued (e.g. Shakespeare, 2006) that 'even in the most accessible world there will always be residual disadvantage attached to many impairments' (ibid., p. 50).

An often-quoted example of barrier removal in relation to people with hearing impairment is a historical study (Groce, 1985) of Martha's Vineyard, Massachusetts, an island off the eastern coast of the United States. Hereditary deafness was common in this isolated community and residents developed a dialect of sign language known as *Martha's Vineyard Sign Language*. It was estimated that by the late 1800s, around 0.7% of the residents were born deaf, nearly 20 times the national average. The sign language is reported to have been commonly used by hearing residents until the mid-1900s enabling deaf residents to be more included in the society. As deaf people could communicate with all their neighbours, it has been suggested, they experienced no disabling barriers and their hearing impairment was not a problem.

However, as Shakespeare (2006) has argued, this does not provide evidence that 'a barrier free environment eliminates disability and equalizes non-disabled and disabled people' (ibid., p. 51). The hearing members of the Martha's Vineyard community, to the extent that they did not stop speaking with other hearing neighbours, were able to communicate more widely in a way in which deaf members of the community could not fully participate. Hearing people had the advantage of two forms of communication, their speech and sign language, and could travel off the island and still communicate with others. In experiencing, appreciating and moving around in the natural environment, hearing people would have had the advantage of hearing natural sounds. These would range from pleasurable ones to sounds of warning and numerous other cues, to what is happening in the environment, not present in the same way for those with hearing impairment.

A variation on the question of the social positioning of deafness seems to relate to the debate and disagreements concerning special schools for deaf children. Some argue that deaf children should be educated in ordinary schools rather than special schools because they have a supposed human right to be educated with hearing children. Others maintain that hearing impairment is not a disability but a characteristic of a linguistic minority and that, therefore, this minority have a 'right' to be educated in special schools where they are not denied the opportunities to communicate with their peers who have hearing impairment. While this suggests a proliferation of supposed rights to the extent that some are no longer compatible with one another, it also relates to social views of deafness.

Other examples of responses to hearing impairment that could be said to remove barriers but that differ from social views include the use of aids to improve hearing. However, these address the barrier of the impairment rather than the attitudes of others and typical ways of doing things that might exacerbate hearing impairment. The 'removal' of hearing impairment through cochlear implants is considered controversial by some commentators for various reasons, including that it can be seen as not accepting the identity of the person as deaf and does not celebrate diversity. Others consider the operation a benefit perhaps because they do not accept the separation of impairment and disability assumed by the social model and regard the implant as a way of removing the impairment.

Orthopaedic Impairments and Removing Barriers

This section defines orthopaedic impairment and examines some practical applications of the notion of removing barriers from several vantage points: the curriculum, resources, accommodation, organization, and therapy and care. The examples given are illustrative rather than exhaustive. Under United States Individuals with Disabilities Education Act, an orthopaedic impairment is defined as a severe impairment affecting adversely the child's educational performance. The Code of Federal Regulations definition is 'impairments caused by congenital anomaly (e.g. club foot, absence of some member etc.), impairments caused by disease (e.g. poliomyelitis, bone tuberculosis etc.) and impairments from other causes (e.g. cerebral palsy, amputations and fractures or burns causing contractures)' (34 CFR, section 300.7 [c] [8], 1999). This definition embraces both orthopaedic conditions as strictly understood in relation to orthopaedics, and also neuromotor impairment.

Aspects of the *curriculum* can be reconsidered for pupils with orthopaedic impairments to remove or reduce constraints. The curriculum can help ensure the best involvement and support of the pupil in activities including art, technology and science where special equipment may be necessary. Within safety requirements, many activities may still be available in physical education for pupils with an orthopaedic impairment. The teacher may seek advice from the physical therapist and occupational therapist and may work with the physical therapist to devise programmes that will engage pupils with orthopaedic impairment. Where special programmes are necessary to develop skills or encourage movement, these can be planned into the pupil's school day to ensure that the pupil still encounters a balanced range of subjects.

Adapted physical education (APE), an individualized programme provided by people having studied requirements of physical education instruction for children with disabilities, is used in the United States. The APE teacher focuses on fundamental motor skills and physical performance of individual pupils and may work with pupils for a specified number of hours each week (Gabbard *et al.*, 1994). The classroom teacher and the APE teacher jointly develop and teach programmes of physical education, leisure and recreation. An approach suggesting the removal of barriers to participation is implied in the selecting and designing of suitable adapted physical activities using adaptive words as a guide. 'Raise and lower' might indicate raising the number of attempts allowed to successfully carry out an activity or lowering the physical height of equipment used in an activity, for example, the balance beam in gymnastics

(Bigge *et al.*, 2001, pp. 474–475). Barrier removal can be used to describe ways that activities can be structured to enable all pupils to participate in physical education lessons (Black and Haskins, 1996). For example, in a 'discrete adapted activity', pupils take part in pairs or practise individually (ibid.). In developing skills for a game in which a bat is used to strike a ball (e.g. soft ball) a pupil with orthopaedic impairment may practise using a larger bat or a lighter ball.

In educators' choice and use of *resources*, guidance from the physical therapist or the occupational therapist can remove potential barriers to a pupil's participation. Furniture will take account of a pupil's stature and need for good posture and support. During the teaching of subjects such as science where pupils might sit on high stools, a stool with a back support and arms may be used. Participation can be aided by ensuring that pupils are properly positioned perhaps using pads and cushions or specially constructed adapted seat inserts. Chairs without legs, corner seats and other types of seating may be employed (Bigge *et al.*, 2001, pp. 199, 201–204).

Mobility and physical access perhaps most obviously represent the potential to remove barriers. Hoists and other devices may support safe moving of the student. A PVC pipe walker or crutches may assist walking. Manual or powered wheelchairs can be used or toys used as mobility aids. Wheelchairs may be adaptable to climbing stairs. Otherwise, wheelchair access ramps and continuous areas of smooth floor surfaces can help ensure better access to classrooms and other facilities.

Barriers can be created if materials and equipment are not accessible or cannot be held or controlled easily. Bigge *et al.*, (2001, pp. 213–218) consider these matters in relation to the location of materials and equipment (e.g. a wheelchair backpack or modular stacking trays for storing materials that the pupil can reach from his desk): work surface modifications and object modifications. Object modifications can be understood in different ways. These include object stabilization (ways in which an object can be controlled or held still), boundaries (such as the periphery of a tray), grasping aids and manipulation aids (Finnie, 1997, pp. 127–160).

The pupil may have his own set of modified equipment for different subjects, for example, guillotine scissors or pencil grips in art lessons. When preparing food, the pupil may use adapted equipment such as a kettle tilting device for safer pouring, food choppers usable with one hand, cookers with special controls, and sinks and cooking surfaces of adjustable height.

Environmental control may involve the use of appliances such as communication devices and computers. Home lighting may be operated in various ways including electrically, by infrared, radio control or ultrasound. Switches enable the individual to gain greater control over the environment and can be activated by pushing, pulling, tilting, puffing, eye blinking and voice (Bigge *et al.*, 2001, pp. 219–221).

To the extent that school *accommodation* can constrain access to facilities or opportunities for independence and self-care, adapting accommodation can be seen as removing barriers. Separate rooms where personal care procedures can be carried out privately may be provided. Toilets may be adapted to take account of various requirements that students with orthopaedic impairment might have such as changing a colostomy bag. Also, the layout and use of school facilities can create hindrances that can be avoided or removed. Corridors can be made free of clutter to allow easy access for users of wheelchairs. In the classrooms and around school, sufficient room can be made for a pupil requiring mobility aids such as a wheelchair, walking frame or sticks to move around easily.

The *organization* of the school and the classroom can create barriers to access and participation, which can be removed. It might be helpful to enable some pupils with orthopaedic impairment to start their journey to the next lesson when corridors are relatively free. Therefore, the school might consider flexible arrival and departure times for lessons. Barriers can be set up by oversolicitous adult care and support, which can get in the way of the pupil socializing and making friends.

Regarding *therapy and care*, the support of services other than education is generally required for the student to function successfully and maintain better life quality (Snell and Brown, 2000). Medical practitioners, physical therapists, occupational therapists, prosthetists and others contribute to the pupil's well-being as well as reducing barriers and extending opportunities. Attitudinal barriers may be created in adults who do not have high enough expectations of a pupil's educational progress and personal and social development and these can be challenged and modified.

Conclusion

This chapter outlined an individual view of difficulty/disorder and examined other approaches as a context for considering a social view of disability/disorder. Examples of the application of a social perspective were given for orthopaedic impairments and hearing impairment. A social contribution may apply better to some types of disability/disorder than others. Relatedly, while a strong social view may be difficult to sustain, a multi-level explanation and understanding disability/disorder informed by social perspectives is likely to be more rsuasive.

Thinking Points

Readers may wish to consider the following:

- the extent to which a social perspective represents a credible view of special education;
- the degree to which a social view represents a credible representation of certain types of disability/disorder, for example, physical impairment and sensory impairment but less of a convincing picture of others, such as profound cognitive impairment or autism
- the degree to which Vygotsky's ideas on development and 'defectology' has relevance for the present day
- the potential for productively bringing together aspects of social views and individual views.

Key Texts

Armstrong, D. (2003) *Experiences of Special Education: Re-evaluating Policy and Practice Through Life Stories*. London: Routledge-Falmer.

Although this book does not provide up-to-date views of participants' experiences in special schools, it presents clearly arguments based on an oppression view of special education.

Barton, L. (Ed.) (2006) *Overcoming Disabling Barriers: 18 Years of Disability and Society*. New York/London: Routledge.

This brings together a selection of articles from the journal 'Disability and Society' and written by authors from the United States, Australia and Europe. The first section on disability studies includes articles on the social model of disability.

Farrell, M. (2006a) *Celebrating the Special School*. New York/London: Routledge.

This presents the positive views of parents and pupils attending present-day special schools. It suggests decisions about education in special schools be informed by the academic progress and personal and social development pupils make there, compared with ordinary schools.

Karpov, Y. V. (2005) *The Neo-Vygotskian Approach to Child Development*. New York: Cambridge University Press.

This book critically presents the way some Russian followers of Vygotsky's ideas have elaborated his ideas. These are essentially attempts to integrate child development (cognitive, motivational and social) with the role of children's activity as mediated by adults in development.

Langford, P. E. (2005) *Vygotsky's Developmental and Educational Psychology*. New York: Psychology Press.

This book provides a historical, cultural and philosophical (Marxist and Hegelian) context for Vygotsky's life and work.

Power, D. and Leigh, G. (Eds) (2004) *Educating Deaf Students: Global Perspectives*. Washington, DC: Gallaudet University Press.

Part 1 deals with 'Contemporary Issues for All Learners'; part 2 covers 'The Early Years'; part 3 'The School Years'; and part 4 'Contemporary Issues in Postsecondary Education'.

Shakespeare, T. (2006) *Disability Rights and Wrongs*. London: Routledge.

This wide-ranging and closely argued book critically examines debates relating to a strong social model of 'disability'.

Thomas, C. (2007) *Sociologies of Disability and Illness: Contested Ideas in Disability Studies and Medical Sociology*. New York/London: Palgrave Macmillan.

The book sets out in historical context, some areas of overlap and differences in medical sociology and disability studies.

Watson, N. (Ed.) (2007) *Disability: Major Themes in Health and Social Welfare*. New York/London: Routledge.

This edited four-volume collection on policy areas includes education and leisure. Volume one concerns the emergence of a social barriers approach and its relationship to social models of disability.

5

Medical

Introduction

This chapter introduces aspects of the discipline of medicine and the medical profession, related professions and issues arising from these. It explains the relationships between medical perspectives and special education. The scope of medical applications to children with disability/disorder is considered with brief reference to sensory impairment, orthopaedic impairment, health impairment, speech difficulties, disorders of conduct, obsessive-compulsive disorder and depression. Fuller examples are then examined. With regard to epilepsy, medical perspectives on the classification of seizures and implications for care and the administration of medication are discussed. Concerning attention deficit hyperactivity disorder (ADHD), the chapter looks into its validity as a medical condition and the use and possible overuse of medication in its management. In relation to traumatic brain injury, the contribution of medicine to treatment, assessment and rehabilitation is outlined.

Medicine and Children with Disorders/Disabilities

(a) Aspects of medicine and the medical profession

Paediatrics, the branch of medicine concerned with child development and childhood diseases, is perhaps most obviously relevant to special education (Candy *et al.*, 2001; Behrman and Kliegman, 2002; Osborn *et al.*, 2005; Kliegman *et al.*, 2007). Paediatrics is generally envisaged in terms of the development and care of children, and 'the nature and treatment of diseases of children' (Anderson, 2007, p. 1421). Reflecting this orientation, paediatric textbooks may cover paediatric principles using a developmental approach, and paediatric conditions using a systems approach, for example, neurology, metabolism, orthopaedics and so on (e.g. Candy *et al.*, 2001). However, underpinning such specialisms as paediatrics are foundational disciplines to medicine such as human anatomy, physiology, pathology and pharmacology. These in turn inform clinical medicine as it applies to children (and adults).

Anatomy, the structure of the human body and its scientific study, is conventionally divided into gross anatomy, histology, embryology and neuroanatomy (Standring, 2005, p. 3). Gross anatomy involves structures distinguishable to the naked eye, and includes surface anatomy (the study of the form of the body surface), endoscopic anatomy (in which the endoscope, an instrument for examining the body cavities, is used) and radiological anatomy (in which radiological techniques such as x-rays are employed) (ibid.). Histology is the study of microscopic tissue structure; embryology concerns the study of embryos and their development; and neuroanatomy is the anatomy of the nervous system.

Physiology concerns the functioning of the body including the processes of organs, cells, tissues and systems and the way they interact (Guyton and Hall, 1997). It has been defined as *the dynamic study of life* and as describing the function of ' . . . living organisms and their organs, cells and molecules' (Boron and Boulpaep, 2003, p. 3). Anatomy and physiology are very closely linked because living structures and their functions are interrelated (ibid.).

Pathology, the study and diagnosis of disease including its causes, mechanisms and consequences (Kumar *et al.*, 2005; Mohan, 2005), can involve the examination of cells, tissues, organs and body fluids. The term also refers to the medical specialism in which such investigations are used to obtain clinically useful information.

Pharmacology (Lissauer and Clayden, 2007; Rang *et al.*, 2007) concerns the understanding of the action of drugs and their effect on the different body systems and organs. It includes knowledge of the desired effects of drugs and understanding of any unwanted effects and drug toxicity. Pharmacokinetics, involving how the body deals with a drug including its absorption, distribution and excretion, includes developmental pharmacokinetics also, which applies this knowledge to infants and children (Kearns *et al.*, 2003).

Drawing on anatomy, physiology, pathology, pharmacology and a range of other knowledge and skills, clinical medicine (Kumar and Clark, 2005;

McPhee and Ganong, 2006) concerns the management and treatment of health problems and considers following aspects:

- aetiology
- prevalence
- diagnosis
- disease course
- prognosis
- treatment.

Aetiology refers to 'the study or theory of the factors that cause disease and the method of their introduction to the host' and to 'the causes or origin of a disease or disorder' (Anderson, 2007, p. 660). For example, in cystic fibrosis, a disorder involving dysfunction of the exocrine glands leading to signs such as chronic pulmonary disease, the cause is a defect in a gene on chromosome 7 (Weinberger, 1993). In some conditions, although certain causes may be known, others may not. In congenital heart disease, aetiology is often unknown. Sometimes one may speak more accurately of precipitating factors, for example, among those associated with asthma are the inhalation of cold air, atmospheric pollution and exercise (Kumar and Clark, 2005, pp. 912–915).

Prevalence, the total number of cases of a disease or condition in a specified population that exists at any one time, may be expressed as the number of cases per 100 000 people. On the basis of such information, conditions may be described on a dimension from very common to very rare. In a particular country, diabetes mellitus may be common, blindness fairly common, Down's syndrome uncommon and autism rare. Prevalence is distinguished from incidence, which is the number of new cases occurring during a specified period. There may be 200 new cases of a disease per 100 000 people per year. If these continue year on year, prevalence will exceed incidence unless people with the condition die at the same rate that new cases appear (Anderson *et al.*, 2003, p. 1505 'prevalence' and p. 919 'incidence').

Diagnosis, 'the determination of the nature of a case of disease', includes clinical diagnosis based on 'signs, symptoms and laboratory findings during life' (Anderson *et al.*, 2003, p. 507). In foetal diagnoses, chromosome analysis allows the identification of chromosomal abnormalities such as trisomy 21 (Down's syndrome). More broadly, diagnosis may involve the doctor drawing on personal observation, signs reported by the patient, physical examination and various investigations depending on the specific circumstances.

The course of a disease or condition is a description of its typical path. Regarding Duchenne muscular dystrophy, a sex-linked recessive trait affecting boys only, traits may become apparent about the age of 3 years, with the child being unable to run properly or keep up athletically with peers. Weakness progresses such that ' . . . arm weakness is evident by 6 years of age, and most boys are confined to a wheelchair by 12 years of age'. By the age of 16, there is little mobility in the arms and respiration difficulties increase (Behrman and Kliegman, 2002, p. 813).

Prognosis, an estimate of the outcome of a disease, is informed by knowledge of its typical course and the patient's age and general condition, and the outcome may vary with the individual. It has been defined as *a forecast as to the probable outcome of an attack of disease* and recovery prospects ' . . . as indicated by the nature and symptoms of the case' (Anderson *et al.*, 2003, p. 1515).

Treatment, the steps taken to cure or prevent a disease, includes a range of interventions. Drugs may be used in connection with various disabilities/disorders. The psychostimulant methylphenidate may be used in cases of ADHD. In asthma therapy, a mainstay is the administration of therapeutic agents delivered directly to the lungs as powders or aerosols. Genetically engineered drugs are sometimes used such as factor VIII concentrate administered by intravenous infusion to treat haemophilia A (Kumar and Clark, 2005, p. 473). Intensive care may be necessary for some conditions such as traumatic brain injury. This enables vital functions such as heart rate, breathing and blood pressure to be monitored, any change in the child's condition detected immediately and suitable action taken. Surgical procedures include the ethically debated (Stewart and Ritter, 2001) insertion of cochlear implants for some children who are deaf and replacing joints in some orthopaedic conditions. Cancer treatment may involve surgery, chemotherapy, radiotherapy and biological/endocrine therapy.

In brief, the study and practice of medicine involves foundational disciplines such as human anatomy and physiology, pathology and pharmacology. These inform clinical medicine, which includes consideration of aetiology, prevalence, diagnosis, disease course, prognosis and treatment. Paediatrics, concerned with child development and childhood diseases, applies this to children.

Community paediatrics is a speciality within paediatrics. Community paediatricians work with children and families in a holistic way, ensuring liaison between educators and other professionals and agencies as needed. One area of community paediatrics is neurodisability. In a particular district, a community paediatrician will be responsible for the care of children with disabilities as part of a team, which may include therapists, community nurses, colleagues from education and welfare services and voluntary agencies.

(b) Related professions

Other professions also make important contributions. The following are among the professions related to medicine and whose members may be involved in supporting children with disabilities and disorders:

- physical therapy/physiotherapy (Farrell, 2003c)
- occupational therapy (ibid.)
- speech and language pathology/therapy (Farrell, 2005g)
- prosthetics and orthotics (Farrell, 2006b)
- podiatry (Farrell, 2006c)
- dietetics (ibid.)
- diagnostic radiography (ibid.).

As implied in the outline of medicine provided in the previous section, doctors make the diagnosis, prescribe treatment and estimate prognosis. They can provide advice to a school in the form of a 'health care plan'. Physical and occupational therapists undertake a detailed functional assessment of a child's abilities and limitations and provide an individualized treatment programme. They may also provide advice to the school on seating, mobility aids and so on.

Members of these related professions, like medical doctors, are usually employed by health care providers. However, there are exceptions such as where schools directly employ and pay their own full-time speech pathologist who may maintain links with the health care provider for personal support, professional supervision and training.

(c) Considerations relating to medical approaches

Those who support a social view of disability sometimes depict medical perspectives in terms of a 'medical model'. This is touched on in the chapter 'Social' of this book. Essentially, a medical model, in the social view, is equated with an individual perspective, which tends to locate the disability within the child. It may take insufficient account of social factors or views that disability may in some senses be socially constructed (Barnes and Mercer, 1996; Booth, 1998; Drake, 1996). Such depictions are sometimes made not only of medicine but also of aspects of other disciplines where it is perceived that an individual approach has the propensity to recognize social factors insufficiently.

Where such social views are held, it may be argued that a distinction can be made between 'impairment', which is taken to mean the physical aspect of a condition, and 'disability', which is taken to refer to the interaction between the impairment and the environment, including the influence of the attitudes and behaviours of others. Social views do not necessarily oppose medical approaches as such, but argue against perspectives that might regard the identity of a person to be excessively defined in terms of the disability/disorder.

Also, while the potential benefits of medical interventions may be recognized, there is a view that the possible complications, discomfort and risk may not always be made as prominent. Where medication is prescribed, the potential benefits as well as possible negative side effects and risks need to be apparent. For obsessive-compulsive disorder, the tricyclic antidepressant clomipramine was shown to lead to significant improvement (DeVeaugh-Geiss *et al.*, 1992) but cardiac monitoring was essential because of the very small risk of sudden death from cardiac arrest (review by Geller *et al.*, 1999). For ADHD, methylphenidate can lead to side effects including insomnia and temporary loss of appetite. In practice, it is important that a thorough assessment is undertaken before medication is used and that effects are continuously monitored, including by school and home.

Surgical procedures such as limb straightening can allow individuals with restricted growth with malformed joints and legs to be more mobile and avoid any worsening effects of the condition (Shakespeare, 2006, p. 108). However, limb lengthening has been described as ' . . . a very stressful procedure causing considerable pain, frequent infections around the sites where pins are inserted into bones, and confinement to a wheelchair for many months (ibid., p. 109).

Medicine in Relation to Special Education

In considering the contribution of medical aspects to special education, it is important that the focus is clear. The remit is not the medical attention that some children need while being educated. Neither is it on the medical attention and treatment that may be necessary to enable the child to benefit from education. Both of these are important; but the focus in relation to medical aspects of special education is more specific. It concerns how medicine and medical information inform the special education and care of children with certain health related conditions.

There needs to be mutual understanding and collaboration between educators and many health personnel who work within a largely medical framework. This is widely recognized as a worthwhile aspiration. However, in practice, this is difficult to achieve because of differences in training, perspectives and roles of the different people working with a child with disability/disorder.

Nevertheless, special educators need to be familiar with basic medical information. Teachers of children with visual impairment require basic knowledge of the anatomy and physiology of the optic nerve and visual system; an understanding of the pathology of various conditions affecting vision; and an appraisal of the assessments used to ascertain vision. Such information is used to help determine the best environment for the child such as suitable lighting and the use of other resources, the use of tactile methods of teaching and learning and other aspects of provision and education (Farrell, 2008b, Chapter 6). Similar understanding is required with regard to hearing impairment and deafblindness. Contextual knowledge and understanding is needed to provide for pupils with orthopaedic impairment, traumatic brain injury and health impairment.

For example, medical aspects of congenital heart condition inform provision including educational provision. A congenital heart condition, a heart abnormality present at birth affecting heart chambers, heart valves or major blood vessels such as the aorta, occurs in about 1% of live births (Kumar and Clark, 2005, p. 832). Although often the aetiology is unknown, genetic and chromosomal abnormalities are among the recognized associations (ibid.). The types of heart condition affecting children include coarctation (narrowing) of part of the aorta, which may require surgery in childhood (ibid., pp. 837–838).

If a child has a congenital heart condition constraining the child's capacity for strenuous physical exertion and having other implications, among possible considerations for education in school are *logistical* ones. Where the school building has stairs, it is important that the classroom and other facilities are on the lower floor or otherwise, the necessity of stair climbing should be minimized, perhaps by using a lift or stair climber. A pupil's belongings may be kept in a locker in a central, accessible area to reduce the need to carry equipment around school. As with all children, *safety* is another prime consideration. Some aspects of lessons, where there may be some inhalation of fumes, such as metal shop or science may have to be avoided. A mask may be used in some practical lessons where dust might be inhaled. Where lessons are physically taxing, the child may need extra adult *support*. In physical education lessons, *alternative activities* that are engaging and participatory may be provided. *Organizational flexibility* may be required such as flexible time scales for the return of homework where fatigue has delayed its return. Supported work at home or home tuition may be arranged if the child is absent from school for long periods. *Specialist resources* include the possible use of postural aids where lessons require long periods of standing.

As may be seen from the example of a congenital heart condition, the implications for special education can include the following:

- logistical
- safety orientated
- support and alternative activities
- organizational flexibility
- specialist resources.

Where medical information suggests requirements in regard to logistical matters, these may relate to the possible fatiguing effects of conditions or physical constraints on mobility. These may make it necessary that the school examines situations where pupils generally use stairs, make long journeys between lessons in tight time limits or where facilities are spread over a large campus area. Where such constraints can be reduced, it is sometimes said that schools are removing 'barriers' to participation. Sometimes the environment can be modified or alternatives used as when a child who has difficulty climbing stairs can use a lift. However, the environment is not always the sole reason for any constraints. For example, the environment does not bring about fatigue on its own. It brings it about in interaction with certain conditions in which usual levels of exertion are very difficult. This is not to say that solutions should not be sought, but that this is likely to involve taking account of the environment and the condition, not just the environment.

Regarding safety procedures, medical conditions highlight the role of general safety precautions for all children. Such procedures also pinpoint particular risks that may be experienced by children having a particular condition. In areas of the curriculum where noxious fumes may be involved, care is taken to avoid or minimize their inhalation. For pupils more prone to the effects of such fumes, such as those with respiratory problems, greater care is needed.

Support and alternative activities may be suitable for pupils with some medical conditions. Some conditions may require the child to avoid rough contact sports but he could participate in alternative forms of exercise such as swimming. Among such conditions is osteogenesis imperfecta (brittle bone syndrome) a group of disorders of which the commonest, type I, is predominantly inherited (Candy *et al.*, 2001, p. 346). Another is haemophilia A, the commonest genetic blood coagulation defect (ibid., p. 256). Organizational flexibility may involve earlier or later starts to lessons, or home or hospital tuition perhaps including the use of video links, the Internet and e-mails. Specialist resources might include a range of physical aids to positioning and movement to enable the fullest participation in lessons.

In addition to the above points, there are implications for special education where medication is prescribed as mentioned in the next two sections.

The Scope of Medical Perspectives in Special Education

The scope of medical perspectives relates to different disabilities/disorders. For a child with visual impairment, assessment information and advice are gleaned from the optician and ophthalmologist as well as specialist teachers. This helps decide the way the classroom teacher presents work and the environment in which the child carries out his studies. The type of visual impairment a child experiences influences the type of illumination used. A child having photophobia requires reduced lighting while others will prefer higher levels of illumination (Farrell, 2008b, Chapter 6). Similarly, for a child with hearing impairment, assessments and advice from the audiologist and specialist teachers will influence the teaching environment and teaching itself (ibid., Chapter 5). If a child is deafblind, contributions from these specialists are also important (ibid, Chapter 7).

For a pupil with orthopaedic impairment or motor difficulties, the contribution of the physical therapist can be extensive. It will include assessment, perhaps direct therapy, and advice to the teacher and others on posture, movement and other matters. Physical therapists and teachers may work together to produce programmes enabling the fullest participation of the child in physical activities and lessons including physical education and games (Black and Haskins, 1996). The occupational therapist similarly will be involved in assessment, direct work and advice. Where physical disability or motor impairment limits the manipulation and exploration of objects, the occupational therapist may give advice and guidance on alternative means of developing three-dimensional understanding. This might involve handling objects using the feet or the mouth if the child has no hands, or using three-dimensional computer simulations.

Educators working with children with health impairments may draw on medical advice as to the best way to help the pupil learn and develop while ensuring safety. The medical doctor's assessment of asthma may lead to advice about what activities may be pursued, the implications of weather conditions – especially cold – and the optimal regime for exercise and rest. The child himself will be involved in ongoing decisions and will be helped to anticipate the need for rest and encouraged and guided to develop skills and knowledge that help manage the condition. As they get older, many children are encouraged to carry their own inhaled medication and to use it as required, for example, prior to exercise.

Approaches to speech difficulties include medical ones (e.g. Martin and Miller, 2003, pp. 40–45). Medical perspectives may include genetic information, as it appears some speech difficulties have a hereditary element. Structural and sensory problems may require medication to be administered, for example, antibiotics for ear infection; or surgery may be recommended for cleft palate.

Regarding various types of disorder/disability, the use of medication has implications for the education of the child. In disorders of conduct, where it has been maintained that medication cannot be justified as the 'first line of treatment' (Fonagy *et al.*, 2005, p.192), teachers need to be aware of the intended effects and the potential side effects of any medication. These include the possible impact on learning and other aspects of behaviour. With disorders of conduct, while traditional neuroleptic medication seems to reduce aggressiveness, side effects include sedation and interference with learning. Atypical anti-psychotic drugs appear to reduce aggressiveness but weight gain is reported. The effectiveness of combinations of psychosocial treatments and stimulant medication together appears greater and more sustained than either on their own. Also, where other strategies are developed and evaluated well, medication may not need to be considered (Fonagy *et al.*, 2005, pp. 182–192).

In research involving children and young people aged 8 to 17 years, obsessive-compulsive behaviours appear to be significantly lowered by the selective serotonin reuptake inhibitor 'fluvoxamine'. Selective serotonin reuptake inhibitors also tended to produce less serious side effects than tricyclics (Riddle *et al.*, 2001). It is recommended that for childhood obsessive-compulsive disorder, the treatment of choice is a combination of selective serotonin reuptake inhibitor medication and cognitive behavioural therapy (March, 1999).

Fuller Example of the Application of Medical Perspective: Epilepsy

This section outlines the nature of epilepsy and its causal and precipitating factors, and where these can be identified. It explains limitations of classification systems for seizures and epilepsies, but indicates the importance of classification for management and care in school and elsewhere.

Epilepsy and causal factors Epilepsy is a neurological condition defined by 'clinical manifestations linked to chronic recurrence of paroxysmal discharges within neuronal networks of the brain . . . ' (Jambaqué *et al.*, 2001, p. 1). Clinical manifestations include ' . . . acute events, the epileptic seizures, and/ or progressive deterioration of motor, sensory or cognitive functions' (ibid.). Seizures are associated with convulsions (violent movements of the limbs or the whole body caused by muscular contractions), muscle spasms, involuntary movements and changes in perception and consciousness.

Often epilepsy is idiopathic, for example, in over two-thirds of cases of epilepsy in a UK community survey, a definite cause was not established (Kumar and Clark, 2005, p. 1221). Understanding of factors contributing to a chronic susceptibility to seizures has been described as 'rudimentary' (Westbrook, 2000, p. 930). Known causes comprise various combinations of ' . . . brain damage, genetic predisposition and maturation phenomena characteristic of the child's brain' (Jambaqué *et al.*, 2001, p. 1). Aetiological factors include genetic predisposition with a low seizure threshold appearing to run in families; perinatal trauma and hypoxia (lack of oxygen); and brain injury (usually sufficient to cause coma). Factors that may precipitate seizures include watching flashing lights such as those associated with some video games particularly when tired ('photosensitive epilepsy') (Candy *et al.*, 2001, p. 318).

Classifications of seizures and epilepsies

1. Seizures.

In the early twenty-first century, the most widely used classification system for seizures was the International Classification of Epileptic Seizures (ICES) revised in 1981 by the Commission on Classification and Terminology of the International League Against Epilepsy (1981). Under this ICES system, seizures may be classified as generalized or partial. There are also unclassified seizures, for example, neonatal seizures (ibid, part III).

A *generalized* seizure is one in which first clinical changes indicate that both hemispheres of the brain are involved. Further clinical classification distinguishes 'absence seizures', 'myoclonic seizures', 'clonic', 'tonic-clonic' or 'atonic' (ibid, part II paraphrased). These terms convey the characteristics and course of the seizure. For example, 'absence seizures' tend to occur suddenly and interrupt ongoing activity and the child may stare blankly. Generalized 'tonic-clonic seizures' comprise tonic (rigid) and clonic (shaking) aspects (ibid., part V, Definition of Terms, paraphrased). A *partial* seizure is one in which it is indicated there is initial activation of neurons in part of one cerebral hemisphere. It is further clinically classified according to whether consciousness is impaired during the seizure, either at the onset or during its course. It is also classified according to whether it evolves into 'generalized' tonic-clonic convulsions (ibid, part I paraphrased).

The ICES 1981 classification assumes a one-to-one relationship between 'electroclinical syndromes' and 'corresponding epilepsy syndromes' (Kellinghaus *et al.*, 2006, p. 217). But the correlation of neuroimaging and video electroencephalography (EEG) results shows the relationship between an electroclinical syndrome and the underlying epileptogenic process is, in fact, variable especially in infants (Nordli *et al.*, 2001). In the context of such 'unresolved issues and controversies' (Kellinghaus *et al.*, 2006, p. 217), a further proposal was put forward by an International League Against Epilepsy Task Force on Classification and Terminology (Engel, 2001). Debate continues about the optimum system. A number of Internet sites give a brief overview of seizure types, for example, www.e-epilepsy.org.uk.

2.   Epilepsies.

The system for classifying the epilepsies proposed by the Commission on Classification and Terminology of the International League Against Epilepsy (1989) is the most widely used. It is based largely on the definition of electroclinical syndromes (Loddenkemper *et al.*, 2006, p. 347). Part I describes temporal lobe, frontal lobe, parietal lobe and occipital lobe epilepsies. Part II deals with definitions, for example, localization-related epilepsies and syndromes, generalized epilepsies and syndromes. These include childhood absence epilepsy, juvenile absence epilepsy, and epilepsy with generalized tonic-clonic seizures on awakening. Part III concerns symptomatic generalized epilepsies of specific etiologies. Part IV includes reference to primary reading epilepsy, that is, reflex epilepsy that is triggered when the individual tries to read (Commission on Classification and Terminology of the International League Against Epilepsy [1989]).

A 2001 ILAE proposal includes five axes for seizure description, seizure type, epilepsy syndrome, aetiology and impairment (Engel, 2001). This structure is an attempt to overcome 'shortcomings and confusion' among three features. The first is EEG features measuring brain activity through the skull reflecting electrical events generated by neurons. The second is clinical seizure symptomatology. The third feature is syndrome classification (Loddenkemper *et al.*, 2006, p. 348). Dividing seizure classification into various axes is partly in response to the lack of strict one-to-one relationship between epilepsy syndromes and seizure types (ibid.). However, limitations to the 2001 proposals have been identified (ibid., pp. 349–353) and the debate continues.

Implications of classification for educators and others Even given the limitations of classification systems for seizures and epilepsies, until better ones are devised educators and others work within existing frameworks. Educators need various pieces of information with regard to a child. These are the type of seizures the child experiences, their frequency, and whether they occur at particular times of the day or night, week or month. Teachers also need to know any potential 'triggers' such as tiredness or certain types of lighting; and how a seizure, should it occur, must be dealt with (Johnson and Parkinson, 2002, p. 7, paraphrased).

If a teacher is present when a seizure occurs, she will need to know what support to provide and what other action to take. Afterwards, she needs to know how to describe the seizure and how to record information that will further inform provision including the management of any subsequent seizures. Pre-printed seizure description forms may be used to help ensure full and systematic recording of observations.

For tonic-clonic seizures, procedures include not moving the child unless he is in danger and placing him in the safety-recovery position. Should a child experience regular tonic-clonic seizures, or other attacks where he may fall and injure his head, he may wear a protective helmet. Knowledge of the physical effects of tonic-clonic seizures, during which the child may lose bladder and bowel control, enables educators and others to plan ahead so that they can respond supportively. The school can seek to ensure privacy during such episodes and can make practical arrangements such as keeping a second supply of the child's clothing easily available to replace any stained clothing.

Staff need to be able to competently and sensitively deal with seizures and carefully record their progress because it has implications for the management of medication and other matters. The teacher needs to know whether there are arrangements for medication to be taken during the day. She needs to be aware of any side effects of medication, and whether there have been any changes in medication and the implications for school activities.

Emergency procedures and protocols are also put in place for very occasional instances such as when after several minutes, a seizure does not look as though it is stopping, or when the child has several seizures within a few minutes (status epilepticus). In managing seizures lasting more than 20 minutes, the child may be administered rectal diazepam (Candy *et al.*, 2001, p. 319). Where such procedures are followed in school, certain arrangements are likely to be in place such as that members of staff will have been trained, parents will have given consent and guidelines will have been agreed upon with the school principal and staff.

The classification of epilepsy in terms of a syndrome, where this is possible, assists in understanding what the cause might be; the possible course of the syndrome, the sort of treatment that might be effective and the prognosis. For example, the Lennox–Gastaut syndrome usually becomes apparent in children aged 1 to 8 years. It is associated with multiple generalized seizure types, typical EEG patterns between attacks and cognitive dysfunction in most individuals. Non-convulsive status epilepticus is common. The seizures are usually resistant to medical treatment (Farrell and Tatum IV, 2006, p. 429).

It will be remembered that Part I of the Commission on Classification and Terminology of the International League Against Epilepsy (1989) described several types of epilepsy according to brain location, including temporal lobe epilepsies. When educating children with frontal lobe epilepsy, the importance of a multidisciplinary approach has been stressed including medication, tutoring as necessary and psychological support (Hernandez *et al.*, 2001, 109). Children with frontal lobe epilepsy tend to be impulsive and have difficulty sustaining effort throughout an activity. They tend to function better when goals are clear and when information is provided step by step, checking understanding along the way. They require help in organizing and planning work and leisure activities. Behaviour modification may be effective, and training in self-management and 'positive feedback' can enable the child to become more autonomous and raise his self-esteem (ibid.).

Such general information can help teachers, parents and others understand the implications of the condition at the same time as they respond to individual differences in relation to a particular child. These implications include possible effects on cognition, language and social skills.

Fuller Example of the Application of Medical Perspective: Attention Deficit Hyperactivity Disorder

This section considers a widely used definition of ADHD and the validity of ADHD as a biological dysfunction; and examines issues relating to the use of medication for children with the condition.

The validity of ADHD as a biological dysfunction The term ADHD emerged from attempts to describe inattentive, overactive and impulsive behaviour.

The *Diagnostic and Statistical Manual of Mental Disorders Fourth Edition Text Revision* (*DSM-IV-TR*) (American Psychiatric Association, 2000, pp. 85–93) definition sets out criteria relating to inattention, hyperactivity and impulsivity. The nine criteria for *inattention* include these: 'often fails to give close attention to details or makes careless mistakes in school work, work or other activities' and 'often has difficulty sustaining attention in tasks or play activities'. Among the six criteria for *hyperactivity* are, 'is often "on the go" or often acts as though "driven by a motor"'. The three criteria for *impulsivity* include 'often has difficulty waiting a turn' (ibid., p. 92).

The diagnostic criteria state that six or more of the nine criteria for inattention *or* six or more of the nine criteria for hyperactivity-impulsivity should have persisted for at least 6 months to an extent that is 'maladaptive and inconsistent with developmental level'. Four further criteria must be met including that 'some impairment from the symptoms is present in two or more settings . . . ' such as at school and home and that 'some hyperactive-impulsive or inattentive symptoms were present before age 7 years' (ibid., p. 92). Clearly, a child can meet the criteria if he manifests different combinations of inattention, hyperactivity and impulsiveness. This influences whether the difficulty is seen as predominantly inattention, or hyperactivity, or impulsivity with hyperactivity. There is debate about whether it is useful to combine these potentially disparate profiles under the wider criterion of ADHD. An alternative view is that it would be better to consider 'hyperactivity-impulsiveness' and 'inattention' as predominantly separate manifestations that may and often do overlap.

The validity and the credibility of ADHD as a distinctive condition are sometimes considered to depend on there being a discernible physical abnormality being established. If it is a real biological dysfunction, it is argued, abnormalities such as neurological indicators should be discernible. Where it is considered that no discernible physical abnormality has been securely established for ADHD purported 'symptoms' can be regarded as little more than a list of behaviours annoying to teachers and parents. Arguing along such lines, Cohen (2006) maintains the diagnosis of ADHD 'cannot have any validity as a label for a genuine biological dysfunction' (ibid., p. 21).

It has been suggested that the classification of ADHD involves identifying the symptoms in medical terms but not the possible causes of the behaviours because the symptoms are synonymous with the condition. This view may be taking insufficient account of possible neurological correlates of ADHD or the apparently related effect of psychostimulants (see the following section). If ADHD is solely the list of purported symptoms, it is difficult to explain why medication seemingly acting on hypothesized brain processes has its effect.

Considerations regarding the use of medication for ADHD Psychostimulants are the most frequently prescribed drugs for children with ADHD and have been demonstrated to be effective in controlling hyperactive and aggressive behaviour in these children (Fonagy *et al.*, 2005, p. 199). The beneficial effects of stimulants for the primary symptoms of 'inattention, hyperactivity, and impulsivity' have been confirmed in more than 100 trials, at least in the short term (ibid., p. 202, and pp. 199–217 for reviews of some of these studies). Methylphenidate is the most frequently used psychostimulant (Swanson *et al.* 1995). Possible side effects for stimulant treatment include loss of appetite, insomnia, changes in mood, nausea and vomiting, and suppression of growth (Fonagy *et al.*, 2002, p. 201).

Where the use of psychostimulant drugs appears effective with ADHD, possible neurological explanations are hypothesized. Methylphenidate may act to increase the release of the neurotransmitter dopamine in individuals where dopamine signals are weak. It is proposed that, as a dopamine reuptake inhibitor, methylphenidate increases the level of dopamine in the brain by partly blocking the dopamine transporter that removes it from the synapses. This amplification of the release of dopamine is thought to improve the individual's attention and ability to focus attention (Vaidya *et al.*, 1998). Neuroimaging investigations have indicated that, for children taking Ritalin, stimulus recognition is improved in terms of better attention to auditory and visual stimuli (Seifert *et al.*, 2003).

The use of medication for pupils with ADHD is debated in part because of the variation in its use. For example, in the United States around 90% of pupils with ADHD receive medication of some kind (Greenhill, 1998), while in the United Kingdom, about 10% of pupils with ADHD are estimated to receive medication (Munden and Arcelus, 1999), with less than 6% being administered methylphenidate (National Institute of Clinical Excellence, 2000).

Concerns are expressed that medication may not always be used according to clear parameters and may be overprescribed. In 1998, a survey investigating the use of stimulants in public elementary schools in Laval, Quebec, Canada (Cohen *et al.*, 1999) found that some 2% of girls and 6% of boys were taking prescribed stimulants. A study conducted in Laval in 1998 (Cohen, 2006) gathered information from focus group discussions in five small groups totalling 29 participants: parents, teachers, school-based psychosocial practitioners, primary care physicians and specialist physicians. It aimed to examine why and how the decision to medicate children arose. The discussions were taken to indicate ' . . . a poorly controlled process of assessment, intervention and follow-up, lacking *explicit* guiding or consensual principles' (ibid., p. 151, italics in original).

Among the parameters under which medication is used are that stimulant treatment should start with a below optimal dose to reduce the risk of side effects, and that the dose should be gradually increased while monitoring 'for effectiveness and any adverse reactions' (Fonagy *et al.*, 2002, p. 200).

All school staff working with children with disability/disorder who are administered medication need to be aware of the expected effects of the medication so that they can contribute to an assessment of its effectiveness in achieving what is intended. If the expectation of administering psychostimulants to a child with ADHD is to improve his ability to concentrate and to focus attention, monitoring needs to establish whether this is happening. At the same time, staff need to be conversant with possible side effects of the medication, so they are part of the monitoring of its safety and effectiveness. School staff need to liaise with parents and others to ensure that an overall picture of the effects of the medication is achieved and maintained. Also, because medication may be used in combination with other approaches such as behavioural interventions, it is not always possible in individual instances to ascribe the proportionate contribution to any improvements to one or the other.

Fuller Example of the Application of Medical Perspective: Traumatic Brain Injury

This section describes traumatic brain injury (TBI) and its causes, medical information relating to it, assessment and rehabilitation.

Traumatic brain injury and its causes The term 'acquired brain injury' may refer to an injury to the brain occurring after birth and caused by an accident or as a result of disease or infections, therefore excluding congenital brain injury (e.g. Walker and Wicks, 2005, pp. 1–2). In this context, 'atraumatic' brain injury is caused by illness and infection while TBI results from accidents or other injuries. Among the most frequent causes of TBI are a traffic accident, fall or sport injury (DiScala, Osberg and Savage, 1997). The injury may arise from an intentional act such as attempted suicide, or child physical abuse or other violent crime. TBI may give rise to neurological problems and can affect attention and memory, the visual system, executive functions, communication and behaviour. Recently published summaries of these effects and the implications for education in school are available (Farrell, 2008b, Chapter 10).

Medical information and traumatic brain injury In educating children who have experienced TBI, teachers and others need to understand the relevance of medical information. This will emerge in discussions at joint meetings of health, social/welfare services and educational personnel and in reports to the school from health personnel. Such discussion and information will establish the prognosis for the particular child. Educators also need to understand the likely effects of TBI on the child's cognitive processes and functioning, and the educational implications of these may be very subtle.

Assessments of the location and severity of traumatic brain injury There are important medical contributions for the identification and assessment of TBI. Non-invasive techniques already described, computerized tomography scans and magnetic resonance imaging scans help determine the type and location of the child's injury after the trauma. Information from these sources is put together with assessments of the child's functioning to provide a more comprehensive picture. Observations are made on the duration of the coma and of post-traumatic amnesia, which help predict the depth and duration of neurological dysfunction, indicating the likely impact on the child's current and subsequent functioning.

In intensive care provision, the *Glasgow Coma Scale* (Teasedale and Jennet, 1974), which has subscales for eye opening, verbal responses and motor responses, is used to detect a child's progress or deterioration. Whether the child is in a coma and if he is, its duration informs judgements about the severity of the brain injury. There is debate about how the end of coma is best signalled: by spontaneous eye opening or by the child being able to follow simple commands. TBI is classified as mild, moderate or severe.

- mild TBI is associated with no loss or only momentary loss of consciousness, or with coma of less than an hour.
- moderate TBI is associated with a coma of 1 to 24 hours.
- severe TBI is associated with coma of 24 hours or more duration.

The length of post-traumatic amnesia is a further predictor of the severity of TBI, indicating likely longer-term effects on memory and cognition. The classification according to duration of post-traumatic amnesia is as follows:

- less than 1 hour is associated with mild TBI.
- 1 to 24 hours is associated with moderate TBI.
- 1 to 7 days is associated with severe TBI.
- 7 days or more is associated with very severe TBI.

Post-traumatic amnesia, as an indicator, takes precedence over other indications where it suggests a higher degree of severity. Seeking to establish the level of severity of TBI in terms of whether it is considered mild, moderate or severe is important in indicating the relative risk of certain problems. Generally, the levels of risk are as follows:

- children with mild TBI tend to avoid long-term complications and do well.
- children with moderate TBI are at high risk of temporary (or permanent) cognitive and behavioural problems.
- children with severe TBI are at very high risk of permanent cognitive and behavioural problems and also of motor problems.

Rehabilitation Rehabilitation involves restoring to someone abilities they once had but lost because of illness or injury. The rehabilitation team carry out evaluations of functioning and difficulties. For example, the *Rancho Los Amigos Cognitive Scales* (Savage and Wolcott, 1995) are used to help recognize and respond to early stages of recovery from TBI.

Aiming to optimize health and functional abilities, rehabilitation commences in the intensive care unit and continues beyond there for as long as necessary. Because rehabilitation involves relearning to do things the child can no longer do; and compensating for inabilities by using abilities (such as helping impaired memory through using visual structures and electronic reminders), it links with education in its broadest sense. So while medical provision in rehabilitation is crucial, educators and others also form an essential part of the rehabilitation team.

The team becomes smaller as the child makes progress. The initial team may include: medical personnel (doctor and nurse), nutritionist or dietician, psychologist, speech and language pathologist/therapist, teacher, occupational therapist, recreational therapist, physical therapist/physiotherapist, a social worker and a swallowing therapist (e.g. a speech pathologist who undertakes swallowing assessments and provides advice on safe feeding). Later the team might comprise a physician, teacher, psychologist and social worker (Schoenbrodt, 2001).

The rehabilitation team might make recommendations leading to modifications in the environment (e.g. at home) and the use of adaptive equipment and assistive devices (e.g. wheelchair, visual aids to memory). Rehabilitation might take place locally on an outpatient basis involving home, hospital and community facilities. Alternatively, it may involve the child staying in an in-patient rehabilitation hospital some distance from home and later using less intensive facilities locally.

For educators and others, it is important to recognize the implications of a range of factors. Neurological problems include post-concussion syndrome, headaches, seizures, and motor impairments. There are effects on attention and memory, the visual system, executive functions, communications and behaviour (for a summary see Farrell, 2008, pp. 140–145). For example, many head injuries involve damage to the frontal lobes. These are involved in the oversight of functions such as decision-making and emotional expression and perform the brain's executive functions including regulating emotional expression. Relatedly, some children with TBI may manifest disruptive behaviour or outbursts of temper, poor self-esteem, anxiety and depression (ibid., p. 144). The school's understanding of a child's emotional ability and his response to such feelings and his management of behaviour contribute much to the child's development and well-being.

Conclusion

The remit of a medical approach and the role of medication, the relationships between medical perspectives and special education, and the scope of the application of medical perspectives were outlined. The chapter used the fuller examples of epilepsy, ADHD, and traumatic brain injury. Issues examined included medical perspectives on classification of symptoms and syndromes and implications for education and care; the use and potential for overuse of medication in provision; and the contribution of a medical perspective and treatment to assessment and rehabilitation.

Thinking Points

Readers may wish to consider the following issues with reference to a particular school or district:

- how effectively medical information provided to schools makes clear the implications for care.
- who translates medical information into possible implications for education and how this is conveyed to educators and others.

- how it is ensured professionals from health, social welfare services and education settings communicate well with one another and work together effectively.

Key Texts

Anderson, D.M. (2007) (31st edn) *Dorland's Illustrated Medical Dictionary*. Philadelphia, PA: Elsevier/Saunders.

A long-established clearly illustrated medical dictionary, with appendices including medical etymology and abbreviations.

Bigge, J.L., Best, S.J. and Heller, K.W. (2001) (4th edn) *Teaching Individuals with Physical, Health or Multiple Disabilities*. Upper Saddle River, NJ: Merrill Prentice-Hall.

This book includes a chapter on 'Physical Disabilities'. The chapter on 'Multiple Disabilities' focuses on cerebral palsy as an example.

Clay, D.L. (2004) *Helping Children with Chronic Health Conditions: A Practical Guide*. New York: The Guilford Press.

Discusses specific health conditions to encourage school participation and social functioning. For example, a chapter on 'Making Accommodations: Developing 504 Plans and Individual Education Plans (IEPs)' gives planning guidance regarding diabetes, asthma, juvenile rheumatoid arthritis and cystic fibrosis.

Johnson, M. and Parkinson, G. (2002) *Epilepsy: A Practical Guide*. London: David Fulton Publishers.

Emphasizes the practical and educational implications of epilepsy.

Lissauer, T. and Clayden, G. (2007) (3rd edn) *Illustrated Textbook of Paediatrics*. London: Elsevier/Mosby.

Taking a mainly systemic approach, this book covers areas such as the child in society, genetics, normal child development, and various systems disorders.

Lloyd, G., Stead, J. and Cohen, D. (Eds) (2006) *Critical New Perspectives in ADHD*. New York: Routledge.

Draws on social constructionist views with some Foucaultian post-modernist threads and examinations of children's 'rights'. David Cohen's chapter, 'How does the decision to medicate children arise in cases of ADHD?' reveals anomalies in the processes for administering stimulant medication.

Schoenbrodt, L. (Ed.) (2001) *Children with Traumatic Brain Injury: A Parent's Guide*. Bethesda, MD: Woodbine House.

This book written primarily for parents is also useful for teachers and others, providing a rich source of information on rehabilitation, education and family adjustment.

Walker, S. and Wicks, B. (2005) *Educating Children with Acquired Brain Injury*. London: David Fulton Publishers.

A well-structured account for teachers, other professionals and parents largely assuming a UK context.

Internet Resources

International League Against Epilepsy www.ilae-epilepsy.org/

6

Neuropsychological

Introduction

This chapter begins with an explanatory note on some of the main cerebral lobes and on the cerebral hemispheres. It then describes neuropsychology, associated research techniques and related assessments including psychological ones. The chapter examines the relationships between neuropsychology and special education. It considers the scope of neuropsychology in relation to types of disability/disorder including depression and autism. Three fuller examples are presented: reading disorder, developmental coordination disorder and mathematics disorder. Finally, the chapter outlines a cognitive hypothesis testing approach involving close multi-disciplinary working.

A Note on Cerebral Lobes and Cerebral Hemispheres

Frontal, temporal, parietal and occipital lobes The cerebrum, the largest part of the brain, is involved in complex processes such as learning and planning and comprises two hemispheres connected by a structure called the corpus callosum. Each hemisphere can be divided into lobes. Four of these lobes approximately correspond in surface area to cranial bones from which they take their names (Standring, 2005, p. 387). They are the

- frontal lobes
- temporal lobes
- parietal lobes
- occipital lobes.

A very simplified outline of some of their functions is as follows.

The *frontal lobe*, which includes the primary motor cortex, pre-motor cortex, and supplementary motor cortex, is the brain's output centre. It is involved with coordinated fine movement and the motor aspect of speech, and includes an area known as Broca's area, named after the French neuro-anatomist Paul Pierre Broca (1824–1880) who associated the area with speech. The frontal lobe is also involved with executive function (involving such tasks as planning, organizing, monitoring and changing behaviour).

The temporal, parietal and occipital lobes are input centres. The *temporal lobe*, which includes the auditory cortex, receives and processes auditory information (hearing and understanding and remembering what is heard). It is implicated for memory, receptive language and musical awareness. Wernicke's area, named after the German neurologist Karl Wernicke (1848–1905), relates to speech comprehension although there has been uncertainty about the extent of the area (Bogen and Bogen, 1976).

The *parietal lobe*, which includes the somatosensory cortex, is important for interpreting sensory information. It is the destination for sensors in skin and joints conveying information about touch and position. Structures within the parietal lobe are implicated for arithmetic, word reading and writing.

The *occipital lobe*, which includes the primary visual cortex, is involved in processing and interpreting visual stimuli. It is the receiving area for nerve cell activity in the retinas of the eyes.

Cerebral hemispheres Turning to the cerebral hemispheres, the surfaces of both right and left cerebral hemispheres have raised areas and fissures. The raised areas are known in the plural as gyri (singular, gyrus) and the fissures are referred to in the plural as sulci (singular, sulcus). The hemispheres are divided by a deep longitudinal fissure, but connected by the corpus callosum. The outer (grey matter) portion of the hemisphere is the cortex where the cell bodies of neurons are located. Beneath the grey matter is the white matter comprising axons (projections from the neurons). Through these axons, which are covered with an insulating myelin sheath, impulses travel to other parts of the brain and to the body, communicating with other nerve cells or muscles.

Generally, the dominant hemisphere is the left hemisphere for nearly all right-handed people and most left-handed people too. The dominant hemisphere controls speech and language, verbal memory, reading and writing, calculations and (usually) the dominant hand. The non-dominant hemisphere is more involved with visual functions and rhythm. It processes information such as memory and perception of shape, pattern, texture, three-dimensional spatial relationships, construction (including drawing and copying) and understanding and expressing emotion.

The left side of the brain controls movements and interprets sensation for the right side of the body and the right side of the brain acts similarly for the left side of the body. As already indicated, the left hemisphere is the dominant one for most people. For most left-handed people, the left hemisphere is likely to control speech and language function although motor control of the left hand is in the right hemisphere. Most cognitive acts involve the coordination of both hemispheres.

For a more detailed but still simplified outline of the frontal, temporal, parietal, and occipital lobes and the cerebral hemispheres, please see Hale and Fiorello (2004, pp. 51–76). For a technical description of the anatomy of these structures with some reference to their function please see Standring (2005, pp. 396–399, frontal lobe; pp. 399–400, parietal lobe; pp. 400–401, temporal lobe; pp. 403–404, occipital lobe).

Neuropsychology

Neuropsychology, 'the study of brain–behaviour relationships' (Dewey and Tupper, 2004, p. xi) involves an understanding of brain anatomy (structure) and physiology (functioning). It seeks to link observed behaviours to areas of the brain used in carrying them out (Lezak *et al.*, 2004). Neuropsychology can also embrace the cellular basis of behaviour and neurochemistry (the study of the chemistry of the nervous system).

The more specific remit of school neuropsychology applies knowledge of brain–behaviour relationships to school-aged children. A school neuro-psychologist, it is suggested, has to be aware, 'not only of brain-behaviour relationships, but of their application in real life settings, both for typical children and those with disabilities' (Hale and Fiorello, 2004, p. 4). In special education, the focus is on aspects of school neuropsychology relevant to the education and development of children with disabilities and disorders.

The school neuropsychologist is part of an interdisciplinary team that might include other psychologists, medical doctors and clinic staff, speech and language pathologists, teachers and others (e.g. Hale and Fiorello, 2004, p. 2). The importance of this is underscored by the multi-disciplinary nature of neuropsychology itself, which seeks to inter-relate aspects of disciplines including neurology, cognitive psychology, genetics and biology. An aim of neuropsychology in relation to special education is to construct a pedagogical theory linking neuropsychological assessment data to effective intervention (Bernstein, 2000).

Neuroanatomical Measurements

Neuroanatomy is a branch of anatomy dealing with the nervous system, and neuroanatomical differences may be cited as typifying some disorders. But the evidence is complex, as studies of the planum temporale ('planum') in the context of reading disorder illustrate. The planum is a region of the surface of the temporal lobe. A seminal paper by Geschwind and Levitsky (1968) reported that the planum was longer on the left side of the brain than on the right side in 65% of brains. Subsequently, left–right asymmetry of the planum has been reported in research on adult brains using neuroimaging techniques (e.g. Good *et al.*, 2001). It has also been reported in studies involving post-mortem examination (e.g. Witelson and Kigar, 1992). Absence of left–right asymmetry of the planum, it is suggested, may be related to verbal ability (Eckert and Leonard, 2003). In young children, planum size and asymmetry have been related to phonological awareness scores (Leonard *et al.*, 1996).

However, the proportion of cases showing a larger planum on the left side of the brain has varied according to the sorts of measurements taken and the techniques employed. The definition of the planum used in different studies has varied (e.g. Shapleske *et al.*, 1999) and this has naturally led to differences in measurements.

After examining such problems, Beaton (2004, p. 182) observes, 'It turns out that the magnitude and even direction of asymmetry between left and right planum temporale depends upon how the planum is defined and on how it is measured'.

Neural Imaging Techniques

Neural imaging techniques used to investigate brain activity, and considered suitable for use with children, include the following:

- electroencephalography (EEG)
- functional magnetic resonance imaging (fMRI) and
- functional near-infrared spectroscopy (fNIRS).

(a) Electroencephalography

EEG measures brain activity through the skull, reflecting electrical events generated by neurones. It involves placing electrodes at specified positions on the child's scalp. In an application using evoked potentials, neuronal electrical events are brought about by specific stimuli and distilled from the EEG record by signal averaging. Stimuli are presented to the individual and the electrical activity that follows is recorded. As stimuli are present many times, the averaging effect cancels out background effects. Early or late responses can be compared in different conditions. For example, a positive peak occurs 300 milliseconds (P300) after the stimulus only if the stimulus has relevance to the individual. While EEG is unable to give a precise spatial location to the examined activity, it is time responsive and records brain activity within milliseconds. For a fuller description please see Mildner (2008, p. 59–60).

(b) Functional magnetic resonance imaging

The fMRI method uses the response of the protons of hydrogen atoms to a strong magnetic field and radio waves. The child lies inside a scanner, a large cylindrical magnet, where there is an extremely strong magnetic field so that the protons of the body, normally taking random directions, line up parallel with one another. A radio wave pulse is then used to misalign the protons. As the protons realign themselves, they produce radio signals, detected by the scanner. These are converted by a computer into an image related to the strength of the radio signals. Because the greatest source of protons in the body is hydrogen atoms in water molecules, the fMRI scan reflects differences in the water content of tissues. In measuring brain activity, it is assumed that changes in blood flow relate closely to changes in fMRI activity. This technique provides good spatial resolution but poorer time sensitivity. Also, it is not clear what exactly the relationship is between neural activity and fMRI responses (Beaton, 2004, p. 204).

(c) Functional near-infrared spectroscopy

The technique of fNIRS involves the use of 'optodes', sensors optically measuring a specified substance. These optodes, giving off near-infrared light, are placed at the same electrode scalp positions used for EEG. This light is absorbed at different rates by the brain tissue, depending on the concentration of haemoglobin (the red oxygen-carrying pigment of red blood cells). Changes of the amount of haemoglobin in brain tissue reflect changes in blood oxygenation level, which is related to blood flow. In this way, fNIRS provides a measure of changes in blood volumes in the brain. The technique gives better spatial accuracy than EEG (but not as good as fMRI) and better time sensitivity than fMRI (but not as good as EEG) (Goswami, 2008, p. xii).

(d) Considerations concerning neuro-electric techniques

Ascertaining correlations between the anatomical and the functional aspects in higher-order cognitive operations is challenging. As well as the techniques already mentioned, another is positron emission tomography (PET) in which increases or decreases in blood flow are tracked through injecting a radioactive tracer into the bloodstream (Frackowiak and Friston, 1994). Considering reviews of both PET studies and of fMRI studies, Bubb (2002, p. 482) observes that functional imaging faces 'a host of methodological difficulties'. These must be successfully negotiated before the particular technique can be used to give a 'testing ground' for neuropsychological theories concerning higher cognitive functions (ibid.). Furthermore, one cannot assume that the pattern of activation shown in the final image is 'a literal description of neurons firing to a particular task demand' (p. 468). A task might be considered to tap into sub-component processes of cognitive functions. However, other operations may be 'conjointly performed' when the task is carried out. Cerebral structures other than those under consideration might also be activated (Sergent *et al.*, 1992, pp. 69, 78).

Assessment in Neuropsychology

(a) Assessments

Assessment and intervention are considered key aspects of school neuropsychology (e.g. Hale and Fiorello, 2004, p. 4). Assessment includes the neuropsychological interpretation of test data (ibid., pp. 1, 85–127).

Comprehensive cognitive and socio-emotional assessment is recommended to help build up a picture of the child's strengths and weaknesses. Tests of intelligence may be interpreted in terms of levels of performance and patterns of performance. The *Wechsler Intelligence Scale for Children* (*WISC-Fourth edition*) (Wechsler, 2003) has been developed using a four-factor model with indices for verbal comprehension, perceptual reasoning, working memory and processing speed. Each has sub-tests (excluding optional ones) as follows:

- verbal comprehension: similarities, vocabulary and comprehension;
- perceptual reasoning: block design, picture concepts and matrix reasoning;

- working memory: digit span and letter-number sequencing;
- processing speed: coding and symbol search.

While it has been reported that nearly 90% of school psychologists use factor scores and the analysis of sub-test profiles when interpreting intelligence tests (Pfeiffer *et al.*, 2000), such scores have to be interpreted with caution.

Also, specific tests seeking to tap neurological processes may be used, for example, the *NEPSY* (Korkman *et al.*, 1998). The *NEPSY* is a neuropsychological (NEuroPSYcholgical) assessment for children aged 3 to 12 years. It assesses five functional domains: attention/executive functions, language, sensori-motor functions, visuospatial processing and memory and learning. Each has core sub-tests, some for children aged 3 to 4; some for children 4 to 12 others for both. These concern the following:

- attention/executive functions: tower, statue, auditory attention and response set, visual attention;
- language: phonological processing, comprehension of instructions, body parts naming, speeded naming;
- sensori-motor functions: fingertip tapping, imitating hand positions, visuo-motor precision;
- visuospatial processing: design copying, arrows, block construction;
- memory and learning: narrative memory, sentence repetition, memory for faces, memory for names.

Examples of sub-test content illustrate the constructs they seek to tap into. Within the attention and executive function domain, the tower sub-test draws on planning, inhibition, problem-solving, monitoring and self-regulation. In the language domain, the comprehension of instruction sub-test involves receptive language, sequencing, grammar and simple motor responses. The finger tapping sub-test within sensori-motor functions seeks to involve simple motor speed and perseverance. The arrows sub-test within visuospatial processing engages spatial processing, visualization, line orientation and inhibition.

One of the express purposes of the *NEPSY* (Korkman *et al.*, 1998) is to provide a tool for identifying and assessing brain damage and dysfunction. It aims to assess the degree to which this impacts on the development of a functional domain and operations within that domain and the limitations it might place on other functional domains. (Ahmad and Warriner, 2001, pp. 240–249 provide a test review.)

(b) Constraints on assessment

There are reservations about the conceptual integrity of aspects of neuropsychological assessments. In the *NEPSY* (Korkman *et al.*, 1998) there is debate about the attention/executive functions domain. The nature of this domain is considered 'conceptually problematic' (Ahmad and Warriner, 2001, p. 242). This may relate to researchers' lack of agreement, and the constitution of the tasks that are intended to measure executive function. A further factor is whether it is possible to measure executive function in very young children (ibid.). It is accepted that it is important to consider the input, processing and output demands of any tests administered and to relate findings to other data. However, there is a difficulty in ascertaining processing demands, because, all that is available are observable and measurable behaviours 'from which to draw inferences about neuropsychological processes' (Hale and Fiorello, 2004, p. 92).

Relationships between Neuropsychology and Special Education

Embedded within relationships between neuropsychology and special education lies the putative connection between psychological and neurological accounts. Links between psychological and neurological explanations are sometimes assumed or implied but are in fact difficult to demonstrate. On the biological neurological side are descriptions of brain structure and functioning and data that appear to show differences between individuals who have a particular disorder and individuals who do not. On the other side are descriptions of theories concerning psychological processes. For example, in the case of autism there are accounts at the neurological and psychological levels.

A difficulty lies in trying to explain the coexistence of the two or more levels of evidence. If there are differences in brain anatomy and physiology between those with and without autism, an explanation is still needed concerning how those associated with autism relate to the psychological manifestations. Given the complex nature of apparent associations, neurological and behavioural explanations are likely to involve multiple possible causal factors. Regarding attention deficit hyperactivity disorder (ADHD), attempts to bring together information from various studies suggest a biological-psychological-social model, implicating brain morphology, cognitive differences, a particular child's circumstances and skills and capacities.

The influence of neuropsychology in special education appears to be increasing. It is as though neuropsychology holds out the prospect of types of disorder and disability being demonstrated to have strong 'within the child' aspects. It is considered to potentially provide evidence that conditions, such as ADHD, may be as much (or more) rooted in the biology and psychology of the child as they might be influenced by social factors.

Neuropsychological explanations might be welcomed in a negative sense. Not reading very well might be thought by some to relate to laziness, poor parenting or other negative influences. But if it can be demonstrated that difficulty with reading is a 'reading disorder' with neurological underpinnings relating to psychological manifestations, it may appear more legitimized. More positively, it is hoped that exploring possible neuropsychological foundations for disorders and disabilities could lead to:

- greater understanding of the conditions including the underlying processes thought to be associated with them;
- better classifications of disabilities/disorders including the identification of possible subtypes; and
- interventions that are better justified and more effective.

The Scope of Neuropsychology and Types of Disability/Disorder

General The scope of neuropsychology can be illustrated with reference to various types of disability/disorder. Depression, autism, ADHD and disorder of written expression are discussed in the present section. Reading disorder, mathematics disorder and developmental coordination disorder are considered as fuller examples in later sections. Neurological and psychological aspects of communication disorders are examined in the 'psycholinguistic' chapter of the present book.

Depression Regarding depression, the interaction of genetic influences (Plomin and McGuffin, 2003) and the environment (Caspi *et al.*, 2003) are considered important elements of any model. Therefore a range of manifestations or components of depression may lead to different 'endophenotypes'. Different symptoms may reflect varied disruption to different underpinnings of brain functioning (Hasler *et al.*, 2004). Against this background, it is suggested that a neuropsychological approach, seeking to relate various types of behaviour to different underlying brain systems, can apply to features of depression

(Folensbee, 2007, p. 173). For example, depressed mood may relate to disruption of serotonin systems (Hasler *et al.*, 2004). (Serotonin is a substance, which, in the brain, is involved in the transmission of nerve impulses between cells and is thought to influence states of consciousness and mood.)

Such an approach may inform the assessment of the aspects of depression manifested and possibly interventions that may be effective in terms of the brain systems involved (Janicak *et al.*, 2001). Possible ways are envisaged (Christensen *et al.*, 2006) in which cognitive-behavioural therapy might be conceptualized in the treatment of depression, influencing associated cognitive deficits such as general attention, mood–memory connections and inhibition. Therapy can seek to replace previous automatic thoughts linked with depression with more positive effortful thinking (Folensbee, 2007, p. 174).

Autism Brain regions most consistently affected in autism include the cerebellum and the limbic system (Lathe, 2006, 71).

There may be abnormalities in the cerebellum. This is a part of the brain situated between the cerebrum and the brain-stem (the lower part of the brain adjoining the spinal cord) (Eliez and Reiss, 2000). The cerebellum is involved in timing, memory and learning and in coordinating cognitive functions (e.g. Rapoport *et al.*, 2000). The cerebellum also has a role in controlling and coordinating articulation (see Obler and Gjerlow, 1999, passim).

The limbic system is a ring-shaped area consisting of clusters of nerve cells within the cortex. It influences the recall and recognition of emotional stimuli, encoding and consolidating memory and the processing of sensations of smell (Adolphs *et al.*, 1995; Gehring and Knight, 2000). However, children with autism tend not to use the amygdala region when making mental inferences (Baron-Cohen *et al.*, 2000). The amygdala is involved in the recall and recognition of emotional stimuli (Adolphs *et al.*, 1995) and is important in evaluating the significance of events in the environment including stimulus and reward associations (Sandring, 2005, p. 411).

It is hypothesized that people with autism do not have a sufficiently developed 'theory of mind'. That is, they experience particular difficulties recognizing and interpreting the emotional and mental states of others, leading to social and communication difficulties (Baron-Cohen, 2000). Children with autism may experience a joint attention deficit (Mundy and Neale, 2001). This involves impairments in the capacities to attend to events jointly with others and impairments in preferring social rather than inanimate events, leading to difficulties in language, social communication, and theory of mind. A further theory implicates executive dysfunction (Ozonoff, 1997). This affects the ability to plan actions, disengage from the external context, restrain unwanted responses, maintain a cognitive focus and remain on task and monitor one's performance.

Attention deficit hyperactivity disorder Attention deficit hyperactivity disorder (ADHD) may be related to dysfunction in the brain's neurotransmission system responsible for making connections between different parts of the brain. Brain-imaging research has indicated abnormalities in the frontal lobes where systems responsible for regulating attention are centred. It is also suggested that hyperactivity results from an underarousal of the mid-brain, leading to inefficient inhibition of movements and sensations. If so, then, where stimulant drugs are effective they may stimulate the mid-brain sufficiently to suppress the overactivity. In up to nearly a third of instances of ADHD, particularly in severe cases, such physiological features are caused by brain disease, brain injury or exposure to toxins.

One psychological theory of ADHD is that there is a dysfunction of the self-regulation mechanism leading to particular difficulty delaying a behavioural response. Another view focuses on the executive functions of mental filtering and checking used when making behavioural decisions. This involves using inner speech, taking one's emotional state into account and recalling knowledge from situations similar to that in which one finds oneself. Characteristics of individuals with ADHD may lead to difficulties with these processes (Barkley, 1997). Another suggestion is that ADHD involves a deficit in the *allocation* of attentional resources as an aspect of executive function. The overarching executive function of self-control is thought to be a shared feature explaining features associated with ADHD: apparent inattentiveness (an aspect of cognitive control) and hyperactivity/impulsivity (an aspect of social-emotional control) (Cutting and Denckla, 2003, p.126). Brain morphology, environmental circumstances and cognitive differences in ability to inhibit responses to stimuli may all influence the emergence of ADHD (Nigg, 2006; Nigg and Hinshaw, 1998).

Disorder of written expression The skills of spelling and handwriting clearly have a bearing on the development of written expression. Even leaving these aside there are still the components of executive functions (Wong, 1991) and semantic knowledge (Berninger, 1994) that are required. The complexity of the processes has perhaps been a factor in constraining research in this area. Possible subtypes of 'written language disorder' are suggested (Sandler *et al.*, 1992).

In research examining 'oral and written discourse' in adolescents with closed head injury, several groups were identified. The first, and largest, group had fine motor and linguistic deficits. The second group were characterized by poor handwriting and visual-spatial skills but good spelling and ability to develop ideas. The third group had memory and attention problems. The fourth group experienced problems with letter production, legibility and sequencing. Many areas of the brain appear to be implicated in the complex activity of written expression. A central factor may be executive and working memory deficits as these have been associated with such features as poor sentence coherence and poor lexical cohesion (Wilson and Proctor, 2000). (Lexical cohesion refers to a sense of unity in a text by which sentences form a coherent whole.)

Fuller Example: Reading Disorder

Reading disorder and related deficits It is suggested that children learning to read English have to develop multiple strategies in parallel to become successful readers. One of these is grapheme–phoneme recoding strategies for reading regular words such as 'big', 'top' and 'cat', which involve linking marks on a page of text with sound in a regular, predictable way. Rhyme analogy strategies are employed to read irregular words such as 'right' and 'sight'. Whole word recognition strategies are used for words such as 'yacht' (Goswami, 2008, p. 347).

Word reading disorders are associated with various difficulties. These include deficits in phonemic awareness; orthographic coding skill (concerning coding the writing system of a language); rapid automatic naming; temporal sequencing of sensory input and processing speed or automaticity individually or in combination (e.g. Wolf, 2001).

A key causal theory of reading disorder is that of a 'phonological deficit'. Where reading disorder is regarded as predominantly a phonological problem, the brains of affected children are thought to be less efficient than typical in processes associated with phonological development. There is debate about whether the difficulties are predominantly at phoneme level (Tallal, 2004) or at syllable level (Goswami, *et al.*, 2002). Relatedly, tasks that children with reading disorder are likely to find difficult are the following:

- phonological awareness tasks such as tapping out syllables;
- tasks that require short-term phonological memory such as digit span; and
- tasks requiring rapid automatic naming of familiar items such as colours or pictures (e.g. Goswami, 2008, p. 349).

Sometimes, literacy and literacy difficulties are considered within a psycholinguistic framework, through the underlying processes of language, mainly phonology and grammar. In developing literacy, children appear to use among other processes, phonological processing, working memory and accessing vocabulary. Relationships between speech processing and processing written language may allow difficulties of written expression to be approached using a psycholinguistic model (Stackhouse, 2001, pp. 1–40; Martin and Miller, 2004, p. 60). An example of developing a literacy programme for a child with a history of speech difficulties is provided by Nathan and Simpson (2001, pp. 249–298).

Anatomical structures Attempts to identify the biological underpinnings of reading disorder have suggested several anatomical structures and systems apparently distinguishing poor readers from control groups. However, differing indications of reading disorder make the interpretation of studies difficult. Among brain areas identified are

- the cerebral hemispheres (activation)
- the cerebellum and
- the corpus callosum.

Cerebral hemispheres Generally, the dominant cerebral hemisphere is the left one for nearly all right-handed people and most left-handed people. As mentioned earlier, the dominant hemisphere controls speech and language, verbal memory, reading and writing and calculations and usually the dominant hand. Therefore, neural networks for language are said to be 'left lateralized' and involve the frontal and temporal areas of the brain. For reading, the left lateralized neural networks involve frontal, temporoparietal and occipitotemporal regions.

Different patterns of activation in some regions of (usually) the left cerebral hemisphere of individuals with reading disorder and others have been identified by functional neuroimaging studies. Shaywitz and colleagues (2002) studied 70 children with dyslexia aged on average 13 years compared to 11-year-old controls. The children were scanned using fMRI while they were carrying out various reading-type tasks: letter identification, single-letter rhyme, non-word rhyming and reading for meaning. Children with dyslexia were found to show underactivation in the left frontal, temporal, parietal and occipital cortex, all areas associated with reading.

Given that the data in such studies is correlational rather than causal, it is unclear whether such anomalies or reading disorder arise first. A congenital defect in brain function or brain anatomy may influence the way the brains of individuals with reading disorder are 'wired'. Or the experience of individuals with reading disorder may have led to functional reorganization of their brain. For example, PET studies with literate and non-literate participants suggest that learning to read and write in childhood ' . . . permanently influences organization of the adult brain with regard to processing the sounds of speech' (Castro-Caldas *et al.*, 1998).

The cerebellum The cerebellum is a part of the brain situated between the cerebrum and the brain stem. A 'cerebellar deficit hypothesis' proposes that some symptoms of reading disorder relate to a deficiency in cerebellar functioning. However, acquired alexia (loss of the ability to understand written language) does not appear to occur as a sole result of cerebellum damage. Also, cerebellar lesions do not appear to effect segmental language skills, which are the skills involved in recognizing and applying knowledge of segmenting and blending sounds in spoken language. It is the impairment of segmental language skills that is considered by some as a core deficit in dyslexia (Beaton, 2004, p. 257). Among stronger evidence of possible cerebellar influence is the co-occurrence of dyslexia and deficits in motor tasks involving both hands, which may relate to cerebellar damage (ibid.).

The corpus callosum The corpus callosum is a structure that connects the majority of the left cerebral hemisphere with the majority of the right cerebral hemisphere. It is thought that it may have a role in aspects of the timing control of the two hands in bimanual motor tasks (Kennerley *et al.*, 2002). One suggestion is that in some people with dyslexia, impaired motor skills may be linked to an impaired callosal transfer system that also shows itself in poor reading.

Biological, cognitive and behavioural levels Frith (1997, p. 13) considers the possibility of connections between various levels of description in relation to reading disorder/dyslexia: biological, cognitive and behavioural levels. In one scenario, there is a genetically determined abnormality of the peri-Sylvian region of the brain. The peri-Sylvian regions are those around the Sylvian fissure, which separates the frontal lobes (concerned with motor output) and the temporal lobes (concerned with auditory processing) and extends to the parietal lobes. The genetically determined abnormality of the peri-Sylvian region is related to a core cognitive deficit of phonological processing. This deficit is further related to behavioural manifestations of poor performance in reading, naming, verbal memory and phonological awareness.

Fuller Examples: Developmental Coordination Disorder

Developmental coordination disorder (DCD) is described as a 'marked impairment of motor coordination', significantly interfering with academic achievement or daily living activities (American Psychiatric Association, 2000, pp. 56–57). Although the cerebellum has been implicated in DCD, it is likely that different levels of causation provide a clearer picture of the condition.

The cerebellum The cerebellum has already been mentioned in connection with reading disorder. It is concerned with maintaining body posture and balance and with coordinating gross and fine motor activity. The cerebellum appears to be involved in timing, memory and learning and in coordinating cognitive functions (e.g. Rapoport *et al.*, 2000). Injury to this part of the brain may, among other effects, cause clumsiness, difficulties with balance and impaired planning and timing of activities (Drubach, 2000). For such reasons, cerebellar dysfunction is considered to be associated with DCD.

Different causal levels Evidence suggests that DCD cannot be attributed to a single direct cause but that causal factors are likely to be multi-dimensional. They might include genetic predisposition, brain structure, prenatal influences and post-natal effects. This suggests that models allowing for many causes might help researchers and others to understand the possible interconnections (Cermak *et al.*, 2002).

In a neuropsychological context, it is important to try to identify and understand the processes that might be involved in movement and difficulties with movement. The perception of vision and movement are implicated. The relationships between vision and perception and between vision and movement are relevant. Equally pertinent are the representation of visual and spatial information. Research examines differences that may arise when movements are intended and when they are not, and features such as the accuracy and speed of movements.

A useful distinction is between motor and non-motor factors. 'Non-motor' refers to the processing of perceptual information in the service of action. 'Motor' concerns control processes responsible for selecting and programming an appropriate motor response, taking account of information from the environment (Wilson and McKenzie, 1998). The relative importance of motor and of non-motor factors in the aetiology of DCD is debated. It has been proposed that influential non-motor factors, in relation to DCD, include the following:

- visuoperceptual deficits
- visuospatial representation deficits
- deficits in kinaesthetic function and
- deficits in visuomotor integration (Wilson, 2005, p. 292).

The main deficit with DCD (Wilson and McKenzie, 1998) appears to be visuospatial processing irrespective of whether a motor response is required or not. Kinaesthetic perception (that is the perception of different types of movement) is also implicated, especially where active movement is involved. A further factor is cross-modal perception (involving different modes such as visual and movement perception).

In line with this, deficits in the visuospatial representation of *intended* movements are thought to be an important part of the explanation of motor clumsiness in children (Wilson, 2005, p. 293). This relates also to the debate about terminology. Sometimes, instead of DCD, the term 'dyspraxia' (from the Greek, 'difficulty in doing') continues to be used. In such instances, definitions tend to focus on the organization, planning and organization of movement. Dyspraxia has been defined as a ' . . . marked impairment in gross and fine motor *organization* (which may or may not influence articulation and speech) which are influenced by poor perceptual regulation' (Dixon and Addy, 2004, p. 9, italics in original). These difficulties present themselves as ' . . . an inability to *plan and organize purposeful movement*' (ibid. italics in original).

In analysing deficits in motor control, research compares children with and without DCD in relation to the temporal and spatial characteristics of their reaching movements to objects/targets in space. Reaction time, movement time, movement accuracy, and movement variability are studied. Using such information, attempts are made to determine how children with DCD plan, organize and carry out motor responses.

Studies of goal-directed arm movements have examined the ability of children with DCD to use visual and kinaesthetic feedback to control their movements (Pryde, 2000). These suggest that characterizing the effects of DCD on manual aiming has to take account of the requirements of the aiming task. For example, relevant features include whether the child is allowed to see his hand movements and the amplitude of movements. It has been argued (Roy *et al.*, 2004, pp. 54–55) that overall, DCD does not affect the initial programming of movement but does affect the processing of feedback information and the integration of feedback from vision and proprioception. (Proprioception is the sense by which one knows the relative position of different parts of the body.) Despite the view that initial programming of movement is not affected, for some children, earlier programming stages do appear to be influenced.

Fuller Examples: Mathematics Disorder

In mathematics disorder, mathematical ability is substantially below that expected for the child's chronological age, intelligence and age-appropriate education. This 'significantly interferes' with academic achievement and daily living that requires mathematical skills (American Psychiatric Association, 2000, p. 53).

Co-occurrence of mathematics disorders and reading disorders The co-occurrence of reading disorders and mathematics disorders has been estimated to be as high as 40% (Light and DeFries, 1995). Given that many children with mathematics problems also have difficulties with reading and writing it has been suggested that in such instances there could be 'similar neuropsychological reasons for their difficulties' (Hale and Fiorello, 2004, p. 209).

Possible types of mathematics disorder and associated cognitive skills Much less neuropsychological research has been conducted for mathematics disorder than for reading disorder. Some supposed subtypes of mathematics disorder appear to be related conceptually to either developmental coordination disorder or reading disorder. For example, spatial dyscalculia may relate to dyspraxic difficulties. Lexical dyscalculia (difficulty reading numbers and symbols of mathematics) and perhaps graphic dyscalculia (difficulty with writing numbers and mathematical symbols) may relate more to dyslexic difficulties. (E.g. Jordan and Hanich, 2003; Jordan, Hanich and Kaplan, 2003).

Conversant with the idea that there are different cognitive skills components of mathematics competency, other types of mathematics disorder have been identified. Mazzocco (2001) proposes three subtypes: semantic memory, procedural and visual-spatial. These subtypes, it is suggested, may not necessarily be separate and may occur together. The semantic memory subtype, which has been associated with reading disorder and language disorder, involves poor number–symbol association and poor automaticity of mathematical facts. Implicating poor use of strategies and algorithms, the procedural subtype has been associated with difficulties with attention and executive functions. Finally, the visual-spatial subtype, involving difficulties with aligning columns, place value, and keeping to the correct operation, has been associated with non-verbal learning difficulties.

Left and right cerebral hemisphere location Regarding the left cerebral hemisphere, it appears from studies of patients that dysfunction of the left parietal area alone can lead to mathematics disorder although both right and left parietal lobes seem to be needed for mathematical skills (Isaacs *et al.*, 2001). Also calculation deficits were associated with less grey matter in the left parietal lobe (ibid). If there is left hemisphere damage to the peri-Sylvian areas, this can impair the retrieval of mathematical facts. However, if there is no impairment to the left inferior (rear) parietal region, calculation skills may be unaffected (Cohen, L. *et al.*, 2000).

Mathematics disorder also appears to relate to right hemisphere damage. There is a high rate of constructional apraxia in individuals with mathematics disorder who have right brain damage. Constructional apraxia is associated with an inability to construct a whole object from its parts and inability to copy simple shapes. It occurs following injury to the right posterior parietal lobe (Mildner, 2008, p. 260). A patient with right hemisphere damage may be unable to spatially align columns correctly and may neglect stimuli in the left visual field (e.g. Basso *et al.*, 2000). Therefore, mathematical information presented in vertical columns would be difficult. Mathematics disorder relating to right hemisphere damage and neglecting stimuli in the left visual field is conversant with the co-occurrence of mathematics disorder and constructional apraxia (Basso *et al.*, 2000).

The respective roles of the left and right hemispheres in relation to mathematical tasks are debated. Reviews indicate support for right hemisphere damage being implicated in mathematics disorder (Rourke, 2000) while other evidence points to left hemisphere damage (McClosky *et al.*, 1991). Hemispheric differences may relate to the nature of the mathematical activity, with patients having left hemisphere damage finding calculation difficult and those with right hemisphere damage having difficulties with constructional aspects of mathematics (Langdon and Warrington, 1997).

Parietal areas The parietal lobe is important for interpreting sensory information. Also, dysfunction of the parietal lobe, especially the left side, can result in problems with skills for computing in arithmetic, sound–symbol association in reading, and perceptual motor difficulties for writing (e.g. Hale and Fiorello, 2004, p. 62). Foetal alcohol syndrome has been associated with mathematical disorder. It is a condition of baby's altered prenatal growth and form seen in mothers who were 'chronically alcoholic' during pregnancy (Anderson, 2007, p. 1855). It has been associated with babies being born with underdeveloped parietal lobes and, as these brain areas are important for numeracy, their underdevelopment is associated with the child later having difficulties with mathematical cognition and with number processing (Kopera-Frye *et al.*, 1996).

Damage to the left parietal lobe can result in Gerstmann syndrome, a condition first described by the Austrian neurologist Joseph Gerstmann (1887–1969). The syndrome is associated with left–right confusion, problems with writing and difficulty with mathematics (Mayer *et al.*, 1999). Several neuroimaging studies suggest that the prefrontal and inferior (rear) parietal areas are involved in mathematical computational skills (e.g. Cowell *et al.*, 2000; Gruber *et al.*, 2001).

Neural systems The verbal system is among neural systems contributing to mathematical cognition (Dehaene *et al.*, 1998). It appears to store verbally rote learned information and number facts such as number bonds and underpins counting and numerical rote learned knowledge such as multiplication tables. If a child with mathematics disorder also has reading disorder having a phonological basis, the verbal system underpinning counting and calculation may be the system affected (Goswami, 2004, p. 179). Another neural system concerned with the representation of number appears to underpin knowledge of numbers and their relations (Dahaene *et al.*, 1999). Located in the intra-parietal areas of the brain, the system is activated by such tasks as number comparisons (numerical, verbal or visual). Visuo-spatial regions may be involved with complex calculations (Zago *et al.*, 2001) where visual-mental imagery may be important.

A Cognitive Hypothesis-Testing Approach

General overview In a cognitive hypothesis-testing model (Hale and Fiorello, 2004, pp. 128–161), individual psychosocial assessment is combined with the development of interventions and monitoring (p. 129). This approach is multi-disciplinary and, as well as the child and his parents, may involve medical, psychological, educational and welfare personnel. A psychologist specializing in neuropsychology may lead the approach, and educators will be a part of the consultation process.

The model involves a cycle in which theory, hypothesis, data collection and interpretation are visited and revisited. The process begins with a consideration of the 'problem' as it presents itself. A hypothesis follows that it is a cognitive problem and suitable psychological assessments are administered and interpreted. A profile of cognitive strengths and weaknesses is developed and further assessments are administered, interpreted and compared. The psychologist, educators and others hold a consultation meeting about possible interventions and one of the plausible interventions is chosen. The effect of the intervention is observed and evaluated. The intervention is modified, continued or discontinued according to the findings (Hale and Fiorello, 2004, pp. 129–130).

One strength of such an approach is that it is able to draw on neuroanatomical information and neural imaging data; neuropsychological assessments and the behavioural observations of educators and others. This information is used to develop and test suitable interventions that aid learning and development. The possible links between hypothesized processes and processing difficulties and possible interventions may not be straightforward. However, monitoring the impact of interventions may provide evidence to support or disconfirm the original hypotheses.

Practical example Hale and Fiorello (2004) provide many examples of the cognitive hypothesis-testing model in action. In one scenario, a pupil is slow to complete written work, and work samples show messy handwriting and evidence of poor spacing and coordination (p. 26). *Wechsler Intelligence Scale for Children* (*WISC-Fourth edition*) (Wechsler, 2003) results show poor performance on processing speed and difficulty with working memory. Among possible hypotheses to account for this are the following:

- slow processing speed (that might reflect difficulties with attention and affect)
- deficits in visual tracking
- deficits in perception
- deficits in visual-motor integration
- deficits in fine motor coordination
- deficits in graphomotor ability
- deficits in executive function.

To further explore these possibilities, further tests might be used to help decide whether visual-motor integration, visual discrimination, or fine motor coordination difficulties were contributing to the problem. A test such as the *NEPSY* (Korkman *et al.*, 1998) sub-tests of attention/executive functions might be employed to help indicate whether attention or executive problems were influential. Classroom behaviours would also be observed to test the various hypotheses. For example, the child's attention during activities that did not involve visual-motor skills (such as listening while the teacher reads a story) could indicate whether attention is a problem. From this information, an intervention is decided and its effects monitored.

Conclusion

Indications of brain activity and its possible relationships with behaviour are interpreted in the context of the ways in which information is gleaned and used. Techniques for attempting to identify, measure and interpret brain activity are shaped by the technology used and the way information is presented. Neuropsychological assessments also make informed assumptions about possible underlying processes. Attempts to draw on these sources of information relate them to possible interventions and also involve assumptions and elements of trial and error although these are informed and modified by subsequent evaluations. Nevertheless, information, interpretation and hypotheses drawing on the fields of neurological research and psychological assessment and developments in neuropsychology are providing insights for the present and exciting possibilities for the future.

Thinking Points

Readers may wish to consider the following:

- the strengths and limitations of techniques used in neuropsychology;
- the extent to which neuropsychology helps understanding, assessment and intervention for particular disabilities/disorders such as reading disorder and developmental coordination disorder.

Key Texts

Beaton, A.A. (2004) *Dyslexia, Reading and the Brain: A Sourcebook of Psychological and Biological Research*. New York: Psychology Press.

This volume presents current research in reading disorder. Cognitive chapters include the role of phonological awareness, auditory perception and the temporal processing deficit hypothesis. Biological chapters include information on laterality and hormones; neuro anatomic aspects and functional brain-imaging.

Coch, D., Dawson, G. and Fischer, K.W. (2007) *Human Behaviour, Learning, and the Developing Brain: Atypical Development*. New York: Guilford Press.

This book outlines work on neurological and cognitive aspects of disorders including autism, attention deficit hyperactivity disorder, dyslexia and dyscalculia. It makes observations about the educational and other interventions that are likely to be effective.

Conn, P.M. (Ed.) (2003) (2nd edn) *Neuroscience in Medicine*. Totowa, NJ: Humana Press.

Chapters include systemic ones as well as ones that focus on particular areas such as the brain-stem and cerebral cortex.

D'Amato, R.C., Fletcher-Janzen, E. and Reynolds, C.R. (Eds) (2005) *Handbook of School Neuropsychology*. Hoboken, NY: John Wiley and Sons.

This text combines theory and practice in school neuropsychology. Sections include brain development, structure and functioning; neuropsychological assessment for intervention; learners with diseases and disorders and neuropsychological interventions in schools.

Dewey, D. and Tupper, D.E. (Eds) (2004) *Developmental Motor Disorders: A Developmental Perspective*. New York: Guilford Press.

Although this book concerns motor disorders relating to a range of conditions, it also contains reports and research and has sections relating specifically to developmental coordination disorder.

Hale, J.B. and Fiorello, C.A. (2004) *School Neuropsychology: A Practitioner's Handbook*. New York: The Guilford Press.

Chapters concern assessment and intervention strategies, neuropsychological approaches to interpreting assessment and neuropsychological principles. The book also outlines possible neuropsychological aspects of several conditions.

Kandel, E., Schwartz, J.H. and Jessel, T.M. (2000) *Principles of Neural Science*. New York: McGraw-Hill.

A well-structured and richly illustrated textbook on general neuroscience, providing comprehensive information on brain structure and functioning. It progresses from information on cell and molecular level biology of the neuron, synaptic transmission and the neural basis of cognition to areas of complex behaviour such as movement and language.

Loring, D.W. (Ed.) (1999) *INS Dictionary of Neuropsychology*. New York: Oxford University Press.

Draws on neuropsychiatric, medical and neuroscientific terminology and is intended mainly for a wide range of professionals.

Miller, D.C. (2007) (2nd edn) *Essentials of Neuropsychological Assessment*. Hoboken, NY: John Wiley and Sons.

An overview of neuropsychological practice in schools. Covers identifying the need for testing, gathering a neurodevelopmental history, choosing suitable assessments, evaluating students and interpreting results.

Morton, J. (2004) *Understanding Developmental Disorders: A Causal Modelling Approach*. United Kingdom: Blackwell Publishing Oxford.

The book develops representations of causal connections in different areas: biological, cognitive, behavioural and environmental. Autism, dyslexia, conduct disorder and hyperactivity are modelled, bringing greater clarity to different theories.

Standring, S. (39th edn) (2005) *Gray's Anatomy: The Anatomical Basis of Clinical Practice*. London: Elsevier Churchill Livingstone.

Section 2 of this standard text concerns neuroanatomy and includes chapters on the cerebellum and cerebral hemispheres.

Yeates, K.O., Ris, M.D., and Taylor, H.G. (2000) *Paediatric Neuropsychology: Research, Theory, and Practice*. New York: Guilford Press.

This covers primary disorders of the central nervous system; CNS dysfunction in other medical disorders; clinical implications and applications and a commentary on trends.

Internet Resources

Among the more easily accessible websites illustrating brain structure and function are the following:

University of Utah, Salt Lake City — Atlases of the brain:
   http://medlib.med.utah/kw/brain_atlas/

Michigan State University — Human Brain Atlas:
   http://www.msu.edu/~brains/humanatlas/

Harvard Medical School — Atlas of the human brain:
   http://www.med.harvard.edu/AANLIB/

Build a Brain
   http://www.stanford.edu/group/hopes/basics/braintut/ab9.html

Digital Anatomist Information System
   http://sig.biostr.washington.edu/projects/da/

7

Psychotherapeutic

Introduction

To avoid undue repetition, this chapter follows a slightly different structure from many of the other chapters in this book. It defines and describes the nature of psychotherapy and the relationship between special education and psychotherapy in general. Next, it outlines three important perspectives in psychotherapy: systems, psychodynamic and cognitive-behavioural approaches. For each of these, the chapter explains the perspective and considers its scope and its relationship to special education. The chapter then concentrates on cognitive-behavioural therapy and related approaches providing several fuller examples. These concern children or adolescents with disorders of conduct; anxiety disorders or depressive disorders.

Psychotherapy and Special Education

Psychotherapy in general As long ago as the 1970s, Meltzoff and Kornreich (1970) succinctly defined psychotherapy in relation to the important aspects of planned techniques, therapist qualifications and client outcomes. Psychotherapy is described as ' . . . the informed and planful application of techniques derived from established psychological principles'. These are given expression by 'persons qualified through training and experience to understand these principles and to apply these techniques . . . ' (ibid., p. 4). The intention is to help individuals, to ' . . . modify such personal characteristics as feelings, values, attitudes and behaviours which are judged by the therapist to be maladaptive or maladjustive' (ibid.).

Different types of psychotherapy, for example, 'behavioural therapy' or 'psychodynamic psychotherapy', can be understood in terms of several key features (Gurman and Messer, 2005, pp. 4–20). These include the concept of personality that is implied or understood, psychological health and pathology, the process of clinical assessment and the practice of therapy. It further includes the therapeutic relationship and the stance of the therapist; curative factors or mechanisms of change; treatment applicability and ethical considerations; and support for the therapy provided by research.

In seeking to identify 'essential' psychotherapies, Gurman and Messer (2005) note that there are hundreds of so-called psychotherapies. But they make the point that the great majority are, in fact, only 'partial methods' or 'single techniques' or 'minor variations' on techniques or approaches that have already been developed (ibid., p. 1). They suggest that about a dozen distinguishable types of therapy can be identified.

Not all of these 'essential psychotherapies' are grounded in a particular view of human personality or behaviour. For example, 'family therapies' describe the people who are the focus of therapy rather than the approach. They may be informed by several perspectives including strategic, systemic, cognitive and behavioural therapy. 'Marital therapies' refer to conjoint therapy with couples and may also include various approaches. 'Brief psychotherapy' describes the shorter-than-usual time span of the intervention and again may be informed by different perspectives.

Special education Provision for special children may be seen in a broad sense as encouraging educational progress, as well as nurturing personal and social development (Farrell, 2003b passim). If a child or young person is receiving psychotherapy, it can be helpful if the school is aware of the aims of the therapy and its potential contribution to the child's ultimate well-being. Within such a framework, educators, therapists and other professionals can work towards similar goals. Therapists and other staff working with special children need to cooperate in several ways. They will liaise with each other, sharing information as necessary about progress or concerns. In the therapist's case, this can be done in a general manner without disclosing the confidentiality of the therapy sessions.

From a management point of view, timetabling and the organization of the school day will need to include time for therapy sessions to take place. The transition from therapy session to classroom and vice versa may need careful handling, as the expectations in each setting are different. Consequently, the child may find it difficult to switch from one to the other. Also, if in therapy sessions, the child has been dealing with intense feelings and issues, the return to regular classroom routine may be difficult.

Among ways of approaching these matters is having a secure system of handing over the child from one setting to the other. This may include a transition period after psychotherapy and before the child rejoins his class group. Where therapy takes place on the school site, the therapist may collect the child from the classroom and return him there at the end of the session. Where the pupil travels to therapy sessions from school, the escort who accompanies him will need to be sensitive to the transition.

Three Approaches

Before examining three distinctive approaches to psychotherapy, it is important to mention that combined approaches may be used. These have been tried with adolescents with conduct disorder including delinquency. They include ones drawing several interventions together in a multiple level package such as 'multi-systemic therapy', which is considered to be a promising intervention for serious young offenders. Multi-systemic therapy, a home-based intervention provided by a single therapist, uses various techniques as required such as family therapy, parent training and behavioural and cognitive approaches. With delinquent adolescents, it has reduced recidivism and improved both family and individual pathology (e.g. Borduin, 1999). Reviews suggest multi-systemic therapy for young delinquents tends to reduce time spent in institutions and frequency of arrests (Wolfenden et al., 2003).

Turning to distinctive approaches, some stand out as being based on foundational views of human personality, behaviour and interaction. These include 'systems', 'psychodynamic', 'cognitive' and 'behavioural' perspectives. Indeed, Reinecke and Freeman (2003) suggest that, 'like behavioural, psychodynamic and systemic models of psychotherapy, cognitive therapy might be best described as a 'school of thought' rather than a single theory' (ibid., p. 229). Cognitive-behavioural approaches have been described as 'hybrids of behavioural strategies and cognitive processes' (Dobson and Dozoiz, 2001, pp. 11–12). To this extent, they can be seen as relating to both behavioural and cognitive 'schools of thought'. Accordingly, the present chapter focuses on three perspectives:

- systems
- psychodynamic
- cognitive-behavioural.

Systems Approach

A systems perspective reflects, ' . . . a view of behaviour which takes account of the context in which it occurs' (Dowling and Osborne, 1994, p. 3). It is an approach to family therapy. More generally, it also provides insights into the way in which a school and a child's family, as systems, might be understood and responded to. This section therefore considers functional family therapy; the family and the school as systems; a joint systems approach involving family and school; and relationships between systems perspectives and special education.

Functional family therapy In general terms, family therapy (Dallo and Draper, 2000) refers to various approaches to group therapy in which the therapist sees all family members at the same session. A family member, for example, a child may be considered to experience some psychosocial disorder. In a systems approach to family therapy (Gurman and Messer, 2003, pp. 400–462), such a problem apparently located in a particular family member may be re-examined. The problem may come to be seen as existing within the family as a whole. Members of the family are enabled to communicate with one another and to try to find solutions to the problem as it appears to them. The therapist may put forward various strategies to encourage family members to behave, think and feel differently.

Functional family therapy developed by Alexander and colleagues (Alexander and Parsons, 1982) is a systems approach, which also draws on learning theory and cognitive theory. It creates a non-judgemental environment in therapy, in which explanations are built up about the interactional function of the behaviour of all family members. In this way, it seeks to help clients understand the role of their behaviour in regulating family relationships. This allows family members to modify their expectations, attitudes, beliefs and emotions, empowering them to feel more capable of making changes. Behaviours, certain expressions of which may be problematic, are considered to fulfil particular outcomes. These are contact/closeness (merging); distance/independence (separating), or vacillation between the two (midpointing).

The steps of the process of functional family therapy are assessment, therapy and education. During assessment, levels of family functioning are evaluated. These allow the therapist to identify family interactions in which the problem behaviours are embedded and functions that are served by the behaviours. In the therapy phase, interventions are employed to try to deal with family resistances and encourage family members to change. Among techniques that may be used in the therapy phase is that of reattribution techniques. These involve encouraging members of the family to re-examine their understandings of the way the family interacts and the problem as it presents itself. In the education aspect, the therapist may introduce intervention such as contingency management, modelling and problem-solving training (Alexander *et al.*, 2000). Recent, fuller summaries of functional family therapy are available (e.g. Gurman and Messer, 2005, pp. 441–442).

Functional family therapy has been used in the treatment of delinquents (Alexander *et al.*, 1988). In this context, it takes the view that an adolescent's difficult behaviour is serving a function. For example, this might be regulating the distance between family members. Consequently, intervention does not just seek to tackle the adolescent's behavioural problems and cognitive dysfunction. It also addresses family interactions and aims to change patterns of interaction and communication to encourage adaptive family functioning.

Family and school as systems More broadly, a systems view of a child's family and his school may be taken to inform approaches to children who appear to experience psychosocial disorders. The school a child attends may be regarded as a system in which it is possible to envisage a child having a problem, but where the problem may also be understood in relation to the school as a whole.

A systems approach may be contrasted to a linear model. A linear model of behaviour seeks a rationale to explain the apparent causes and effects of behaviour, which it regards as an individual phenomenon. On the other hand, a systems approach sees behaviour as existing within a context and takes an interactional and holistic view. It is suggested that through a sort of circular causality, sequences of interactions contribute to the continuation of a 'problem'. Consequently, it becomes more pertinent to ask *how* a problem arises than to enquire *why* it happens (Dowling and Osborne, 1994, p. 5). If a parent, brother, sister or a teacher decides to 'punctuate' the circle of interaction by focusing on a point in the cycle, this can give a possibly spurious impression of a linear cause and effect.

To take a school example, there may be a cycle of interaction that perpetuates regular conflict between a particular pupil and a certain teacher. The teacher may punctuate the circle at the point of a pupil's perceived rude and uncooperative behaviour in the classroom, seeing the problem as residing predominantly within the pupil. By contrast, the pupil may punctuate the circle at the point of the teacher's perceived negative and demeaning attitude towards him, seeing the situation as being largely precipitated by the teacher. Neither the pupil nor the teacher is 'correct' in their interpretation in any absolute sense. In fact, it is considered that there is no absolute perspective from which behaviour can be viewed and evaluated.

It is important that the system is coherent and that its pieces fit together in a way that is internally and externally balanced in relation to the environment. In the context of the school system, there may be self-regulating aspects of dysfunctional individual behaviour. Consequently, components of the school system may sustain unacceptable conduct. Examining this possibility may lead to modifying elements of routine and procedure. This could result in the school's aims being fulfilled, but without sustaining the conflict with a pupil.

Family and school are seen as 'open systems' in that they ' . . . cannot be viewed without reference to their influence on the environment in which they exist' (ibid., p. 6). The 'reciprocal influence' of the family and school, which are closely interlinked over a long period, determines how the two systems view one another.

A joint systems approach involving family and school It has been suggested that the following are among common elements that school and family share: hierarchical organization, rules, culture (including the ethos of an organization) and belief systems.

Regarding hierarchical organization, in the family, it appears important there is a responsible adult in charge. This adult establishes consistent rules and communicates these to children, helping them feel secure and able to understand the consequences of any rule infringement. Similarly, in schools, hierarchy is important. However, the organizational structure may influence a pupil's perception and behaviour in a way that leads him to be seen as problematical to those striving to maintain the structure (ibid., p. 8).

Both families and schools have and require rules. A school tends to make these public, explicit and the subject of whole-school policies. In the family, rules may not be as explicitly stated as this but are evident nonetheless. School culture relates to its ethos, conveyed in the way things are done, almost unconsciously. Similarly, in the family, there is a culture and an implicit expectation that things are done in a certain manner. Belief systems include the explicit and implicit beliefs and values that influence day-to-day interaction and behaviour and apply in both school and family, although the particular beliefs and values may differ.

A 'joint systems approach' seeks to understand the child's family and the school as systems and explores ways of taking into account interrelationships between them (Dowling and Osborne, 1994 passim). The aims of a joint systems approach to family and school have been summarized as follows:

- facilitating communication between school, staff and family members
- clarifying differences in perceptions of the problem by focusing on how it occurs rather than on why it happens
- negotiating commonly agreed goals
- beginning to explore specific steps towards change (ibid., p. 15).

Systems perspectives and special education A systems perspective of provision for special children takes a wider view of apparent problems than some other perspectives. It would not assume the problem was, as it were, located within the child. It implies examining the school and family contexts of the pupil's 'problem' behaviour to avoid pre-emptively identifying the difficulties as solely within the child. This can lead to a school modifying its views of the identification and assessment of behavioural and emotional disorders such as disorders of conduct.

A specialist worker, perhaps a family therapist, who stands outside the family and school systems, may be involved where there are perceived problems with a child. In some schools, a family-school liaison worker might draw insights from a systems approach. The worker may not be trained in family therapy. However, he may work pragmatically on the principle that where there is a perceived problem, it is generally better that the family and school systems communicate with each other, trying to see the other's point of view.

Regarding provision, it may help ensure the school has considered a range of possibilities and acted on them before being confident that the 'problem' can be best addressed as though it were predominantly within the child. For example, an approach outlined by Daniels and Williams (2000) developed and applied a framework for intervention for schools (Ali *et al.*, 1997), which addressed behaviour problems at different levels. It initially concentrated on a behaviour environment plan (BEP) aimed at school and classroom factors. Only at a later stage did it turn to an additional individual behaviour plan. One of the central principles was that ' . . . problems with behaviour in education settings are usually a product of complex interaction between the individual, school, family, community and wider society' (Daniels and Williams, 2000, p. 222). Three levels of intervention are proposed in which, particularly, at level 1, systems perspectives are applied.

Level 1 is the initial referral part of the process. It does not propose developing individual education plans. Rather it focuses on the environment in which the behaviour arises and may relate to groups of pupils as well as individual pupils. The process involves carrying out a behavioural audit aiming to achieve the optimum environment. This is one that would be achieved

' . . . if every environmental improvement that it is reasonable to expect were made' (ibid., p. 222). A checklist is completed covering factors that affect the environment including the classroom and the playground. These factors might be whole-school policies, physical factors, classroom organization and the personal style of the teacher. Once the checklist is completed, the teacher may decide to tackle an issue through developing a BEP. A baseline measure of the behaviour causing concern is taken so that the effectiveness of the BEP is judged according to changes in the behaviour as well as modifications to the environment. The plan runs for 6 weeks.

If after 6 weeks, concern about the behaviour continues even after the BEP has been implemented, the process moves to level 2 of the framework. At this level, individual behaviour plans are introduced while the BEP continue to be applied. The individual plan might involve interventions such as individual counselling or reward systems. If necessary, level 3 of the framework is introduced, in which help, support and advice from a specialist such as a school/educational psychologist is called upon.

Psychodynamic Approach

Psychodynamic perspectives The term 'psychodynamic' concerns 'emotional conflict or conflicts taking place within a person's internal, unconscious world or mind' (Ayers and Prytys, 2002, p. 168). Among important contributions to a psychodynamic perspective in the present context are those of Melanie Klein, Donald Winnicott and John Bowlby. These are briefly outlined below. The section then considers a particular type of psychodynamic psychotherapy, 'focal psychodynamic psychotherapy', which is effective with children experiencing mild anxiety and depressive disorder. Arts therapies and play therapy that have a psychodynamic orientation are considered next. Finally, the section describes particular applications to special education developed from the work of Winnicott and Bowlby.

Melanie Klein, Donald Winnicott and John Bowlby Melanie Klein (Klein, 1932), ([various dates]/1964; [1957]/1975), through her clinical work and observation with children, sought to develop the hypotheses put forward by Sigmund Freud. Freud's reported clinical work (Freud, [1940]/2002, pp. 175–236; 1923) had been almost exclusively with adults. Klein considered that she was extending the ideas of Sigmund Freud who hypothesized that older children (aged around 5 or 6 years) struggled with deep incestuous wishes. Klein believed that very young children (aged around 2 or 3 years) and even infants experienced fantasies of incestuous union and of frightening punishments. However, these fantasies were in a much more primitive form. Deep differences developed between the views of Klein and of Sigmund's daughter Anna Freud (Freud, 1945; [various dates]/1998) and their followers. Klein believed that children can be analysed through interpreting their play in a similar way to that in which free association is analysed in adults. Anna Freud considered that very young children could not be analysed because their 'ego' is insufficiently developed to cope with in-depth interpretations of instinctual conflicts (Mitchell and Black, 1995, p. 86).

Winnicott (1958, 1965) is associated with 'object relations' theory. He developed theories of the early mother–child relationship and their connection with an individual's later healthy development or dysfunction. He focused on a state of 'false self disorder' affecting the adult patient's sense of being a person, linking this to the patient's infant relationship with the mother. The infant's earliest state of mind, he termed *unintegration*. As the infant's needs and wishes emerge from the unintegrated drift of consciousness they are met by a 'good enough' mother. The mother creates a 'holding environment' in which the baby is protected without knowing it. As the mother gradually emerges from her absorption with her infant, she does not meet the baby's needs as seamlessly. The baby gradually comes to realize that his desires are not omnipotent but that his mother provides for him, and that he is dependent on her. This experience of objective reality is added to the infant's experience of subjective omnipotence. A 'transitional object' (e.g. a toy) is an object, which becomes an extension of the child's self. It lies somewhere between the child's two experiences of the mother that the child creates in subjective omnipotence and the mother acting for herself in the objective world. Transitional experience connects the subjective omnipotence aspects of the self to the world of other people's subjectivity. Where the mother is not able to provide a 'good enough' environment, the core of personhood is suspended. The child develops a premature concern with the external world, which constrains his own subjectivity. The true self becomes separated from a false compliant self. Later, a holding environment might be found enabling the individual to develop authentic experience and a sense of self. In the analytic setting, the analyst provides the adult patient with this 'good enough' environment. This is a holding environment in which the patient's suspended self-development can be re-awoken so the true self can emerge (Mitchell and Black, 1995, pp. 124–134).

Psychoanalyst John Bowlby placed great importance on the bond between child and mother, which he termed *attachment*. His theory of attachment relates to the biological survival of the species and secures the safety of the infant in a loving environment (Bowlby, 1965, 1969, 1973, 1980). He proposed five instinctive responses that lead to greater 'proximity' to the mother and that mediate attachment. These responses are sucking, smiling, clinging, crying and following. Bowlby took the view that the child's attachment to the mother is instinctual and primary (not derivative of the mother providing for the child's needs). His researches into early experience of loss of and separation indicated they lead to mourning. This appears to support the importance of the primacy of the child's bond with the mother. Emotional security is built up through early childhood experiences and relates to the confidence the child has in the availability of attachment figures. Different forms of anxiety all relate to the basic anxiety about the separation from the object of attachment. All defences relate back to detachment, what has been called a *deactivation of the fundamental and central need for attachment* (Mitchell and Black, 1995, p. 137).

Focal psychodynamic psychotherapy At the University of Pisa, a study evaluated the effectiveness of a programme of family work. It involved 58 children with relatively mild anxiety disorder or dysthymic disorder (which involves a chronically depressed mood). Treatments comprised 11 sessions of 'focal psychodynamic psychotherapy'. This began with five sessions involving the whole family in which the therapist explored the dynamic formulation of the child's conflicts in terms of family relationships. Next came five sessions with only the child. In these, the therapist aimed to help the child make connections between his feelings and unconscious conflicts about the relationship with his parents. The final session again included the whole family, and the therapist once more set out the dynamic formulation of the child's conflicts rooted in family relationships. A control group was referred for community treatment. Of the children in the study, 60% were in the clinical range of the *Child Behaviour Checklist* (Achenbach and Edelbrock, 1983). In the treatment group, this was reduced to 34% at follow-up testing. In the control group, the percentage increased to 65% (Muratori *et al.*, 2002).

Arts therapies and play therapy Several therapies draw on psychodynamic perspectives. These include some approaches to music therapy, art therapy, drama therapy and movement therapy, sometimes collectively referred to as *arts therapies*. Arts therapies use different approaches, perspectives and aims that can include therapeutic ones, as well as programmes promoting wellness in the general population. Some approaches to play therapy involve psychodynamic orientations. Also, psychodynamic approaches and perspectives are influential for some arts therapists. Indeed, it has been said that the idea of the unconscious has been 'central to some areas of the arts therapies: their thinking and their methodology' (Jones, 2005, p. 126).

Some arts therapists work on the basis that there are 'ways of engaging with the unconscious which can bring about change or healing' (ibid., p. 128). Art making and arts products within therapy are considered to relate to the unconscious in ways 'fundamental to the recovery of health, or the improvement or maintenance of well being' (ibid., p. 128). In the United Kingdom, research (Karkou, 1999a, b passim) has indicated that the main theoretic influences in arts therapies included those of Winnicott (1958, 1965) and Melanie Klein ([1957]/1975).

Where possible, the effectiveness of psychotherapies is evaluated in line with the current trend towards evidence-based practice. There is a perceived dichotomy between seeking to use objective approaches to assess the efficacy of art therapies and the more fluid nature of therapeutic encounters themselves. This makes developing evidence-based practice challenging. Attempts include examining ways in which drama therapists ascertain whether the client is 'getting any better', for example, experiencing improved well-being (Valente and Fontana, 1997, p. 29). This might be suggested by client self-reports, projective techniques and reports by other group members. In art therapy, evaluation may involve a review and of pictures with the client, which may uncover 'connections and links that have previously been unconscious' (Schaverien, 1995, p. 28).

Psychodynamic perspectives in education To the extent that a psychodynamic approach implies underlying unconscious or subconscious forces influencing behaviour, the general connections with special education are only tangential. Settings for special education may encourage more open communication from pupils and may provide activities that may be communicative and expressive such as drama, aspects of physical education and play; but there are important differences between such activities and their therapeutic counterparts. Drama is not drama therapy and play is not play therapy. The aim of each is different, and the training and perspectives of educators and therapists also differ substantially.

In some very specialist settings, psychodynamic interpretations may be used in day-to-day living as well as in individual sessions. The Mulberry Bush School in the United Kingdom (www.mulberrybush.oxon.sch.uk) is a special school, which continues and develops the work of its founder and psychotherapist Barbara Dockar-Drysdale (1991, 1993). She, in turn, developed her approach from the work of the psychoanalyst and paediatrician Winnicott (1958, 1965).

The school works on the principle that the children have missed the 'building blocks' of nurturing experiences and seeks to offer them the opportunity to re-experience caring and clear relationships with adults and other children. Among the ways the adults do this is through 'planned environment therapy', using opportunities associated with group living to give the child clear expectations, routines and rules about how to live and get on with others (for a fuller description of the school, please see Farrell, 2006a, p. 66).

In mainstream settings, the development of a form of early intervention known as nurture groups (Boxall, 2002) has its foundations in the attachment theory of John Bowlby. These groups, based in mainstream schools, are intended for children whose emotional, social and behavioural 'needs' cannot be addressed in a mainstream classroom. The intention is to return the children to mainstream classes as soon as it is considered appropriate. The group might comprise a teacher and an assistant and 10 to 12 children. It is hypothesized that these children have not had early experiences that would have enabled them to function appropriately for their age socially and emotionally.

The relationship between the child and the adults is seen as important to the child developing a sense of self. Social development is encouraged and concentrates on the emotional aspects of interactions between child and caregiver. Therefore, a nurture group emphasizes emotional growth. It provides a range of experiences in an environment that provides security, predictable routines, clear boundaries and repeated planned opportunities for learning (Boxall, 2002). The adults might 'model' suitable positive behaviour in a structure that is right for the child's developmental level. Through this provision, it is suggested the child is able to develop an attachment to the adult, receive approval and experience positive outcomes.

Cognitive-Behavioural Approach

A cognitive-behavioural perspective This section examines a cognitive-behavioural viewpoint and its application. The cognitive and behavioural elements of this combined approach are explained. Next, three cognitive-behavioural interventions are outlined: rational-emotive behavioural therapy, cognitive therapy and problem-solving dialogues and training. Finally, cognitive-behavioural approaches and special education are considered.

Cognitive and behavioural elements Defining a cognitive-behavioural perspective may be approached by considering its two components. A behavioural perspective defines personality with reference to individual behaviours and these behaviours are assumed to arise ' . . . primarily as a result of an individual's learning history' (Antony and Roemer, 2003, p. 186). However, behaviour therapy is not inevitably viewed as a unified approach and numerous behavioural strategies are used in treating psychological problems (ibid., p. 182).

The model underlying cognitive therapy has been described as a 'cognitive-constructivist' model of human behaviour (Reinecke and Freeman, 2003, p. 226). This is founded on 'psychological constructivism', which has been defined as

' . . . a family of theories about mind and mentation that (1) emphasize the active and proactive nature of all perception, learning and knowing; (2) acknowledge the structural and functional primacy of abstract (tacit) over concrete (explicit) processes in all sentient and sapient experience; and (3) view learning, knowing and memory as phenomena that reflect the ongoing attempts of body and mind to organize (and endlessly reorganize) their own patterns of action and experience . . . '
(Mahoney, 1991, p. 95).

Differences are apparent in the two perspectives. Behavioural approaches such as operant conditioning (Skinner, [1953]/1965, pp. 62–69) regard behavioural reactions and emotional reactions as the result of reinforcement history and environmental contingencies. By contrast, a cognitive-constructivist model sees behaviour as ' . . . goal directed, purposive, active, and adaptive' (Reinecke and Freeman, 2003, p. 226). However, it has been suggested behavioural therapists may find in the cognitive therapy model 'a brief, active, directive, collaborative, psychoeducational model of psychotherapy that is empirically based and has as its goal direct behavioural change' (ibid., p. 224).

In fact, while there may be differences in models and perspectives, in practice, the merging of cognitive therapy and behavioural therapy has ' . . . become more the rule than the exception' (Reinecke and Freeman, 2003, p. 224). It has been proposed that cognitive-behavioural approaches represent, ' . . . hybrids of behavioural strategies and cognitive processes, with the goal of achieving behavioural change' (Dobson and Dozoiz, 2001, p. 11–12). From this perspective, behaviour is considered to be influenced by cognition (attitudes and assumptions) and by cognitive appraisal (the process of thinking and reasoning).

Cognitive-behavioural   interventions Cognitive-behavioural   interventions involve monitoring cognitions; seeking connections between thoughts, feelings and behaviour; and seeking to replace negative cognitions with positive ones. Examples that might further indicate some of the rationale of cognitive-behavioural therapies are as follows:

- rational-emotive behavioural therapy
- cognitive therapy
- problem-solving dialogues and training.

Rational-emotive behavioural therapy Rational-emotive behavioural therapy focuses on rational and irrational beliefs (Ellis *et al.*, 1997). Psychosocial disturbances are regarded predominantly as self-created and arising from beliefs, interpretations and evaluations of what occurs in an individual's life. Beliefs held about oneself, others and one's environment, can influence thoughts, emotions and behaviour. These beliefs, whether positive or negative in their effect, can be modified. Rational beliefs are self-enhancing and their consequences are 'healthy' negative emotions such as sorrow and concern. Irrational beliefs, characterized by absolutist thoughts and inferences that cannot be substantiated, lead to 'unhealthy' negative emotions such as anger, anxiety and guilt. They are self-defeating and contribute towards psychosocial problems. These problems, it is argued, are brought about by absolutist demands: directed at oneself (ego disturbance) or concerning conditions (discomfort disturbance). A cognitive analysis may be used in terms of: an activating event such as perceptions and inferences; rational and irrational beliefs; and emotional and behavioural consequences.

Adaptive behaviour is encouraged by correcting or modifying irrational thinking as the approach considers that disturbances are brought about mainly by current beliefs rather than past events and memories. Change is brought about as the child works on his irrational beliefs through dialogue with the therapist. The beliefs are identified, discussed and challenged and are tested empirically, logically and pragmatically.

Cognitive therapy Cognitive therapy (Beck *et al.*, 1979) concerns the cognitive processes of perceiving, thinking and reasoning and their effect on behaviour and emotions. Individuals construct their own experiences and beliefs and the latter can be sampled by self-reports and other means. Central notions are automatic thoughts, cognitive schema and cognitive deficits and distortions.

Automatic thoughts, unlike voluntary thoughts, appear to arise spontaneously, are difficult to control and may be distressing. Cognitive schemas formed in early learning experiences are deep cognitive processes. They determine an individual's view of himself, his view of the world and his relationships with others. Once activated, cognitive schemas are maintained and reinforced by cognitive distortions (such as overgeneralizing), which bias the selection of information to support existing schemas. Cognitive deficits, such as in memory or perception, also help maintain schemas and may involve, for example, the inability to recognize sufficiently the consequences of one's actions. These processes lead to thinking and reasoning becoming inflexible and judgements becoming absolute (typified by perceptions of language such as 'must' or 'ought').

Psychosocial problems arise as exaggerations of normal responses. The therapist, given the active involvement and motivation of the child, encourages him to reappraise beliefs logically and empirically. This includes looking for alternative explanations for events, different ways of acting and responding and different ways of behaving.

Problem-solving dialogues and training Problem-solving dialogues and training work on the assumption that the child lacks problem-solving skills necessary for effective social functioning. Such approaches have cognitive and behavioural elements and use structured programmes to help the child with psychosocial problems. Problem-solving skills training (D'Zurilla, 1986) involves being aware of the problem; defining and formulating it; putting forward alternative solutions; deciding the approach; and testing the solution. Participants are trained to identify problems, prevent their initial impulses, produce several alternatives, consider possible consequences, plan their solutions and evaluate them.

Cognitive-behavioural perspectives and special education A cognitive-behavioural approach, in liaison with the psychotherapist, can be supported in a setting where a child receives special education. Educators might encourage more positive interpretations of events where a child tends to view them very negatively. 'Self talk', a type of internal monologue, might be introduced as a strategy and used in therapy to aid the child's learning and development. This can be used to manage anxiety. Consider a pupil that might be anxious in certain situation where the anxiety is not related to any apparent 'real' cause. He may first be taught to recognize the starting signs of the anxiety, perhaps increased heart rate or sweating palms. On recognizing these signs, the pupil is taught to intervene using self-talk. This may be agreed and scripted so that the pupil knows it very well. It is likely to include certain aspects such as encouraging calmness, challenging negative interpretations of events or circumstances and seeking to replace a negative interpretation with a plausible and likely alternative explanation. A pupil who becomes very anxious when he thinks a certain teacher is trying to ridicule him might learn a script such as the following.

'I will keep calm. The teacher has just asked me if I will be able to manage the homework. I think she is being sarcastic. But she might be just checking so she can help me before the lesson ends. I will say that I don't understand everything and ask the teacher if she will explain part of it again'.

Self-talk can be encouraged and reinforced in different settings including the classroom. Similarly, strategies for anger management can be supported and encouraged in schools.

As indicated earlier, cognitive-behavioural interventions involve monitoring cognitions, seeking connections between thoughts, feelings and behaviour and seeking to replace negative cognitions with positive ones.

A cognitive-behavioural approach has been employed in training programmes for parents of children with attention deficit hyperactivity disorder. Parents have been taught special child management techniques and given information about attention deficit hyperactivity disorder. At the same time, cognitive therapy techniques have been used to aid the parents' acceptance, management and understanding of attention deficit hyperactivity disorder (Anastopoulos and Farley, 2003, pp. 187–203). Parent training plus medication appears superior to only medication for certain outcomes (e.g. family functioning) and for some children (e.g. ones that are also anxious) and their families (ibid., p. 202). Parent training tends to improve parents' self-esteem as they learn to cope better and reduces their stress. Furthermore, it appears to increase the child's compliance and shortens task completion time.

Fuller Examples

The fuller examples that conclude this chapter all involve cognitive-behavioural approaches. Cognitive-behavioural therapy is particularly widely used and its effectiveness is being increasingly demonstrated. Where it is preferred to other approaches such as psychodynamic ones, relevant factors may include the shorter time involved in treatments and relatedly, the lower cost of treatment. The fuller examples relate to the following:

- disorders of conduct
- anxiety disorders
- depressive disorders.

Cognitive-Behavioural Therapy and Disorders of Conduct

Cognitive-behavioural therapy has been used effectively with children with conduct disorder. An approach for children aged 2 to 13 years with conduct disorder involved problem-solving skills training for the children (e.g. using 'stop and think' self-statements) and for parents, training to help them manage the child's behaviour (e.g. using positive reinforcement) (Kazdin, 2003, pp. 241–262). The intervention focused on individual characteristics as well as 'external and interactional events' to promote socially acceptable behaviour. Among individual facets were cognitive and behavioural repertoires and 'predispositions' to respond to potentially difficult situations. External and internal interactional events included the way that other people responded before and after the child's behaviour, that is, antecedents and consequences from others (ibid., p. 258).

Two interventions that are used in cognitive-behavioural approaches are social skills training and anger management. Social skills training involves establishing the social skills that the child or young person lacks or has to a limited degree. The training involves instruction, prompting, reinforcement, modelling, role-play and other elements of behavioural and social learning perspectives. The individual also has to be motivated to perform the skill. Following up the training involves encouraging the child or young person to demonstrate the skills in real-life situations. Anger management may combine aspects of behavioural interventions such as positive reinforcement and time out and cognitive approaches such as self-instruction and stress-inoculation training, where the individual is taught to gradually deal with increasingly stressful situations without resorting to anger.

As will be apparent from the above descriptions, social skills training and anger management training may draw on cognitive-behavioural frameworks. One rationale is that conduct disturbance relates to deficits in information processing and that a child with conduct disorder tends to have distorted appraisals of social events. It is suggested that he will therefore benefit from treatments that seek to modify these distortions and that lead to better ability to regulate his emotional responses. One approach to anger management training for aggressive children used a 'contextual social cognitive' model of prevention (Lochman *et al.*, 2003, p. 264). It took the view that the child factors and parent factors were potential mediators for adolescent antisocial behaviour. Among child factors might be lack of social competence. Possible parent factors included poor child discipline. This particular model of intervention included an 'Anger Coping Program', with sessions such as 'using self instruction', 'perspective taking', 'choices and consequences' and 'steps for problem solving' (ibid, p. 267).

A school-based strategy, 'Coping Power' (Lochman and Wells, 1996) involved primary school children with conduct problems. Thirty-three structured sessions were administered during school days. Besides engaging themselves with problem-solving elements of the programme, children reviewed examples of social interactions, discussing social cues and motives. Particular skills were practised to manage anger arousal and anger control strategies such as self-talk were used.

Evidence indicates that training in social skills and anger management can help reduce *mild* conduct problems in pre-adolescents (Quinn *et al.*, 1999 provide a review).

Cognitive-Behavioural Therapy and Anxiety Disorders

Some cognitive-behavioural therapy packages have been effective in treating certain anxiety disorders in children (Toren *et al.*, 2000). For example, a 'child-focused treatment' of anxiety (Kendall *et al.*, 2003, pp. 81–100) was used to treat, 'disturbingly anxious' 8 to 13 year olds. It involved several elements. Child–therapist relationships were important. The package also involved education into the physiological signs of anxiety, the normality of anxiety and 'behavioural skills to address the management of anxiety' (ibid., p. 97). An initial educational (preparation) phase was followed by an exposure (practice) phase.

In one study, individual cognitive-behavioural therapy was compared with individual cognitive-behavioural therapy plus family cognitive behavioural work (Barrett *et al.*, 1996). Seventy-six children aged 7 to 14 years were allocated to one of the three conditions (cognitive-behavioural therapy only; cognitive-behavioural therapy plus family management; waiting list control). Cognitive-behavioural therapy plus family intervention was found to be the superior condition, confirming earlier research by others.

Approaches drawing on group cognitive-behavioural therapy may be helpful with children and adolescents with separation anxiety disorder. An open trial of parent–child group cognitive-behavioural therapy for children with anxiety disorders was conducted. Almost all had separation anxiety disorder and half had overanxious disorder of childhood (now subsumed under the diagnostic criteria for generalized anxiety disorder) and/or phobias. Twenty-four children and their parents took part in ten sessions using cognitive-behavioural therapy approaches. Seventy percent of these no longer met the diagnostic criteria by the end of treatment; and three years later, this applied to 91% of them (Toren *et al.*, 2000).

Regarding interventions for obsessive-compulsive behaviour, medication is effective. However, cognitive-behavioural therapy, involving exposure and response prevention, is also used. A small-scale open study involved cognitive-behavioural therapy with 14 children and adolescents meeting the criteria for obsessive-compulsive behaviour. The intervention led to 12 of the patients having at least a 50% reduction in the severity of symptoms. Furthermore, these gains were maintained after a 9-month follow-up (Franklin *et al.*, 1998). A recommended treatment of choice for childhood obsessive-compulsive behaviour is a combination of medication (selective serotonin reuptake inhibitors) and cognitive-behavioural therapy (March, 1999).

Cognitive-behavioural therapy, including gradual exposure techniques, can be effective in treating circumscribed phobias such as school refusal, especially in younger children (King *et al.*, 2001). One randomly controlled trial of cognitive-behavioural treatment involved 34 children aged 5 to 15 years with school phobia. Those assigned to cognitive-behavioural therapy showed significantly greater improvement during treatment compared with a waiting list control. The cognitive-behavioural therapy involved six individual therapy sessions over a period of 4 weeks and a gradual return to school (King *et al.*, 1998).

It will be seen that cognitive-behavioural approaches are effective with several types of anxiety disorder including separation anxiety disorder, obsessive-compulsive behaviour and circumscribed phobias.

Cognitive-Behavioural Therapy and Depressive Disorders

Cognitive-behavioural therapy appears effective for treating adolescents with mild or moderate depression whether treatment is provided individually or in a group. Where there was no response to treatment of the usual duration, providing a longer course of cognitive-behavioural therapy or booster sessions reduced relapse and improved recovery (Clarke *et al.*, 1999).

The programme 'Primary and Secondary Control Enhancement Training for youth depression' is used for treating depressed children and young people aged 8 to 15 years. This programme draws on the cognitive-behavioural tradition (Weisz *et al.*, 2003, pp. 165–183). It takes a two-process model of control and coping:

- 'Primary control' involves attempts to cope by making objective conditions (such as the activities in which one participates and one's acceptance by other people) conform to one's wishes.

- 'Secondary control' refers to efforts to cope by adjusting oneself to fit the objective conditions (e.g. adjusting one's beliefs, expectations and interpretations of events).

The programme involves treatment sessions and assignments that are taken home.

A series of studies compared cognitive-behavioural therapy, systemic-behavioural family therapy and nondirective support for 107 adolescents experiencing depression. These indicated that cognitive-behavioural therapy showed the greatest improvement, particularly for those adolescents also experiencing anxiety. Where the mother was clinically depressed, the treatment outcome for the adolescent was worse. In these circumstances, cognitive-behavioural therapy was no better than the other conditions. At a 2-year follow-up, the superiority of cognitive-behavioural therapy had not been maintained. The finding that co-occurring maternal depression reduced the treatment efficacy suggests that any such maternal depression should be concurrently treated (Brent *et al.*, 1998).

Conclusion

The chapter examined the nature of psychotherapy and systems, psychodynamic and cognitive-behavioural approaches and looked at their relationships to special education and their scope. Cognitive-behavioural therapy has particular application to disorders of conduct, certain anxiety disorders and depressive disorders.

Thinking Points

Readers may wish to consider the following:

- differences and similarities in systems, psychodynamic and cognitive-behavioural 'schools of thought'
- differences and similarities in the application of systems therapy, psychodynamic therapy and cognitive-behavioural therapy
- ways in which therapists, educators and others may work together to maximize the effectiveness of interventions.

Key Texts

Abela, J. R. Z. and Hankin, B. L. (Eds) (2008) *Handbook of Depression in Children and Adolescents*. New York: Guilford Press.

The parts of this book cover epidemiology, aetiology, treatment, prevention and special populations. The treatment sections include cognitive-behavioural approaches, psychopharmacological treatment, the ACTION treatment programme, positive psychotherapy and interpersonal psychotherapy.

Bloomquist, M. and Schnell, M. (2005) *Helping Children with Aggression and Conduct Problems*. New York: Guilford Press.

This describes interventions found effective with children aged 3 to 12 years with aggression and conduct problems. These include social competence training, parent and family skills building and school-based approaches. Risk factors and protective factors are also described.

Dobson, K. S. (Ed.) (2003) (2nd edn) *Handbook of Cognitive-Behavioural Therapies*. New York: Guilford Press.

Part One of this book deals with conceptual issues. Part Two describes several therapies including 'Problem solving therapies' (Chapter 7) and 'Rational emotive behaviour therapy' (Chapter 2001). A further chapter 'Cognitive behavioural therapy with youth' outlines several approaches including relaxation training, affective education and cognitive restructuring.

Folensbee, R. W. (2007) *The Neuroscience of Psychological Therapies*. Cambridge: Cambridge University Press.

The book considers brain functioning and brain behaviour connections in relation to the practice of psychotherapy. It concerns basic processes (e.g. affect and anxiety) and the process of psychotherapy (e.g. affect in therapy, anxiety and change).

Fonagy, P., Target, M., Cottrell, D., Phillips, J. *et al.* (2002) *What Works for Whom? A Critical Review of Treatments for Children and Adolescents*. New York: Guilford Press.

This text includes the chapters 'Anxiety Disorders', 'Depressive Disorders', 'Disturbance of Conduct' and 'Attention-Deficit/ Hyperactivity Disorder' as well as a concluding chapter examining the effectiveness of various interventions including cognitive-behavioural, psychodynamic and family/systemic therapies.

Gurman, A. S. and Messer, S. B. (Eds) (2003) (2nd edn) *Essential Psychotherapies: Theory and Practice*. New York: Guilford Press.

Readers may find these chapters particularly relevant to the present context: 'Contemporary Issues in the Theory and Practice of Psychotherapy: A Framework for Comparative Study' (Chapter 1); 'The Theory and Practice of Traditional Psychoanalytic Treatment' (Chapter 2); 'Behaviour Therapy' (Chapter 6); 'Cognitive Therapy' (Chapter 7) and 'Family Therapies' (Chapter 11).

Kendall, P. C. (2006) (3rd edn) (Ed.) *Child and Adolescent Therapy: Cognitive-Behavioural Procedures*. New York: Guilford Press.

This book includes sections on guiding theory for cognitive-behavioural theory, externalizing disorders, internalizing disorders, special populations and special topics.

Mitchell, S. A. and Black, M. J. (1995) *Freud and Beyond: A History of Modern Psychoanalytic Thought*. New York: Basic Book.

This readable introduction considers 'Sigmund Freud and the Classical Psychoanalytical Tradition'; 'Ego Psychology'; 'Melanie Klein and Contemporary Kleinian Theory'; and 'The British Object Relations School: W. R. D. Fairbairn and D. W. Winnicott' as well as other developments. The final two chapters consider controversies in theory and technique.

8

Behavioural/Observational

Introduction

This chapter first considers learning theory through the work of Thorndyke on learning by trial and accidental success; Pavlov on classical conditioning; Watson on conditioning emotional responses; and Skinner on operant conditioning. Next, the chapter looks at observational learning and modelling through Bandura's work and social cognitive theory. For both learning theory and observational learning, their relationship to special education and their scope is reviewed. Fuller examples are examined of the joint application of learning theory and observational learning/modelling to conduct disorder and autism.

Behavioural Approaches

(a) Thorndyke and learning by trial and accidental success

Thorndyke (1911]/1965) describes experiments in which a cat is placed in a box from which it can get out only through performing certain actions. It might have to turn a wooden button to open a door on the box (p. 31). Thorndyke found that if the same cat was repeatedly returned to a box, it progressively took less time to get out (to escape or to reach food), eventually doing so immediately. He suggests the cat forms associations between the action leading to the door opening and getting out and the previous experience leads to the cat forming the associations quicker (p. 48). A 'law of effect' was proposed. Part of this is, "Of several responses made to the same situation, those which are accompanied . . . by satisfaction to the animal will . . . be more firmly connected with the situation, so that, when it recurs, they will be more likely to recur" (p. 244). Conversely, responses accompanied by discomfort are only weakly connected with the situation so that, when the situation recurs, the response is less likely to do so. A further, 'law of exercise' states that a response to a situation is more strongly connected with it, ' . . . in proportion to the number of times it has been connected with that situation and to the average vigour and duration of the connections' (p. 244). Thorndyke believed these laws (and instinct) could explain imitation in animals and humans (pp. 251–257). For him, learning involves making and rewarding connections between stimulus and response or avoiding and punishing such connections (p. 266).

(b) Pavlov and classical conditioning

Pavlov's ([1926]/1960) investigations into the physiology of the cerebral cortex in dogs included a series of experiments exploring what came to be called *classical conditioning*. A dog presented with food exhibited a salivation reflex response connected with digestion. The food was the unconditioned stimulus and the salivation was the unconditioned response because they occurred naturally. If the food was presented on several occasions accompanied by a sound such as a bell, the salivating reflex could subsequently be elicited using the sound of the bell alone, without the presence of food. In these circumstances, the bell was known as the conditioned stimulus because the dog had learned to connect it with anticipated food. The salivation was called the conditioned response because it occurred in response to a learned connection. This is a process of stimulus substitution in which a stimulus, formerly neutral, acquires the power to elicit a response, which before was elicited by another stimulus. The change is brought about by the neutral stimulus being reinforced by the effective stimulus (ibid. e.g. lectures 2 and 3 pp. 16–47). Pavlov also studied the effect of different time intervals between the stimulus and the reinforcement, and the degree to which the properties of different stimuli could exert control. He examined the process of 'extinction' whereby the conditioned stimulus, when it is no longer reinforced, loses its power to evoke the response (ibid. e.g. lecture 4, pp. 48–67).

(c) Watson and conditioned emotional responses

Watson and Morgan (1917) theorized that original infant emotional reaction patterns are fear, rage and love. Later, mainly owing to conditioned reflex factors (they hypothesized) these emotions and their admixtures are elicited by an increasing range of stimuli. Watson and Rayner (1920) sought to demonstrate conditioned emotional responses through experiments on Albert B., an infant brought up mainly in a hospital environment (ibid., p. 1). The experiments began when Albert was 8 months old. He was shown various real animals and items, for example, a white rat, a rabbit and cotton wool and indicated no fear of them. When the infant was nearly 9 months old, the researchers established that he showed fear when a noise, made by striking a hammer on a steel bar, was made outside his line of vision. During the period when Albert was just over 11 months old, until he was nearly 13 months old, Watson and Rayner sought to establish whether fear of an animal such as a white rat could be conditioned by linking its presentation with striking the steel bar. After several pairings of Albert touching the rat and the noise, he became reluctant to touch it and eventually showed fear in its presence even in the absence of the cacophony. Some days later, when Albert was shown a white rabbit and it was placed in contact with him, he became frightened, suggesting transference of the appearance and the touch of the rabbit and the rat. Watson and Rayner suggest many phobias are direct or transferred conditioned emotional reactions (p. 14). However, this overlooks methodological flaws in the experiments such as that fear responses apparently generalized to associated items were sometimes 'topped up' by being conditioned directly (Harris, 1979).

(d) Skinner and operant conditioning

In animal experiments, Skinner ([1953]/1965) demonstrated 'operant conditioning'. Learning can occur if the researcher identifies a desired learning outcome and the animal is rewarded for behaviours (operants) progressively approximating the target behaviour (ibid., pp. 62–66, p. 90). Rats were trained using a cage with a lever and a food trough. The target learning outcome (e.g. for the rat to depress the lever) is broken into smaller components called 'operants'. Importantly, 'operant behaviour . . . is *emitted*, rather than *elicited*' (p. 107, italics in original). Following might be the operants: the rat spontaneously (and fortuitously) turns towards the lever; approaches it; touches it; and presses it. Initially, if the rat approaches the lever, a food pellet (the reward or reinforcement) is released into the trough. This behaviour is rewarded until it is consolidated. Later, the food pellet is only delivered if the rat touches the lever. Later still food appears only if the animal presses the lever. The process of rewarding successive approximations towards the target behaviour is called 'shaping' (p. 92). Skinner later discovered that shaping was more effective if the reward followed several correct responses rather than every correct one. Such findings led to the development of schedules of reinforcement.

The behaviour of a pigeon stretching its neck might be reinforced by a light being switched on. 'The stimulus (the light) is the occasion upon which a response (stretching the neck) is followed by a reinforcement (the food)' (p. 108). Eventually the response is more likely to occur when the light is on, through a process of 'discrimination' (p. 108). The researcher can then alter the probability of a response by presenting/removing the discriminative stimulus. The discriminative stimulus alters the probability of the occurrence of a response (p. 110).

Positive reinforcement involves a 'correct' response being followed by a reward and therefore being reinforced. In negative reinforcement, an unpleasant stimulus is removed to reinforce behaviour; that is, it involves the presence of an unpleasant stimulus and then its removal when the required behaviour is produced (p. 73).

Punishment involves the presentation of an adverse stimulus or the removal of a pleasant stimulus to discourage certain behaviour (pp. 182–193). If a particular response is followed by an aversive stimulus, any stimulus accompanying the response is conditioned becoming an 'aversive stimulus' (p. 188). A child on seeing a hot stove may approach it and try to touch. The parent shouts at the child and startles him. This adverse stimulus, if effective, discourages the unwanted response of approaching the hot stove. Approaching the stove becomes conditioned to be an aversive stimulus. Skinner states, '*Any behaviour which reinforces this conditioned aversive stimulus will be reinforced*' (p. 188, italics in original). Therefore it is necessary to specify the behaviour of 'doing something else'. In the example this would be moving away from the hot stove. An effect of punishment is to, ' . . . establish aversive conditions which are avoided by any behaviour of 'doing something else' (p. 189). An individual can also be punished for not doing something (pp. 189–190).

Behaviour can be reduced in frequency or eliminated if another behaviour incompatible with it is reinforced. Sociable behaviour might be reinforced to reduce the incidence of withdrawn behaviour (p. 192). Extinction occurs when the behaviour is no longer reinforced and gradually fades. Primary reinforcers include food, water, sexual contact and escape from injurious conditions (p. 83). Conditioned reinforcers involve the pairing of a stimulus that is reinforcing with one that initially is not, so that the non-reinforcing stimulus becomes reinforcing. This is concerned not with eliciting a response but with reinforcing it (p. 76). If a hungry pigeon is fed every time a light is switched on, the light in time becomes a conditioned reinforcer able to condition an operant in the same way as food.

Generalized reinforcement occurs when a conditioned reinforcer is paired with more than one primary reinforcer. If money or tokens are the reinforcer, subsequent control of behaviour is relatively independent of passing deprivations (e.g. lack of food). Skinner argues that we are reinforced irrespective of any deprivation when we successfully control the physical environment (p. 77). He maintains, 'Eventually, generalized reinforcers are effective even though the primary reinforcers upon which they are based no longer accompany them' (p. 81). An example is approval for its own sake. The reinforcement of responses 'increases the probability of all responses containing the same elements' (p. 94).

Differential reinforcement involves the reinforcing of certain behaviours, not others, and has the effect of increasing the frequency of the reinforced behaviour (pp. 95–98). Intermittent reinforcement is of various types. Interval reinforcement involves reinforcing behaviour at regular intervals, say every minute (pp. 100–102). In ratio reinforcement, the schedule of reinforcement depends on the manifestation of the behaviour. For example, in fixed ratio reinforcement, every say 20th occurrence of a specified behaviour may be reinforced (p. 102). Schedules may combine interval and ratio reinforcement so reinforcement is determined by both passage of time and 'the number of unreinforced responses emitted' (p. 105). (See also Pierce and Cheney, 2008.)

(e) Evaluation of behavioural approaches

The examples provided so far concern mainly the application of behavioural approaches to animals, except for the controversial single case study involving Albert B. Naturally, it cannot be assumed that such approaches apply to children and adults. Examples provided later in the chapter, however, indicate that in some circumstances, approaches derived from such early work are effective in modifying the behaviour and assisting the learning of some children. There is very wide research base supporting this that is so well established that reviews and evaluations done decades ago tend to stand.

For example, Rutherford and Polsgrove (1981) reviewed the use of behaviour contracts with 'behaviourally disordered and delinquent' children and young people. Classroom group contingencies were analysed by Litow and Pumroy (1975). Token economies in the classroom were reviewed by O'Leary and Drabman (1971). Rutherford and Nelson (1982) reviewed the literature on the use of time out for 'behaviourally disordered' pupils in classrooms; and response cost in school settings was considered by Walker (1983). Schedules of differential reinforcement in relation to a person's degree of intellectual disability have been the subject of more recent review (Whitaker, 1996).

Reservations remain however. One of these is difficulty with generalizing behaviour, despite the fact that the importance of this has long been recognized. New behaviour may be acquired in a particular setting; for example, social skills may be learned in a residential school through behavioural methods (see later in the chapter). Where the methods used to encourage the behaviour, such as token economy systems, cease to be used, the behaviour may not persist. Therefore, in a different setting such as the child's home, where such methods may not be practicable, the new behaviour does not continue. Attempts to avoid such failures of generalization include arranging for the behaviour to be reinforced by naturally occurring rewards such as praise that can be offered in many settings. It is rare for stimulus and response generalization to be built into a programme of intervention (Rutherford and Nelson, 1988). Also, in practice, behavioural approaches may be combined with other strategies such as cognitive interventions where the child's ways of thinking are challenged.

Observational Learning and Modelling

(a) Social learning theory and social cognitive theory

In *Social Learning Theory* (Bandura, 1977) Bandura sets out a theory of learning placing emphasis on cognitive process in which observational learning is important. Also important is perceived self-efficacy, the individual's belief that he is able to influence or control his behaviour or outcomes. This can affect behaviour, motivation, thinking, feelings and performance. Later, in *Social Foundations of Thought and Action* (Bandura, 1986), Bandura sets much of this in the context of what he calls a 'social cognitive theory' (which is the book's subtitle). In considering observational learning and modelling, it is largely to this second book that the present chapter refers although readers may find these concepts and applications referred to elsewhere (Ayers and Prytys, 2002, p. 197–198) as aspects of 'social learning theory'.

Bandura (1986) recognized the limitations trying to explain complex behaviour with reference solely to conditioning (ibid., pp. 12–18). Complex behaviours are acquired faster than would be expected if conditioning were the only explanation. Also, common experience suggests that observation is an important aid to learning. Taking a social cognitive perspective, Bandura sets out a theoretical framework for analysing motivation, thought and action. All three aspects (Bandura, 1986, p. 51) play their part and interact with one another:

- behaviour
- personal features including cognitive ones
- the environment.

Bandura states, ' . . . behaviour, cognitive and other personal factors, and environmental influences all operate interactively as determinants of each other' (Bandura, 1986, p. 23). While he refers to the model as one of 'reciprocal determinism' (Bandura, 1986, p. 23), determinism in this context signifies, ' . . . the production of effects by certain factors'. It does not necessarily imply, ' . . . actions being completely determined by a prior sequence of causes operating independently of the individual' (pp. 23–24).

(b) Observational learning and modelling

Within social cognitive theory, observational learning is important and is governed by four 'constituent processes' (Bandura, 1986, p. 51) as follows:

- attentional processes
- retention processes
- production processes
- motivational processes.

Attentional processes are influenced by a person's cognitive skills and other attributes of the observer, the properties of the modelled activities (such as their complexity) and other features (Bandura, 1986, pp. 51–55). For example, a model that is more attractive or interesting to the observer is likely to gain greater attention.

Retention processes involve the observed behaviour being retained in a symbolic form so they can be drawn on in the future (Bandura, 1986, pp. 55–63). This implies the learner transforming what is observed into pertinent symbols to capture the 'essential features and structures' of the modelled activities (ibid., p. 56). Representation may be in words or images. Rehearsal of what has been observed, either by action or through cognitive rehearsal, augments learning and retention.

Production processes (Bandura, 1986, pp. 63–68) involve 'converting the symbolic conceptions into appropriate actions' (ibid., p. 63). Because most modelled activities are represented as conceptions and rules of action, the production of behaviour involves organizing responses in time and space in compliance with these conceptions. Feedback through corrective modelling can help the learners achieve the desired standard of performance in the activity, a principle used extensively in sports training.

Motivational processes (Bandura, 1986, pp. 68–69) influence the performance of observationally learned behaviour through 'direct, vicarious and self-produced' incentives (ibid., p. 68). Individuals are more likely to produce modelled behaviour if it results in positive outcomes than if it leads to negative ones. Similarly, observed outcomes for other people affect learners' behaviours as they vicariously experience the consequences. Personal standards of behaviour act as a motivator.

Bandura (1986) maintains that most of human behaviour is learned by observation through modelling; however, modelling is not mere imitation. He notes, "By observing others, one forms rules of behaviour, and on future occasions this coded information serves as a guide for action' (p. 27). Words and images are vehicles of modelling as symbolic models and ' . . . modelling can transmit simultaneously knowledge of wide applicability to vast numbers of people through the medium of symbolic models' (ibid., p. 47). Also, in skill acquisition, modelling is better regarded 'as rule learning than as response mimicry' (ibid., p. 48). The breadth of the influence of modelling is made clear. Bandura (1986) argues that, 'Powerful modelling influences can simultaneously change observers' behaviour, thought patterns, emotional reactions, and evaluation' (ibid., p. 48). Also, ' . . . modelling influences can serve as instructors, inhibitors, disinhibitors, facilitators, stimulus enhancers, and emotional arousers' (ibid., p. 50).

(c) Evaluation of social cognitive theory

Among considerations relating to social cognitive theory is that modelling tends to influence behaviour where the child identifies with the person being observed. This identification cannot be guaranteed in interventions. The child may also be modelling his behaviour on others whose behaviour is not what is intended by the intervention. Furthermore, in interventions to encourage self-control through group cognitive-behavioural self-control training and other methods, the benefits do not always generalize to other settings (see the study described in the section 'Fuller Example of Application of Observational Learning and Learning Theory: Conduct Disorder' involving children screened for disruptive behaviour; Barkley *et al.*, 2000).

Relationships between Learning Theory and Observational Learning to Special Education

The relationships between learning theory and special education are complex and equivocal. On the one hand, learning theory strives to be scientific and observational and tends to focus on behaviour, having little to say about purported inner states and cognition. This appears to be a limited view of the complexities of human life and learning. After enjoying wide currency up to the 1950s, behavioural approaches were overextended when attempts were made to explain language acquisition by reference to operant conditioning, chaining and related factors. Skinner's (1957) perspective was convincingly criticized by Chomsky (1959).

On the other hand, behavioural strategies underpinned by learning theory are demonstrated to work in many settings and have contributed to approaches in special education and education generally. For example, token economy systems are used for some children with disorders of conduct. Besides this, the contribution of the behavioural elements in the development of cognitive-behavioural approaches and psychotherapy is extensive. In such approaches, recognition of the importance of changing behaviour as well as working on supposed cognitions constitute a strong and widely used strategy.

Perhaps the most conspicuous legacy of the early approaches, especially the work of Skinner is the modern-day use of applied behaviour analysis. These elements are also described in terms of functional assessment and functional analysis. The approach typically (Arthur-Kelly, Lyons, Butterfield and Gordon, 2007, Chapter 8) involves various elements. It is important to observe, carefully define and measure behaviour. The target behaviour (the behaviour the educator is aiming to change) has to be precisely defined so that there is consistency in observations when interventions are tried and further observations are made to see if the target behaviour is increasing or decreasing. An example of possible unwanted target behaviour might be, a pupil persistently spitting on the classroom floor, or moving around the class without permission and touching other pupils. An example of desired target behaviour might be the pupil sitting quietly in his own seat. An ABC record may be made of the antecedents (A) to the target behaviour, the behaviour itself (B) and its consequences (C).

A baseline measure of the behaviour that is desired to change is taken so that there is a basis on which to judge the effectiveness of interventions. The baseline might include measures of the frequency and duration of the behaviour as well as other measures (Alberto and Troutman, 2005). The educator then identifies the range of reinforcers that are likely to be effective in modifying the behaviour. These may be positive (e.g. praise, a token, food and a favourite activity) or negative (e.g. detention). Crucially, the reinforcement must be immediate, contingent on the pupil's behaviour and motivating (Arthur-Kelly, Lyons, Butterfield and Gordon, 2007, Chapter 8). A schedule of reinforcement is devised which might involve, for example, reinforcing the behaviour every time it occurs initially, then gradually reducing the frequency of reinforcements as the behaviour is modified. Built into the programme are ways of eventually replacing the more artificial reinforcers with naturally occurring ones (such as praise). These naturally occurring reinforcers are given with the artificial reinforcers so that the two become paired and the behaviour eventually becomes sustained by the natural reinforcer once the artificial one is no longer used.

Among strategies for increasing desirable behaviour are, shaping, negative reinforcement, token economies (where token are given as immediate rein-forcement that can be later traded for rewards) and contracts. Strategies to reduce unwanted behaviour include reinforcing behaviour that is incompatible with the unwanted behaviour (rewarding sitting down if the aim is to reduce out of seat behaviour), extinction (e.g. ignoring the unwanted behaviour), overcorrection (including restitutional overcorrection in which the student puts something right that he has damaged or done wrongly), response cost (e.g. losing points in a token economy system) and time out (removing the opportunity of the reinforcement of unwanted behaviour) (Arthur-Kelly *et al.*, 2007, Chapter 8).

Among adaptations of applied behaviour analysis are cognitive-behavioural approaches (Kaplan and Carter, 1995). (See also the 'Psychotherapeutic' chapter of this book.) In classroom terms these might imply both using behavioural methods to shape behaviour as well as encouraging students to use strategies such as anger management and self-instruction. Another application is functional analysis and assessment (Larson and Maag, 1998; Reid and Maag, 1998). This involves establishing the goal for the student of any unwanted behaviour and seeking to enable the student to reach the same goal without exhibiting the behaviour. For example, if the student misbehaves to get attention from the teacher, ways of giving the student the attention that do not involve unwanted behaviour are found. Often the situation is more complex and a careful analysis of the context in which the behaviour occurs is necessary as well as examining what might be the triggers for the unwanted behaviour. Adjustments to the context and management of the possible triggers are tried and tested to see if they are having a positive effect on behaviour. This method has been used with students with very challenging behaviour (Sigafoos *et al.*, 2003).

Observational learning and modelling in the context of social cognitive theory in some respects addresses some of the perceived limitations of a more constrained learning theory. It does so by taking into greater account observational learning functioning as a force in its own right as well as being partly explainable by learning theory. The social and cognitive contexts of learning and behaviour are taken into greater account and used to change behaviour and enhance learning. Again the contribution of this approach is reported across areas of special education and general education (Farrell, 2008b). For example, role-play is used to encourage better communication skills or ways of dealing with anger.

The Scope of Application of Learning Theory and Observational Learning

Examples of the scope of behavioural and observational learning under-pinnings include elective mutism; phobias; difficulties with grammar, comprehension and pragmatics; and attention deficit hyperactivity disorder (ADHD).

Elective mutism (selective mutism) has been defined as a 'persistent fail-ure to speak in specific social situations where speaking is expected, despite speaking in other situations' (American Psychiatric Association, 2000, pp. 125–127). The child might not speak at school and might speak at home. Elective mutism has been found to be responsive to family-based behavioural treatment (Carr, 2006). This typically involves the child and a family member, with whom the child will speak, having planned conversations in a venue where the child is usually mute, such as the school classroom. Initially, these conversations might take place in the classroom when it is empty. Incremen-tally, people in whose presence the child does not usually speak in that setting (e.g. other pupils and the teacher) join the child and family member. As the child comes to be increasingly able to continue conversation with the family member in the presence of these others, the teacher and pupils gradually parti-cipate in the conversation. Eventually, the child and family member move further apart until the child is conversing with others in the classroom with the family member present by the classroom door. Finally when the child feels ready, he asks the family member to leave and collect him after school (ibid., p. 521; Sage and Sluckin, 2004).

Types of phobia include specific phobia (e.g. claustrophobia) and social phobia (American Psychiatric Association, 2000). A *specific phobia* is a persistent unreasonable fear of certain situations, activities or objects leading to their avoidance. *Social phobia* is a marked, persistent, unreasonable fear of social situations or performance situations where the child may be embarrassed (ibid., p. 450). Behavioural interventions can be effective for many phobic children (Ollendick and King, 1998 provided a review). Treatments of discrete phobias may involve desensitization through either images of what is feared or *in vivo* treatment using the real feared item or situation. School refusal has been effectively treated by 'flooding' in which the child is quickly returned to school, although there is ethical debate about such intervention (Fonagy *et al.*, 2005, p. 87). Operant conditioning-related contingency management has been demonstrated to be effective with young children with phobias (Menzies and Clarke, 1993). In one study, mainly of school refusers of secondary school age, behavioural treatment led to significantly better rates of maintenance in school than home tutoring or inpatient treatment (Blagg and Yule, 1984). Turning to social learning theory, childhood phobias have been effectively treated through modelling (Bandura, 1977) especially participant modelling involving *in vivo* exposure and the modelling of exposure by others (Blanchard, 1970).

Where a child has difficulties with grammar, elements of social learning theory contribute to the strategy of sentence recasting in which an adult responds to a child's utterance by modifying it. While the adult response maintains the meaning, context, referents and main lexical items of the child's utterance, it modifies sentence constituents (e.g. verb) or changes the sentence modality (e.g. declarative to interrogative). The recasting often corrects errors in the child's utterance (Fey and Proctor-Williams, 2001, p. 179). In this conversational naturally occurring procedure, the adult does not try to get the child to correct his (the child's) original utterance. The implication seems that if the child is exposed frequently to the corrected sentences, he will learn them if he takes the opportunity to later imitate the adult, perhaps also identifying with the adult. The strategy of 'elicited imitation' draws on the social learning principle of imitation (as well as on conditioning) to help children having problems with grammar. An adult shows the child a non-verbal stimulus such as a picture; says an utterance related to the picture and asks the child to repeat it. The child tries to repeat the utterance and the adult rewards a correct response. If the child is wrong the adult repeats the correct utterance and asks him to try again. Gradually, the adult utterance and reward are phased out so that the child responds correctly to only the picture and a question (Fey and Proctor-Williams, 2001, p. 180–183).

Strategies aimed at helping difficulties with comprehension may draw on imitation, modelling and conditioning. The pupil may be taught to sit still and look at the speaker as prerequisites of listening as well as being encouraged to listen to what is said. The teacher and assistant can set up role-play sessions in which the two of them model good listening behaviour while pupils carefully observe. The teacher can then arrange that each pupil follows this up with a partner (adult or child) practising the observed skills, which the teacher monitors and praises. Later as and when pupils spontaneously demonstrate good listening skills elsewhere, these are also recognized and praised.

Observation and modelling are also used to help with difficulties in pragmatics. Role-play sessions or video/DVD examples can illustrate common aspects of non-verbal communication, which can then be discussed with small pupil groups. Similarly, examples of intention can be explored so aspects such as humour can begin to be developed.

For ADHD, behavioural interventions alone appear to be less effective than stimulant medication alone. However, behavioural methods enable the dose of medication to be reduced while maintaining similar improvements. The effects of behaviour management training and the psychostimulant, methylphenidate were tested as single and combined treatments in relation to the classroom performance of children with ADHD. Performance comprised classroom behaviour, accuracy and academic productivity (Carlson *et al.*, 1992). An 8-week programme involved 24 boys aged 6 to 12 years. The research design crossed two doses (0.3 mg and 0.6 mg) of methylphenidate (Ritalin) with two classroom settings: behaviour modification (token economy, time out and home report card); and no behaviour modification. A combination of behaviour modification and 0.3 mg of methylphenidate provided maximal behaviour modification, nearly as much as 0.6 mg of methylphenidate alone.

Response cost can be effective with ADHD and has been incorporated into an attention training system. This is a battery operated feedback module placed on the child's desk, displaying the running total of points earned by a child in a specified period. For each minute the child is on task, a point is added; but each time the teacher sees the child off task, she presses a remote control button and a red light is on, on the module, alerting the child that a point has been deducted. At the end of the agreed period, the points are totalled and converted to a reward.

Behaviour management techniques can be linked to the implications of functional behavioural assessment. If a pupil regularly produces a product in art that is well below what he could achieve, a functional behavioural analysis may suggest this function to enable the child to finish the task quickly to be able to physically move to other activities. In response, the environment might be modified to enable better work by agreeing with the pupil that it be completed in two phases with a brief recess. This would be monitored to ensure the objective was reached thereby confirming or disconfirming the hypothesis. With many behavioural approaches, booster sessions and the reinforced opportunity to use the skills in the necessary setting may encourage generalization. Also schedules of reinforcement can be gradually changed towards the natural reinforcement found in the classroom, for example, moving from tokens/tangible rewards to teacher praise.

Fuller Example of Application of Observational Learning and Learning Theory: Conduct Disorder

Barkley and colleagues (2000) carried out a study, involving 158 children screened for disruptive behaviour of which 57% met clinical criteria for oppositional defiant disorder, 12% met clinical criteria for conduct disorder and more than 50% met criteria for ADHD. The effects of behavioural interventions, parent training and the combined treatments were compared and these were compared with a control group. Among the classroom interventions were a token system, overcorrection, response cost, time out, group cognitive-behavioural self-control training, group anger-control training, group social skills training and support for home-based reinforcement. The multiple behavioural interventions were associated with positive outcome measures such as teacher ratings indicating less child aggression. However, approaches do not appear to generalize to other settings such as the child's home or to continue beyond the end of the programme. No effects were discernable for parent training, perhaps because parents had not sought it out themselves.

Behavioural and observational learning principles are evident in the Teaching Family Model used by many group homes for aggressive and delinquent adolescents in the United States (Kirigin, 1996). Treatment includes academic tutoring, a reinforcement system for monitoring school behaviour, a multi-level points system, social skills training and self-government procedures. While there is evidence of benefits during the programme, effects tended to be lost when participants left, indicating difficulties of generalization.

Modelling theory suggests that aggression is learnt through observation and modelling (Bandura and Walters, 1959). This may involve parents' aggressive behaviour as, notably, the fathers of aggressive boys are typically aggressive themselves. Accordingly, interventions include helping parents model appropriate behaviour for their children, or providing alternatives through foster care or residential settings.

Using elements of social learning theory and conditioning, the 'Oregon Social Learning Center Program' (Patterson and Forgatch, 1995) addresses aggression and non-compliance in children aged 3 through 12 years. Parents learn to identify and monitor (in daily 1-hour periods over a week) their child's behaviour focusing on a few behaviours that concern them. The programme then introduces a positive reinforcement system of points underpinned by reinforcers (e.g. treats and social reinforcement including praise). Parents are taught to use the strategies of time out for non-compliance and aggressive behaviour, mild punishments (chores) and response cost (loss of privileges). The programme involves teaching problem-solving and negotiation strategies to alleviate family crises and marital difficulties (Patterson and Chamberlain, 1988).

The 'Incredible Years Training Series' (Webster-Stratton and Reid, 2003, pp. 224–240) seeks to improve parents' competence, for example, by encouraging parents to work together, increasing positive parenting and reducing negative parenting. It comprises training curricula for

- parents;
- children aged 2 to 8 years;
- teachers.

Problem-solving skills training (PSST), derived from the work of Spivak and Sure (1978) involves about 20 clinic-based individual sessions in which a therapist examines the ways in which a child with conduct problems tends to respond to interpersonal situations. It encourages a structured approach to solve problems. PSST builds on observations that aggressive children tend to attribute hostile intentions to others and anticipate rejection more than typically developing children; and that children with conduct problems are limited in creating different solutions to interpersonal problems and divining others' motivations. Accordingly, PSST seeks to influence interpersonal cognition, aiming to help these children develop better interpersonal and cognitive problem-solving skills. Children are taught to recognize and alter how they think about and respond to social situations, perhaps using modelling and role-play. PSST uses structured tasks related to real-life situations, and social behaviours are encouraged by modelling and direct reinforcement.

Fuller Example of Application of Observational Learning and Learning Theory: Autism

The application of observational learning and of learning theory to interventions with children and young people with autism is evident in several approaches. In the following text, the Lovaas programmes, discrete trial training, pivotal response training, Learning Experiences – An Alternative Program for Pre-schoolers and Parents (LEAP), time delay procedures and joint action routines are considered briefly.

The Lovaas programme [Lovaas, 1987 and the Lovaas Institute for Early Intervention (www.lovaas.com)] is based on the principles of Applied Behavioural Analysis and uses behavioural methods to teach skills and to reduce unwanted behaviour. Because some types of behaviour, such as obsessive behaviour, are considered to be in excess, and others, such as communication and social skills in deficit, the programme seeks to decrease such excess behaviours and increase deficit behaviours. The child is usually taught at home, one to one, by a therapist trained in the use of the programme, and by his parents and volunteers. The child generally sits opposite to the therapist at a table and the therapist gives instructions supported by physical prompts if necessary. Required responses are rewarded and unwanted responses ignored or given time out. Teaching takes place in short sessions of 10–15 minutes, followed by a period of play, then by a further work session. Target behaviours are specified (e.g. repeating a word) and a sequence presented to teach it. The first three goals are, 'come here', 'sit down' and 'look at me' and these are followed by work such as matching, labelling objects, imitation and pre-school academic skills. The programme, it is recommended, should start before the child is 42 months old. This early intervention programme has, generated 'some controversy' (Magg, 2007, p. 260).

Discrete trial training/training (DTT) (Committee on Educational Interventions for Children with Autism, 2001) provides a structured and therapist-led intervention. It involves breaking behaviour into smaller steps, teaching one sub-skill at a time, shaping required behaviours until they are well learned and prompt fading. Reinforcement is directly related to the task. The approach comprises presentation, response, consequence and pause. There is an adult *presentation* (a stimulus such as an environmental cue or an instruction cueing the child to perform the required behaviour). The child's *response* occurs as a result of the cue. A *consequence* (a reward) follows this response. There is a brief *pause* after the consequence and before the next instruction. If the presentation fails to have the desired effect, the adult may prompt the child or model the action required. Regular teaching may use the basic 'presentation, response, consequence, pause' structure informally and for many purposes; but DTT programmes use this model predominantly and do so more intensively and for longer periods. DTT programmes may teach a different content, one example being its use in the Lovaas programme beginning with early receptive language and leading to skill programmes in self-help, in school and in the community.

Pivotal response training is intended to improve the social-emotional and communicative behaviour of young children with autistic spectrum disorders. It does not teach one behaviour at a time, but targets pivotal areas of a child's functioning that are likely to lead to broader changes in non-targeted behaviours. Procedures are used to structure the environment to teach these pivotal skills so that broader areas of social and communicative functioning are improved (Koegel and Koegel, 1995). Two key areas are 'motivation' and 'responsivity to multiple cues'. For example, a child's motivation may be increased to learn new skills and to initiate social contacts and respond to others doing so. More generally, motivation is increased through approaches such as turn taking, giving the child choices and reinforcing attempts, not just success. This is intended to help the child respond to opportunities that arise day to day to learn and interact. Pivotal response training uses a model of Applied Behaviour Analysis involving positive child-centred and family-centred procedures. It may involve short sessions, perhaps from 10 minutes to an hour, several times a week. It includes using varied tasks that encompass mastered and novel activities; ensuring adequate modelling of the required behaviour such as turn taking; using naturally occurring reinforcers such as responding meaningfully to a child's requests (e.g. helping a child obtain an item when it is requested); and using activities the child prefers and allowing choices within these activities. These are incorporated into day-to-day teaching and learning opportunities in natural settings.

Learning Experiences–An Alternative Program for Preschoolers and Parents (LEAP) (Strain and Hoyson, 2000) includes aspects of behavioural methods and observational learning. It is used in preschooling classes in which children with autism learn with children who are developing typically for their age. Parents are taught how to use behavioural skills with their child at home and in the community. One of the principles is that the children with autism, being educated with typically developing peers, have the opportunity to learn from models of appropriate social skills and have more opportunities to interact with their peers with no disabilities. Among the features of the approach are that typically developing peers are taught to help the social and language skills of children with autism. Also, data is collected each day on Individual Education Programme objectives to inform the next day's teaching plans. A LEAP classroom might typically have about four children with autism and perhaps ten who do not, and as well as the usual staffing, a special education teacher who helps the children with autism throughout the day.

Improving the communication skills of children with autism is likely to include work on using intonation, non-verbal communication, reducing echolalia and correcting the common reversal of pronouns. Approaches may use structured behavioural training and are likely to take a long time. To increase spontaneous verbalization for children with autism, one intervention is time delay (Ingenmey and Van Houten, 1991; Matson *et al.*, 1993). Time delay procedure to develop spontaneous requests might involve presenting the child with a target stimulus to be requested such as a toy or food. The adult immediately models the response (e.g. a request for the toy). When the child is able to imitate the response without error, the adult delays the prompting, lengthening the time delay at each trial. A response, spontaneous or imitated, is reinforced by giving the child the item. As the stimulus/model interval increases, the child is expected to initiate the request independently before the prompt is given.

Joint action routines (Prizant *et al.*, 2000) use regularly occurring day-to-day routines that encourage communication, for example, laying a table, making a snack or setting out equipment for a game. The activity generally involves clear discrete parts and a predictable sequence. Consider the task of laying one's own place setting a table. The adult might gather together items but require the child to request each (table mat, knife, fork, plate, cup and so on). It should be clear who does what, for example, the child might request each item, then set it in its proper place. Initially, the routine has to be established before the adult progresses to request responses from the child. The adult may demonstrate what to do (to encourage modelling) and then communicate the desire that the child does part of the routine, conveying the expectation of taking turns.

To encourage communication the adult might pause in the routine and say the word she wants the child to say (e.g. 'plate'). If the child says the word, the activity continues. If not, the adult tries several more times and if there is still no response, she models the required response and carries on with the activity. Once the routine is established and the child knows the previously modelled response, the response might be elicited by offering the child a choice where one of the responses is the previously modelled one. The adult, holding up two items, one which the child requires and one he does not, asks, 'What do you want, the plate or the ball?' 'The adult maintains consistency until the response is securely learned by carefully following routines and using the same words. Once the routine is secure, learning opportunities for responses can be created by unexpectedly changing the routine so a response is necessary.

Conclusion

The chapter examined behavioural approaches to learning with reference to learning theory and observational learning and modelling. Examples of application were provided for elective mutism; phobias; difficulties with grammar, comprehension and pragmatics; and ADHD. Learning theory and observational learning/modelling were considered together in their application to conduct disorder and autism.

Thinking Points

Readers may wish to consider the following:

- the extent to which learning theory and social learning theory offer an adequate explanation of simple human behaviour and complex human behaviour;
- the degree to which social learning theory explains complex human behaviour;
- why applications of learning theory can be effective in modifying behaviour but have limitations for the generalization of newly learned behaviour.

Key Texts

Alberto, P. A. and Troutman, A. C. (2005) (7th edn) *Applied Behavioural Analysis for Teachers*. Columbus, OH: Merrill/Prentice Hall.

A practically oriented book covering the concepts and techniques of behaviour management. It includes: identifying the target behaviour, collecting and presenting behaviour data, functional assessment, experimental design, arranging antecedents and consequences, generalizing changes in behaviour and ethical issues.

Arthur-Kelly, M., Lyons, G., Butterfield, N. and Gordon, C. (2007) (2nd edn) *Classroom Management: Creating Positive Learning Environments*. Melbourne, Australia: Thompson Learning.

This book sets out an integrated model of classroom management involving ecological, preventative and interventionist perspectives. Preventative practices include curriculum, teaching, communication and classroom organization. Psychosocial and behavioural interventions are considered. Chapter 8 concerns, 'Intervening Using Behavioural Strategies'.

Bloomquist, M. and Schnell, M. (2005) *Helping Children with Aggression and Conduct Problems*. New York: Guilford Press.

Describes interventions effective in children aged 3 to 12 years with aggression and conduct problems. These include social competence training, parent and family skills building and school-based approaches.

Gabriels, R. and Hill, D. E. (2007) *Growing Up with Autism: Working with School Age Children and Adolescents*. New York: Guilford Press.

Offers guidance for supporting positive behaviour, social skills and communication and dealing with issues of mental and physical health and sexuality.

Hersen, M. (Ed.) (2002) *Clinical Behaviour Therapy: Adults and Children*. Hoboken, NY: John Wiley and Sons.

Intended mainly as a casebook in the training of clinical professionals.

Kazdin, A.E. (2001) (5th edn) *Behavior Modification in Applied Settings*. Pacific Grove, CA: Brooks/Cole.

Sets out behaviour modification principles and how they can apply in school, the home and clinic as well as at work. It draws on both applied research approaches and clinical intervention techniques.

Nelson, W. M., Finch, A. J. and Hart, K. J. (Eds) (2006) *Conduct Disorders: A Practitioners Guide to Comparative Treatment*. New York: Springer

Provides a broad picture of approaches and models used with conduct disorder. Chapters include psychoanalytical approaches to treatment; family therapy; cognitive-developmental psychotherapy; behavioural treatment; cognitive-behavioural psychotherapy; multi-systemic therapy; continuum of residential treatment care; and comparative treatments.

Pierce, W. D. and Cheney, C. D. (2008) (4th edn) *Behaviour Analysis and Learning*. New York: Psychology Press

Covers the principles of behavioural analysis and learned behaviour and includes chapters on 'applied behaviour analysis' and 'verbal behaviour'.

9

Developmental

Introduction

This chapter concerns child development, particularly cognitive development. It focuses on Piaget's theory as an example of a developmental cognitive theory. The chapter first outlines issues concerning child development and developmental milestones before describing Piaget's theory. It then looks at the relationships between child cognitive development, especially Piaget's theory, and special education. It examines the scope of child cognitive development, particularly genetic epistemology. Finally, the chapter looks at Piaget's sensorimotor period in more detail, exploring its relevance to the development of programmes for children with profound cognitive impairment.

Child Development and Developmental Milestones

Development may be seen as a process of growth by which a child matures in various ways: physical, motor, sensory, cognitive, emotional and social. It has been defined in the context of maturation as follows. 'The term *maturation* implies both *growth,* a measurement of physical characteristics over time and *development*, the acquisition of metabolic functions, synaptic circuits, reflexes, secretory and other cellular functions, sensory awareness, motor skills, language and intellect' (Sarnat and Flores-Sarnat, 2006, p. 13, italics in original). Cognitive development, the particular focus of this chapter, concerns the development of attention, memory, learning, language, concepts and reasoning.

Child development as a framework of expected progress seeks to describe development as universally as possible. Especially regarding a particular society where expectations and values are similar and a specified period such as the present day, it is considered possible to make generalizations about children's expected progress and development.

Another assumption is that in a particular society, children are subject to broadly similar types of stimulation, for example, in their home environment. However, it is accepted that a child in a materially, culturally and linguistically impoverished home environment is unlikely to progress as well as one in a setting that is richer in these areas. The difficulties of estimating the relative contributions of the environment and apparent cognitive and other abilities are evident in debates around assessing mild cognitive impairment (American Psychiatric Association, 2000, p. 42; Greenspan, 2006). One issue is the extent to which mild cognitive impairment might relate to environmental impoverishment or 'within child' factors, given the two interact. Such judgements may affect educational provision. Education may simply provide a rich and stimulating environment to compensate for an impoverished home environment enabling the child to develop well. Or if there are 'cognitive impairments', these may require specific interventions such as greater emphasis than is age-typical on developing concrete operations (using concrete examples in mental operations) and extending these towards logical thought, less dependent on concrete exemplars (Farrell, 2008b, Chapter 4).

Further assumptions are made concerning areas of development, for example, cognitive, fine motor and mobility development. These may be differently interpreted or described in different frameworks, although the overlap may be clear if the framework is precisely described. Also, it is accepted that the various strands of development interrelate. Cognitive development is influenced by motor development. If a child is less able to move and explore his surroundings perhaps because of motor impairment, this can constrain his exploring and relating motor information and sensory information. For a child with motor disabilities, implications arise for not only motor development but also perceptual development, cognitive development, communication and social and emotional development (Lewis, 2003, pp. 153–191).

Child development theories and frameworks often use terms such as 'stages' or 'periods' to express the expectation that development will take place within a certain time span and in a specified sequence. The idea of 'readiness' suggests that certain levels of physical maturation have to be reached before particular skills can be learned (Luxem and Christopherson, 1994).

It is recognized that there are wide variations in the rates at which different children progress, even within a specified society at a particular time. However, it is also accepted that a period is reached where a slower progress than is typically expected or a lack of progress may indicate difficulties. On one hand, slower than usual development may be temporary and when the child later develops typically, it is retrospectively seen that there was no cause for concern. On the other hand, slower than expected development may indicate problems which if not dealt with in a timely manner can exacerbate difficulties later. There is a balance between being neither too precipitate nor too dilatory in intervening.

Indicators of progress are often expressed as 'milestones', which a child developing typically is expected to reach within a certain age range. Milestones for gross and fine motor development (Bayley, 1993) may indicate an average age for the development of a skill and the age range within which the skill usually develops. The average age at which a child builds a tower of two cubes in the Bayley framework is 11 months 3 weeks. In the age range of 10 to 19 months, 90% of children develop this skill. A variety of milestones are presented in Berk (2006) and include gross motor development in early and middle childhood (p. 175); the development of touch, taste, smell, balance and hearing (p. 153); visual development in infancy (p. 161); cognitive attainments (pp. 230, 242, 246); language development (p. 388); and emotional development (p. 411).

When a child does not achieve expected milestones within the typical age range, he may be considered as having a 'developmental delay'. The profile of such a delay may be broad or relate to a specific area. Distinctions are made between 'delay', where the course of development of the child is the same as for other children but slower and 'difference', where the development does not occur in the usual sequence.

Cognitive Developmental Theory: Piaget's Theory

Among the currently influential theories of cognitive development the emphasis is on social/cultural, biological and constructivist ones. It is suggested (Goswami, 2008, p. 374) that contemporary theories of cognitive development have to acknowledge all these elements: social influences, biological aspects and constraints and knowledge construction. For example, Vygotsky's theory concerns the importance of social and cultural influences, the importance of language and the role of adults in mediating cultural learning (chapter titled 'Social' in this book). In neuroscience, connectionist modelling has provided a framework in which cognitive development and constraints to learning can be understood. Computer networks are presented as being analogous to neuron networks and seek to model how simple on–off nodes in a connected network can lead to complex cognition (Goswami, 2008, pp. 402–407). Neuroconstructivism seeks to explain how the brain learns in terms of bio-logical constraints on the patterns of neural activation that make up mental representations (Westermann *et al.*, 2007). Turning to constructivist theories, those developed by Swiss biologist Jean Piaget has been the most influential (Gallagher and Reid, 1981, pp. 231–236).

Piaget developed a stage-related theory of cognitive (especially logical) development and affective development (Piaget and Inhelder, 1966/1969; Piaget, 1970). Cognitive or intellectual development was envisaged in terms of gradual and progressive adaptations, for which the child was innately prepared, leading to adult reasoning. This process of adaptation involves a reciprocal interaction between the child and his environment.

As a survival mechanism, children act on their environment through physical activity to control aspects of it. To the degree they are able to act appropriately towards aspects of the environment, they can be said to understand them. The knowledge that a child has can 'assimilate' those features of the environ-ment. However, the environment also acts upon the child's cognitive struct-ures ('schemas') by coming up with new features requiring the cognitive structures to change to 'accommodate' these features. Essentially, assimilation concerns interpretation and accommodation has to do with the adaptation of cognitive schemes (general concepts). A baby may explore a ball that is soft and pliant and assimilate its properties but may later manipulate a similar looking ball that turns out to be hard and resilient and will accommodate these features. In cognitive development, there is a striving towards adaptation in which schemas most closely represent to the child an external reality in which he can operate. The motivation to learn comes from the disparity between an existing schema and incoming information, which requires the child to 'accommodate' it.

Assimilation and accommodation are the mechanisms of 'equilibration', a self-regulatory process enabling external experience to be incorporated into internal structures (Gallagher and Reid, 1981, p. 233). Piaget sees learning as an 'internal process of construction' (ibid., p. 2), which involves knowledge being gained through direct experience of the environment. However, learning also occurs from interplay among maturation, experience and equilibration (p. 172). Piaget identified typical ways of responding, considered to be associated with qualitatively different sequential stages of cognitive development. The sequence was believed to be universal and invariable because it was determined by maturational factors. Piaget's stages were considered to occur at approximate ages as follows:

- the sensorimotor stage (0–2 years)
- the pre-operational stage (2–7 years)
- the concrete operational stage (7–11 years)
- the formal operational stage (11–12 years onwards).

In the sensorimotor stage (Piaget and Inhelder, 1966/1969, pp. 3–27), babies develop from exhibiting reflex survival behaviours such as sucking and grasping to forming a very basic notion of causality and their role in making things happen. These 'cognitive substructures' constructed by the child form a basis for subsequent perceptive and intellectual development (ibid., p. 3). This stage is described in detail later in the chapter.

In the pre-operational stage (ibid., p. 128), while children develop physically, become fully mobile and become more competent communicators, their thinking is still limited by egocentricity. The child's judgements are based on sensory evidence, a logic-lacking reversibility and a focus on one aspect to the exclusion of others. If a child is shown two identical transparent beakers holding the same amount of coloured liquid, he will recognize their equality. However, if the liquid in one beaker is poured into a narrower container so the liquid level is higher, the child will claim that this container contains more liquid. Such responses are taken to indicate the child's inability to recognize that matter maintains or 'conserves' its volume even in different forms.

The two operational stages (concrete and formal) involve the use of organized systems of mental actions that interrelate. They transform reality through 'internalised actions' grouped into 'coherent, reversible systems' (ibid., p. 93). In the concrete operational stage, complex and systematic mental problem-solving (in which mental representations are used) can take place in relation to concrete and actual events. A child may know that Peter has a garden plot bigger than David's and that David's plot is bigger than Jenny's. If asked who has the smallest plot, he might work out the answer by mentally picturing Peter's plot, then David's plot and then Jenny's plot. He would then recognize that Jenny's plot was the smallest.

After the age of 11 or 12, in the formal operations stage, concrete operations are restructured and subordinated to new structures enabling the child to reason hypothetically (ibid., p. 152). The child becomes able to use the form of logical systems to create and test hypotheses about real or imagined events.

In a scientific task, a child will be able to work out the rule relating weight and distance from the centre of the fulcrum using a balance scale.

It is argued that sensorimotor cognition, contrary to Piaget's hypotheses, is not redeveloped in the mental realm. Instead, what appears important is sensori motor knowledge being augmented by further experience either through action or through language. Logical development may also depend on children's ability to reflect metacognitively on their knowledge and the extent to which they can inhibit competing knowledge that is interfering with their applying the logic (Goswami, 2008, p. 386).

In line with the earlier suggestion that current theories need to draw on social, knowledge construction and biological elements, 'neo-Piagetian' perspectives (Morra *et al.*, 2007) tend to be informed by neuropsychology. They take a constructivist approach to cognitive development and regard cognitive development as divided into qualitatively different stages. However, they tend to relate increasingly complex stages with the child's information processing system rather than with logical properties. Links are also made with neuropsychology (ibid.).

Relationships Between Child Development and Piaget's Theory and Special Education

Child development and special education Interpretations of disability/disorder are often linked to notions of typical child development. Levels of cognitive impairment (profound, severe to moderate and mild) may be related to the extent of difference from age-typical development and functioning. Degrees of hearing impairment or visual impairment are assessed in terms of normal sight or hearing. Orthopaedic and motor impairments are determined according to typical physical development and mobility. Descriptions of health impairments are framed with reference to optimal states of health and functioning. Conduct disorder can be seen as personal and social development anti-pathetic to social norms or the safety of others. Disorders relating to reading, writing and mathematics are defined with regard to what is expected typically of a child of the same age.

However, the relationships between child development and special education are complex. The framework and milestones for typical child development inform assessments that a child has a disability/disorder and suggest that intervention may be necessary to encourage development and well-being. However, on the other hand, knowledge of the developmental course associated with different disabilities/disorders informs interventions. Consequently, knowledge of atypical development as well as typical development is important. Indeed, as Lewis (2003) notes, understanding how a certain disability may change the course of development in individual children can aid understanding of the processes of typical development. It may 'throw light on pre-requisites for particular developments (ibid., p. 1). She also recognizes this requires vigilance that one is predominantly observing the developmental consequences of the disability and that the 'difference' is not due to other factors.

As long ago as the 1980s, Walker and Crawley (1983) suggested five different ways in which the development of special children might relate to that of typically developing children: delayed, abnormal, compensatory, absent and normal. Delayed development refers to a child passing through similar developmental stages involving the same processes as a typically developing child but at a slower pace. This may mean that the child does not reach a point where development is equal to that of a typically developing child. Abnormal/different development involves the child developing in a way that is different to typical development. In language development, for example, a distinction is sometimes made between delay and language disorder. It is considered to be language delay if the language of a child is similar to that expected of a younger child, but language disorder is defined in terms of being different to what is expected both qualitatively and quantitatively. However, the distinction is not as clear-cut as it might appear at first (Farrell, 2008b, Chapter 14).

Compensatory development implies that a child reaches or moves towards the same developmental goals as a typically developing child but via different routes (see references to aspects of Vygotsky's work in the chapter titled 'Social' in this book). Absent development refers to the lack of development of a child in a particular area, for example, a child with profound cognitive impairment may not achieve spoken language, although, of course, there may be development in other forms of communication. Where the development of a child is normal, this refers to an area of development that is unaffected by the disability/disorder and develops at age-typical rates and involves the same processes as for all children. For a young person with conduct disorder, motor skills may develop at a typical rate and in a typical way.

As Lewis (2003, p. 338) points out, one, some or all of these types of development may be evident in a particular child because the disability/disorder may affect different areas of development in different ways. Also, where a child develops differently from a typically developing child, this variation is likely to relate to the disability/disorder. However, it may also relate to some other consequence of the disability/disorder such as an alternative route to development not being available for a reason unrelated to the disability (ibid.). For example, alternative electronic means of communication may not be immediately available for a child with very severe speech difficulties.

Piaget's theory and special education Accounts of typical development, including cognitive development, cannot always be directly related to the development and learning of special children. Neither are the relationships between genetic epistemology and special education straightforward. Criticisms of Piaget's theory include that children's development is more rapid than the age ranges associated with the developmental stages suggest; that the within-child view of maturation might underplay the importance of the environment in stimulating development; and that the influence of language on cognitive development may be underestimated.

However, aspects of Piaget's theory have remained useful orientations for researchers and educators regarding the development of children's thinking. Piaget's stages (bearing in mind their variability which Piaget himself recognized) may be related to the development of children with cognitive impairment, helping educators understand the possible ways in which cognition might be developing. It has been suggested that pupils with mild cognitive impairment generally show thought processes typical of concrete operations; and pupils with moderate-to-severe cognitive impairment generally show processes characteristic of pre-operations. Those with profound cognitive impairment are likely to develop within the sensorimotor stage (e.g. Inhelder, 1968 passim). Attempts to adapt Piaget's framework need to take into account that children with cognitive impairment may in some ways develop differently from typically developing children and not just more slowly.

The Scope of Child Development and Piaget's Theory

The scope of child development in general In special education, child developmental perspectives provide a framework of typical development, which can inform perspectives of how a special child is developing in relation to cognitive, psychosocial, motor, sensory and physical development. Ways in which the development of special children might relate to that of typically developing children, that is, delayed, abnormal, compensatory, absent and normal

(Walker and Crawley, 1983) have relevance to the interpretation of such perspectives.

The development of special children can also inform the understandings of typical development, given careful interpretation. Lewis (2003) suggests that the range of findings that the development of blind children differs from that of typically developing children in various ways makes the study of blind children significant for general theories of development (ibid., p. 338).

The importance of the congruence of other senses than sight for typical development may attract insufficient attention because of the central importance attached to vision. Yet the development of blind children encourages one to recognize the importance of the other senses and their congruence and overlap, as it is this that helps a blind child to make sense of the environment. Millar (1994), considering spatial understanding, suggests that a blind child may use information from a range of converging sources (hearing, touch, smell, taste and movement) comparably to the information processed by sighted children. These congruent and overlapping sources and modalities relate to what the child already knows to help build spatial understanding. This also suggests that educators should take particular care that a child with visual impairment experiences a range of information. This should be in different modalities and from different sources that overlap and have redundancy to help the child integrate the information to make sense of the environment.

The scope of Piaget's theory Criticisms of Piaget's theory influence its perceived scope. The ages Piaget considered to be typical of his various stages may be somewhat conservative (Wood, 1998). Linked with this is a degree of reinterpretation of his experimental data. Among Piaget's data were experiments indicating the child's stage, for example, his lack of conservation of matter at the pre-operational stage. Repeating these experiments has indicated that the language the experimenter uses and how the child perceives what is being requested of him, influences outcomes. It has been demonstrated that some young children can reason at a more advanced level than Piaget had been able to show (Donaldson, 1978). Similarly, Piaget may have underestimated the capacity of newborn infants for imitating and remembering, evidence for which was not available in Piaget's time (Goswami, 1998). Within the sensorimotor stage, the age at which infants develop cognitive representations has been demonstrated to be much earlier than Piaget was able to show (Goswami, 2008, Chapters 1 and 2, summarizes some of this evidence).

Interpretations of Piaget's theory can lead to the assumption that maturational 'within child' factors largely account for slower-than-typical cognitive development. Contrastingly, Vygotsky ([various dates]/1978) emphasizes the importance of a child interacting with others who are more advanced thinkers in helping intellectual development. While Piaget did not regard language as having a facilitating effect on thought, the interaction of language and thought is now considered influential in cognitive development. Although Piaget's theory embraced interaction between the child and the environment, the environment seemed to take a rather passive role. The potential for modifications in the child's environment to enhance development may not have been given sufficient attention.

Research suggests that special children follow the same sequence of stages of cognitive development as typically developing children, but with more regressions and oscillations in development. Also, special children working within the sensorimotor stage may show different levels of response to different materials or tasks so that there is not the same consistency in performance as with younger typically developing children (Hodapp, 1998). For children with profound cognitive impairment, Piaget's work suggests the importance of sensory stimulation (visual, auditory, touch, taste and smell) and motor stimulation (movement, balance and coordination) in intellectual development. However, while Piaget would regard the child's maturation as being largely a matter of unfolding development, modern applications of his ideas allow for the importance of structuring the environment to encourage such development.

Fuller Example: The Sensorimotor Period and Profound Cognitive Impairment

The final two sections look in detail at the sensorimotor period and examine how an understanding of it might inform the education of children with profound cognitive impairment. All references in the section titled 'The Sensorimotor Period', unless otherwise stated, are from *The Psychology of the Child* (Piaget and Inhelder, [1966]/1969). The ages at which Piaget and Inhelder considered developments to be apparent are given, but more recent research has pushed back these ages so that often they cannot be taken as a reliable guide for age-typical development.

The Sensorimotor Period

The nature of the sensorimotor period In Piaget's view, mental development in the first 2 years of life is vital as the child constructs cognitive substructures and affective reactions. These form the basis for later perceptual, cognitive and emotional development. The intelligence that develops in this period succeeds in solving many 'problems of action' such as reaching for hidden objects by constructing a system of 'action schemes' and organizing reality in terms of structures of space, time and causality (p. 4). These constructions are made with the support of perceptions and movements and therefore through the sensorimotor coordination of actions. All this Piaget argued develops in the absence of language representative thought, although Piaget may have underestimated the ages at which the infant's capacity for representative thought can be discerned.

Through assimilation, information about reality is treated or modified so it becomes incorporated ' . . . into the structure of the subject'. Each newly established connection is 'integrated into an existing schematism' (p. 5). The organizing activity of the child is as important as the connections inherent in the external stimuli. Indeed, the child only becomes aware of these connections to the degree to which he can assimilate them by referring to his existing structures. The sensorimotor period is envisaged in six stages.

Stages of the sensorimotor period In the first stage of the sensorimotor period, the 'modification of reflexes stage' (0–4 weeks), certain reflexes in the newborn child that have future importance such as the sucking reflex are consolidated by functional exercise. After a few days, the baby finds the nipple more easily than initially in a sort of 'functional assimilation'. This leads to further similar activities such as sucking on other things which Piaget calls 'generalized assimilation' and to distinguishing the nipple from other objects (p. 7).

The second stage is the stage of 'primary circular reactions' (about 1–4 months). The 'circular reactions' are repetitive behaviours and they are designated as 'primary' because they are concerned with one's self. They recreate sensory experiences. The repetitive behaviour, for example, thumb sucking, is based on a general sensorimotor scheme in which the infant does not yet differentiate means (e.g. movements of the arm, hand and mouth) and ends (thumb sucking). The end is reached only by the movements leading to it (p. 8).

The third stage (about 4–10 months) is the stage of 'secondary circular reactions'. These are repetitive behaviours involving the outside world, for example, the infant might repeatedly drop an item (which is returned to him). They recreate events. Piaget uses the example of a toy suspended above the baby's cot that has a cord that shakes rattles when pulled. The infant may catch the cord, which has the effect of sounding the rattles. He repeats the action several times motivated by the result but does not differentiate the end result from the means used. However, later, if a new toy is hung above the cradle, the child looks for the cord indicating that he is starting to differentiate means and ends. Even if the child hears only the mechanical sounds, he will look for and try to pull the now non-existent cord. In using the same means to try to achieve different ends, the child is on the threshold of intelligent action, even though holding an incorrect belief in causality without any physical connection.

Complete acts of practical intelligence are discernible in the fourth stage (about 10–12 months), that of 'the coordination of circular reactions'. The baby can coordinate several actions to achieve a goal. He will lift a screen that masks a hidden item. In carrying out such an action, the child sets out to get a particular result, independent of the means he is going to use. The coordination of means and ends is new and created differently for each novel situation, justifying the notion of intelligent behaviour. Even so, the means used derive only from known schemes of assimilation (p. 11).

A new pattern emerges in the fifth stage of 'tertiary circular reactions' (about 12–18 months). The baby can use trial and error to see the outcomes of certain actions. For example, an item might be placed on a rug beyond the child's reach. The child accidentally or in trying to reach the item grasps the rug and observes the relationship between pulling the rug and the object moving. Gradually, the child comes to pull the rug to reach the object. In doing this, the child is beginning to search for new means by differentiation from schemes already known and comes to discover spatial and causal relations between the objects he manipulates.

In the sixth stage, the 'interiorisation of schemes' (about 18 months to 2 years) the child develops cognitive representations of actions and their outcomes. He is able to find new means not just by external or physical groping and trial and error but by 'internalised combinations' also, leading to 'sudden comprehension' (pp. 11–12). The child has a small box with a slightly open drawer that has an item. At first he tries to open the box by physical groping as in the fifth stage. When this fails, he stops and examines the situation carefully then suddenly slips his finger into the crack and succeeds in opening the box. This cognitive representation of actions and their consequences, Piaget believed, marked the beginning of conceptual thought.

The permanent object, space, time and causality Sensorimotor systems of assimilation culminate in 'structures of ordering and assembling' that make up a substructure for the future operations of thought. Sensorimotor intelligence also organizes reality. It does this through building up the categories of action ' . . . the schemes of the permanent object, space, time, and causality', which form substructures of the notions that will later correspond to them (p. 13). None of the categories is given at the outset and the child's early world is centred on his own body and actions. However, during the first 18 months, the child gradually comes to recognize himself as an object among others in a world that is made up of permanent objects structured in time and space and working under causality.

During the second year, the child builds up recognition that the world consists of permanent objects. The child is increasingly able to solve 'displacement' problems in which an item is put in a different place other than where it was originally. About 5 to 7 months, if the child is about to grasp an item and the adult covers it with a cloth, the child behaves as if the object no longer exists. At a later age, when the child has learnt to look for a hidden object, the permanence of the object is still not discerned. An item might be hidden behind a screen to the child's right and the child finds it. Then the adult, while the child watches, hides the item behind a screen to the child's left. Often the child will still look for the object behind the first screen as though the position of the object were dependent on where he had previously found it rather than the changes in place that are independent of the child's action. By the age of 9 or 10 months, however, the child will tend to look for the item in the place to which it has been moved. Later still, the child can solve more complicated situations (p. 15). If an item is hidden under a cloth and the child removes this and finds another screen beneath it, he will remove that screen. The child has learnt both that the object continues to exist when out of sight and where the object does, in fact, go. The formation of the scheme of the permanent object is related to the spatial–temporal and causal organization of the world. For Piaget, the solving of such problems indicated that the child had a cognitive representation of the object distinct from sensory perception and unconnected to motor action. More recent evidence from neuroimaging studies indicates that cognitive representations and object permanence occur at a much earlier age than Piaget was able to demonstrate (Goswami, 2008, p. 377 and passim).

Piaget maintains that, initially, there are several 'spaces' centred on the child's own body such as buccal spaces (specifically the cheek but more generally the mouth) and postural spaces (relating to the child's own position). He also specifies certain impressions of time such as waiting. These remain only partial until the formation of the scheme of the permanent object has led to the distinction between changes of physical state and changes of position and in movement. Behaviour patterns of localization and of search for the permanent object and displacements are eventually organized into a fundamental structure constituting the framework of practical space. When the child understands the properties of space, he can solve 'detour' problems, that is, problems involving getting to the same place by different routes. A child can recover a ball that has rolled under the sofa by working out where it must have gone. The organization of positions/displacements in space goes together with grasping sequences in time because displacements are made physically step by step and one at a time (pp. 16–17).

Causality develops only after a long evolution. Even when the child is able to manipulate objects, he knows only the cause of his own action and is unaware of the need for spatial contact (p. 18). Eventually, the child becomes able to recognize causes other than those situated in his own actions. He recognizes the causal relationships in various objects. The causal relationships between two objects or their actions presuppose a physical and spatial connection.

Piaget's view that the development of object permanence takes around 18 months to achieve is not supported by evidence indicating object permanence develops much earlier. In one experiment, a screen is rotated and is expected to come into contact with a hidden object. Babies aged 5 months look reliably longer when the screen appears to pass through the hidden object apparently expecting the continued existence of the object (Baillargeon *et al.*, 1985).

The symbolic function About the age of 2 years, the symbolic function appears, involving the ability to represent something. The signified 'something' might be an object, event or conceptual scheme. This is represented by a 'signifier', which is differentiated and serves only 'a representative purpose'. Examples are language, a mental image or a representative gesture (p. 51). More complex manifestations of symbolic function are deferred imitation, symbolic play, drawing, mental images and image memories and language (p. 91).

An early indication of the symbolic function appears to be deferred imitation that starts after the disappearance of the 'model'. In sensorimotor imitation, the child begins by imitating perhaps a hand movement while the 'model' is still present. He may later continue when the model is absent, although this does not imply representation in thought. However, Piaget and Inhelder cite a child 16 months old who imitates the actions of an angry playmate several hours after the playmate's departure. This suggests the beginning of representation and the imitative gesture as the beginning of the differentiated signifier (p. 53).

Implications for Profound Cognitive Impairment

Provision for pupils with profound cognitive impairment predominantly includes behavioural elements such as task analytic assessment and instruction. However, aspects of genetic epistemology shed light on approaches for these pupils. Piaget's theory can help an understanding of very early development that can illuminate work with children with profound cognitive impairment in encouraging sensory and motor development.

This is not to suggest necessarily a direct translation of explanations of possible developments in an infant to an older child with profound cognitive impairment. Neither is it implied that pupils with profound cognitive impairment never develop beyond the sensorimotor period. However, sensorimotor development underpins later development in typically developing children and a pupil with profound cognitive impairment is likely to spend a considerable time responding and exploring in ways typical of this stage. Suggestions in the present section are not directly taken from Piaget and Inhelder's work, but indicate how it might relate to children with profound cognitive impairment.

When educating pupils with profound cognitive impairment, monitoring behavioural state is a precursor. Guess *et al.* (1990) found that when they observed a group of students with 'profoundly handicapping conditions' the students were awake and alert for only about half their time in school. It is important that educators capture times when pupils are alert and capitalize on these.

Curriculum and assessment Allowing for Piaget's underestimation of the ages in which different aspects of development in the sensorimotor stage might be considered to be apparent in typical development, the sequence of the sub-stages may still be a useful orientation. If approached with care, these sub-stages can also inform interpretations of the cognitive development of a pupil with profound cognitive impairment. These in turn can inform aspects of the curriculum and assessment.

The educator might look at a range of responses of the pupil in different settings and with different activities and materials and consider whether the pupil's responses are best characterized as being typical of a certain sub-stage. Is the child showing 'modification of reflexes' such as mouthing different objects? Is there evidence of 'primary circular reactions' connected with the child's own body? Does it appear that the child behaves in a way that indicates 'secondary circular reactions', for example, engaging in repeated activities beyond his own body? Can the child, as in 'coordination of circular reactions', put together several actions to reach a goal such as moving two obstructing objects to reach a third? Does he use trial and error, as in 'tertiary circular reactions', to see the outcomes of certain actions? Is there, as in 'interiorization of schemes', evidence of mental working out of problems such as how a container opens?

Using careful observation, the educator can assess the sub-stage at which the pupil appears to be functioning. Although Piaget considered the sub-stages as naturally evolving, later views accept the possibility of encouraging and accelerating progress through education.

Taking this view, activities that might consolidate progress in that sub-stage can then be provided and encouraged. If the pupil is demonstrating 'secondary circular reactions', these might be encouraged and widened to different reactions, objects and situations. If the apparent 'secondary circular reactions' are obsessive in nature, they have the potential to hinder learning and development. So opportunities to extend the repertoire might also have the added benefit of diversifying potentially stultifying behaviour. The secondary circular reactions might be developed in potentially meaningful and appropriate situations such as throwing and catching a ball with a partner in a physical education session or mixing ingredients in a cookery session. The educator can then consider whether encouraging activities typical of the next sub-stage might be suitable. In the present example, this would be the 'coordination of circular reactions' encouraging the pupil to put together several actions to reach a goal such as in self-care routines.

Such an approach does not preclude using other strategies to assess the level at which the pupil is functioning; for example, strategies used in cognitive psychology more widely. With regard to perception, visual preference techniques (e.g. Franz, 1966) involve showing a child say two items and noting which one he prefers to look at. This indicates that the child is able to distinguish between the two items. Using a habituation paradigm involves presenting the child with a stimulus; for example, the sound of a door closing until he gradually pays little attention to it. If a new sound, say, of footsteps crossing a room are presented and the child pays revitalized attention, this suggests that the child can discriminate between the two sounds. Slater *et al.* (1983) used a habituation paradigm to indicate that newborn infants can discriminate between a cross and a circle.

In making observations and assessments and considering interventions, educators may have a working assumption that the pupil with profound cognitive impairment may be developing in a similar way to a typically developing child but more slowly. However, this it is not assumed in all instances. The curriculum and other aspects of provision will also take account of idiosyncratic development and the effect of other disabilities.

More broadly, activities will include those that encourage and provide opportunities for sensory experiences and motor experiences and their development. Physical therapy is likely to be planned into provision to ensure that the movement the child has is optimized and that the best forms of physical support and positioning are used. Functional activities will be planned and encouraged including communication and self-care and social and interpersonal skills in response to impairments in adaptive functioning (American Psychiatric Association, 2000, p. 49).

Interaction with the environment Assimilation involving the emerging knowledge that the child has and accommodation involving his environment making demands of the schemas to modify themselves (Piaget and Inhelder, [1966]/1969, p. 5) can be useful orientations for work with pupils with profound cognitive impairment. The educator might provide an object for the pupil to explore perhaps a soft ball. In closely observing the pupil's reactions, the educator might develop a working assumption that the child has expectations of the object suggesting a schema. The child might look at the ball; hold out his hands a suitable width apart to receive it and when he holds, it might do so with suitable pressure to retain it in his grasp. All these may suggest suitable adaptations to the qualities of the ball. At another time the pupil may be given a similar looking ball but which is hard and his responses may suggest that he has a less well-developed schema for such an object. The child may find it more difficult to exert the right pressure to hold it securely. It might also suggest that on reaching for the hard ball, the child had an expectation of it being soft, based on the previous experience with the similar soft ball. These expectations were not met and the child had to adapt accordingly.

Assimilation and accommodation can provide hypotheses for the educator to use in further interactions with the pupil. Does the pupil have a schema for soft items and a less developed one for hard items? Does he retain an expectation and therefore a memory of a previously experienced soft item?

Does he recognize the similarities in size and shape of the previous soft ball and carry this over to expectations of the second ball, which he recognizes as having similar size and shape?

Sensorimotor coordination A theme of the sensorimotor stage is the coordination of movement and the senses of vision, hearing, touch, smell and taste. Children with profound cognitive impairment often experience additional impairments, for example, to sight, hearing and movement. This makes it more difficult for the child to explore the environment by himself and makes it essential that educators encourage development by using the senses available and trying to help the child coordinate the sensory data and make it available, accessible and in some way meaningful.

Multi-sensory teaching and learning, along with the child's movements involved in exploring, are employed to encourage the use and integration of all the senses available. Swimming and hydrotherapy provide opportunities to explore the water itself, the rubberized surfaces of the poolside and various buoyancy aids. A visit to a sensory garden gives a chance to move around in an area where one can see, smell and touch various safe plants. There are limitations to stimulating senses to provide sensory perceptions for their own sake (Ouvry and Saunders, 2001, p. 245). However, where there is an underpinning of a potentially meaningful situation, such approaches can be useful. Sensory experiences can then provide opportunities for conceptual learning and help the pupil understand better the surroundings, daily activities and everyday experiences (Carpenter, 1994).

For example, movement and sensory experiences can be incorporated into activities that have their own meaning and context such as functional or leisure activities. Putting items of the lunch table can involve beginning to recognize the different textures and colours of cutlery, tablemats and crockery if sufficient time is allowed for this. Where texture and colour are used to help identify place settings for different pupils, this can serve as an aid to the task also. Preparing food offers numerous examples of stimulating the senses, creating routines and building experiences that may become meaningful, even leaving aside the pleasure of eating what has been prepared! Many self-care and social skills can also be approached in this way.

Repetition and routine The child's earliest development is characterized by repeated actions, for example, Piaget's primary and secondary circular reactions. Later, in the fourth sub-stage of the sensorimotor stage, there is a 'coordination of circular reactions' where an infant can coordinate several actions to achieve a goal (Piaget and Inhelder, [1966]/1969, p. 11). The educator may use repetition and routine to extend the repertoire of the pupil with profound cognitive impairment. Later, this may be extended to enable the student to achieve a goal in different ways. When the pupil's capacity to explore is limited, repeated experience structured and encouraged by the educator can provide important experience.

More generally, school routines may be used to extend pupils' understanding and skills by building on the familiar. Resources associated with such routines can gradually acquire meaning by being associated with well-known activities. Training shoes regularly used by a pupil in physical education sessions may come to be associated with these times. Routines can also lead to several items being connected. In food preparation, the use of items (bread, butter and spread) one after another may come to be seen as part of the activity. Giving pupils the opportunity to see and touch utensils and observe and participate in the food preparation process can help them build up a concept of 'lunchtime'.

Object permanence Piaget and Inhelder ([1966]/1969, passim) convey the stages by which object permanence becomes secure. Sensory and motoric activities are important in helping develop object permanence. To begin to integrate the experiences that facilitate object permanence, the pupil needs to be positioned to be able to attend what is before him. Hence comfortable positioning is necessary. This may involve the use as appropriate, of positioning devices such as standing frames or inclined wedges, to enable the child to adopt a prone position on the floor. Positions may need to be regularly changed to ensure that they continue to be comfortable and aid maximum attention.

Specific activities involving the educator showing then, hiding an interesting object and noting the child's response can give an indication of whether the pupil has any expectation that the object continues to exist once it is out of sight. Games of 'peek-a-boo' can be used in this way. The pupil can be encouraged to reach out for objects and touch and handle them. For a pupil who has motor difficulties, changes of position and viewpoint help provide the different vantage points that other pupils might create for themselves. The planned co-occurrence of motor experiences and sensory experiences can facilitate the child's development of object permanence.

Causality and communication Piaget and Inhelder (1966/1969, p. 18) propose that, after a 'magical-phenominalist' perception of causality, the child is able to recognize causes other than those situated in his own actions. For pupils with profound cognitive impairment, it is important to provide an environment conducive to communication and development, where contingency awareness can be established.

For children with profound cognitive impairment, some early responses may be spontaneous. However, where an adult in turn regularly and reliably responds to them, they can come to have communicative significance. These sorts of consequences are of course part of how communication develops and is encouraged for all children (Pease, 2000, pp. 41–42). It may take a long time before such patterns of response become established and the adult communication partner needs to be alert and sensitive to the pupil's behaviour and reactions.

Using switch-operated reinforcers, children may be prompted to use the switch so that they will experience their action and its consequences repeatedly and begin to link the two. Relatedly, a 'responsive environment' (Ware, 2003) can help social, intellectual and communicative development through ensuring pupils with cognitive impairment 'get responses to their actions, get the opportunity to give responses to the actions of others, and have the opportunity to take the lead in interaction' (ibid., p. 1). This can be used in pre-meditated teaching and also to capitalize on the spontaneous actions of children.

Pupils may be taught to make choices through adult prompting and/or the use of a switch-activated reinforcer. Prompting may be used to teach switch activation and/or discrimination between different choices (Ware, 2005, p. 73). Multiple micro-switches can enhance different responses in children with profound disabilities with a wider range of response opportunities and more differentiated inputs from the environment producing higher levels of responding (Lancioni *et al.*, 2002).

Conclusion

Child development frameworks, the assumptions involved in them and their strengths and limitations require careful consideration. Within such a context, a child cognitive developmental framework, such as Piaget's, can provide helpful structures for assessing and encouraging the development of special children.

Thinking Points

Readers may wish to consider the following:

- the extent to which Piaget's conception of the sensorimotor period reflects early age-typical infant development;
- the degree to which the observations relating to the sensorimotor period can inform understanding of the development of learners with profound cognitive impairment;
- implications for provision for learners with profound cognitive impairment.

Key Texts

Aird, R. (2001) *The Education and Care of Children with Severe, Profound and Multiple Learning Difficulties.* London: David Fulton Publishers.

Discusses severe learning difficulties (moderate-to-severe cognitive impairment) and profound learning difficulties (profound cognitive impairment). Includes discussion on ensuring the curriculum being broad and responsive to the learning and other 'needs' of the pupils.

Berk, L. E. (2006) (7th edn) *Child Development.* London: Pearson (Pearson International Edition).

A wide-ranging introduction to child development for undergraduate and graduate students.

Crone, D. A. and Horner, R. H. (2003) *Building Positive Behaviour Support Systems in Schools: Functional Behavioural Assessment.* New York: Guilford Press.

Includes case examples of developing and using functional behavioural assessments within school systems. Appendices provide supportive charts and proformas.

Perret-Clermont, A-N. and Barrelet, J-M. (Eds) (2007) *Jean Piaget and Neuchâtel: The Learner and Scholar.* New York: Guilford Press.

A cultural and socio-historical perspective of Piaget's development and contribution to child development and epistemology.

Goswami, U. (2008) *Cognitive Development: The Learning Brain.* New York/Hove: Psychology Press.

Summarizes a wide range of information on child cognitive development relating these to the theories of Piaget and Vygotsky and to theories in developmental cognitive neuroscience.

Lewis, V. (2003) (2nd edn) *Development and Disability*. Malden, MA/Oxford: United Kingdom.

Focuses on the development of deaf children, blind children, children with motor disabilities, children with autism, children with Down's syndrome and practical and theoretical implications.

Meadows S (2006) (2nd edn) *The Child as Thinker: The Development and Acquisition of Cognition in Childhood*. London: Routledge.

Chapter 4, 'Models of cognition in childhood: Metaphors, achievements and problems' compactly outlines and criticizes aspects of Piaget's theory.

Morra, S., Gobbo, C., Marini, Z. and Sheese, R. (2007) *Cognitive Development: Neo-Piagetian Perspectives*. New York/Hove: Psychology Press.

After a historical introduction, this book reviews the main theories and findings associated with developments beyond Piaget, including applications to education and child problem- solving.

Pressley, M. and McCormick, C. B. (2007) *Child and Adolescent Development for Educators*. New York: Guilford Press.

Chapters include ones on biological development, cognitive development (Piaget's theory and information processing theory), social theories and socio-cultural theories.

Tilstone, C. and Layton, L. with Anderson, A., Gerrish, R., Morgan, J. and Williams. A. (2004) *Child development and Teaching Pupils with Special Educational Needs*. London/New York: Routledge.

Introduces the work of selected theorists (cognitive developmental, psychoanalytical, learning/social learning); examines educational implications of the theories; and looks at areas of development (e.g. cognition and learning) in relation to disabilities/disorders.

10

Psycholinguistic

Introduction

After emphasizing its multi-disciplinary nature, this chapter outlines some of the key aspects of psycholinguistics: linguistics, neuropsychology and the development of models of brain architecture. It examines definitions of psycholinguistics, introducing some of the research techniques used. Relationships between psycholinguistics and special education are considered with reference to a particular psycholinguistic framework incorporating input processing, lexical representations, output processing and intervention. The chapter illustrates the scope of psycholinguistics applied to special education with reference to intonation, word finding, semantics and grammar. Fuller examples are considered for persisting speech difficulties (PSDs) and for specific language impairment (SLI).

Although literacy and literacy problems, often considered within a psycholinguistic framework, are not covered in this chapter, reading disorder is examined in the chapter, 'Neuropsychological' of this book.

Psycholinguistics: Aspects, Definitions and Research Methods

(a) Aspects of psycholinguistics

The multidisciplinary nature of psycholinguistics Psycholinguistics overlaps with several areas of study including psychology, neuroscience, phonetics, language pathology and computer modelling (Field, 2004, p. ix). A further contributory area is discourse analysis (ibid.), which concerns how meaning is built not in grammatical units but in larger units. As a form of analysis it can be applied to the use of written, spoken or signed language. Several disciplines of the social sciences have shown interest in discourse analysis including sociology and social psychology. The various approaches tend to be concerned with the social context in which the discourse takes place (Gee, 2005).

A broad view of the psycholinguistics might include the following:

- language processing
- lexical storage and retrieval
- infant language acquisition
- special circumstances such as disability/disorder
- the brain and language
- second language acquisition and use (Field, 2004, p. xi summarized).

Mildner (2008, p. 249), while writing of cognitive neuroscience and communication, refers to the coming together of the 'hard' sciences such as neurology, molecular biology, biochemistry, physiology and physics with fields such as psychology, linguistics, phonetics and speech communication. This has been associated with the emergence of new terms such as neurolinguistics, biopsychology and cognitive neuroscience. Even more important has been the ' . . . increasing interest, understanding, appreciation, and cooperation among scientists of various research disciplines' (ibid.). To the extent that psycholinguistics involves the study of brain–behaviour relationships, it is closely aligned to neuropsychology applied to communication.

Psycholinguistics draws on linguistics, neurology and psychology (especially cognitive developmental psychology) and is indeed called a 'developmental cognitive neurolinguistic' framework sometimes (Martin and Miller, 2003, p. 11). The remaining subsections concern, respectively, linguistics, neuropsychology and computer modelling of brain architecture.

Linguistics Linguistics, as the scientific study of language, covers a broad area with several recognized branches (Aronoff and Rees-Miller, 2000, passim). Phonetics (Ladefoged, 1993) concerns the way in which speech sounds are made and perceived; phonology (Carr, 1993) has to do with units of sound in the context of a theory of languages as systems. Morphology (Mathews, 1991) relates to the grammatical elements of words such as plural endings in English, while syntax (Burton-Roberts, 1997) deals with the relationships between units including words within a sentence. Semantics (Lyons, 1995) involves the study of meaning or more specifically 'the way meaning is organized in language'

(Crystal and Varley, 1998, p. 47). Pragmatics (Bishop, 2000) concerns the use of language, or more precisely, 'the study of factors that govern our choice of language (the sounds, constructions, words) in social interaction, and the effects of our choices upon others' (Crystal and Varley, 1998, p. 48; www.asha.org).

In modern linguistics, it has been suggested that phonology and grammar have been studied for the longest period, semantics followed and pragmatics came to prominence relatively late in the 1980s (Crystal and Varley, 1998, p. 48). Models of language structure sometimes distinguish structure and language use. Within language structure, the formal features of language are observed in a spoken utterance classified into three types, namely, *phonology*, *grammar* and *semantics*. Language use refers to pragmatics. A further area of study within linguistics is the relationships between language and the brain (Obler and Gjerlow, 1999), which in turn relates to neuropsychology.

Neuropsychology Cognitive developmental psychology involves the psychological study of cognitive processes such as memory, attention and perception in the context of human development. It has been briefly defined as 'The study of human mental processes and their contribution to thinking, sensation and behaviour' (Field, 2004, p. 62). An aspect of cognitive psychology is an information-processing approach seeking to map the mental processing of information as particular cognitive tasks are carried out. Evidence from neurology may be related to psychological studies such as those of memory, attention and perception, as in neuropsychology.

Neuropsychology has been described as 'the study of brain–behaviour relationships' (Dewey and Tupper, 2004, p. xi). It seeks to link observed behaviours, such as using language, to areas of the brain used in carrying out those behaviours (Lezak *et al.*, 2004). As the 'Neuropsychological' chapter in this book indicates, the difficulties and complexities of demonstrating any supposed relationships between behaviour and brain structure and function are considerable.

Although broadly the brain controls cognitive aspects of producing and comprehending language and the motor aspects of articulation, the interrelationships of structures supporting communication are important. As Mildner (2008) points out, 'Although speech and language are primarily left-hemisphere activities, they need the right hemisphere to proceed optimally' (ibid., p. 249). In addition, speech and language are ' . . . equally difficult if not entirely impossible without subcortical and peripheral structures' (ibid.).

Models of brain architecture Connectionist models make an important contribution to computer modelling. The brain is regarded as transmitting information through interconnected neural networks. Therefore, connectionist models are made in a way that resembles this configuration. The assumptions of this approach are summarized by Field (2004). They are that, ' . . . a model which resembles the brain potentially provides a more plausible account than one that does not' and that ' . . . by using this kind of architecture, we may gain incidental insights into at least some of the brain's functions' (ibid., p. 73).

Connectionist models typically comprise numerous simple processing nodes (units) linked by many connections. Activation passes along the connections spreading from one unit to another with an ease determined by the strength of the connections. This strength in turn relates to the frequency with which the connection is used. Connections to a frequent word become stronger over time; hence, the word is more quickly activated than less frequent ones. The model is intended to be analogous to the activation of electrical impulses (and chemical processes) involved in passing information via brain neurons.

An example of the architecture of one type of connectionist model is that of parallel distributed processing. In this model, the representation of a word form is distributed across several units, whereas in earlier models, the word representation tended to be located in a single unit (Whitney, 1998, pp. 105–108). A connectionist model of speech recognition with correspondences to phonetic features, phonemes and words is the trace model (McClelland and Elman, 1986). Among its limitations is that it is unable to generalize to different speaking rates because it assumes fixed timing patterns between its levels and that it does not account for learning (Mildner, 2008, p. 96).

(b) Definitions of psycholinguistics

It has been proposed that psycholinguistics (Field, 2004, p. ix) ' . . . provides insights into how we assemble our own speech and writing and how we understand that of others; into how we store and use vocabulary; into how we manage to acquire a language in the first place; and into how language can fail us'. In definitions of psycholinguistics, descriptions of its goals, assessment strategies, approaches and sources, a common theme is reference to 'underlying' features.

Psycholinguistics has been said to concern ' . . . the processes underlying the production, perception, and comprehension of language' (Weismer, 2006, p. 93). The primary goal of psycholinguistics has been said to be 'elucidating psychological mechanisms of language use' (Traxler and Gernsbacher, 2006, p. 8). In assessment, psycholinguistics investigates 'underlying skills' (Stackhouse and Wells, 1997, p. 25) and in interventions seeks to target 'the underlying sources of the difficulties rather than the symptoms alone' (Stackhouse and Wells, 2001, p. 412). Similarly, psycholinguistic perspectives seek to understand children's speech difficulties in terms of 'underlying points of breakdown in a speech-processing chain or model' (Pascoe *et al.*, 2006, p. 4). Aitchison (2008) states, 'The common aim of all those who call themselves psycholinguists is to find out about the structures and processes which underlie a human's ability to speak and understand language' (ibid., p. 1).

Four elements of the approach have been suggested (Dockrell and McShane, 1993):

- the cognitive/neuronal architecture
- mental representations
- the processing of tasks
- the output.

The cognitive/neuronal 'architecture', or the way the brain is organized for language, relates to mental representations and may include the notions of working memory and long-term memory. Working memory (Gathercole and Baddeley, 1993) is considered to hold short-term information for current use and therefore allows auditory and visual information to be stored and used immediately. Long-term memory (Kellogg, 1995), by which data is stored for longer periods, includes storage of the lexicon, word knowledge and linguistic competence. Long-term memory provides short-term memory with information as necessary and receives information from short-term memory for long-term storage.

Mental representations concern the way information is stored. Pre-lexical processing is taken to imply ' . . . some sort of transformation of acoustic-phonetic information into abstract representations' (Mildner, 2008, p. 25). More broadly, information on a word's speech sound sequence would be expected to be stored as a phonological mental representation and information on a facial expression as a visual mental representation. Perception is clearly important because the way sounds, sights and movement are perceived influences the information to be stored. The 'mental lexicon' has been defined as ' . . . mental representation of the words any individual has at her/his disposal' (ibid., p. 194). The notion of a 'lexicon', the vocabulary system mentally stored as an entry for each item, relates to the processing approach of psycholinguistics and its structure is the subject of debate (ibid., p. 274).

The processing of tasks is mainly automatic, allowing information to be manipulated and understood. However, with new material, children appear to develop conscious processing strategies such as strategies for approaching the pronunciation of a new word. For the output to be correct, it is important that the person has access to the stored information and can retrieve it and there may be mental representations for organizing output.

The output of speech production is thought to depend on representations that organize the programming of motor speech acts (Martin and Miller, 2003, p. 11). One model of speech production (Levelt, 1989) suggests three processes: conceptualizing, formulating and articulating. A conceptualizer chooses a proposition, selects and orders information and relates it to previous information. A formulator translates the conceptual structure into a linguistic structure through grammatical and phonological encoding and other processes to form an articulatory plan. This representation of how the proposed utterance is to be articulated is stored in an 'articulatory buffer'. The articulator retrieves internal speech from the buffer and converts these into motor commands to the muscles that control the respiratory system, the larynx and the articulators.

(c) Research techniques in psycholinguistics

Data gathered and interpreted to inform theories, models, assessment and other aspects of psycholinguistics come from various sources. Where there has been damage to a particular area of the brain, the recording of spoken language can help identify speech impairments and classify them. Neuropsychological data on language may be obtained, for example, from brain imaging techniques as described in the chapter, 'Neuropsychological' of this book. Discourse analysis may be used on recorded connected speech to study how it is planned and carried out. Computer modelling has already been mentioned as a method of seeking to understand possible mental processes. Naturally occurring data or experimentally induced information may be used.

The way lexical items are stored and retrieved and how speech is assembled may be studied through analysing slips of the tongue made by typically developing speakers. The errors might be selection errors such as the substitution of one word for another, which can suggest how words might be stored and retrieved. The substituted word might be associated with the target word by similarity of form or meaning or both. Alternatively, the errors might be assemblage errors where the correct lexical item is retrieved or a series of words is intended but the order is incorrect. Such slips of the tongue may be recorded in naturally occurring speech or may be studied experimentally.

Experimental procedures are used to examine other features. Response times can indicate the demands that ambiguities make on working memory. Response time may be measured by asking the child to press a button in response to a specified occurrence. The child might be played a recorded text and asked to respond whenever he hears a specified word (or phoneme). If the response is slower when the word coincides with semantic or syntactic ambiguities in the text, the experimenter can measure the increased demands these ambiguities place on working memory. Repetition tasks may also be used to study working memory. The child might be asked to repeat words or non-words after the experimenter, with the span increasing gradually until the child can no longer repeat accurately. This is taken as an indication of memory capacity.

Gating (Grosjean, 1980) is a method used to study the mental lexicon and its organization, activation and functioning. The child is played a sentence fragment prepared from a recorded sentence by computer software. Further fragments (usually of 20 ms in duration) are added, making the segment progressively longer. Each time the child is asked to say what he heard and what he thinks the complete sentence was. This is continued until the sentence has been correctly guessed or until the entire recorded sentence has been played. The procedure indicates the amount and sort of information needed before a correct response is obtained.

To study spoken language perception and to indicate possible language deficits, the technique of shadowing may be used. A child is presented with different stimuli in the left and right earphones and asked to repeat simultaneously the message he hears in one of the ears. That is, the child tries to verbally 'shadow' what is heard. Should a change be made to the message in the unattended ear, for example, if the voice changes from female to male, the child typically hesitates or begins to lose the thread of the message he is repeating. Shadowing is more successful if the stimuli are different, for example, if the voices have a different pitch (Coren and Ward, 1989).

Priming and interference are used in tests in which a stimulus is used to facilitate or interfere with another. The relationship may be phonological, syntactic, lexical or semantic. The degree of facilitation or interference is measured by the time the child takes to respond to the second stimulus. This provides information about the organization and relationship between the first stimulus (the prime) and the second (target) stimulus. For example, if the child is presented briefly with a word, followed soon after by another likely to be associated with it, the second word will be detected quicker if there is such an association. This can indicate the temporal sequence and the extent of interference between the two competing cognitive processes/representations of different stimuli. However, it provides limited information about how the processes and representations function (Westbury, 1998).

Relationships between Psycholinguistics and Special Education

Overview of a particular psycholinguistic framework This section focuses on the speech-processing applications of a psycholinguistic framework proposed by Stackhouse and Wells (1997). It is current, fairly comprehensive and has application to children with speech (and literacy) difficulties, offering a hypothesis testing approach to investigate speech-processing skills. Unless otherwise specified, references in this section are to this framework. It involves 'a psycholinguistic assessment framework, a theoretical model of speech processing, and a developmental phase model for speech and metaphonological awareness' (p. 239).

Key aspects include 'lexical representation' (a means of keeping information about words) and a 'lexicon' (a store of words). It is assumed that a child receives information about an utterance, remembers it, stores it in various lexical representations within the lexicon and then chooses and produces spoken and written words. This is represented as an input channel of information via the auditory system and a channel for output information through organs involved in articulating speech. 'Top down' processing concerns an activity using previously stored information (lexical representations), whereas 'bottom up' processing does not (p. 8). Within the lexicon, information about a word is stored in semantic, phonological, grammatical and orthographic representation and motor programme, that is, a set of instructions for pronouncing a word that is sent to the mouth (pp. 10–11).

Children with speech difficulties have one or more problems in this speech-processing system: at the level of input, representation or output, this is reflected in assessment, the profile of difficulties and subsequent remediation. The framework strives to establish where the speech-processing skills are breaking down and how this could be affecting speech and literacy development. Levels of processing and routes between them are represented by an information-processing model (pp. 144–187), but it does not claim neuroanatomical reality. Findings using the model need to be informed by knowledge of typical child development to gain a fuller grasp of the nature of speech-processing difficulties and what can be done to remediate them. A progression through several phases is identified (pre-lexical, whole word, systematic simplification, assembly and metaphonolgical phases) (pp. 190–215, 221–232). Children with speech difficulties are viewed as having static, difficult or slow development through these phases.

Input processing Input processing involves peripheral auditory processing, speech/non-speech discrimination, phonological recognition and phonetic discrimination. Peripheral auditory processing, being able to hear the full range of sounds involved in speech, is understood in the context of general auditory ability. Some children have normal peripheral hearing but experience difficulties with 'higher level' auditory processing (p. 148). Normally a pre-linguistic level of processing discriminates environmental sounds and speech sounds before the latter are forwarded for further decoding. However, a child with acquired language problems (e.g. after an accident) may retain unimpaired hearing acuity but be unable to distinguish speech and environmental noises.

Should speech/non-speech discrimination be normal, the child has to determine that the speech is part of the language with which he is familiar. This involves recognizing phonological features specific to, for example, English that aid the segmentation of the input into 'words, syllables and smaller units' (p. 152) and identifying each of these units accurately. A level of processing is conjectured at which speech input is recognized as English and sent on for further decoding and non-English speech is not. The child distinguishes between these by 'phonological recognition', matching the input against an 'inventory' of English phonetic patterns, thus filtering out unfamiliar phonetic sequences (p. 149). Should the input contain unfamiliar phonetic material, for example, from an unfamiliar accent of English, the child has to be able to phonologically sort this material out, for example, mapping the percept onto 'new articulatory routines' to try to reproduce the unfamiliar sound (p. 152).

Lexical representations Lexical representation involves the connected components of phonological representation, semantic representation, motor programme, grammatical representation, orthographic representation and orthographic programme (pp. 152–153, p. 157).

A child might be shown two pictures, one of a clown and one of a crown. The adult says one of the words and the child has to decide which has been said. To comply, the child has to recognize the pictures via the visual system, access the semantic representation of each word, thus activating previous knowledge about its 'phonological structure and content' (pp. 152–153). This *phonological representation* is regarded as part of the child's stored knowledge of each word from memory and contains only information needed to distinguish it from other words. This is mainly its acoustic/auditory properties and visual information from the shape of the lips when the sound is made (p. 162).

Phonological representations are considered to have a hierarchical structure: syllable, onset and rhyme, and nucleus and coda. *Semantic representation* is a necessary part of the child's knowledge of a word. Without knowledge of meaning, the child cannot access the phonological representation of, say, 'clown' on seeing a picture. One cannot go from visual stimulus to phonological representation without first accessing the semantic representation.

The *motor program* consists of a series of 'gestural targets' for the tongue, lips, soft palate and vocal folds stored in the lexical representation, made to achieve an acceptable pronunciation of the word. Both phonological representation and semantic representation are linked to the motor programme. Some speech production activities, for example, spontaneous speech do not require input processing of auditory information. Because the spoken output is generated from the semantic representation, the word uttered being already known, phonological representation is unnecessary for recognition (p. 162).

The lexical representation also contains *grammatical information* and, once the child begins to learn to read and spell, *orthographic information (representation and programme)*. The grammatical and semantic representations are linked, the grammatical class of a word being closely concerned with its meaning. In English, the phonological and orthographic aspects are linked because of the often-predictable relationships between phonological units and graphemes.

Output processing Output processing involves motor programming, motor planning and motor execution. Motor programming represents the component of the model where new motor programmes are created, for example, when the speaker has to produce previously unfamiliar words. It may be understood as a store from which phonological units are selected and as a process of assembling them into new combinations (p. 163). Motor planning is the level of processing where motor programmes of individual words are 'assembled into a single utterance plan' (p. 165).

Regarding motor execution, the motor plan is executed and an acoustic signal produced. If there are anatomical problems with any part of the vocal tract, or if the innervation of these organs is affected, speech production can be influenced (p. 166). Fuller descriptions of motor execution and the physical basis of a 'communication chain' are provided by Crystal and Varley (1998, pp. 115–129), in terms of respiration, phonation and articulation (tongue and soft palate).

Intervention Several *principles* have been identified based on theoretical rationale and linking short-term aims/objectives with intervention tasks. These include 'work on the system', reinforcing the point that although weaknesses with particular levels and connections can be identified, it does not make sense to target these as if they occurred in isolation. An intervention activating stronger levels of processing can help strengthen weaker ones (Stackhouse and Wells, 2001, p. 52). A '*task*' refers to any materials used for the intervention, the procedure followed, the feedback provided for the child and any technique used to support speech processing such as cued articulation. Changes in any of these components can alter the 'psycholinguistic nature' of the task (ibid., p. 67).

A psycholinguistic framework helps ensure sufficient emphasis on the input and storage aspects of speech processing and links with medical, educational, phonological and other perspectives in seeking a coordinated structure. A role is recognized for articulatory approaches and phonological therapy to improve a child's speech production and enhance intelligibility (Pascoe *et al.*, 2006, p. 13). Indeed phonological intervention can be seen as linking intervention and cognition. One goal of phonological intervention is 'facilitating cognitive reorganization of the child's phonological system and . . . phonologically oriented processing strategies' (Grunwell, 1985, p. 99).

A psycholinguistic framework allows a methodical approach to language disorder in terms of perception, storage, access, retrieval and output. A child having problems with attention may miss some of what is said so that processing is inaccurate. For a child with hearing impairment, information may be imperfectly received; hence, information that is processed may not be that which educators assume. Another child may be able to hear well but may be unable to discriminate between some sounds or to process them in the right order. Alternatively, a child may receive, process and store information adequately but be unable to produce the expected 'output'. If a child's processes of motor planning or motor organization are weak, he may have problems producing sounds in the way he heard them. Accordingly, a feature of language causing concern may have different causes, suggesting different strategies of intervention. Imperfect speech may be related to problems receiving or processing information or difficulties in production.

A psycholinguistic framework enables areas of respective weakness and strength to be identified so that strengths can be used and consolidated to support skills and areas of weakness are tackled. However, excessive focus on apparent areas of breakdown may be unhelpful as aspects of speech are often interrelated. Often, there is ' . . . an interrelationship between all levels of processing so that there is feedback into the speech sound system, enabling a certain amount of monitoring at a non-conscious level' (Martin and Miller, 2003, p. 44).

In educating a child with speech difficulties, interventions may be planned and delivered jointly by the speech pathologist, teacher, assistants, parents and others using a consultative model. This may have an economic or pragmatic rationale where there is a shortage of speech pathologists but may work better for children with less severe difficulties than for children with PSDs. Trained assistants working closely with the speech pathologist may contribute to assessment and interventions. A psycholinguistic framework may include individual task-based interventions and group-based support and intervention.

The Scope of a Psycholinguistic Approach

The psycholinguistic framework was originally developed in studies of children with specific phonological impairment and verbal dyspraxia. However, it may be used with a wide range of children with communication difficulties where these appear to be related to speech-processing problems. These include children with acquired speech and language difficulties associated with epilepsy (Vance, 1997) or children with semantic pragmatic difficulties or autistic features (Popple and Wellington, 2001, pp. 299–329). For a child with hearing impairment, the approach can help identify different levels of processing implicated in a child's speech output errors and difficulties with lexical retrieval (Ebbels, 2000).

Intonation Prosody may be understood as combining the features of tone, duration and intensity and although pauses may be included as part of prosody, they require units larger than a single word (Mildner, 2008, p. 185). As part of phonology, prosodic structures and systems mediate between 'the phonetic substance of speech' and 'a wide range of lexical, grammatical and pragmatic functions' (Wells and Peppé, 2001, p. 366).

Mildner (2008) summarizes neurological evidence and research into tone and prosody. She suggests that laterality of particular functions is based on the degree of involvement of properties such as 'temporal sequence, timing, duration or frequency' (p. 190). The left hemisphere may be more active when material is more time dependent or requires sequential processing. The right hemisphere may be implicated more when material is not dependent on temporal factors (ibid.).

A psycholinguistic approach where prosody is atypical seeks to identify the underlying level of deficit by examining different levels of processing. A battery has been devised to assess children's intonation, the *Profiling Elements of*

Prosodic Systems—Children (PEPS-C). At the time of writing this book, the test was not published but is described in a published article (Peppé and McCann, 2003). Case studies suggest that the relationships between prosodic input and output in children are not always straightforward (Wells and Peppé, 2001, p. 395).

Word finding A word-finding difficulty occurs when a target word exists in a child's receptive vocabulary but the child cannot produce the word 'quickly and easily on demand' (Constable, 2001, p. 330). A psycholinguistic approach aims at establishing how the difficulty arises in lexical development and what causes particular words to be difficult to find (p. 334). In a single-word naming task, problems can arise at the levels of semantic representation, the motor programme or in motor execution (p. 336). Teaching and therapy targets may address underlying input- and output-processing skills, memory, lexical updating (improving the accuracy of stored information) and 'compensatory strategies to improve coping behaviour' (p. 355).

Semantics When subjects carried out semantic processing tasks, magnetic resonance imaging (MRI) investigations indicated several places of activity in the inferior temporal and parietal lobes and in the superior frontal lobe (Frackowiak, 1994b). Studies using event-evoked potential (see the chapter 'Neuropsychological' in this book for an explanation of this technique) have indicated that semantic and syntactic (and morphological) processes are processed in different systems (Friederici *et al.*, 1993).

The meaning of words can be included as part of the examination of the processes of language. It is suggested that children use strategies to store, access and retrieve meaning in language and that where it can be established where the process breaks down this might suggest strategies for intervention. However, information about developmental patterns for naming is still being gathered and underlying causes of semantic difficulties are unclear (Dockrell *et al.*, 1998, p. 453).

Grammar Neurologically, syntactic processing has been considered to be a strongly left-lateralized language function (Mildner, 2008, p. 210). However, it has been suggested that sentence comprehension may activate other cortical regions that do not process only specifically linguistic information (Just *et al.*, 2004).

In Stackhouse and Wells' (1997) model, lexical representation includes a grammatical component. This specifies, for example, how a word is used in sentences or changed into a plural, but not where grammatical coding takes place in utterances beyond single words. Also, attempts have been made to conceptualize connected speech within the model. At each level of the model, connected speech (as well as single word) tasks can take place. On the input side, auditory discrimination tasks can be carried out for discriminating between two sentences where a word differs at the end of the sentence. The speech-processing routes are the same as for single-word tasks, but there is an extra complexity in processing continuous speech (Pascoe *et al.*, 2006, pp. 176–179). At the level of motor planning, motor programmes for individual words are assembled into an overall plan for speech production. Using case studies of children, links have been explored between speech processing and deficits in grammar, pragmatics and semantics (Chiat, 2000).

Fuller Example: Persisting Speech Difficulties

General PSDs have been defined as 'difficulties in the normal development of speech that do not resolve as the child matures or even after they receive specific help with these problems' (Pascoe *et al.*, 2006, p. 2). They include articulation, phonological and fluency difficulties. For some children there may be an identifiable aetiology such as cleft lip, but for others there will be no known cause and it is apparent that the group is heterogeneous (ibid., p. 3). However, PSDs appear to sometimes run in families and a mutation in a gene (FOXP2) is thought to be associated with apraxia in individuals with the affected gene (Vargha-Khadem *et al.*, 2005). Factors may include medical, genetic, psycholinguistic or social ones (ibid., p. 13).

PSDs are usually identifiable taking into account a child's age (typically 5 or 6 years of age and older), the primary nature of the speech difficulties and associated difficulties such as problems acquiring literacy and psychosocial difficulties (ibid., pp. 3–9). In terms of a psycholinguistic perspective, children with PSDs are thought to have 'multiple, and often severe, levels of breakdown throughout the system' (ibid., p. 10).

Segments in single words For assessment and intervention, segments in single words are chosen as stimuli. Approaches to stimuli design and selection include developmental, complexity, functional and systemic perspectives (Pascoe *et al.*, 2006, p. 63). Where a developmental perspective is adopted, norms are available for typical speech development in different countries (McLeod, 2002), which can inform the selection of stimuli for intervention. The speech of older children with PSDs may be disordered rather than delayed, limiting the usefulness of developmental norms.

A 'complexity' approach involves the assumption that earlier segments are not a prerequisite of later segments. More complex targets are tackled earlier than a developmental approach would suggest. A sort of downward generalization is assumed to take place and a child's whole speech system is considered to be more rapidly changed. In a functional perspective, the focus is practicality. The child's name or other core vocabulary may be selected as a target, or there may be efforts to stabilize the production of high-frequency words. In the systemic perspective, it is argued that long-lasting changes in a child's speech system require that work be undertaken of the whole speech system. This involves focusing on contrasts made explicit in interventions, for example, using minimal or maximal pairs.

Consonant clusters We may now turn to consonant clusters in single words (e.g. sky, basket and flask). Consonant clusters emerge later than single consonants, slowly and with greater accuracy developing between the ages of 3 years and 6 months and 8 years (McLeod *et al.*, 2001). A psycholinguistic framework may explore the development of consonant cluster perception and a child's ability to discriminate between related clusters and how this relates to production. Bridgeman and Snowling (1988) compared the perception of consonant clusters of children with dyspraxia and children with typically developing speech and aged 7–11 years. The tasks involved the auditory discrimination of word-final consonant clusters [st] and [ts] in words and non words in a same/difference paradigm. Both groups were able to discriminate real words equally well. However, children with dyspraxia did worse than controls in discriminating cluster sequences in non-words. This was interpreted as the children having difficulties with sequential aspects of phonological processing.

Regarding intervention, a psycholinguistic approach suggests first determining the level or levels at which there is breakdown and then concentrating on the phonological units affected at each level. One child may be unable to perceive the difference between particular clusters, whereas another may have problems with motor programming; however, the outcome of poor production may be the same. There is debate about whether consonant clusters should be chosen as early intervention targets. They can result in greater generalization throughout the child's system and better intelligibility, although different clusters, such as [s] sequences, appear to have different effects on generalization (Barlow, 2001).

Connected speech Connected speech, consisting of segmental and prosodic processes (Pascoe *et al.*, 2006, pp. 168–173), is not simply a sequence of the segments that comprise it. This is because each segment of speech influences the segments surrounding it. The importance of taking connected speech into account in planning speech pathology/therapy intervention is increasingly recognized. Camarata (1998) suggests that where children are assessed in a single-word context, this is likely to show speech competence at its highest. Therefore, a child's speech should be assessed in syntactic contexts too.

Children with PSDs may require intervention at the level of connected speech as well as at individual word level in order for their functional speech to be more intelligible. This is because they may not generalize gains from individual word interventions spontaneously to connected speech (Pascoe *et al.*, 2006, p. 176). Also children with PSDs may be more motivated by interventions aimed at connected speech because it has greater functional relevance.

Case studies Single-case studies illustrate some current approaches and the following all-used pre- and post-therapy assessment. In these studies, 'generalization' refers to the degree to which an area targeted in an intervention leads to changes beyond what was the focus. 'Across-item generalization' is that occurring from treated stimuli to untreated (but matched) stimuli. 'Across-task generalization' extends from a treated task such as speech to an untreated one such as spelling.

Gibbon and Wood (2003) in a study of an 8-year-old boy with long-standing articulation disorder used electropalatography, a technique monitoring contact between the tongue and hard palate during articulation and speech. The outcome measure was of velar production (involving the back of the tongue and the soft palate as when making the sound *k* in English) in single-word speech. This led to significant progress in the use of velars in single words. A detailed history was taken before intervention and a long-term follow-up was made. There was across-item generalization and across-task generalization from single-word speech to connected speech.

Best (2005) reported case studies of five children (two boys aged 6 and 10 years and three girls, one aged 8 and two aged 9 years) with word-finding difficulties. A computerized aid was used to encourage word-finding skills assessed through the outcome of picture naming of single words and led to significant improvement for all children. Control procedures included long-term follow-up. There was across-item generalization for two children and across-task generalization for one child in reading.

Pascoe *et al.* (2005) presented a case study of a 6-year-old girl with unintelligible speech. The intervention comprised minimal pair work on final consonant production and connected speech work using graded sentences. This led to significant progress as indicated in the use of final consonants in single words and connected speech.

Control procedures included long-term follow-up. There was across-item generalization and across-task generalization from speech to spelling.

Fuller Example: Specific Language Impairment

Specific language impairment The term SLI is intended to distinguish children who have a deficit in spoken language ability but do not have symptoms associated with other developmental disorders. The disorder is not associated with hearing impairment, physical disability or cognitive impairment (Adams *et al.*, 1997). The language difficulty of children with SLI is persistent and 'seems to be out of proportion with other aspects of development' (Martin and Miller, 2003, p. 21). It is associated with a 'discrepancy between the verbal and non-verbal scores in a standardized assessment' (Macintyre and Deponio, 2003, pp. 68–69). Children with SLI have difficulties communicating what they want and the difficulty is usually apparent before the child starts school, suggesting early diagnosis is helpful and the support of a speech and language pathologist/therapist is necessary (pp. 68–69). Some children experience difficulties only with expressive language and appear to have normal comprehension. Their problems range from lack of use of the past tense or lack of use of plurals to 'extreme difficulty in forming words or organizing speech' (p. 99). Others have difficulty only with comprehension. They may produce fluent speech but have problems in processing speech. Other children have problems with both expressive and receptive language (p. 99).

The distinctions between expressive difficulties and both receptive and expressive difficulties are reflected in the criteria for communication disorders in the *Diagnostic and Statistical Manual of Mental Disorders Fourth Edition Text Revision* (American Psychiatric Association, 2000). An essential feature of expressive language disorder is an impairment of expressive language development, 'as demonstrated by scores on standardized individually administered measures of expressive language development substantially below those obtained from standardized measures of both non-verbal intellectual capacity and receptive language development' (ibid., p. 58). The difficulties may occur in verbal language or in sign language. For 'mixed receptive–expressive language disorder', an essential feature is impairment in both receptive and expressive language development. This is indicated by scores on standardized individually administered measures of both receptive and expressive language development that are ' . . . substantially below those obtained from standardized measures of non-verbal intellectual capacity' (p. 62).

Prevalence of SLI is about 7% (Tomblin *et al.*, 1997) in epidemiological studies and there is a male : female ratio of 1.5 to 1. Although there appears to be a genetic component, the causes of SLI may be multifactorial (Leonard and Deevy, 2006, p. 1144). When children with SLI reach school age, they often experience reading difficulties (Catts *et al.*, 2002).

Inconsistency in producing tense and agreement morphemes Leonard and Deevy (2006, pp. 1143–1171) provide an interesting perspective of SLI in children on which the remainder of this section draws. Regarding English-speaking children with SLI, a common profile appears to be a mild-to-moderate deficit in semantic and phonological areas and a more serious deficit in morphosyntax, especially the expression of tense and agreement. Children with SLI have difficulties with the following:

- grammatical morphemes such as the past tense 'ed' (e.g. call*ed*);
- present third person singular 's' (e.g. call*s*);
- copula and auxiliary forms of 'is', 'are', 'am', 'was' and 'were'.

However, it has been argued that children with SLI rarely use these morphemes in an *in*appropriate context and their difficulty with tense and agreement morphemes may be the *inconsistency* of producing them (ibid., p. 1149). This particular difficulty with tense and agreement, expressed as tense and agreement variability, appears to be an important distinguishing feature of SLI. Theories and models have been put forward to explain it. Leonard and Deevy (2006, pp. 1150–1161) describe two approaches, one drawing on linguistic theory and the other relating to processing.

The extended optional infinitive account The first perspective drawing on linguistic theory suggests that children with SLI have poorer grammatical grasp than typically developing children. An 'extended optional infinitive' (EOI) account (Rice *et al.*, 1998) argues that children learning languages such as English pass through a period of grammatical development where they treat morphemes as 'optional' in main clauses. Children understand the function of tense and where it is applied but do not grasp the fact that it has to be applied universally. Where tense is not selected in such instances, the child uses a non-finite form. Leonard and Deevy (2006, p. 1150) suggest a child saying 'Chris play basketball yesterday' is similar to the non-finite adult sentence, 'We saw Chris play basketball yesterday'. While age typically developing children pass through this stage, children with SLI appear to stay longer. Among perceived limitations of such approaches is they do not fully account for variability such as reliable differences that have been found between groups of children or between languages despite all the children being at an optional period of development (ibid., p. 1157).

A processing limitations account The second view, which concerns processing, assumes children with SLI have the potential to grasp the pertinent details of language but have processing limitations making storing, retrieving or applying them inconsistent. These (general or specific) limitations appear to relate to reduced speed of processing and limited capacity. General processing approaches may propose a generalized slowing for SLI (Kail, 1994). A single mechanism is thought to be responsible for processing rate in different domains affecting tasks in different domains and the individual steps of a complex task. Regarding capacity, one model proposes two short-term storage systems that are modality specific for verbal and for visual information and a central executive component. The latter partly coordinates the flow of information in working memory (Baddeley, 1986). Experimental evidence has been taken to suggest children with SLI have a reduced storage capacity in phonological memory. Other models indicate a more general capacity deficit. As with linguistic accounts, the processing models have not achieved universal acceptance.

Possible future research Leonard and Deevy (2006, pp. 1162–1165) suggest future research might usefully seek to bring together the two approaches relating to linguistic knowledge and processing capacity. What is evident in both types of account, however, is the focus on underlying psychological processes that are intended to account for tense and agreement, a key feature of SLI.

Conclusion

Relationships between psycholinguistics and special education were considered with reference to input processing, lexical representations, output processing and interventions. The various levels of explanation and evidence such as neuropsychological, linguistic and relating to brain architecture can provide multilevel descriptions. These have the potential to be mutually reinforcing and to provide richer accounts than if explanatory evidence is limited to one level of description.

Thinking Points

Readers may wish to consider the following:

- the strengths and weaknesses of a psycholinguistic approach towards different types of communication disorders (speech, grammar, semantics and pragmatics);
- the extent to which the approach convincingly relates assessment to intervention;
- the extent to which an essentially process-based approach clarifies understanding of disorders.

Key Texts

Aitchison, J. (2008) *The Articulate Mammal: An Introduction to Psycholinguistics*. New York/London: Routledge.

This book provides a readable summary of some recent developments and interests in psycholinguistics including language acquisition, the link between language knowledge and use and producing and comprehending speech.

Crystal, D. and Varley R. (1998) (4th edn) *Introduction to Language Pathology*. London: Whurr.

This book provides an introduction to communication and communication disability taking into account information-processing approaches to language disorders. It concerns child and adult communication. Chapter 6 provides a brief discussion of the classification of language pathologies.

Field, J. (2004) *Psycholinguistics: Key Concepts*. New York/London: Routledge.

Intended for the general reader as well as the student, this book provides an introductory guide in A to Z format to the main terms and concepts in psycholinguistics, suggesting further reading for main areas.

Kandel, E., Schwartz, J. H. and Jessel, T. M. (2000) *Principles of Neural Science*. New York: McGraw-Hill.

Chapter 59 of this textbook on general neuroscience concerns language and the aphasias.

Mildner, V. (2007) *The Cognitive Neuroscience of Human Communication*. New York: Lawrence Erlbaum Associates.

This book looks into research methods used in the neuroscience related to communication and covers a wide range of topics relating to speech and language. Chapter 5 describes the central nervous system in terms of principles, theories, models of structure, development and functioning. Chapter 6 gives an account of lateralization and localization of functions.

Pascoe, M., Stackhouse, J. and Wells, B. (2006) *Children's Speech and Literacy Difficulties Book 3: Persisting Speech Difficulties in Children*. London: Wiley.

This book concerns school age children with persisting speech difficulties and looks into the psycholinguistic nature of these difficulties and at the design and outcome measurement of intervention programmes, which mainly draw on psycholinguistic and linguistic approaches.

Stackhouse, J. and Wells, B. (1997) *Children's Speech and Literacy Difficulties Book 1: A Psycholinguistic Framework*. London: Wiley.

This presents the principles of psycholinguistic investigation using a developmental psycholinguistic model and suggesting a hypothesis testing approach. It is intended mainly for those involved in speech pathology, education, psychology and clinical linguistics.

Stackhouse, J. and Wells, B. (Eds) (2001) *Children's Speech and Literacy Difficulties Book 2: Identification and Intervention*. London: Wiley.

Following on from book 1, this text suggests how information gleaned using a psycholinguistic framework might be used to plan interventions for children with speech, word-finding and phonological awareness problems. Case studies are used to illustrate.

Traxler, M. and Gernsbacher, M. A. (Eds) (2006) (2nd edn) *Handbook of Psycholinguistics*. San Diego, CA: Academic Press.

Sections comprise 'language production', 'language comprehension' and 'language development'. Chapter 30 concerns 'Comprehension: Cognitive and Linguistic Issues in the Study of Children with Specific Language Impairment'.

Internet Resources

An example of the Internet resources available is the American Speech-Language Association (ASHA) site (www.asha.org). ASHA is a professional and accrediting association for speech-language pathologists and audiologist in the United States and elsewhere. An A to Z topic index on this site leads to a list of definitions and resources, access to some of which is limited to members of the organization.

11

Technological

Introduction

This chapter explores how technology may be used in special education to enhance teaching and learning and to increase pupils' independence and autonomy. It pays particular attention to information and communications technology (ICT). The chapter considers definitions and descriptions of technology. It highlights the importance of teacher education in extending the effective use of technology for pupils in schools. The chapter outlines ways in which technology can be classified, for example, according to curriculum requirements. Such frameworks can inform school audits and ensure optimum use.

The relationships between technology and special education are examined. The chapter indicates the scope of the application of technology with reference to several disorders/disabilities. It then examines the use of technology for visual impairment, orthopaedic and motor impairment and speech disorder more completely.

In different countries, information about technological aids, including ICT, is available from a variety of sources. Consequently, the chapter provides only a few examples of particular manufacturers or software. Up-to-date information can be obtained from national and regional advice centres for technology; from the catalogues of companies that manufacture the technology; from the Internet and from specialists such as technicians, physical therapists and occupational therapists.

Technology and Its Effective Use

In general education texts 'information technology' has been defined in terms of 'information handled by modern technology, particularly the computer'.

Definitions have also drawn attention to the application of technology to subjects of the curriculum and cross-curricular activities (Farrell *et al.*, 1995, p. 113). It is recognized that technology has wide applications to areas of the curriculum ranging from 'historical and geographical databases' to 'computer-aided design' to the 'shaping of reading skills' (ibid., p. 54). A key use of technology whether it involves word processing, art software, spreadsheets, e-mails, the Internet, local and regional learning networks or multimedia CD-ROMs is to 'individualise learning and make it more stimulating and motivating' (Farrell, 1999, p. 103).

The importance of the Internet and other forms of electronic communication has led to the term 'information and communications technology' being commonly used. In the context of the school curriculum, in England, ICT refers to ' . . . the range of tools and techniques relating to computer-based hardware and software; to communications including both directed and broadcast; to information sources such as CD-ROM and the Internet, and to associated technologies such as robots, video conferencing and digital TV' (Qualifications and Curriculum Authority, 1999b, p. 184). It includes the use of palm top and lap top computers, interactive white boards, still and video digital cameras and many other applications. However, teachers are not always confident or competent in using these and many need guidance (Farrell, 2001a, p. 44).

With particular reference to special education, technological aids include resources ranging from 'adaptive equipment' and 'aids to hearing' to 'information and communications technology' and 'multisensory environments' (Farrell, 2003a, passim). In this chapter, a broad definition of technology is adopted to include a wide range of resources and aids including computer technology that enhance or enable learning or increase autonomy.

It has already been suggested that teachers are not always confident or competent in using technology (Farrell, 2001a, p. 44, see also Brodin and Lindstrom, 2003). This can constrain the wider and more effective use of technology in schools. Therefore it is particularly important that teachers and others receive the training and support necessary to enable them to competently use technology themselves. Only then are teachers likely to see the opportunities for using and adapting technology to aid learning and participation for pupils with disability/disorder. This may still require that from time to time the teacher seeks advice from technicians and others specialists who will be more conversant with current changes and improvements in technology. But the teacher will still require a basis of knowledge both of different types of disability/disorder and the ways technology can be used effectively.

Another constraint in some countries and areas is the cost of technology. In many instances the cost of hardware appears to have fallen and the cost of software appears to have risen. Although the total costs in relation to what technology can do may have fallen, the outlay for modern technology is still substantial. This makes it all the more important that teachers are trained to fully use what is available. Sometimes, pupils will be more conversant with the latest modern technology than their teachers and parents. It is clear however that as Hasselbring and Williams Glaser (2000) state of technology ' . . . the barriers of inadequate training and cost must first be overcome before more widespread use can become a reality' (ibid. p. 102).

Ways of Considering Technology

The effective use of technology begins with establishing what is likely to benefit the learner. Educators ask what the child can do and what they cannot do (or find very difficult to do). But it is not necessary to begin from square one for every child. Some generalizations can be made about the sorts of technology that is likely to be useful for different types of disability/disorder. This is considered in later sections when the scope of technology is examined in relation to several types of disability/disorder, and when fuller examples of visual impairment, orthopaedic and motor impairment and speech disorder are considered. Of course, some general observations need to be informed by the particular circumstances and strengths and weaknesses of an individual pupil.

As well as taking into account the requirements of the pupil, educators also have to consider what technology can do (and what it cannot). They have to bear in mind the requirements of the curriculum. Furthermore, the notion of 'access' needs to be examined along with what technology can do to improve it. Therefore the present section examines technology in terms of the following:

- qualities of technology
- curriculum requirements
- access.

There is some overlap across these suggested frameworks and some technology can be placed in different groupings. But for schools and others several benefits of classifying technology are evident. It aids understanding of this rapidly expanding and complicated area. It provides a structure for audits of resources to ensure that technology is used in a comprehensive way. Relatedly, the groupings can help identify where the school has gaps or strengths in technology provision. Classifying also helps schools and others consider alternatives to approaches they currently use.

(a) Qualities of technology

Possible qualities of information and communications technology that have been suggested (Hardy, 2000, pp. 14–17) are as follows:

- automaticity
- capacity and range
- provisionality
- interactivity and
- sociability.

Automaticity refers to the speed and automatic facilities associated with information and communications technology. These are used to allow the pupil to concentrate on the main learning objectives (Hardy, 2000, pp. 14–15). It is important that information and communications technology is used to remove the unnecessary drudgery of tasks, not to carry out processes of which the pupil has no understanding. Once the pupil understands addition he might justifiably use a calculator. Where the learning objective (perhaps in a science lesson) is interpreting information, using a calculator would enable the pupil to more quickly perform otherwise time-consuming and tedious calculations. He could then better concentrate on the main objective of understanding the information. In other words, technology is used to deal with tasks that the pupil understands and could do unaided but which would consume time. The time saved is used for the pupil to concentrate on the main learning point of the lesson.

The *capacity and range* of ICT allows large quantities of information to be easily stored, retrieved and used (ibid., p. 15). An example is multimedia CD-ROMs such as encyclopaedias using text, photographs and diagrams, video clips, audio clips and interactive features. Such features can be motivating and informative if software is chosen well and regularly updated.

Provisionality refers to the quality of allowing provisional attempts to be made at tasks (p. 16). In word processing, work can be drafted in the knowledge that it can be reordered, checked, corrected and polished until the pupil is satisfied with the results. When making designs, several attempts can be made and these can be adjusted and compared before decisions are made about the best outcome.

Interactivity allows pupils to be more actively involved in their learning than they might otherwise be (ibid.). Multi-media facilities can reward the pupil's correct responses through sounds, pictures and so on. Virtual reality plans of a school can allow pupils to find their way to different areas using alternative routes and practise these in virtual space before trying them in the physical world.

Sociability of ICT concerns the way it can be used to encourage interactions between a pupil and others. It can encourage 'learning through collaboration, and the interpersonal and social skills gained from group work' (ibid.). Although the use of computers can be solitary and isolating, ICT does have the potential to be used in a social way. A pupil sending e-mails and text messages allows contact with pupils in other countries to enliven geography, history and other aspects of the curriculum. Video conferencing for pupils in hospital schools can reduce feelings of isolation from their regular school. Group work such as collaborative writing and planning can be helped if a small group of pupils share a computer screen. Where ICT is used to facilitate communication, this has clear social implications as the use of speech synthesizers and other aids to communication illustrate.

If a school reviews equipment using as guidance the qualities of technology, this may help it identify whether its existing equipment is being used to its fullest potential. This can suggest ways of using existing technology more fully and more flexibly. Developing sociability, not always associated with ICT, may be one quality that a school can exploit better. Given the tensions between the potential of technology to isolate or to enhance social relations, the teacher will need to plan carefully to ensure that social disadvantages are minimized and social advantages maximized.

(b) Curriculum requirements

Another way of considering technology is in relation to elements of the school curriculum. The school may take a typical aspect of technology such as the use of interactive CD-ROMs and ensure there are stimulating and engaging examples for all curriculum subjects and areas.

Or the school may examine each curriculum subject and see if a suitable range of technology is available. Is there suitable technology in science to involve pupils with disabilities/disorders such as measuring scales with a magnified closed circuit television display for pupils with visual impairment? Does English have multimedia software to reinforce phonics work for pupils with reading disorder?

As well as subjects such as science and English, aspects of the curriculum may be examined, for example, communication or handwriting. For communication, a switch, several switches or a touch screen may be used for pupils with communication difficulties to produce words or pre-programmed phrases or sentences. The range of messages from which a pupil might choose can be carefully selected so that they are relevant and required in real situations throughout the day.

Where handwriting is very difficult for a pupil, word processing may be used, perhaps with keyboards adapted to the pupil's movement capabilities. Predictive writing technology can be sometimes employed so the pupil does not always have to write out complete sentences. Alternatively words and phrases can be produced by using an overlay keyboard.

Prerequisites of learning and skills considered to underpin learning (such as attention or a grasp of cause and effect) can be developed using technology. Attention may be encouraged by the use of interactive software that stimulates and rewards attention. Technology can also help the pupil establishing relationships between events. This might include simple effects such as the pupil activating a switch to trigger a particular sound or image. Cause and effect links can be used to communicate as when a pupil learns that activating a switch or a choice of switches produces certain communications such as pre programmed words or phrases.

A school audit using categories relating to the curriculum can be a convenient way of enabling subject/aspect curriculum co-ordinators to check that they are using technology optimally. A senior manager might take a cross-curricular overview, including a review of skills across the curriculum and underpinning aspects of learning. This can help ensure that opportunities beyond usual subject/aspect areas of the curriculum are not missed. It can also encourage collaborative work where teachers working on different subject areas collaborate to develop skills necessary to their subjects. A science teacher and a history teacher might work together to develop technology-assisted opportunities for pupils to develop understanding of time. This would be part of an overall aim to integrate learning and understanding.

(c) Access

With regard to access provided by technology, among kinds that have been identified (Day, 1995) are 'physical' and 'cognitive'. (Day also suggested 'supportive' access, which is not considered here.)

Physical access concerns using technology to try to enable a pupil to take part despite physical difficulties. A contemporary way of expressing this, informed by social views of disability/disorder, is to say that the educator is reducing physical 'barriers' to learning. This attempts to put the focus on modifying the environment rather than on what the pupil finds difficult to do. Whatever weight is placed on the contribution of the environment or the abilities of the pupil, the aim is to ensure participation and learning.

A pupil may not be able to physically handle objects easily, which limits his understanding of mathematical concepts such as shape. As an alternative, the pupil can use a computer showing three-dimensional graphics so that he can manipulate shapes on the screen, perhaps using an adaptation known as a roller ball. This raises particular challenge to educators. Where a pupil can feely handle objects and shapes, the proprioceptive sense (the understanding of body position), sensory information (especially sight and hearing) and vestibular sense (relating to balance) are used. Information from these sources is integrated to help the child develop a cognitive 'schema' of a shape or item (Farrell, 2005a). Computer aided learning does not reproduce this coordination of senses and information. Therefore the educator will need to ensure, perhaps through also helping the pupil handle physical objects, that computer-aided 'manipulation' becomes meaningful.

To allow *cognitive access*, technology is used to present curriculum content in ways that make it more accessible. In relation to cognitive access, three approaches have been suggested for pupils with cognitive impairments (Detheridge and Stevens, 2001, p. 164). The first is 'simplifying the writing process'. This might involve using an on-screen grid of words, or symbols and phrases that pupils can transfer to their own text to assist the writing process. The second suggested form of cognitive access is 'allowing pupils to explore ideas and try things out before committing themselves to the final outcome'. An example is using word processors that allow redrafting and editing before deciding to print off the final version. Finally, cognitive access can be helped by 'presenting information in small quantities that can be easily assimilated'. This might involve using talking book or CD-ROMs presenting manageable pieces of information, often enhanced with pictures, video clips, animation, spoken commentary or music.

An important distinction emerges between access to *information* and access to *learning* (Woodward and Ferretti, 2007, p. 445). Access to information may not be the same as access to learning. Technology may allow access to print for a pupil with reading disorder by transforming the printed word into the spoken word. But this does not enable the pupil to learn to read print. The educator needs to be clear when technology is being used to aid access to information and take steps to make sure that learning is also taking place. Technology is a tool to assist learning. It does not ensure that learning takes place. Despite potential pitfalls, this classification of technology may be used as an audit of existing equipment and as an indication of gaps in equipment and provision.

Relationships Between Technology and Special Education

In the United States, the *Individuals with Disabilities Education Act 1990* (Public Law 101-476) states that students with disabilities should have access to assistive technology equipment and related services. The federal mandate in the reauthorization of the Individuals with Disabilities Education Act (IDEA) was to consider assistive technology when planning the individual education plan of every pupil.

But it may not be always recognized that there is a case for using technology. It may be easier to recognize opportunities to use technology to aid learning in certain circumstances more than in others (Edyburn, 2006, p. 21). It may be easier to see the need to use technology, where a pupil has an obvious physical disability perhaps sustained after an accident than if the pupil has reading difficulties that have persisted over a long period. Edyburn maintains that educators may continue to expect achievement in reading from a child, ' . . . using the same visual, perceptual and cognitive functions as everyone else, despite a plethora of data that points to an impairment in those organic systems' (ibid., p. 22). Where there is a specific incident such as an accident that creates difficulties, it is clearer when to intervene than when a child fails to progress over a long period, for example, in reading. In the first case, there is often an obvious need for different ways of doing things including the consideration of assistive technology. In the second instance, there is no obvious moment when such reconsideration takes place.

Even where the role of technology is recognized, its use may still not be optimal. An important consideration is the 'interface' between the user and the technology. Where a child has a prosthetic appliance, the fitting, comfort and easy use of the appliance are self evidently important. The importance of other interfaces may not be as immediately clear. Where a piece of technology is intended to improve the communication of a child with profound cognitive impairment, the child must be able to understand it at some level so that its use quickly becomes part of his repertoire. Any skills necessary to use a device need to be taught. Allowances and adjustments will need to be made if the child has a condition that leads to changes in skills or requirements such as a debilitating condition or a disability/disorder that varies from day to day. This suggests regular evaluations and adjustments.

The contribution of technology to special education can also be understood with regard to remediation and compensation (Edyburn, 2002 passim and 2006, p. 22). Remediation includes such approaches as extra tuition time and using different instructional approaches, perhaps informed by breaking a task into very small steps to ascertain the point at which understanding or skill breaks down. Where such steps fail to have the desired impact or have very little effect, compensation may be used to help the pupil reach the required levels of performance. The decisions about remediation versus compensation need not be an 'either–or' dilemma. The judgement can be seen as a sort of balance in which estimates are made about the proportion of time that might be optimally spent on each and this can be adjusted over time depending on the progress the pupil makes (ibid., p. 22).

As the cost of technology reduces and its capacity increases, ICT is increasingly available to support pupils in schools in all areas. However, there may be room for debate about how fairly support is provided in different geographical areas and in poorer and more affluent areas of a particular country. Such measures as the number of pupils per computer (expressed as a ratio) provides a start in examining this issue. But within the school an assessment of the perceived requirements of different pupils and their particular access is also important. A pupil by pupil audit, updated regularly, is one way of gathering the basic information needed to help ensure that resources are being matched to what pupils require to develop and progress.

Also important is the access of pupils to ICT at home and elsewhere. Here a divide of access is more likely between poorer and more affluent families and between families who may be confident in using these technologies and those who may not. Schemes exist whereby schools and local school boards/local authorities provide help with these technologies either through grants or through loaning or providing equipment. A catalyst for such developments is likely to be the increasing use of portable equipment with wireless connections enabling pupils to have access to information (from the school's intranet resources or the Internet) from home and elsewhere.

More broadly, the relationships between technology and special education appear rather different from many other foundational aspects of special education. Social theories seek to explain how disabilities/disorders come to be seen the way they are (Shakespeare, 2006), while Vygotsky's ideas (Carton, [various dates]/1993) suggest how disability/disorder might influence overall child development. Neuropsychological approaches endeavour to find links between neurological findings and psychological states to inform the understanding of disability/disorder and possible interventions (Hale and Fiorello, 2004). By apparent contrast, technological approaches seem to focus on ways of providing practical help and widening the control an individual has over his environment. But technology can also help the understanding of disability/disorder.

For technology to be developed, the function it is seeking to assist or replace generally has to be well analysed and understood. If computer software is to be effectively used to assist writing for a pupil with disorder of written expression, the nature of the pupil's difficulty needs to be carefully examined first. It is necessary to identify the areas of particular difficulty and the points where the process breaks down. Then the type of information or structure likely to help the pupil has to be worked out. Next the assistive technology is tried and progress monitored to see if it is effective, with modifications being made if it is less effective than anticipated. Pupil case conferences, resource planning, auditing and institutional planning all form part of this approach.

Similarly, supports for movement and posture for a child with orthopaedic impairment are put in place after a thorough professional assessment of the difficulties and what can be best done to alleviate them or compensate for them. This is likely to involve an assessment made by specialists such as a physical therapist and an occupational therapist and others including technicians. Such interventions at the cognitive level or at the physical/motor level require a deep understanding of the nature of the difficulty and an equally thorough understanding of the capabilities of the technology that is likely to assist. It will be seen that the use of suitable technology is not just a practical and pragmatic process. It also requires that cognitive process and physical capabilities are analysed and better understood.

The relationships between technology and special education appear to be secured in legislation. Yet opportunities to use technology to benefit pupils with disability/disorder may be missed or may not be used optimally. A balance between remediation and compensation is sought. As the cost of suitable technology decreases in many applications, issues about its fair allocation persist. While the use of technology may seem essentially practical and pragmatic, it can inform understandings of disability/disorder too.

The Range of Applications of Technology

General points The range of applications of technology considered in the following section relates to different types of disability/disorder, as do the subsequent sections in which fuller examples of the use of technology are examined. Focusing on types of disability/disorder can be particularly helpful.

The teacher needs to reflect upon the likely implications of a disorder/disability, the particular characteristics of the individual pupil and the general requirements of all pupils. For a pupil with autism, communication, social skills and flexibility in behaviour are likely to be particularly difficult. The factors that are often common to the disorder/disability are considered also with factors particular to the individual pupil to provide a picture of his relative strengths and weaknesses.

The teacher might consider what particular skills and abilities require help and support. In looking at the range of support that can be provided by technology, the teacher and others look at whether technology offers the right sort of solutions. If it appears it might, then they can proceed to a more specific consideration of potentially suitable technology. The purpose of using the technology and the expected benefits of its use are kept to the fore. Once the technology is introduced, the school monitors and evaluates its impact to help ensure that the expected benefits are being achieved. If they are not achieved the situation is reconsidered.

Related to this is the potential for refining the applications of technology as more becomes known about the implications for learning of particular disabilities/disorders. If a profile of processing difficulties is identified in relation to reading disorder, this can inform the support provided by technology. Should phonological impairment be a factor in the pupil's reading difficulties, then technology that supports the pupil in blending and segmenting sounds and gives him plenty of practice and success can be helpful.

If visual tracking is a problem in reading some material and then writing notes, technology can compensate. The teacher can ensure that whatever she writes on a classroom white board is reproduced on a laptop computer beside the pupil. This recognizes that tracking from the nearby laptop to the note-taking paper is easier than tracking from the distant whiteboard to the paper. The laptop computer screen can also be positioned at an angle approaching the horizontal so it is on the same plane as the pupil's writing surface, making any copying or note-taking easier.

A focus on the processes of learning rather than concentrating too closely on the eventually desired outcome may contribute towards teaching that is more sensitive to what the pupil can already do and understand. This in turn could be more likely to lead to the desired learning outcomes. Care is taken that this does not develop into a fragmented concentration on component processes obscuring the point of what is being learned.

Types of disability/disorder Considering the applications of technology in terms of the type of disorder/disability can act as an audit of what a school provides. It may be especially useful where a school, ordinary or special, educates pupils with a range of disorders/disabilities. The review of technology refers to the type of disorder/disability, not to any purported 'type' of child, so that where a pupil has several disorders/disabilities, the best use of technology is considered in the particular pupil context. Such a review can be supplemented by other kinds of audits mentioned earlier to ensure that all suitable uses and benefits of technology are being exploited (qualities of technology, curriculum requirements and access).

The following is a list of disorders/disabilities for which technology is used:

- cognitive impairment
- health impairment
- traumatic brain injury
- hearing impairment
- reading disorder
- disorder of written expression
- mathematics disorder
- developmental coordination disorder
- difficulties with language comprehension.

Where a pupil has *cognitive impairment*, making choices an aspect of communication may be encouraged by using a switch-activated reinforcer. The educator may prompt the pupil to use switch activation or/and discrimination between different choices (Ware, 2005, p. 73). Multiple microswitches can enhance different responses in children with profound cognitive impairment. The wider range of response opportunities and the more differentiated input from the environment lead to higher levels of responding (Lancioni *et al.*, 2002). For an activity in school or beyond, a digital still camera or video camera can be used to record events and very soon after the activity images can be transferred to a computer and projected.

For pupils with profound cognitive impairment who may not have developed an understanding of symbolic communication, this may not 'get across' what the teacher assumes. The teacher or other adult will need to observe the pupils' responses to try to determine what the images seem to be conveying. This is because the images are a form of symbolic communication that the student may not recognize or understand. For pupils with profound cognitive impairment and for pupils with moderate to severe cognitive impairment, multi-sensory environments have been a part of provision, often in the form of a sensory stimulation room. These aim to provide a user-friendly setting. These rooms may include devices that respond to touch or sound by producing sounds or visual effects. There may be an optikinetics projector, a glass fibre optic light tail and a transmitter of sound effects or music. Drawing on behavioural principles, this may encourage responses from pupils who are reluctant to respond to other forms of environmental stimulation. The rooms may help pupils to relax if they are under stress. However, schools do not always use such provision critically and the supposed benefits to development and well-being need to be evaluated to ensure that they are a reality.

Health impairments include a wide range of conditions and levels of severity. Pupils educated in hospital who may be reluctant to move from the ward to the classroom following an operation may be helped by videoconferencing facilities. This can enable a pupil to communicate with staff and pupils and have some experience of the classroom environment and activity. Hospital schools have developed 'virtual classrooms' to increase the opportunities for a pupil to interact with other pupils and work collaboratively. Internet projects in hospital education can help pupils keep contact with the 'outside' world and to obtain materials to support their course work (Department for Education and Skills, 2001a, p. 37).

For a pupil with *traumatic brain injury*, resources may include adaptive equipment such as a wheelchair (which may be used temporarily or for some activities and not others) and environmental modifications. Technology may be used to help manual dexterity. Depending on the exact nature and consequences of the traumatic brain injury, resources associated with orthopaedic impairment may be used.

For *hearing impairments*, various aids are available. A conventional hearing aid comprises of a microphone to receive sound, an amplifier and a receiver to transmit signals from the amplifier to the ear. Hearing impairment often affects certain frequencies more than others and the hearing aid does not differentially rectify these frequencies but amplifies all equally.

As well as conventional hearing aids, radio aids are also employed (Pagliano, 2002). A radio aid consists of a microphone and a transmitter that are worn by the speaker and a radio receiver worn by the listener. The speaker's voice is picked up by the microphone and converted into a radio signal, which is broadcast to the receiver tuned to the suitable frequency. Radio aids work effectively despite any background noise in the classroom and have enabled pupils with hearing impairment to be educated in an ordinary school classroom.

An induction loop system may also be used. The teacher wears a microphone, which sends out signals that are amplified and passed round a wire loop, which goes round the classroom. However, it tends not to encourage communication between the pupil with hearing impairment and other pupils; and there may be silent points in the classroom. A cochlear implant involves surgery to implant electrodes on or in the cochlea and fit an external receiver in the temporal bone (Turnbull *et al.*, 2002) and their fitting has been subject to ethical debate (Stewart and Ritter, 2001).

Regarding *reading disorder*, computer software that supports reading is employed. For a pupil who is unable to independently read his text-books, text-to-speech software enabling him to listen to information 'read' by the computer and other aids may be used. These include ReadPlease (www.readplease.com), Kurzweil 3000 (www.kurzweiledu.com) and Read and Write Gold (www.texthelp.com) (Edyburn, 2006, pp. 23–25 for information about software to help with memory, reading, writing, mathematics and current events). Materials such as printed lessons and computer activities associated with particular programmes may be used. Printed or computer-displayed symbols may be employed. To help with organizational difficulties that may be concurrent with reading disorder or may be related to problems with memory, technological reminders from simple mobile telephone triggers to web-based reminder services through e-mail or telephone messages can help.

Among technological resources used for *disorder of written expression* is computer software to help with essay structure. Where graphical symbols are used the relevant resources are required. The extent of structuring the task of essay writing and the degree of prompting can be varied from pupil to pupil and as the individual pupil progresses over time.

Should a pupil experience *mathematics disorder*/dyscalculia, computational difficulties can be compensated for using web-based support such as WebMath (www.webmath.com) (see also Edyburn, 2002, pp. 23–25). For 'low achieving adolescents', CD-ROMs were used to enliven practical mathematical problems such as purchasing food and building an animal cage from spare wood. The project included practical calculations and problem-solving culminating in building an animal cage (Bottge *et al.*, 2003). While such projects are innovative in their use of technology, it is difficult to separate the contribution of technology to achievement because of its use as a background facilitator (Woodward and Ferretti, 2007, p. 444).

For a pupil with *developmental coordination disorder*, aids to more fluent writing include pencil grips and illuminating pens (that light up either when writing pressure is excessive or insufficient) (Farrell, 2008b, p. 265).

Where there are disabilities relating to *language comprehension*, the teacher might employ visual aids. She might encourage the pupil to use other sensory channels of communication to supplement the usual mode of auditory comprehension. For some pupils signing boards may be used to enable kinaesthetic and visual memory to supplement comprehension. Communication boards and computer technology can therefore be useful here.

Fuller Examples of the Use of Technology

The chapter next examines fuller examples of the use of technology applied to the following:

- visual impairment
- orthopaedic impairment
- speech disorder.

Although it is not a type of disability/disorder, challenging behaviour is also considered.

Visual Impairment

The earlier 'Legal and typological' chapter pointed out that the term visual impairment indicates a continuum of loss of sight, which usually includes blindness. Blindness is defined in different ways, in part depending on the user and the purpose of the definition (Sardegna *et al.*, 2002, p. 28). In the present context, 'blindness' refers to a level of sight loss of children who depend mainly on tactile methods of learning, while 'low vision' is used in relation to children whose education involves predominantly sighted methods. Technology helps children using mainly tactile and those using predominantly sighted methods. For a student with visual impairment, applications of technology include the following:

- lighting
- low vision devices
- storage of and access to information.

Ensuring correct *lighting* is assisted by technology. Lighting blinds, louvres and tinted glass are used to control natural light and dimmer switches to adjust artificial ambient lighting. The school will need to ensure that lighting does not produce glare and should control artificial and natural lighting so the level is suitable for various classroom areas. As well as ambient lighting around school being important, so is task lighting to maximize the use of the pupil's near vision while studying. The type of visual impairment influences what is considered to be suitable illumination: while some pupils will prefer higher levels of illumination, those having photophobia require reduced lighting.

Turning to *low vision devices*, those most suitable for a pupil are determined through consultation that is likely to involve the child, parents, an optometrist, a specialist teacher of the visually impaired and a specialist in rehabilitation. Magnification can be achieved by increasing the size of the image of the object; decreasing the working distance to the object; and increasing the visual angle – perhaps a multi-lens device such as a telescope. Equipment includes various magnifiers, spectacle-mounted devices, telescopic devices and closed circuit television. For closed circuit television, a television camera is fitted to a movable table and connected to a video display monitor.

Using resources to aid *rapid and efficient access to information* is an important aspect of study skills and a way of gaining greater independence. Study can be made easier and more manageable if a tone indexing facility on audio recordings is used. CD-ROMs offer quick access to information through synthesized speech or large character displays. The technology can be supplemented by non-technological ways of ensuring a pupil has easy access to work he has produced. The pupil can have a series of easily labelled files for different areas of study, keeping work on numbered pages.

Computer technology allows a pupil with visual impairment to write an essay by speaking it into a computer. It offers access in several ways, through sight (e.g. using a magnified or large print), hearing (e.g. speech synthesis) and touch (e.g. converting conventional print text into Braille).

To gain access to information from Internet sites, the content is downloaded onto the computer and then read by a screen reader using speech synthesis, magnification or Braille. Optical character machines and scanners enable the pupil to read from printed text by translating it into synthesized speech. CD-ROMs with electronic or spoken versions of the same text and CD-ROM writers and recorders are available. Specialist tape recorders used by pupils with visual impairment include multi-track models with speed control, voice indexing facility and control switches with tactile markings. Through a tone indexing facility, signals can be inserted onto a tape and heard when the tape is rewound or fast-forwarded. Pocket memo recorders may have such a tone indexing facility and may be voice activated. Digital software such as the Digital Accessible Information SYstem (DAISY) (www.daisy.org) and MP3 are increasingly used. A talking computer or calculator can help with calculations.

Mobility can be assisted by technology. Electronic travel aids (used by about 1% of visually impaired people) include electronic canes, devices held in the hand, or mounted on the chest or head, spectacles or on a wheelchair. They require special training to be used safely and effectively. The main principle is that the equipment emits light beams or ultrasound waves that contact objects in the person's path. The device then emits a sound or vibrates. They may use the world-wide positioning system, a digital map database and a digital compass (Sardegna *et al.*, 2002, p. 77).

For further information, please see Mason and McCall, 1997; Farrell, 2008b, the chapter on 'Visual impairment' and various entries in (Sardegna *et al.*, 2002).

Orthopaedic Impairment and Motor Impairment

As described in the earlier chapter 'Legal and typological', an orthopaedic impairment may be regarded as a severe impairment adversely affecting the child's educational performance. In the United States, the Code of Federal Regulations definition recognizes impairments caused by 'congenital anomaly' 'disease' and 'other causes' (34 CFR, section 300.7 [c] [8], 1999). Under this definition, the term 'orthopaedic' includes neuromotor impairment.

The use of technology and other resources for children with orthopaedic impairment as broadly defined often requires guidance from a physical therapist or occupational therapist or other specialists. Below, technology is considered in relation to the following:

- environmental access
- environmental control
- supports for physical aspects of academic tasks.

Environmental access includes ensuring better access to classrooms and other facilities. This may involve wheelchair access ramps and continuous areas of smooth floor surfaces to enable movement, while corridors and other routes need to be free of clutter to allow easy access. Manual or powered wheelchairs may be used or toys such as a hand-propelled wheeler can be used as aids to mobility (Bigge *et al.*, 2001, pp. 206–208, 211–212). The iBOT powered wheelchairs, using self-balancing technology, are designed to climb stairs that have a handrail and where the user has a strong grip, by rotating two sets of powered wheels about each other. They allow travel over uneven terrain and sandy beaches and the user can position himself to be at the same eye level as a standing person of typical height. Computerized architectural simulations of a school building have been used for pupils in wheelchairs to help them 'experience' the layout of a school and plan and practice routes through the school before trying them out in reality.

Environmental control may involve the use of appliances such as electronic communication devices. Home lighting may be operated in various ways including electrically, by infrared, radio control or ultra sound. Switches operated by different movements and pressures can increase the individual's control of surroundings. Environmental control in a broader sense includes being able to manipulate objects in the environment including day-to-day equipment. In what Finnie (1997, pp. 127–160) presents as an aspect of 'object modification', the pupil may have his own set of equipment for various school subjects and activities and some of these may be modified. In food preparation lessons various technological aids may be employed: a kettle-tilting device to ensure safer pouring of hot liquids; food choppers adapted to be used with one hand; a cooker with special controls and sinks and cooking surfaces adjustable to different heights. Some of these items improve safety as well as enable tasks to be managed.

Support for physical aspects of academic tasks can be varied. For pupils who have difficulties with the physical task of writing, the pupil may use predictive writing software to reduce the amount of time he has to spend on the mechanics of word processing. Outside lesson times, for example, for homework or other independent work, speech-to-text software may be used supplemented by student training to get the best results. Telephone dictation services may also be bought, where the student dictates his work and the operative e-mail drafts or the finished product to the pupil for checking.

In brief, technology can improve environmental access where equipment such as wheelchairs are used, especially where the environment can also be modified to aid access. It can aid control of the environment and make it safer. Technology can provide access to some academic tasks but the tension between providing access and encouraging learning arises, as has been mentioned earlier. The use of predictive writing software is an example of a compromise where the pupil still needs to use word processing skills and reading and writing skills and learn new ones but does not have the physical grind of word processing everything.

Speech Impairment

Communication disorders can be considered as difficulties with speech, grammar, comprehension, semantics (meaning) and pragmatics (language use) (Farrell, 2008, pp. 197-241). Language and speech are not of course synonymous terms. Language can take the form of writing or signs as well as speech. In this context, speech has been defined as 'the mechanical aspect of communication' and 'the ability to produce the words, sounds and phrases' (Thompson, 2003, p. 10). Speech difficulties arise where communication is impaired by the child's capacity for speech perhaps because of physical difficulties with articulation; difficulties making the sound contrasts that convey meaning; or difficulties controlling pitch. (For a fuller discussion of speech disorders and provision for them please see Farrell, 2008, pp. 197–212.)

Where a child has very severe communication difficulties of which speech difficulties are an aspect, dedicated communication devices may be used. The term 'dedicated' indicates that these devices are used with the key purpose of communication and the software and hardware are designed with features that are essential for communication. Communication systems may consist of a computer with input options, communication software and a speech synthesizer. The system may speak programmed messages when the pupil activates locations marked by symbols.

Symbols may also be used as a form of communication using electronic or non-electronic devices. Among commercially available symbol sets are Widget Literacy symbols (www.widget.com) and Blissymbols (www.blissymbolics.us). The term symbol usually refers to a system of graphic communication, with each symbol standing for a concept such as an object or activity. With all symbol use, care is needed to ensure that the pupil makes the link between the real and intended object, activity or person and the symbol, as, although some symbols may seem obvious, they may not be so to a child. Non-electronic equipment includes communication grids in which several symbols can be set out, for example, in a sequence to indicate a sequence of activities. But electronic devices allow greater capacity and flexibility in such devices.

For children with speech impairments and motor difficulties there are particular considerations to be taken into account when symbols are used. To ensure communication is as effective as possible, educators need to consider the following:

- how the child will indicate a selection (pointing, using a head stick, eye pointing, light pointing);
- the vocabulary content available;
- the output method

(Bigge *et al.*, 2001, pp. 242–250).

It will be seen that technology can offer alternatives when speech is very severely impaired. The pupil can operate devices that produce simulated speech or can indicate graphic symbols to communicate. But the pupil still needs to have the motivation to communicate. He needs the cognitive ability to be able to grasp the abstract nature of symbols. He also needs to be able to physically operate the equipment.

Conclusion

This chapter has used a wide definition of technology and considered its relationships to special education, the scope of the application of technology and fuller examples of its use. Technology of many kinds can be indispensable in some areas of special education. Whether aiding physical movement, allowing greater control of the environment or enabling better access to the curriculum, the effective use of technology is an essential aspect of provision. Nevertheless, the teacher needs to critically view technology to ensure it is being used where it can best enhance learning, access to learning and development.

Thinking Points

Readers may wish to consider the following:

- the child's capabilities and functions that the use of technology is seeking to assist;
- the different forms of technology and their application to enable educational progress and help personal and social development;
- the extent to which pupils with different types of disability/disorder can benefit from particular types of technology;
- how technology audits can help ensure that a comprehensive, effective range of technology is provided.

Key Texts

Abbott, C. (Ed.) (2002) *Special Educational Needs and the Internet: Issues in Inclusive Education*. London: Routledge-Falmer.

This text covers in its several parts the gathering and publishing of information; communication with others and policy and management issues. Many contributors are teachers or resource providers, providing the book with a strong practical orientation.

Bigge, J. L., Best S. J. and Heller, K. W. (2001) (4th edn) *Teaching Individuals with Physical, Health or Multiple Disabilities*. Upper Saddle River, NJ: Merrill-Prentice Hall.

This book includes many examples of the use of technology for pupils with physical disabilities and health impairments.

Cockerill, H. and Carrollfew, L. (2007) *Communicating without Speech: Practical Augmentative and Alternative Communication for Children*. New York: Blackwell Publishing.

Intended mainly for health professionals such as speech and language pathologist/therapist, this book is also relevant for other professionals including teachers. It concerns children who do not develop adequate speech because of complex neurological conditions or learning disabilities and may require alternative and augmentative communication systems.

Edyburn, D., Higgins, K. and Boone, R. (Eds) (2005) *Handbook of Special Education Technology Research and Practice*. Whitefish Bay, WI: Knowledge by Design Incorporated.

Concerns research and practice in special educational technology and intended for special education teachers, administrators, teacher educators, technology specialists and researchers. Includes chapters on history, law and policy; access; assistive technology; disability specific technology applications; instructional design and technology and instruction.

Hardy, C. (2000) *Information and Communications Technology for All*. London: David Fulton Publishers.

This assumes an England context. Chapters include ones on curriculum access; evaluating software; and carrying out an ICT assessment.

Judge, S. L. and Parette, H. P. (1998) *Assistive Technology for Children: A Guide to Family-Centred Services*. Cambridge, MA: Brookline Books.

Explains a range of assistive devices and their capabilities. Covers evaluating children's requirements; selecting and providing devices and training children, parents and the teacher to use the technology.

Mason, H. and McCall, S. with Arter, C. McLinden, M. and Stone, J. (1997) (Eds) *Visual Impairment: Access to Education for Children and Young People*. London: David Fulton Publishers.

Includes chapters on 'Low Vision Devices for Children and Young People with a Visual Impairment', 'The Preparation of Raised Diagrams', 'Access through Technology' and (with reference to pupils with multiple disabilities and visual impairment) 'Educational Technology'.

Sardegna, J., Shelly, S., Rutzen, A. R. and Steidl, S. M. (2002) (2nd edn) *The Encyclopaedia of Blindness and Vision Impairment*. New York: Facts on File Library of Health and Living.

In A to Z format, this book covers issues and topics relating to blindness. It includes medical, educational, economic and legal information. There are many entries on adaptive aids. Appendices such as lists of companies and federal agencies assume a mainly US readership but suggested Internet sites are internationally accessible.

Internet Resources

www.nectac.org/topics/atech/bibliography.asp
This site leads to a 'Selected Bibliography of Articles and Books on Assistive Technology'. NECTAC is the National Early Childhood Technical Assistance Centre. It is a programme of the FPG Child Development Institute at the University of North Carolina at Chapel Hill, NC. (FPG is named after Frank Porter Graham, a past president of the university.) The institute is a multidisciplinary centre for studying young children and their families.

12

Pedagogical

This chapter first explores the nature of pedagogy and provides examples. It then examines pedagogy in relation to special education, in particular, the issue of distinctive pedagogy for different types of disability/disorder. The scope of pedagogy for special education is considered with reference to a wide range of disorders/disabilities. Fuller examples are examined for mild cognitive impairment and moderate to severe cognitive impairment.

The Nature of Pedagogy

If the school curriculum, the 'what' of education, sets out the knowledge, skills and attitudes it is intended a school will convey and encourage, then pedagogy is taken to refer to the methodology or the 'how' of teaching. Pedagogy is what the teacher plans and carries out, in the classroom and elsewhere, to promote and encourage pupils' learning. It is, 'the *way* in which the content of education, whether it is the knowledge, skills or attitudes, is learned by the pupil and taught or facilitated by the teacher' (Farrell *et al.*, 1995, p. 4, italics added).

Pedagogy may involve the teacher emphasizing certain sensory modalities in presenting information (or encouraging the pupil to use particular sensory modes in communicating or responding). A child who is blind may write in Braille, communicating in a medium interpreted through touch rather than sight. A pupil with moderate to severe cognitive impairment may find information presented visually easier to understand and remember than information presented orally (Farrell, 2008b). In learning to read, a child with Down's syndrome, who has difficulty with short-term auditory memory, may find that a visual icon or pictogram helps make a connection enabling the child to link letter sounds to letter names. Also, the partly visual activity of learning to read may help reinforce and encourage language skills (Alton, 2001).

Pedagogy may involve approaches distinctive to a particular disability/disorder such as 'Structured Teaching' used with children with autism. This is an aspect of Division Treatment and Education of Autistic and related Communication handicapped CHildren (TEACCH) (www.teacch.com), a programme used in the state of North Carolina and elsewhere for people with autistic spectrum disorders and their families (Schopler, 1997). Within this programme, Structured Teaching is 'designed to address the major neurological differences in autism' (Mezibov and Howley, 2003, p. 8). It involves organizing the classroom to reduce visual and auditory distractions, consequently helping the child focus and ensuring that the teaching process and teaching styles are suitable. Visual information is used to make things more meaningful and to encourage learning and independence. The main purpose is to 'increase independence and to manage behaviour' (ibid., p. 9) by adjusting the child's environment, taking into account the cognitive skills, needs and interests of pupils having autistic spectrum disorder.

Pedagogy in special education may emphasize an approach used also with children who do not have a disorder/disability, for example, having a slower pace in lessons for pupils with mild cognitive impairment. Related to this, teaching that appears qualitatively different for pupils with disorders/disabilities is sometimes considered a variation on a continuum of teaching strategies characterized by 'more intensive and explicit teaching', representing the 'greater degree of adaptations' to common teaching approaches used with all children (Lewis and Norwich, 2005, pp. 5–6). In providing examples to learn concepts, such as 'big' and 'small', a more intensive version might provide many different examples while emphasizing what is distinctive about them whereas the low-intensity version might provide few. Although this view questions presenting such approaches dichotomously, it recognizes that teaching 'geared to pupils with learning difficulties might be inappropriate for average or high attaining pupils' (ibid., p. 6).

In brief, pedagogy may be depicted as follows:

01.   emphasizing particular sensory modalities or using alternative sensory modalities;

02.   using approaches different to those used with most children;

03.   using approaches similar to those for all children but with a particular emphasis or intensity.

Examples of Pedagogy

Referring to work reported as early as 1898, Thorndyke ([[1911]/1965]/ 1965) discusses 'explanation, imitation and actual performance' (ibid., p. 149) and later suggests that all learning can be divided into 'learning by trial and accidental success', 'learning by imitation' and 'learning by ideas' (ibid., p. 174).

A more recent attempt to delineate aspects of pedagogy was undertaken by Tharp (1993, pp. 271–272). In the context of an interpretation of Vygotsky's zone of proximal development (ZPD), these approaches were seen as ways of bringing the pupil's performance through the ZPD, enabling independent capacity. The seven means were as follows:

01.   modelling
02.   feedback
03.   contingency management
04.   instructing
05.   questioning
06.   cognitive structuring
07.   task structuring.

Modelling in this context involves another person providing some behaviour for the pupil to copy. The pupil sees the way the teacher has performed, remembers it and uses it as a benchmark to reach. *Feedback* is a process of the teacher (or facilitator) giving the pupil information about how he is doing compared with the required performance. It enables the pupil to compare his present attempts with the standard required and to correct himself to move closer to the benchmark. As the pupil becomes able to provide his own feedback the process of self-correction can be more ongoing.

Contingency management refers to the application of principles of behaviour management to modify behaviour using rewards, punishments, the withdrawal of expected rewards and other techniques. *Instructing* entails asking for a particular action. The teacher might request the pupil in workshop making a dovetail joint to mark out the wood as part of a sequence. In this way, in a situation in which the pupil knows how to carry out some parts of the overall task, the teacher points out the correct behaviour, provides necessary information and aids in decision-making.

Questioning involves the teacher asking the pupil for a verbal response and requires the pupil to carry out a mental operation that he might not have done unaided. It also gives the teacher information about what the pupil does and does not know and his level of understanding. *Cognitive structuring* entails explaining. The teacher helps provide wider structures of cause and effect, interrelation, belief systems or other frameworks to help the pupil organize the new learning and integrate this with what is already known.

Finally, *task structuring* refers to shaping a task into components. This may include chunking together information such as dividing a sequence of numbers, for example, a telephone number to be memorized into groups of three numbers. Sequencing implies finding an order for what is to be learned that facilitates learning, for example, a chronological sequence for learning a skill. Segregating suggests separating information to make it more manageable and learnable. Such strategies modify the task so that the parts of it are within the ZPD even if the task as a whole is not.

Part of the meaning of pedagogy is instructional methods. Algozine and Ysseldyke (2006a, pp. 38–48) identify several that are used for pupils with disorder/disability. They are as follows:

01. behaviour therapy
02. precision teaching
03. ability training
04. direct instruction
05. cognitive behaviour modification
06. cognitive skills training
07. critical thinking
08. counselling therapy
09. learning strategies
10. cooperative learning
11. peer directed learning.

While *behaviour therapy* is mentioned by Algozine and Ysseldyke (2006a, p. 38) they refer mainly to operant conditioning. *Precision teaching* consists of small steps of teaching and assessment with behavioural underpinnings. *Ability training* refers to training in the abilities that contribute to broader skills. Visual tracking from left to right may be taught to improve reading performance in languages such as English that are read in that direction. *Direct instruction* includes attack strategy training. *Cognitive behaviour modification* includes self-statements to improve performance. A pupil who is easily distracted may memorize and be regularly encouraged to use a script such as, 'Am I paying attention?'

Cognitive skills training consists of the knowledge, comprehension and application, analysis, synthesis and evaluation. *Critical thinking* includes approaches such as comparing and contrasting the veracity of sources of information and coming to reasoned judgements about information and beliefs. *Counselling therapy* refers to client-centred therapy, for example, intended to help pupil's application and self-esteem. *Learning strategies* embrace such elements as mnemonics to aid memorization.

Cooperative learning might, for example, involve three or four pupils, each with pieces of information necessary to complete a task, who therefore have to work closely together to be successful. *Peer-directed learning* might include peer tutoring or class-wide peer tutoring, where pairs of pupils in a whole class take turns to be teacher or pupil for a session, for example, to help each other learn facts or tables.

Pedagogy in Special Education

(a) The question of distinctive pedagogy

It is debated whether for different types of disability/disorder, distinctive types of pedagogy can be identified. A start to considering this issue may be made by revisiting the outlines of pedagogy provided by Tharp ((1993)) and by Algozine and Ysseldyke (2006a).

Of the seven ways of facilitating learning suggested by Tharp (1993, pp. 271–272), perhaps all except contingency management can be immediately associated with all children whether or not they have disability/disorder.

Of the 11 examples of instructional methods suggested by Algozine and Ysseldyke (2006a, pp. 38–48) many are used with pupils who do not have a disability/disorder. For example, direct instruction, critical thinking, cognitive skills training, learning strategies, cooperative learning and peer-directed learning may be found in everyday classroom activity.

Ability training, working on apparent component skills, while it might be used with pupils finding particular difficulties with learning, is not employed only with pupils having disability/disorder. Similarly, counselling therapy in the sense used by Algozine and Ysseldyke (2006a, pp. 38–48) referring to client-centred therapy may be used with pupils including those with a disability/disorder for various reasons.

Precision teaching using small steps of teaching and assessment with behavioural underpinnings is more likely to be used where a pupil has considerable difficulties with learning that may involve the identification of a disability/disorder.

Behaviour therapy referring mainly to operant conditioning is used in a structured way with some pupils with disabilities/disorder, for example, pupils with conduct disorders.

Cognitive-behavioural approaches, what Algozine and Ysseldyke (2006a, pp. 38–48) call cognitive behaviour modification, is used with some children not having disability/disorder but may be used more intensively with pupils with disorders.

If one attempts to draw from the pedagogies suggested by both Tharp (1993, pp. 271–272), and Algozine and Ysseldyke (2006a, pp. 38–48), those that appear particularly distinctive for pupils with disabilities/disorder, two approaches emerge. The first is contingency management, an essentially behavioural approach. Precision teaching may be considered as a particular application of such an approach although it does have other elements. The second approach is a cognitive-behavioural one.

(b) Pedagogic principles and types of disability/disorder

Another way of approaching the question of distinctive pedagogy for pupils with disability/disorder is through seeking pedagogic principles. Lewis and Norwich (2005, passim) consider ways in which children may be considered to have needs common to all learners, needs unique to themselves (a unique differences position) and needs that may be shared by an identified sub group such as those with disability/disorders (a general differences position). Focusing on two positions relating to difference, (the general difference position and the unique difference position), they question the usefulness of some groupings of pupils with disability/disorder in relation to 'pedagogic *principles*' (ibid., p. 216, italics added).

In their *general difference* position, group-specific needs of pupils with disability/disorder are brought to the fore although needs common to all learners and needs unique to individual learners remain important. The *unique difference* position emphasizes differences unique to a particular child, de-emphasizes common pedagogic needs and rejects the notion of group-specific needs. As well as by definition, having needs common to all children, learners are regarded as also being uniquely different. Differences between individuals are accommodated in terms of personal uniqueness and their dependence on social context. Common pedagogic needs are approached through general principles that enable individual variations to be possible within a common framework (Lewis and Norwich, 2005, pp. 3–4).

In Lewis and Norwich's edited volume, different contributors considered whether differences between learners, by disability/disorder, could be identified

and linked with the learner's needs for differential teaching. Contributors
nized a general differences position (acknowledging group-specific differ
for the following:

- autistic spectrum disorder;
- attention deficit hyperactivity disorder;
- deafness;
- visual impairment;
- profound and multiple learning difficulties/profound cognitive impairment.

A more individual differences position (rejecting group specific differences)
was preferred for the following:

- deafblindness;
- severe to moderate cognitive impairment/ severe learning difficulty;
- communication disorders/ speech, language and communication needs;
- dyslexia/ reading disorder;
- social, emotional and behavioural difficulties;
- moderate learning difficulties/ mild cognitive impairment (pp. 215–216).

'Down's syndrome' and 'low attainment', not distinctively identified in
American or English special education classifications, were also considered.
Possibly prematurely, given that a general difference position was supported for
5 of the 11 disabilities/disorders often considered in classifications, Lewis and
Norwich (2005) conclude, 'the traditional special needs categories . . . have
limited usefulness in the context of planning, or monitoring, teaching and
learning in most areas' (p. 220).

Perhaps it is not surprising that a group difference position was not held
for such a broad and amorphous group as 'behavioural, emotional and social
difficulties' (although attention deficit hyperactivity disorder was considered
separately). This includes children and young people experiencing disruptive
behaviour disorders, anxiety and depression. Once these are considered separately, a case can be made for group difference position for each. It can also
be argued (Farrell, 2008b, passim) that a 'group difference position' can be
maintained for other types of disorder too, and not only for pedagogy but also
for wider provision.

Of course, this is not to suggest that common needs and unique needs are
not considered in developing pedagogy. For children with a disability/disorder
some approaches may be common to all children, some especially effective
with children with the disorder and some approaches for particular children

with the disorder that may be individual to them. Neither does it imply that some elements of approaches that appear to work well with children with a certain disorder as a group as it were may not always be unsuitable for other children, although sometimes they may.

If children with mild cognitive impairment learn effectively where the curriculum level is significantly below that followed by typical children of the same age, where lessons are slower in pace and where concrete learning is emphasized beyond what is age typical, it does not follow that this profile of provision is suitable for all children who do not have mild cognitive impairment.

(c) Evidence-based practice

To the extent that types of disability/disorder and elements of distinctive provision can be brought together, this relates to evidence-based practice.

An enactment of the *No Child Left behind Act 2002* in the United States is that all students including those with disabilities will perform at a proficient level on state academic assessment tests and will demonstrate annual progress. Evidence-based practice clearly can inform efforts to meet these sorts of aspirations, although identifying, implementing and evaluating effective, valid practices is very challenging.

Simpson (2005), in examining evidence-based practice specifically in relation to autism, makes points pertinent to disability/disorder more broadly. In best practice, products and materials will be validated through research using random samples, control groups and experimental groups and peers will review evidence (ibid., p. 141–2 paraphrased). But where there are 'limited student samples, heterogeneous clinical education programmes, and the need for flexibility in matching research designs to specific questions and issues . . . ' (ibid., p. 142), other methods such as single subject design validation or correlational methods may be appropriate.

Also, families and professionals have to decide on the suitability of an intervention or approach for a particular child looking at different alternatives. They will need to consider the efficacy and anticipated outcomes for a particular intervention. Specifically, they may consider whether the anticipated outcomes are conversant with the pupil's needs, the potential risks (including risks to family cohesion of long-term, intensive interventions) and the most effective means of evaluation (Simpson, 2005, p. 143 paraphrased).

The Scope of Pedagogy in Special Education

Profound cognitive impairment For learners with profound cognitive impairment, pedagogy is supported by the learning environment being organized and routines being finely tuned so that they encourage and are responsive to the smallest signs of interest and responsiveness on the part of the pupil. Through the use of multi-sensory methods, the teacher aims to stimulate the pupil's senses and provide a range of experiences that, over a period of time, may come to have coherence as a sequence or as part of a wider whole. Participating in preparing a snack and being encouraged to use all the senses, the pupil may in time come to comprehend the parts of the experience as a sequence leading to the food being ready to eat (Farrell, 2008b, Chapter 2). Approaches to communication draw on research into and experience of early infant communication such as eye contact and turn taking (e.g. Nind and Hewett, 2001). To communicate well, the adult communication partner needs to be sensitive to the child's smallest response. Such child responses might, through the adult's own response, become invested with communicative intent. Task analysis approaches are used and for some young people with profound cognitive impairment, community-based vocational training skills may be developed.

Sensory impairment There is debate about the relative merits of oral, sign, bilingual and total communication methods for pupils with hearing impairment, and approaches to communication reflect this. Preferences for oral or sign bilingual methods also influence literacy teaching. In the teaching and learning of mathematics, presentational order, early emphasis on counting, avoiding potential confusions and where deaf children have spatial strengths, making best use of this are important (Stewart and Kluwin, 2001).

For children with visual impairment, pedagogy involves teaching mobility and orientation; tactile representation and hands on experience; teaching the pupil ways of securing rapid access to information; developing speaking and listening in the context of very limited or absent visual cues, aids to self-help and independence skills; reading using tactile approaches such as Braille and writing using tactile code (Koenig and Holbrook, 2000; Mason *et al.*, 1997).

Regarding deafblind children, structured opportunities to interact with others, the environment, objects, places and activities are provided. Specialist approaches are used to encourage and develop communication and include co-creative communication, resonance work and co-active movement. Non-symbolic communication is developed using reflexive responses, signals, and place or object cues. Symbolic communication is encouraged through objects of reference, tactile symbols and Moon script, manual sign language and communication books (Aitken *et al.*, 2000; Smith and Levack, 1997).

Disruptive behaviour disorder, attention deficit hyperactivity disorder, anxiety and depression For children aged 3 to 10 years with disruptive behaviour disorders, classroom contingency management can be effective (Barkley *et al.*, 2000). While many behavioural interventions led to benefits such as showing less aggression, such approaches have not been shown to generalize to other settings or to continue beyond the end of the programmes concerned. Teachers can work with therapists and also aid the development of personal and social skills and self-control through what they teach and how they teach it. Approaches can draw on or use programmes such as an 'Anger Coping Program' for aggressive children including sessions such as 'using self-instruction', 'perspective taking', 'choices and consequences' and 'steps for problem-solving' (Lochman *et al.*, 2003). Another school-based strategy, 'Coping Power' (Lochman and Wells, 1996) involves primary school children with conduct problems reviewing examples of social interactions and discussing social cues and motives. It appears social skills training and anger management coping skills training can help reduce *mild* conduct problems in pre-adolescents (Quinn *et al.*, 1999 provide a review). Similarly, teachers can contribute to helping children develop interpersonal problem-solving skills, perhaps informed by such approaches as problem-solving skills training (PSST) developed from the work of Spivak and Sure (1978).

For adolescents with conduct disorder, various interventions may be used. Among school-based interventions is Gang Resistance Education Training (GREAT), which has shown significant effects (Esbensen and Osgood, 1999). Law enforcement officers taught a 9-week curriculum to middle school students that included exercises and interactive approaches intended to underline the consequences of gang violence. Activities taught goal setting, conflict resolution and standing up to peer pressure. Participating students had lower levels of self-reported delinquency and gang membership than a comparison group. It is probably too simplistic, given the multiple causes of conduct disorders to expect direct links between school-related variables and delinquency. Yet the school is an important setting for programmes for conduct disorder and delinquency and there may be potential for drawing on school-based mental health resources to modify the school environment to change characteristics associated with delinquency (Fonagy *et al.* 2002, p. 171).

For children with attention deficit hyperactivity disorder, effective responses include optimum breaks and a supportive structure in the classroom and a classroom layout that reduces potential distractions. It is important there are clear routines, clear instructions and guidance; and active, experiential learning is also helpful. Social skills teaching and the development of compensatory skills are used (Weyandt, 2007).

Regarding anxiety disorders, provision includes therapy which teachers need to be conversant with and support. Certain cognitive-behavioural therapy (CBT) packages have effectively treated children's generalized anxiety disorder and other anxiety disorders (Toren *et al.*, 2000). For depression, again therapy is an important part of provision and teachers need to be aware of the therapy and be supportive of it. Interventions such as CBT for adolescents with depression can be effective, when any depression experienced by the young person's mother is also treated (Fonagy *et al.*, 2002). Such interventions for adolescents tend to be effective for mild depression but evidence is less compelling for interventions for more severe depression whether in children or adolescents. More generally, for pupils with anxiety or depression, teaching methods can contribute to developing a calm ethos. The curriculum and organization of the school in support of teaching and learning can offer opportunities for pupils to communicate openly and with trust, and there may be more formal arrangements for counselling by trained teachers or others.

Communication disorders In pedagogical provision for phonological disorders, broad approaches are employed to raise phonological awareness, and specific programmes are also deployed. Error analysis and articulation exercises and individual task-based programmes are used. For some pupils, communicating through methods other than speech is necessary, for example, using signs and symbols (see Farrell, 2008b, Chapter 14 for fuller details).

Difficulties with syntax and morphology are provided for by sentence recasting (Fey and Proctor-Williams, 2000, p. 179), elicited imitation and modelling (Bishop and Leonard, 2000, Chapter 10). Also helpful is ensuring that teacher communication is clear and straightforward, without being stilted. Where the child has problems with auditory memory, auditory sequencing, attention and reading and writing, remediating work is undertaken. In parallel, the teacher can more directly help the pupil improve grammatical skills and understanding.

Difficulties with comprehension are helped by teaching in modes to maintain the pupil's attention and providing reminders; explicitly teaching the pupil's listening behaviour; reducing processing demands; supporting (through discussion and explanation) pragmatic understanding and sensory and other aids.

Allowing sufficient time to respond helps ensure that comprehension can be checked (Ellis Weismer and Schrader, 1993).

Regarding semantic difficulties, to take just one aspect, children having labelling difficulties may benefit from individual tutoring to enable making links between the spoken word and the object or other phenomena; explicit teaching to direct attention to an object or event being labelled and explicit teaching and structured experiences to encourage recognition of object permanence (for further details, see Farrell, 2008b, Chapter 13).

Pragmatic difficulties are helped by providing basic skills and knowledge; providing models of grammatical cohesion devices; teaching and practizing indications of speakers' intentions; and conversational skills building (MacKay and Anderson, 2000).

Autistic spectrum disorder Approaches used for pupils with autism include 'Structured teaching' (Mezibov and Howley, 2003), which includes organizing the pupil's classroom to reduce visual and auditory distractions to help the child focus and using visual information to help make the environment more meaningful and encourage independence. The Lovaas programme (Lovaas, 1987 and the Lovaas Institute for Early Intervention [www.lovaas.com]) draws on principles of applied behavioural analysis and uses behavioural approaches to both teach skills and reduce unwanted behaviour.

Discrete trial teaching (Committee on Educational Interventions for Children with Autism, 2001), a structured and therapist-led intervention, involves breaking behaviour into smaller parts, teaching one sub-skill before moving on to another, shaping required behaviours until they are securely learned and prompt fading. Reinforcement is directly related to the task.

Developmental coordination disorder With regard to developmental coordination disorder, focuses for provision have been handwriting, including help with posture and pencil grip/pressure and assisting eye–hand coordination for writing; multi-sensory approaches to improve form consistency and strategies for teaching the writing of letter shapes (Dixon and Addy, 2004). In physical education, which can be daunting for a pupil with developmental coordination disorder, the teacher and physiotherapist may work together to develop suitable activities, and lessons can be planned to enable the participation of the pupil. Practical strategies and aids are developed to improve personal and social skills. Adapted clothing can be worn to allow quicker changing for sports and other physical activities.

Disorders of reading, writing and mathematics For *reading disorder*, strategies often relate to purported underlying difficulties: phonological difficulties, visual difficulties and visual processing difficulties; auditory perception and auditory processing difficulties; short-term verbal memory difficulties and sequencing difficulties (relating to temporal order). As well as working on associated difficulties, interventions directly tackle reading often through teaching phonological skills necessary for using a phonemic code, and sound–symbol correspondences (Swanson *et al.*, 2003).

Provision for disorder of *written expression* and problems with *spelling*, includes remediating sequencing and improving coordination skills for handwriting. Cursive script can be taught and there are suggestions of the possible sequence in which letters might best be taught (Pollock *et al.*, 2004). For writing composition, approaches may be frameworks for writing, reducing task demands, note taking, and writing for a purpose. Spelling provision uses multi-sensory aspects, directed spelling thinking activity (Graham *et al.*, 2000), repetition and target words.

Provision for *mathematics disorder* focuses on prerequisite skills and how they may be taught as well as on general interventions. Other strategies draw on the influence of related conditions, particularly developmental coordination disorder and reading disorder (Westwood, 2000, 2003).

Orthopaedic impairment, health impairment and traumatic brain injury Pedagogy for pupils with *orthopaedic impairment* is not in itself distinctive from the pedagogy for children not having a disability/disorder. However, the teacher and others need to use and understand resources that help the pupil gain access to the curriculum and learning activities. Educators will work closely with the physical therapist and the occupational therapist. Comfortable correct positioning and supports that enable this are important. Hoists and other devices may be required for the safe moving of the student. Tables and other surfaces such as cookers may have adjustable heights. Object modifications may be needed, for example, to ensure boundaries and that the items can be handled (Bigge *et al.*, 2001, passim).

The impact of *health impairments* other than orthopaedic impairments can differ from time to time because of variations in the condition. Different demands of the curriculum or the child's peer group also have an effect. The child's educational provision consequently has to respond to changes in the child's physical and motor abilities and be sensitive to effects of the medical condition including physical and psychological ones. Particular requirements arise for certain conditions such as, for a child with epilepsy, having a structured framework and routine in which to locate information to help the student with processing information (Clay, 2004).

Among teaching and learning approaches for a child with *traumatic brain injury* are using routines and clear instructions and other means to help with the pupil's attention and helping the pupil remember, for example, by presenting information several times to allow the pupil to rehearse it more. Texts used for teaching and other materials can be simplified where the child has visual perception problems. Requirements for written work might be reduced and extra time allowed for its completion. Self-talk can be taught to help the child control impulses and self-monitoring can be encouraged (Schoenbrodt, 2001; Walker and Wicks, 2005).

Fuller Examples of Pedagogy: Mild Cognitive Impairment

Mild cognitive impairment is a contested type of disability/disorder in part because it is not always clear to what extent there is cognitive impairment and to what degree the child is responding to a perhaps cognitively impoverished environment. Although this is probably the most difficult impairment for which to argue that there is a specific pedagogy, a case can still be made that there is, and that the wider provision in which teaching and learning are set is distinctive too. These contexts for learning and wider provision include the curriculum, resources, therapy and classroom organization.

The context of learning for children with mild cognitive impairment is set by the curriculum which has content typical for pupils several years younger but chosen in a form that is appropriate to the chronological age of the pupil with moderate to severe cognitive impairment. The curriculum tends to be the subject based with a particular emphasis on subjects that are of central importance themselves but also allow fuller access to other areas of the curriculum. These core areas are English/literacy; speaking and listening; mathematics/numeracy; computer use/information and communications technology; and personal, social and health education. The focus on these may be achieved by allocating more time in the curriculum and also by ensuring that elements of them are tracked into other subjects. For example, in food preparation, mathematics may be planned into an activity so that weighing ingredients and timing the cooking provide practical applications of and opportunities to put into practice mathematical skills and knowledge.

The curriculum relates strongly to pedagogy in that it emphasizes concrete, participatory and practical activities. Complex concepts are presented in smaller parts but taking care that learning is not therefore fragmented. A spiral model in which topics are revisited at a more complex level is sometimes used. Assessment is conversant with the curriculum because it is in small enough steps to ensure that progress is recognized.

Organizationally, pupils may be taught in smaller groups to allow extra attention and encouragement and this may be in a mainstream school, in a unit within a mainstream school or in a special school.

Therapeutically, to the degree that pupils with mild cognitive impairment have communication disorders, the support of a speech and language pathologist/speech therapist may be necessary, as well as practical approaches to help communication outlined in subsequently. Learners with mild cognitive impairment may also experience conduct or mood disorders. In such instances, strategies that can be effective with these disorders can help. For children aged 3 to 10 years with disruptive behaviour disorders, social skills training and anger management skills training (Quinn *et al.*, 1999 provide a review), problem-solving skills training (Kazdin and Wasser, 2000) and classroom contingency management are among provisions found to be effective. Cognitive-behavioural programmes have been used with pupils with general anxiety disorder (Toren *et al.*, 2000). Behavioural interventions and cognitive-behavioural therapy have been used with phobias (Ollendick and King, 1998 provide a review).

Turning to pedagogy directly, speaking and listening is developed using practical experiences such as taking in different settings and to different people. Role-play may be used to practise appropriate forms of social address and social skills of conversation such as turn-taking and showing an interest in what others are saying. Given the concrete nature of the understanding of children with moderate to severe cognitive impairment, it helps to have real objects to talk about and discuss, so when talking about diet, the presence of real food or at least pictures of items being discussed helps as far as is practicable. More abstract topics such as freedom can be started by looking at concrete examples/pictures of people or animals that are free and those that are not in the latter case, for example, people in prison or battery-fed hens.

Also, difficulty with abstract concepts can be lessened if the teacher and others use concrete objects and examples to illustrate points. In history, plenty of visual aids and artefacts and physical reflections of time such as time lines can be helpful. In geography, visits to see land formations and features coupled with plenty of visual aids such as films and objects will enable concepts to be better grasped. The regularity and intensity of such underpinning is likely to be much greater than for pupils of a similar chronological age.

Literacy can be aided through interventions such as 'Phonological awareness training' (evaluated in Brooks, 2002, p. 106; Wilson and Frederickson, 1995). This uses a pupil's existing knowledge of letter sounds and words so in reading and spelling new words containing identically written endings present less of a difficulty. 'Reading intervention' (Hatcher, 2000) has also been evaluated with pupils having mild cognitive impairment/moderate learning difficulties and uses a combination of phonological training and reading (Brooks, 2002, pp. 38–9, 110). Pupils are helped to isolate phonemes within words to enable them to recognize, for example, that certain letters can represent specific sounds.

In mathematics, concrete and visual apparatus can be helpful (Panter, 2001). This might include measuring real liquids, classifying real objects, using real money and measuring real areas for a purpose such as a carpet or garden. From such structured experience, the pupil gradually comes to be able to think concretely by visualizing items, for example, visualizing the order of the height of three people when told their height, relative to one another in pairs.

Where there are concurrent difficulties with communication, the involvement of a speech and language pathologist/therapist may be necessary. Approaches that are generally used with pupils having communication difficulties are drawn on as necessary. Where there are pragmatic difficulties interventions such as the *Social Use of Language Programme* (Rinaldi, 2001) has been used to encourage the communication skills of young people with mild cognitive impairment.

To help develop social and personal skills and understanding, programmes may be used to practise and encourage these. With small groups of pupils with mild cognitive impairment, to help improve social and personal skills, Cornish and Ross (2003) used techniques such as rehearsal, modelling and reinforcement to teach students to use speech (internal and external) to influence their behaviour. The programme also taught suitable social behaviour and problem-solving skills.

Self-regulatory approaches involve the teacher providing encouragement and structures to enable pupils to develop and evaluate their problem-solving strategies. The work of Borkowski and colleagues (2006) indicates that self-regulation is considered fundamental to most learning problems of individuals with cognitive impairment. They often do not use strategies efficiently, or who may not suitably generalize newly acquired strategies, perhaps because of immature forms of self-regulation. The context and choice of classroom tasks may help increase the self-regulatory functioning of pupils with cognitive impairment. Small group work appears to facilitate children's active monitoring better than teacher-directed instruction (Stright and Supplee, 2002). The teacher or parent may show the child self-monitoring skills and he may practise these using role-play, applying them with support and encouragement at home and at school and elsewhere.

Because pupils with mild cognitive impairment tend to have difficulties with generalizing knowledge and skills (Meese, 2001), it helps if the teacher ensures that material to be learned is relevant to pupil's daily life and routines. This can enable new learning to be consolidated because its application is repeatedly practised. If the pupil has practised using money in role-play, regular opportunities to use the skill on shopping trips or visits can help consolidate the knowledge and generalize it to different situations.

Fuller Examples of Pedagogy: Moderate to Severe Cognitive Impairment

Pedagogy for pupils with moderate to severe cognitive impairment is set in the context of a curriculum that takes account of the pupil working at a content level typical of pupils considerably younger. Whereas the curriculum for pupils with mild cognitive impairment tends to be subject based, that for pupils with moderate to severe cognitive impairment tends to be typified by 'functional academic content' (Wehmeyer with Sands *et al.*, 2002, pp. 190–203) and its areas may not coincide with that of usual curriculum subjects. Care is taken that the content however is presented in ways that are appropriate for the pupil's chronological age.

Communication is likely to be closely related to and built on day-to-day requirements. Functional literacy may include learning to read and understand short newspaper cuttings, signs such as those for well-known shops and social signs and symbols such as those for toilet, pedestrian road safety signs, danger signs and others. Functional writing may include writing a note for shopping, listing things that need to be done during the day, or writing an e-mail (see also Algozzine and Ysseldyke, 2006, p. 38–41). Similar functional approaches tend to be taken for areas such as numeracy, personal and social education, leisure pursuits, health care, potential occupational tasks and so on. Using local transport, using community facilities, shopping, cooking, using a restaurant, orientating oneself in a comparatively new geographical area and other practical activities are also part of the curriculum. Developing an understanding of the roles of others in the local community in a practical way (for example by meeting them) is also important.

Assessment is in small steps to ensure that progress is recognized and acknowledged. Assessments are made across different areas of learning and this is related to cross-curricular planning that ensures that skills and understanding are developed coherently and systematically. For example, a mathematical skill such as telling the time is reinforced and eventually assessed in different contexts such as timing oneself in a physical activity, planning a trip, getting somewhere on time, checking the activities during the day and so on. To help ensure learning is generalized, assessments may be made with different adults, in different places and at different times of the day and in different circumstances.

Many countries use curriculum-related assessments and/or standardized assessment of various aspects of attainment and development. In England, curriculum-related assessments are available to recognize progress below level 1 of the National Curriculum, the so-called 'P' scales (performance scales) (Qualifications and Curriculum Authority, 2001a, 2001b, 2001c). These assess progress that is typical of a child working below the age of 5 years and are used where much older pupils are still working at these levels. Commercially available packages may be used for more detailed assessments.

Turning to pedagogy directly, where pupils with moderate to severe cognitive impairment do not have visual impairments, provision may capitalize on visual input.

The classroom can be organized so the best use is made of pupils' senses of sight (and hearing). The classroom can be arranged so pupils can notice and respond to visual cues and the teacher may need to keep this in mind as the day progresses and furniture may be rearranged for different activities.

A pupil with moderate to severe cognitive impairment may have difficulties with phonological awareness (awareness that relates speech sounds to changes in meaning); problems with auditory memory, and hearing impairment. In such instances, approaches to literacy using whole word sight recognition, including the use of graphical symbols, are preferred to ones using phonological methods.

Butler and colleagues (2001) in reviewing strategies for teaching mathematics, found that for students with moderate mental retardation, predominant approaches involved structured direct instruction. Numeracy teaching can also capitalize on visual strengths using real life contexts and encouraging problem-solving, especially where the pupil has poor auditory memory.

For children with Down's syndrome it has been suggested that where the pupil has difficulty with short-term auditory memory, an icon or pictogram can aid connections, enabling the child to link letter sounds to letter names. Also, teaching reading may help reinforce and encourage language skills (Alton, 2001). Where there are particular difficulties linking sounds and written marks, whole word approaches use the possibly stronger visual skills of pupils by linking the sight of the whole word with the spoken response.

Where manual signing is used, this also can use the strengths of visual input and has the benefit that the adult can help and modify incorrect signs visually/three dimensionally.

Children with severe cognitive impairments tend to have limitations in their expressive communication skills (Mar and Sall, 1999). It is important the school setting encourages the child to communicate through such means as daily structure, like a brief arrival greeting session, snack times and recess activities, group activities and paired activities.

A behaviour interruption strategy (Carter and Grunsell, 2001) may be judiciously used to encourage communication. This involves first establishing a secure routine for an activity between the pupil and adult. Then later the routine is interrupted in a way that requires the pupil to communicate to re-establish it. Once the pupil has responded, the routine continues. Routines that the pupil enjoys tend to be used such as making a snack or completing a construction.

Alternative and augmentative communication may be used. A range of skills and knowledge is necessary for such systems to work and an assessment may be made to ensure that these are in place or can be achieved. These include linguistic skills such as learning what pictures and symbols mean and combining symbols into sentences; technical skills for operating the communication system, such as the layout of symbols; knowledge and skills in social rules of interaction; and skills to communicate effectively beyond the limits of competence in augmentative and alternative communication (Light, 1989).

Alternative and augmentative communication may include the use of pictures, symbols, signing, speech synthesizers and objects of reference. Visual symbols use visual input and are often used in connection with computer technology. Symbols are used to support emerging literacy (King-de Baun, 1990). They can be used so they relate to language sequencing skills (as pupils select and place the symbols in order), and for reading and writing. A communication aid speech synthesizer having a bank of words and the flexibility to create new words or a device such as a 'BIGmac', which enables short phrases to be programmed into it, allowing a pupil to participate and respond may be used.

'Talking mats' are one way of supplementing alternative and augmentative communication (www.speechmag.com/archives). A textured mat on which various card symbols can be attached and three sets of symbols concerning 'issues', 'emotions' and 'influences' are used. The pupil can indicate which symbol is intended in various ways including, if he has a physical impairment, eye pointing. Quite a variety of communication can be achieved through the innovative and flexible use of these symbols. Different halves of the mat can be headed by a smiling face and a frowning face and beneath them the pupil can indicate and sort things and experiences he likes and dislikes.

Developing autonomy and independence is clearly central. This has been alluded to with regard to practical activities and functional learning of community and other skills. Routine is important for making sure learning is secure and as a foundation to build on learning experiences. However, choice provides important opportunities to do things differently, to explore and to assert independence. Choices can be offered throughout the school day, in snack times, when alternative activities are available for leisure, when there is a choice of adult or other pupils with whom to work and so on. After deciding the nature of the weather, the pupil can choose clothing to wear before going out for recess and see the consequences of the choices made.

More complex decision-making can be encouraged and the pupil's processes of thinking can be explored, so both the adult and the pupil himself become more aware of them. The pupil can be asked to complete several tasks during a work period but be given the choice about the order in which they will be completed. Having chosen, the adult can explore with the pupil the basis of the choices. Were favourite activities chosen first or saved until last? Were short activities that are easier to complete interspersed with longer, more complicated ones? These leads can contribute to an understanding of time planning and study skills.

Without making the choices and decision-making too planned and defeating the object, the teacher can, from time to time, assess the range of opportunities for choices both offered by the school and taken up by the teacher. A matrix can be made listing the opportunities for choices in a typical day (or a particular day) and the extent to which the pupil has used them. Scheduled activities can be listed down on one side (numeracy, visit to library) and the range of choices across the top (e.g. chooses between two items, decides with whom to work).

Children with cognitive impairment tend to have difficulties using strategies for remembering and monitoring their performance (Henry and Maclean, 2002). Copeland and Hughes (2002), reviewing several studies, considered the effects of encouraging and guiding pupils' goal/target setting on their performance. Giving the pupils information on the accuracy of their performance was an important factor in the success of the approaches. Pupils were often reminded of their targets or given an indication of their progress through visual cues.

Various kinds of support and therapy may be provided for areas of development such as physical development, where the physical therapist and/or the occupational therapist may be involved in assessing, working with the teacher and others and acting in a consultancy role. A speech and language pathologist may contribute to help with phonological difficulties and other aspects of language development.

It is suggested that most people with *moderate* cognitive impairment tend to be able to benefit from training in social and occupational skills (American Psychiatric Association, 2000, p. 43). Individuals with *severe* mental retardation tend to profit to a limited degree from teaching in 'pre-academic subjects' like 'simple counting' and can learn skills such as basic social sight-reading (ibid., p. 44). McDonnell *et al.*, (1993) in a study relating to vocational instruction indicated significant student gains for high school students with 'moderate to profound mental retardation'. Accordingly, the school can provide and arrange a variety of work placements for pupils. It can also contribute to better workplace skills through helping the student develop skills such as following directions, being punctual, staying on task and completing assignments. These can be directly taught as well as encouraged in settings where they are put into practice (Algozzine and Ysseldyke, 2006b, p. 49–50).

Conclusion

Given the nature of pedagogy and its role in special education, especially in relation to special pedagogies for different types of disability/disorder, it is perhaps expected that the scope of its application is wide. The fuller examples of mild cognitive impairment and moderate to severe cognitive impairment indicate difference in types of disability/disorder often considered very similar.

Thinking Points

Readers may wish to consider the following:

- the extent to which within the context of providing for learning needs common to all children and unique needs for a particular child, distinctive pedagogy can be articulated for different types of disorder/disability.

Key Texts

Algozzine, B. and Ysseldyke, E. (2006a) *Effective Instruction for Students with Special Needs: A Practical Guide for Every Teacher*. Thousand Oaks, CA: Corwin Press.

Part of a series but focusing on issues relating to teaching and learning for students with disability/disorder.

Algozzine, B. and Ysseldyke, E. (2006b) *Teaching Students with Mental Retardation: A Practical Guide for Teachers*. Thousand Oaks, CA: Corwin Press.

Part of a series and concerns teaching and learning for students with mental retardation.

Farrell, M. (2005a) *The Effective Teacher's Guide to Dyslexia and Other Specific Learning Difficulties*. New York and London: Routledge.

This covers reading disorder/dyslexia, developmental coordination disorder/dyspraxia, and mathematics disorder/dyscalculia.

Farrell, M. (2005b) *The Effective Teacher's Guide to Moderate, Severe and Profound Learning Difficulties*. New York and London: Routledge.

This book concerns moderate learning difficulties (mild cognitive impairment), severe learning difficulties (moderate to severe cognitive impairment) and profound learning difficulties (profound cognitive impairment).

Farrell, M. (2005c) *The Effective Teacher's Guide to Autism and Communication Difficulties*. New York and London: Routledge.

The book focuses on autism, difficulties with speech, difficulties with grammar, difficulties with meaning, difficulties with the use of language and difficulties with comprehension.

Farrell, M. (2005d) *The Effective Teacher's Guide to Sensory Impairment and Physical Disabilities*. New York and London: Routledge.

Concerns visual impairment, hearing impairment, deafblindness, physical and motor disability and medical conditions.

Farrell, M. (2005e) *The Effective Teacher's Guide to Behavioural, Emotional and Social Difficulties*. New York and London: Routledge.

With regard to behavioural, emotional and social difficulties, the book considers systems, cognitive, behavioural and psychodynamic approaches and examines provision for attention deficit hyperactivity disorder.

Norwich, B. and Kelly, N. (2004) *Moderate Learning Difficulties and the Future of Inclusion*. London: Routledge Falmer.

Considers broad issues concerning moderate to severe cognitive impairment/moderate learning difficulties including justifications for and limitations of this category. It looks at studies and perspectives relating to inclusion and 'moderate learning difficulty'.

Wehmeyer, M. L. with Sands, D. J., Knowlton, H. E. and Kozleski, E. B. (2002) *Providing Access to the General Curriculum: Teaching Students with Mental Retardation.* Baltimore, MD: Paul H Brookes.

This text offers a functional model and a 'supports' view of cognitive impairment. It examines a universal design for the curriculum, individualized learning and personalized planning.

13

Conclusion

The conclusion chapter reminds readers of the definition of special education and its aims and methods in relation to foundational disciplines. It summarizes and reflects upon the contributions of the various foundations including for identification and provision. The chapter considers interrelationships between the foundations, reflecting the theme of multidisciplinary understanding and practice.

Special Education and Progress and Development

Special education was earlier stated to refer to distinctive provision, including education, for pupils with disability/disorder. It is informed by a range of foundational disciplines and encourages academic progress and personal and social development (Farrell, 2001a, 2005f). Indeed, it would be rather odd to envisage educational progress and better personal and social development (and evidence of these) not being the touchstone of any education system. Special education has identifiable aims and methods.

Among the aims of special education mentioned in the introduction to this book with regard to pupils with disability/disorder was 'identifying foundational disciplines that contribute to promoting learning and development' and 'ensuring that elements of provision informed by these foundations promotes the learning and development'.

The methods of special education included refining existing approaches that work and developing promising approaches drawing on aspects of evidence-based practice and using inductive and deductive strategies (Farrell, 2008b, passim). However, considering disciplines and perspectives underpinning special education and critically examining their relevance for provision and understanding was also important. This is in part what this book has attempted to do.

The Foundations

This book attempted to show the relevance aspects of certain disciplines to contemporary special education and how they contribute to the understanding and practice of special education. Eleven of these 'foundational' areas as listed under were examined:

- legal/typological
- terminological
- social
- medical
- neuropsychological
- psychotherapeutic
- behavioural/observational
- developmental
- psycholinguistic
- technological
- pedagogical.

Legal/Typological In considering legal and typological matters, it was suggested that the context of the legal framework of a particular country strongly influences what is understood by 'special education'. Examples of the systems in the United States and England illustrated such frameworks. However, legal structures and definitions and guidance provided by government and others also delineate different types of disability/disorder. The considerable overlap between the frameworks in the two countries considered indicates that there can be much agreement on this matter. However, differences also arise, for example, the inclusion of traumatic brain injury in the US framework but its absence as a specific category in the English structure.

In addition, types of disorder may be categorized and understood differently as suggested by attention deficit hyperactivity disorder being considered a health impairment in the United States and as a behavioural, emotional and social difficulty in England. It may be that the typology currently used in a particular country changes over time, as new information leads to different ways of seeing disability/disorder. Autism, Asperger's syndrome, semantic-pragmatic disorder and related conditions are now commonly grouped as 'autistic spectrum disorders'.

Variations in typology from country to country and within one country over a period of time help remind researchers, professionals and parents that attempts to delineate disability/disorder are not sacrosanct but challengeable and modifiable. Although typologies are necessary to help ensure provision is suitable, it cannot be assumed that at any one time the best possible understanding of the parameters of conditions has been ascertained. While legal and typological frameworks describe the current understanding of disability/disorder, they can also circumscribe understanding. They can appear as though they are the only and final way to see the field, which they are not.

Terminological Examining the language of those involved in an activity or profession or anyone of a range of what are sometimes called 'discourses' can be revealing. It is perhaps hardest to recognize the effects of the language that one lives with as part of one's profession or everyday life. The Biblical caution about seeing a mote in someone else's eye and missing the beam in one's own is all too painfully accurate. Awareness of connotation, the under-/overextension of terms and more broadly, conceptual analysis can help those involved in special education to both clarify matters and to be critical of the field. In day-to-day work and activities, attention may not always be paid to the concepts and assumptions within special education. Yet to examine and challenge these from time to time can be fruitful, leading to greater understanding and clarity.

Sometimes analysis serves not just to sharpen clarity but also to probe areas where there may be crooked thinking. When educators and others speak of 'meeting needs', the implications of an adult deciding the child's supposed needs are not always recognized. The adult's judgement may or may not be correct. It may project supposed needs onto a child that are merely what the adult thinks ought to happen. It may be patronizing to the child and his parents. If the sometimes hidden implications of terms are questioned, it may lead to a more honest appraisal of what different people, including the child, think ought to happen in his education. In such contexts, clarifying terms can lead to different actions.

Social Social perspectives of disability/disorder and of special education at their most penetrating can assist recognition of the contribution of within child factors, environmental factors and the interaction between the two. For educators whose daily work involves arranging the environment of the child to enhance learning, such insights are not always new. At their least insightful, however, social views of disability/disorder seem to be as blinkered as the caricatures of the 'medical model' they often criticize. Solely social explanations of disability/disorder can be as unconvincing as purely individual explanations (if ever such explanations were proffered).

Medical Medical foundations of special education interrelate with education in a complex manner. The medical care and medication that is deemed necessary influence the work of the teacher in several ways. It may require close working with medical personnel. The teacher and others may need training and advice to fully understand the implications of medical conditions and the implications on the curriculum, learning, behaviour, classroom organization and other matters.

Traumatic brain injury is an example of where this is essential. It is appropriate that there is debate about the possible overuse of medication and discussion of the consequences and alternatives. Social perspectives of treatments can be particularly helpful here, for example, in discussions of the possible social pressures that might be influencing the increasing use of medication for children with attention deficit hyperactivity disorder.

Neuropsychological The basis on which neurological and psychological assessments and explanations are built repays critical consideration. One reason is that neurology and psychological work related to it can seem seductively revealing. It might appear that the techniques involved are simply opening a window on the activities of the brain that is as uncomplicated as it is accurate. But this is not so. Careful scrutiny of neuropsychological evidence is necessary to weigh up the implications of findings. Yet findings from neuropsychology can be illuminating so long as these limitations are borne in mind. For example, a wide range of evidence informs the theory that reading disorder is related to phonological processing deficits. This evidence is being subjected to careful criticism and scrutiny.

Psychotherapeutic Psychotherapeutic contributions to special education are perhaps most evident in relation to disorders of conduct, anxiety, depression and other psychosocial disorders. Attempts have been made to relate psychotherapy to neurological findings. Among implications for educators is that they liaise closely with colleagues who deliver psychotherapy so that education and therapy are harmoniously linked in provision. In addition, educators may need training to understand the aims and advantages as well as the limitations of therapy better. Similarly, therapists need to understand and support teaching aims. Potential for extending common ground is evident in similar approaches, for example, the use of behavioural techniques such as token economy in the classroom and in behavioural approaches to therapy.

Behavioural/Observational Tensions exist in learning theory in relation to special education. There are understandable reservations about explanations of human learning and development that seek to focus so strongly on behaviour. Yet empirical evidence indicates that in some situations and with some conditions, behavioural approaches are effective. The success of cognitive-behavioural approaches in psychotherapy suggests that the behavioural element is important. Nevertheless, the approaches of observational learning and modelling may be more convincing to practitioners who have reservations about behavioural explanations.

Developmental The close relationships between typical and atypical child development and special education are evident in general child developmental frameworks and in the relevance of genetic epistemology. The work of Piaget and Inhelder and others subsequently has provided a framework in which normal development can be understood and further examined. The judicious reference to this framework when considering the development and learning of children with cognitive impairment continues to provide insights for special education.

Psycholinguistic Psycholinguistics brings together evidence from psychology and linguistics as well as neurology. In examining or inferring processes of communication in relation to perception, storage, access, retrieval and output, psycholinguistics offers the opportunity to identify where communication difficulties occur. The focus therefore is not only on the outcomes but also on how the outcomes might be explained and remediated with reference to underlying processes. Trying to identify relative weaknesses and strengths in the process of communication also opens up the possibility of harnessing strengths to help with weaknesses. However, the interrelated nature of the parts and aspects of communication militate against identifying difficulties directly and simply with processing problems without carefully testing hypotheses.

Technological Technological foundations relate to practical assessments and interventions to extend the learning, mobility and capabilities of pupils with disability/disorder. They also encourage careful reflection on the functions that are normally carried out by the body and brain that require support or alternatives provided by technology. The insights and expertise of specialists such as technicians, physical therapists, occupational therapists and others working in partnership with teachers are particularly important.

Pedagogical Pedagogy draws on other foundational areas in looking for interventions that lead to better development and learning. At the same time, it seeks its own evidence that approaches do in fact work. It cannot be assumed that because there appears to be a strong neuropsychological explanation of aspects of mathematics disorder, that this will translate directly and inevitably into successful pedagogical approaches. The pedagogical methods require testing and evaluating in their own right. Where pedagogy works in practice and where there appears to be a convincing explanation as to how it might be having its effect that draws on other foundational aspects of special education, the intervention is more credible and more likely to be effective.

Some Further Implications

A framework for understanding special education has been suggested (Farrell, 2008b, passim), which involves several areas:

- definition of the type of disability/disorder
- prevalence
- causal and related factors
- identification and assessment
- provision (curriculum and assessment, pedagogy, resources, therapy and organization).

This section examines how the foundational areas considered in this book might relate to the various aspects of this structure.

Definitions The foundational discipline of terminology can be focused on definitions to help ensure that the definition is clear and as explicit as possible. Its implications can be explored in such a way. For example, the definition of attention deficit hyperactivity disorder can be interrogated and it has been suggested that it is little more than a list of behaviours that irritate teachers (Cohen, 2006, p. 21). Social views of disability/disorder may also question the validity of a definition. Also legal and terminological aspects have clear relevance for determining definitions of disability/disorder. For some types of disability/disorder, the definition is informed by medical foundations, for example, health impairments are defined according to medical criteria. Similarly, conditions such as epilepsy are defined with reference to neuropsychological features, although there is debate about the parameters of the definitions of seizures and epilepsies. Developmental considerations are often part of definitions where a disability/disorder is described in terms of difference from expected age norms. Psycholinguistics also informs definitions of communication disorder both in the behaviours and the processes associated with conditions.

Prevalence The main foundational disciplines with regard to prevalence are similar to those concerned with definition and those involved with identification and assessment. This is for the obvious reason that prevalence is dependent on defining a type of disability/disorder clearly and then seeking to identify and assess it according to agreed criteria.

Causal and related factors Establishing the causes of types of disability/disorder often concerns trying to establish relationships between descriptions of the disorder/disability at different levels: biological, cognitive, behavioural and environmental (Morton, 2004, passim). Accordingly, medical, neuropsychological, psycholinguistic, behavioural and social foundations contribute to this. A full account of reading disorder would provide causal links at genetic, neurological, cognitive and behavioural level and would specify the influence of the environment at different levels, for example, the impact of the environment on cognitive development.

Identification and assessment It is implied in the present book that it is worthwhile and important to agree and seek to continually develop, criticize and refine a typology of disability/disorder. This might be anathema for those wishing to see categorization come to an end in an emancipatory celebration of diversity. However, it is difficult to avoid in the light of a parent wanting some kind of explanation for the confusing and exhausting behaviour of a child who is later identified as having autism. The arguments for and against classification and considerations of the provision associated with different types of disability/disorder have been touched on in this book and are considered in more detail elsewhere (Farrell, 2008b, Chapter 1).

Developments in foundational areas, for example psychotherapy, may lead to a reorganizing of the present typology of disability/disorder in some respects, for example, in the understanding of the multiple factors contributing to disorders of conduct. Subsequent work in psycholinguistics could lead to a reshaping of the ways in which various communication disorders are classified and understood, for example, the relationships between semantic-pragmatic disorder and autistic spectrum disorder. Advances in neuropsychology may help explain some of the shared underpinnings of reading disorder, mathematics disorder, disorder of written expression and developmental coordination disorder.

So far as identification and assessment of disability/disorder within special education is concerned, the foundations are influential. Legal/typological structures are an expression of the way society has agreed to delineate special education, although it is open to modification, for example, in the light of new knowledge. The recognition of particular conditions or classifications can differ in different countries as with traumatic brain injury mentioned earlier.

Terminological analysis can help clarify the concepts related to disability/ disorder generally with implications for identification. It may be recognized that parental or school 'wants' can be presented as children's supposed 'needs', leading to unfair distribution of support and funding to the detriment of pupils with disability/disorder. This might suggest that the school board/local authority is taking greater care in agreeing with parents, schools and local education personnel about the criteria relating to different types of disability/disorder.

Some social views of identification and assessment might question the identification and even the existence of some of the 'new' conditions and the apparent rise in their incidence. Also, some of the assumptions that might be made in naively individualistic perspectives are challenged.

Medical ways of identifying disability/disorder can inform special educational provision, although the links are not always direct. The influence of medical diagnosis may need to be filtered through a consideration of the implications for pedagogy. Neuropsychological identification similarly may need to be examined to see the implications, for example, of suggestions that there may be a phonological deficit in some instances of reading disorder.

Psychotherapeutic approaches have their own ways of identifying and assessing that inform treatment, as in the case of a cognitive-behavioural analysis of certain conditions and behaviours and related interventions. Behavioural and imitative views also inform identification and assessment in their own terms. Developmental frameworks and theories help set disability/disorder in the context of typical development and also provide information about atypical development. Identification and assessment operate within these parameters.

Especially in relation to communication difficulties, psycholinguistic approaches help suggest processes that may be influencing functioning and open up the possibilities of a deeper level of assessment and explanation. Technological approaches can work within a pragmatic framework where different technologies are tried and adapted to help identify more clearly the functional nature of a child's difficulties. Pedagogy can also operate in a framework of ongoing assessment of the effectiveness of approaches.

Provision Special education refers to 'distinctive provision, including education, for pupils with disability/disorder' and provision may involve the curriculum, pedagogy, school and classroom organization, resources and therapy (Farrell, 2008b, Chapter 1 and passim). Using this framework, it is possible to identify evidence-based approaches or approaches informed by professional consensus as briefly outlined in the chapter 'Pedagogical'. With regard to developmental coordination disorder, one key focus has been handwriting, including help with posture, pencil grip/pressure and assisting eye–hand coordination for writing (Dixon and Addy, 2004). In physical education, the teacher and physiotherapist work together to develop suitable activities and the lessons are planned to enable the participation of the pupil. Practical strategies and aids are developed to improve personal and social skills.

Social perspectives inform provision built on evidence and professional consensus in several ways. These include family therapy, social interpretations/interventions relating to what might otherwise be seen as within child behaviour and general systemic ways of providing support. Specifically, medical provision may be provided within school. The implications of medical conditions such as health impairments, orthopaedic impairments and traumatic brain injury affect approaches to teaching and learning.

Neuropsychological evidence influences provision in that it affects the understanding of certain conditions such as mathematics disorder and developmental coordination disorder where possible underlying processes can be supported or compensated for in teaching and learning. Psychotherapeutic methods offer their own provision and treatment and, as indicated, can inform such matters as curriculum, organization and supportive pedagogy. Behavioural and imitative perspectives influence provision quite directly in informing methods of teaching and learning as well as school and classroom organization.

Development frameworks, used judiciously, may suggest next steps or different steps of learning and development and how these might be supported. In this way they may inform the structure of the curriculum. Psycholinguistic frameworks influence provision where they indicate that possible underlying processes relating to communication difficulties are understood and are one of the foci for intervention. They may inform the structure and content of the curriculum.

Technological intervention and support are a key part of intervention for many children with difficulties/disorders. As part of the resources provided or maintained by the school, they are sometimes seen in relation to improved 'access' to the physical environment and to the curriculum. Pedagogical approaches, influenced by other foundations, are of course a central part of provision.

Interrelationships Between the Foundations

One may try to position foundations of special education in a biological–psychological–social range. In the broadest sense, legal frameworks can be seen as the expression of understandings of special education and disability/disorder and can also shape what is meant by these terms. Typological frameworks can also be seen in a similar way, although for some commentators typologies of disability/disorder may represent an over individualistic view. Such legal and typological frameworks are foundational in a particular sense, not because they represent some underlying feature of special education but because they influence and perhaps even determine perspectives of what special education comprises. This is not to imply that legal structures are insusceptible to modification or that typologies are set in stone. However, for the period they are agreed and accepted, they shape the landscape of special education.

Terminological issues permeate all levels and can lead to greater clarity in discussions of biological, psychological and social perspectives. The importance placed on clarifying language and the tacit acceptance that language can mould debate can be balanced against more prosaic attempts to ensure terms are understood better.

Social views clearly position themselves in the social part of any continuum, but more sophisticated social views take account of other foundations including biological and psychological ones. Vygotsky's work suggests that ways in biological impairments and psychological processes might interact. Multilevel explanations and the principles of multiprofessional working also suggest the importance of taking social, psychological and biological perspectives into account.

Medical perspectives tend to take a biological view, but of course medicine has for a long time been concerned with environmental influences and preventative measures relating to the environment. The psychological impact of health impairments and the effect of disabilities and disorders on psychological health and self-esteem are also recognized widely.

Neuropsychological foundations relate to specific evidence of brain activity and proposed links with psychological processes and behaviour. Psychotherapeutic underpinnings draw on behavioural and cognitive-behavioural as well as psychodynamic considerations and thus fit behavioural and psychological explanations. Attempts have also been made to relate psychotherapies to neurology.

Behavioural and imitative foundations draw on behaviour and cognition. Developmental frameworks including genetic epistemology link with biology and psychology. Psycholinguistic underpinnings draw on behavioural aspects and descriptions in linguistics as well as psychological and neurological explanations of processes related to communication. Technological foundations stem from physical and neurological understandings as well as psychological factors. Pedagogical contributions draw on several other foundational areas while requiring their own justification and evaluation.

It will be seen that, while the foundations considered in this book can be understood in relation to a biological–psychological–social continuum, attempts to place them too rigidly in that continuum misses the several ways in which they can be understood. The continued relating of these foundations in different ways is likely to lead to further insights and clearer explanations informing special education. One way of approaching this matter is to consider types of disability/disorder individually and examine the extent to which the various foundations in different combinations aid understanding and intervention. For pupils with autistic spectrum disorder, 'behavioural' foundations might be among the more relevant underpinnings.

Conclusion

Special education relates in many complex ways with the foundational disciplines considered in this book. The foundations themselves also interrelate, reflecting the theme of multidisciplinary understanding and practice.

Thinking Points

Readers may wish to consider the following:

- whether special education can be usefully represented as being underpinned by various disciplines and approaches;
- whether the proposed foundations suggested in this book are sufficiently compressive;
- the extent to which foundational disciplines contribute to understanding and developing provision for pupils with disability/disorder;
- how the various foundations might be further related and the implications for multiprofessional working and training.

Bibliography

Abbe, K., Yokoyama, S. J. and Yorifuji, S. (1993) Repetitive speech disorder resulting from infarcts in the paramedian thalami and midbrain. *Journal of Neurology, Neurosurgery and Psychiatry* **56**: 1024–1026.

Abberley, P. (1987) The concepts of oppression and the development of social theory of disability. *Disability, Handicap and Society* **2**: 5–19.

Achenbach, T. M. and Edelbrock, C. S. (1983) *Manual for the Child Behaviour Checklist and Revised Child Behaviour Profile*. Burlington: Department of Psychiatry, University of Vermont.

Adams, C., Byers Brown, B. and Edwards, M. (1997) (2nd edn) *Developmental Disorders of Language*. London: Whurr Publishers.

Adolphs, R., Tranel, D., Damasio, H. and Damasio, A. R. (1995) Fear and the human amygdala. *Journal of Neuroscience* **15**: 5879–5891.

Ahmad, S. A. and Warriner, E. M. (2001) Review of the NEPSY: A developmental neuropsychological assessment. *The Clinical Neuropsychologist* **15** (2): 240–249.

Aitchison, J. (1987) *Words in the Mind: An Introduction to the Mental Lexicon*. Oxford: Basil Blackwell Publishers.

Aitchison, J. (2008) *The Articulate Mammal: An Introduction to Psycholinguistics*. New York/ London: Routledge.

Aitken S., Buultjens M., Clark C. *et al.* (Eds) (2000) *Teaching Children Who Are Deafblind: Contact, Communication and Learning*. London: David Fulton Publishers.

Alberto, P. A. and Troutman, A. C. (2005) (7th edn) *Applied Behavioural Analysis for Teachers*. Columbus, OH: Merrill Prentice Hall.

Alexander, J. F. and Parsons, B. V. (1982) *Functional Family Therapy*. Monterey, CA: Brooks/Cole Publishing.

Alexander, J. F., Waldron, H. B., Newberry, A. M. and Liddle, N. (1988) Family approaches to treating delinquents. In: Nunnally, E. W., Chilman, C. S. and Cox, F. M. (Eds.) *Mental Illness, Delinquency, Addictions and Neglect*, 128–146. Newbury Park, CA: Sage Publications.

Alexander, J. F., Pugh, C., Parsons, B. and Sexton, T. L. (Eds) (2000) *Functional Family Therapy*. Golden, CO: Venture Publishing.

Algozzine, B. and Ysseldyke, E. (2006a) *Effective Instruction for Students with Special Needs: A Practical Guide for Every Teacher*. Thousand Oaks, CA: Corwin Press.

Algozzine, B. and Ysseldyke, E. (2006b) *Teaching Students with Mental Retardation: A Practical Guide for Teachers*. Thousand Oaks, CA: Corwin Press.

Ali, D., Best, C., Bonathan, M., *et al.* (1997) *Behavior in Schools: A Framework for Intervention.* Birmingham: Birmingham Education Department.

Alston, P. (1984) Conjuring up new human rights: A proposal for quality control. *American Journal of International Law* 78: 607–621.

Allen, J. (1996) Foucault and special educational needs: A box of tools for analysing children's experiences of mainstreaming. *Disability and Society* 11 (2): 219–233.

Allen, J., Brown, S. and Riddell, S. (1998) Permission to speak? Theorising special education inside the classroom. In: Clarke, C., Dyson, A. and Millward, A. (Eds) *Theorising Special Education.* London: Routledge.

Alton, S. (2001) Children with Down's syndrome and short term auditory memory. *Down's Syndrome Association Journal* 95 (winter): 4–9.

American Psychiatric Association (2000) (4th edn) *Diagnostic and Statistical Manual of Mental Disorders*, Text Revision, (DSM–IV–TR). Arlington, VA: APA.

Amundsen, R. (1992) Disability, handicap and the environment. *Journal of Social Philosophy* 23 (1): 105–118.

Anastopoulos, A. D. and Farley, S. E. (2003) A cognitive-behavioural training program for parents of children with attention-deficit/hyperactivity disorder. In: Kazdin, A. E. and Weisz, T. R. (Eds) *Evidence Based Psychotherapies for Children and Adolescents*, 187–203. New York: Guilford Press.

Anderson, D. M. (Chief lexicographer) (2007) (31st edn) *Dorlands Illustrated Medical Dictionary.* Philadelphia, PA: Elsevier Science/WB Saunders.

Anderson, D. M., Novak, P. D., Jefferson, K. and Elliott, M. (2003) (30th edition) *Dorlands Illustrated Medical Dictionary.* Philadelphia, PA: WB Saunders.

Antony, M. M. and Roemer, L. (2003) Behaviour therapy. In: Gurman A. S. and Messer S. B. (Eds) *Essential Psychotherapies: Theory and Practice.* New York: Guilford Press.

American Psychiatric Association (2000) (4th edn) *Diagnostic and Statistical Manual of Mental Disorders*, Text Revision. Washington, DC: APA.

Armstrong, D. (2003) *Experiences of Special Education: Re-evaluating Policy and Practice Through Life Stories.* London: RoutledgeFalmer.

Aronoff, M. and Rees-Miller, J. (2000) *The Handbook of Linguistics.* New York/ London: Blackwell.

Asperger, A. (1944) Autistischen psychopathen in kindesalter. *Archiv fur Psychiatrie und Nervenkrankheiten* 177: 76–136.

Austin, J. L. ([1962]/1971) *How to do things with words.* Oxford: Oxford University Press (Originally published in 1962 by The Clarendon Press, Oxford).

Ayers, H. and Prytys, C. (2002) *An A to Z Practical Guide to Emotional and Behavioural Difficulties.* London: David Fulton Publishers.

Baddeley, A. (1986) Working memory and comprehension. In: Broadbent D., McGaugh J., Kosslyn M., *et al.* (Eds) *Working Memory*, 33–74. Oxford: Oxford University Press.

Baillargeon, R., Spelke, E. S. and Wasserman, S. (1985) Object permanence in 5-month old infants. *Cognition* **20**: 191–208.

Bandura, A. (1977) *Social Learning Theory*. Englewood Cliffs, NJ: Prentice-Hall.

Bandura, A. (1986) *Social Foundations of Thought and Action: A Social Cognitive Theory*. Englewood Cliffs, NJ: Prentice-Hall.

Bandura, A. and Walters, R. H. (1959) *Adolescent Aggression*. New York: Ronald Press.

Barkley, R. (1997) *ADHD and the Nature of Self Control*. New York: Guilford Press.

Barkley, R. A., Shelton, T. L., Crosswait, C. C. *et al.* (2000) Multi-method psychoeducational intervention for preschool children with disruptive behaviour: Preliminary results at post treatment. *Journal of Child Psychology and Psychiatry* **41**: 319–332.

Barlow, J. (2001) The structure of /s/ sequences: Evidence from a disordered system. *Journal of Child Language* **28**: 291–324.

Baroff, G. S. and Olley, J. G. (1999) (3rd edn) *Mental Retardation: Nature, Causes and Management*. Philadelphia, PA: Brunner/Mazel.

Baron-Cohen, S., Ring, H. A., Bullmore, E. T. *et al.* (2000) The amygdala theory of autism. *Neuroscience and Biobehavioural Reviews* **24**: 355–364.

Barnes, C. and Mercer, G. (1996) *Exploring the Divide: Illness and Disability*. Leeds: Disability Press.

Barrett, P. M., Dadds, M. R. and Rapee, R. M. (1996) Family treatment for childhood anxiety: A controlled trial. *Journal of Consulting and Clinical Psychology* **64**: 333–342.

Barrow, R. and Woods, R. (1982) (2nd edn) *An Introduction to Philosophy of Education*. London: Methuen.

Basso, A., Burgio, F. and Caporali, A. (2000) Acalculia, aphasia and spatial disorder in left and right brain damaged patients. *Cortex* **36**: 265–280.

Bayley, N. (1993) (2nd edn) *Bayley Scales of Infant Development*. New York: The Psychological Corporation.

Bigge, J. L., Stump, C. S., Spagna, M. E. *et al.* (1999) *Curriculum, Assessment and Instruction for Students with Disabilities*. Belmont, CA: Wadsworth.

Beaton, A. A. (2002) Dyslexia and the cerebellar deficit hypothesis. *Cortex* **38**: 479–490.

Beaton, A. A. (2004) *Dyslexia, Reading and the Brain: A Sourcebook of Psychological and Biological Research*. New York: Psychology Press.

Beck, A. T., Rich, A. J., Shaw, B. F. and Emery, G. (1979) *Cognitive Theory of Depression*. New York: Wiley.

Bee, H. (2000) (9th edn) *The Developing Child*. Needham Heights, MA: Allyn and Bacon.

Behrman, R. E. and Kliegman, R. M. (2002) (4th edn) *Nelson Essentials of Pediatrics*. Philadelphia, PA: W B Saunders.

Beitchman, J. H. and Young, A. R. (1997) Learning disorders with a special emphasis on reading disorders: A review of the past ten years. *Journal of the American Academy of Child and Adolescent Psychiatry* **40**: 75–82.

Benn, S. I. and Peters, R. S. (1959) *Social Principles and the Democratic State.* London: George Allen and Unwin.

Berger, P. and Luckmann, T. (1971) *The Social Construction of Reality.* Harmondsworth: Penguin Books.

Berninger, V. W. (1994) Future directions for research on writing disabilities: integrating endogenous and exogenous variables. In: Lyon, G. R. (Ed.) *Frames of Reference for the Assessment of Learning Disabilities,* 419–440. Baltimore, MD: Brookes.

Bernstein, J. H. (2000) Developmental neuropsychological assessment. In: Yeates K. O., Ris M. D. and Taylor H. G. (Eds) *Paediatric Neuropsychology: Research, Theory and Practice,* 405–438. New York: Guilford Press.

Bernstein, G. A. and Borchardt, C. M. (1991) Anxiety disorders of childhood and adolescence: A critical review. *Journal of the American Academy of Child and Adolescent Psychiatry* **30**: 519–532.

Best, W. (2005) Investigation of new intervention for children with word-finding problems. *International Journal of Language and Communication Disorders* **40** (3): 279–318.

Bhatnager, S. and Andy, O. (1989) Alleviation of stuttering with human certremedian thalamic stimulation. *Journal of Neurosurgery and Psychiatry* **52**: 1182–1184.

Bigge, J. L., Best, S. J. and Heller, K. W. (2001) (4th edn) *Teaching Individuals with Physical, Health or Multiple Disabilities.* Upper Saddle River, NJ: Merrill-Prentice Hall.

Birmaher, B., Ryan, N. D., Williamson, D. E. *et al.* (1996) Childhood and adolescent depression: A review of the past ten years. Part 1. *Journal of the American Academy of Child and Adolescent Psychiatry* **35**: 1427–1439.

Bishop, D. V. M. (2000) Pragmatic language impairment: A correlate of SLI, a distinct subgroup, or a part of the autistic continuum? In: Bishop, D. V. M. and Leonard, L. B. (Eds) *Speech and Language Impairments in Children: Causes, Characteristics, Intervention and Outcome.* Philadelphia, PA; Hove: Psychology Press.

Bishop D. V. M. and Leonard L. B. (Eds) (2000) *Speech and Language Impairments in Children: Causes, Characteristics, Intervention and Outcome.* Philadelphia, PA; Hove: Psychology Press.

Black, K. and Haskins, D. (1996) Including all children in TOP PLAY and BT TOP SPORT. *British Journal of Physical Education* **9**: 11, Primary PE Focus, Winter edition.

Blagg, N. R. and Yule, W. (1984) The behavioural treatment of school refusal: A comparative study. *Behaviour Research and Therapy* **22**: 119–127.

Blanchard, E. B. (1970) Relative contributions of modelling, informational influences, and physical contact in extinction of phobic behaviour. *Journal of Abnormal Psychology* **76**: 55–61.

Bogen, J. E. and Bogen, G. M. (1976) Wernickes region – where is it? *Annals of the New York Academy of Sciences* **280**: 834–843.

Booth, T. (1998) The poverty of special education: Theories to the rescue? In: Clarke, C., Dyson, A. and Millward A. (Eds) *Theorising Special Education*. London: Routledge.

Borduin, C. M. (1999) Multi-systemic treatment of criminality and violence in adolescents. *Journal of the American Academy for Child and Adolescent Psychiatry* **38**: 242–249.

Borkowski, J. G., Carothers, S. S., Howard, K. *et al.* (2006) Intellectual assessment and intellectual disability. In: Jacobson, J. W., Mulick, J. A. and Rojhan, J. (Eds) *Handbook of Mental Retardation and Developmental Abilities*. New York: Springer.

Bottge, B., Heinrichs, M., Chan, S. *et al.* (2003) Effects of video-based and applied problems on the procedural math skills of average and low achieving adolescents. *Journal of Special Educational Technology* **18** (2): 5–22.

Boulpaep, E. L. and Boron, W. F. (2003) *Medical Physiology: A Cellular and Molecular Approach*. Philadelphia, PA: Saunders.

Bowe, F. (1978) *Handicapping America*. New York: Harper & Row.

Bowlby, J. (1965) (2nd edn) *Child Care and the Growth of Love*. Harmondsworth: Penguin Books.

Bowlby, J. (1969) *Attachment and Loss, Volume 1: Attachment*. London: Hogarth Press.

Bowlby, J. (1973) *Attachment and Loss, Volume 2: Separation, Anxiety and Anger*. London: Hogarth Press.

Bowlby, J. (1980) *Attachment and Loss Volume 3: Loss, Sadness and Depression*. London: Hogarth Press.

Boxall, M. (2002) *Nurture Groups in School: Principles and Practice*. London: Paul Chapman Publishing.

Brent, D. A., Kolko, D., Birmaher, B. *et al.* (1998) Predictors of treatment efficacy in a clinical trial of three psychosocial treatments for adolescent depression. *Journal of the American Academy for Child and Adolescent Psychiatry* **37**: 906–914.

Bridgeman, E. and Snowling, M. (1988) The perception of phoneme sequence: A comparison of dyspraxic and normal children. *British Journal of Disorders of Communication* **23** (3): 245–252.

Brodin, J. and Lindstrom, P. (2003) What about ICT in special education? Special educators evaluate information and communications technology as a learning tool. *European Journal of Special Needs Education* **18** (1): 71–87.

Brodmann, K. ([1909]1994) *Vergleichende Lokalisationslehre der Grosshirnrinde in ihren Prinzipien Dargestellt auf Grund des Zellenbaues*. Leipzig: Johann Ambrosius Barth Verlag. Translated from German as *Brodman's Localisation of the Cerebral Cortex* by L. Garey and published in London by Smith-Gordon.

Brooks, G. (2002) *What Works for Reading Difficulties? The Effectiveness of Intervention Schemes*. London: Department of Education and Science.

Bubb, D. N. (2002) Methodological issues confronting PET and fMRI studies of cognitive function. *Cognitive Neuropsychology* **17**: 467–484.

Burton-Roberts, N. (1997) (2nd edn) *Analysing Sentences: An Introduction to English Syntax*. London: Longman.

Butler, F. M., Miller, S. P., Lee, K. and Pierce, T. (2001) Teaching mathematics to students with mild to moderate mental retardation: A review of the literature. *Mental Retardation* **39** (1): 20–31.

Camarata, S. (1998) Connecting Speech and Language: Clinical applications. In: Paul R. (Ed.) *Exploring the Speech–Language Connection*. Baltimore: Brookes.

Candy, D., Davies, G. and Ross, E. (2001) *Clinical Paediatrics and Child Health*. Edinburgh: Harcourt, WB Saunders.

Carlson, C. L., Pelham, W. E., Milich, R. and Dixon, J. (1992) Single and combined effects of methylphenidate and behaviour therapy on the classroom performance of children with attention deficit hyperactivity disorder. *Journal of Abnormal Child Psychology* **20**: 213–232.

Carpenter, B. (1994) Finding a home for the sensory curriculum. *PMLD Link* **19**: 2–3.

Carr, P. (1993) *Phonology*. London: Macmillan.

Carr, A. (2006) (2nd edn) *The Handbook of Child and Adolescent Clinical Psychology: A Contextual Approach*. London: Routledge.

Carter, M. and Grunsell, J. (2001) The behaviour chain interruption strategy: A review of research and discussion of future directions. *Journal for the Association of the Severely Handicapped* **26** (1): 37–49.

Caspi, A., Sugden, K., Moffitt, T. E. *et al.* (2003) Influence of life stress on depression: Moderation by a polymorphism in the 5-HTT gene. *Science* **301**: 386–389.

Castro-Caldas, A., Peterson, K. M., Reis, A. *et al.* (1998) The illiterate brain: Learning to read and write during childhood influences the functional organization of the adult brain. *Brain* **121**: 1053–1063.

Catts, H., Fey, M., Tomblin, J. B. *et al.* (2002) A longitudinal investigation of reading outcomes in children with language impairments. *Journal of Speech, Language and Hearing Research* **45**: 1142–1157.

Cavanaugh, M. (2002) *Against Equality of Opportunity*. Oxford: Oxford University Press.

Cermak, S. A. and Larkin, D. (2002) *Developmental Coordination Disorder*. Albany, NY: Delmar Thompson Learning.

Cestnick, L. and Coltheart, M. (1999) The relationship between language-processing deficits and visual processing deficits in developmental dyslexia. *Cognition* **71**: 231–255.

Cermak, S. A., Gubbay, S. S. and Larkin, D. (2002) What is developmental co-ordination disorder? In: Cermak, S. A. and Larkin, D. (Eds) *Developmental Co-ordination Disorder*. Albany, NY: Delmar.

Chiat, S. (2000) *Understanding Children with Language Problems*. Cambridge: Cambridge University Press.

Chomsky, N. (1959) A review of Skinner's verbal behaviour. *Language* **35**: 26–58.

Christensen, B. K., Carney, C. E. and Segal, Z. V. (2006) Cognitive processing models of depression. In: Stein, D. J., Kupfer, D. J. and Schatzberg, A. F. (Eds) *Textbook of Mood Disorders*, 131–144. Washington, DC: American Psychiatric Publishing.

Clarke, C., Dyson, A. and Millward, A. (1998) (Eds) *Theorising Special Education*. London: Routledge.

Clarke, G. N., Rohde, P., Lewinsohn, P. M. *et al.* (1999) Cognitive-behavioural treatment of adolescent depression: Efficacy of acute group treatment and booster sessions. *Journal of the American Academy for Child and Adolescent Psychiatry* **38**: 272–279.

Clay, D. L. (2004) *Helping Children with Chronic Health Conditions: A Practical Guide*. New York: Guilford Press.

Coch, D., Dawson, G. and Fischer, K. W. (2007) *Human Behaviour, Learning, and the Developing Brain: A Typical Development*. New York: Guilford Press.

Cohen, D. (2006) How does the decision to medicate children arise in cases of ADHD? Views of parents and professionals in Canada. In: Lloyd G., Stead J. and Cohen D. (Eds) *Critical New Perspectives in ADHD*. New York: Routledge.

Cohen, D., Clapperton, I., Gref, P. *et al.* (1999) *DAH: Perceptions de Acteurs et Utilisation de Psychostimulants*. Laval, QC: Regional Health and Social Services Board of Laval.

Cohen, L., Dehaene, S., Chochon, F. *et al.* (2000) Language and calculation within the parietal lobe: A combined cognitive, anatomical and fMRI study. *Neuropsychology* **38**: 1426–1440.

Commission on Classification and Terminology of the International League against Epilepsy (1981) Proposal for the revised clinical and electroencephalographic classification of epileptic seizures. *Epilepsia* **22**: 489–501.

Commission on Classification and Terminology of the International League Against Epilepsy (1989) Proposal for revised classification of epilepsies and epileptic syndromes. *Epilepsia* **30**: 389–399.

Committee on Educational Interventions for Children with Autism (2001) *Educating Children with Autism*. Washington, DC: National Academy Press.

Conn, P. M. (Ed.) (2003) (2nd edn) *Neuroscience in Medicine*. Totowa, NJ: Humana Press.

Constable, A. (2001) A psycholinguistic approach to word-finding difficulties. In: Stackhouse J. and Wells B. (Eds) *Children's Speech and Literacy Difficulties Book 2: Identification and Intervention*, 330–365. London: Wiley.

Copeland, S. R. and Hughes, C. (2000) Acquisition of a picture prompt strategy to increase independent performance. *Education and Training in Mental Retardation and Developmental Disabilities* **35** (3): 294–305.

Coren, S. and Ward, L. M. (1989) *Sensation and Perception*. San Diego, CA: Harcourt Brace Jovanovich.

Cowell, S. F., Egan, G. F., Code, C. *et al.* (2000) The functional neuroanatomy of simple calculation and number repetition: A parametric PET activation study. *Neuroimage* **12**: 565–573.

Cramb, A. (2004) Slopping out staff may sue. *The Daily Telegraph*, 1 June 2004 page 5, columns 5–7.

Crystal, D. and Varley, R. (1998) (4th edn) *Introduction to Language Pathology*. London: Whurr Publishers.

Cutting, L. E. and Denckla, M. B. (2003) Attention: relationships between attention-deficit hyperactivity disorder and learning disability. In: Swanson, H.L., Harris, K.R. and Graham, S. (Eds) *Handbook of Learning Disabilities*. New York: Guilford Press.

Dallo, R. and Draper, R. (2000) *An Introduction to Family Therapy*. Oxford: Oxford University Press.

Danermark, B. and Gellerstedt, L. C. (2004) Social justice: Redistribution and recognition – a non reductionist perspective on disability. *Disability and Society* **19** (4): 339–353.

Daniels, A. and Williams, H. (2000) Reducing the need for exclusions and statements for behaviour: The framework for intervention. Part 1. *Educational Psychology in Practice* **15**: 220–227.

Daniels, H. (Ed.) (2006) (2nd edn) *An Introduction to Vygotsky*. New York: Guilford Press.

Day, J. (Ed.) (1995) (2nd edn) *Access Technology: Making the Right Choice*. Coventry: National Council for Educational Technology.

Dehaene, S., Dehaene-Lambertz, G. and Cohen, L. (1998) Abstract representations of numbers in the animal and human brain. *Trend in Neuroscience* **21** (8): 355–361.

Department for Education and Skills (2001a) *Access to Education for Children and Young People with Medical Needs*. London: DfES.

Department for Education and Skills (2001b) *Special Educational Needs Code of Practice*. London: DfES.

Department for Education and Skills (2001c) *The National Numeracy Strategy Guidance to Support Pupils with Dyslexia and Dyscalculia*. London: DfES.

Department for Education and Skills (2005) (2nd edn) *Data Collection by Special Educational Need*. London: DfES.

Detheridge, T. and Stevens, C. (2001) Information and communication technology. In: Carpenter B., Ashdown R. and Bovair K. (Eds) *Enabling Access: Effective Teaching and Learning for Pupils with Learning Difficulties*, 156–169. London: David Fulton Publishers.

DeVeaugh-Geiss, J., Moroz, G., Beiderman, J. *et al.* (1992) Clomipramine in child and adolescent obsessive-compulsive disorder: A multicenter trail. *Journal of the American Academy of Child and Adolescent Psychiatry* **31**: 45–49.

Dewey, D. and Tupper, D. E. (Eds) (2004) *Developmental Motor Disorders: A Neuropsychological Perspective*. New York: Guilford Press.

Dewey, J. (1899,1976) The school and society. In: Boydston J. A. (Ed.) *John Dewey: The Middle Works 1899–1924, 1*. Carbondale, IL: Southern Illinois University Press.

DiScala, C., Osberg, J. and Savage, R. (1997) Children hospitalised for traumatic brain injury: Transition to post acute care. *Journal of Head Trauma Rehabilitation* **12** (3): 1–19.

Dixon, G. and Addy, L. M. (2004) *Making Inclusion Work for Children with Dyspraxia: Practical Strategies for Teachers*. London: RoutledgeFalmer.

Dobson, K. S. and Dozoiz, D. J. A. (2001) Historical and philosophical bases of cognitive-behavioural therapies. In: Dobson K. S. (Ed.) *Handbook of Cognitive-Behavioural Therapies* (2nd edn). New York: Guilford Press.

Dockar-Drysdale, B. (1991) *The Provision of Primary Experience: Winnicottian Work with Children and Adolescents*. London: Free Association Press.

Dockar-Drysdale, B. (1993) *Therapy and Consultation in Childcare*. London: Free Association Press.

Dockrell, J. and McShane, J. (1993) *Children's Learning Difficulties: A Cognitive Approach*. Oxford: Blackwell.

Dockrell, J., Messer, D., George, R. and Wilson, G. (1998) Children with word-finding difficulties – prevalence, presentation and naming problems. *International Journal of Language and Communication Disorders* **33** (4): 445–454.

Doll, R. C. (1996) (9th edn) *Curriculum Improvement: Decision Making and Process*. Needham Heights, MA: Allyn and Bacon.

Donaldson, M. (1978) *Children's Minds*. London: Routledge.

Dowling, E. and Osborne, E. (Eds) (1994) (2nd edn) *The Family and the School: A Joint Systems Approach to Problems with Children*. London: Routledge.

Drake, R. (1996) A critique of the role of traditional charities. In: Barton L. (Ed.) *Disability and Society: Emerging Issues and Insights*. London: Longman.

Drubach, D. (2000) *The Brain Explained*. Upper Saddle River, NJ: Prentice Hall.

DZurilla, T. J. (1986) *Problem Solving Therapy*. New York: Springer.

Ebbels, S. (2000) Psycholinguistic profiling of a hearing impaired child. *Child Language Teaching and Therapy* **16** (1): 3–22.

Eckert, M. A. and Leonard, C. M. (2003) Developmental disorders: Dyslexia. In: Hugdahl, K. and Davidson, R. J. (Eds) *The Asymmetrical Brain*, 651–679. Cambridge, MA: MIT Press.

Edyburn, D. L. (2002) Remediation vs. compensation: A critical decision point in assistive technology consideration (Essay). www.connsensebulletin.com/edyburnv4n3.html.

Edyburn, D. L. (2006) Assistive technology and mild disabilities. *Special Education Technology Practice* **8** (4): 18–28.

Eliez, S. and Reiss, A. L. (2000) Annotation: MRI neuroimaging of childhood psychiatric disorders: A selective review. *Journal of Child Psychology and Psychiatry* **41**: 679–694.

Ellis, A., Gordon, J., Neenan, M. and Palmer, S. (1997) *Stress Counselling: A Rational Emotive Behaviour Approach*. London: Cassell.

Ellis Weismer, S. and Schrader, T. (1993) Discourse characteristics of and verbal reasoning: Wait time effects on the performance of children with language learning disabilities. *Exceptionality Education Canada* **3**: 71–92.

Engel, J. (1998) Classifications of the international league against epilepsy: Time for reappraisal. *Epilepsia* **39**: 1014–1017.

Engel, J. (2001) A proposed diagnostic scheme for people with epileptic seizures and with epilepsy: Report of the ILAE Task Force on Classification and Terminology. *Epilepsia* **42**: 796–803.

Esbensen, F. A. and Osgood, D. W. (1999) Gang resistance education and training (GREAT): Results from the national evaluation. *Journal of Research in Crime and Delinquency* **36**: 194–225.

Farrell, K. and Tatum, W. O. IV (2006) Encephalopathic generalized epilepsy and Lennox-Gastaut syndrome. In: Wyllie, E., Gupta, A. and Lachhwani, D. K. (Eds) *The Treatment of Epilepsy: Principles and Practice* (4th edn). Philadelphia, PA: Lippincott Williams & Wilkins.

Farrell, M. (1999) *Key Issues for Primary Schools*. London: Routledge.

Farrell, M. (2001a) *Key Issues for Secondary Schools*. London: Routledge.

Farrell, M. (2001b) *Standards and Special Educational Needs*. London: Continuum.

Farrell, M. (2003a) (3rd edn) *The Special Education Handbook*. London: David Fulton Publishers.

Farrell, M. (2003b) *Understanding Special Educational Needs: A Guide for Student Teachers*. New York, London: Routledge.

Farrell, M. (2003c) The role of the physiotherapist and occupational therapist. *Croner Special Educational Needs Briefing*, 22, 1–4.

Farrell, M. (2004a) *Special Educational Needs: A Resource for Practitioners*. London: Sage Publications.

Farrell, M. (2004b) *Inclusion at the Crossroads: Concepts and Values in Special Education*. London: David Fulton Publishers.

Farrell, M. (2005a) *The Effective Teachers Guide to Dyslexia and Other Specific Learning Difficulties*. New York, London: Routledge.

Farrell, M. (2005b) *The Effective Teacher's Guide to Moderate, Severe and Profound Learning Difficulties*. New York, London: Routledge.

Farrell, M. (2005c) *The Effective Teacher's Guide to Autism and Communication Difficulties*. New York, London: Routledge.

Farrell, M. (2005d) *The Effective Teacher's Guide to Sensory Impairment and Physical Disabilities*. New York, London: Routledge.

Farrell, M. (2005e) *The Effective Teacher's Guide to Behavioural, Emotional and Social Difficulties*. New York, London: Routledge.

Farrell, M. (2005f) *Key Issues in Special Education: Raising Pupils' Achievement and Attainment*. New York, London: Routledge.

Farrell, M. (2005g) Speech and language therapy. *Croner Special Educational Needs Briefing*, **37**: 2–4.

Farrell, M. (2006a) *Celebrating the Special School*. London: David Fulton Publishers.

Farrell, M. (2006b) Professionals working for pupils with SEN. *Croner Special Educational Needs Briefing*, **39**: 2–4.

Farrell, M. (2006c) A vision for inclusion. *Croner Special Educational Needs Briefing*, **45**: 2–4.

Farrell, M. (2008a) *The Special School's Handbook: Key Issues for All*. London: Routledge, National Association for Special Education.

Farrell, M. (2008b) *Educating Special Children: An Introduction to Provision for Pupils with Disabilities and Disorders*. New York, London: Routledge.

Farrell, M., Kerry, T. and Kerry, C. (1995) *The Blackwell Handbook of Education*. Oxford: Blackwell.

Ferguson, P. M. and Ferguson, D. L. (1995) The interpretivist view of special education and disability: The value of telling stories. In: Skrtic, T. M. (Ed.) *Disability and Democracy: Reconstructing (Special) Education for Post-Modernity*. New York: Teachers College Press.

Fey, M. E. and Proctor-Williams, K. (2001) Recasting, elicited imitation and modelling in grammar intervention for children with specific language impairment. In: Bishop, D. V. M. and Leonard, L. B. (Eds) *Speech and Language Impairments in Children: Causes, Characteristics, Intervention and Outcome*. New York: Psychology Press.

Filipek, P. A. (1999) Neuroimaging in the developmental disorders: The state of the science. *Journal of Child Psychology and Psychiatry* **40**: 113–128.

Finnie, N. (1997) *Handling the Young Child with Cerebral Palsy at Home*. Oxford: Butterworth-Heinemann.

Folensbee, R. W. (2007) *The Neuroscience of Psychological Therapies*. New York: Cambridge University Press.

Fonagy, P., Target, M., Cottrell, D., Phillips, J. and Kurtz, Z. (2005) *What Works for Whom? A Critical Review of Treatments for Children and Adolescents*. New York: The Guilford Press.

Foucault, M. (1977) Intellectuals and power: A conversation between Michel Foucault and Giles Deleuze. In: Bouchard, D. (Ed.) *Language, Counter-memory, Practice: Selected Essays and Interviews by Michel Foucault*. Oxford: Blackwell.

Foucault, M. (1982) The subject of power. In: Dreyfus H. and Rabinow P. (Eds) *Michel Foucault: Beyond Structuralism and Hermeneutics*. Brighton: Harvester.

Fox, P. T., Ingham, J., Zamarripa, F. *et al.* (2000) Brain correlates of stuttering and syllable production – a PET performance-correlation analysis. *Brain* **123**: 1985–2004.

Foxen, T. and McBrien, J. (1981) *Training Staff in Behavioural Methods: Trainee Workbook*. Manchester: Manchester University Press.

Frackowiak, R. S. J. and Friston, K. J. (1994) Functional neuroanatomy of the human brain: Positron emission tomography – a new neuroanatomical technique. *Journal of Anatomy* **184**: 211–225.

Frackowiak, R. S. J. (1994b) Functional mapping of verbal memory and language. *Trends in Neurosciences* **17** (3): 109–115.

Franklin, M. E., Kozak, M. J., Cashman, L. A. *et al.* (1998) Cognitive-behavioural treatment of paediatric obsessive-compulsive disorder: An open clinic trial. *Journal of the American Academy of Child and Adolescent Psychiatry* **37**: 412–419.

Franz, R. L. (1966) Pattern discrimination and selective attention as determinants of perceptual development from birth. In: Kidd, A. H. and Rivoire, J. J. (Eds) *Perceptual Development in Children*, 143–173. New York: International Universities Press.

Freud, A. (1945a) Adolescence. *The Psychoanalytic Study of the Child* **13**: 255–278.

Freud, A. (1945b) Indications for child analysis. *The Psychoanalytic Study of the Child* **1**: 127–149.

Freud, A. ([various dates])/(1998) *Selected Writings – Anna Freud*. In: Richard, E. and Ruth, F. (Eds) London: Penguin.

Freud, S. (1923) *The Ego and the Id*. Penguin Freud Library XI, Harmondsworth.

Freud, S. ([1940] 2002) *An Outline of Psychoanalysis* (translation by Helena Ragg-Kirkby). London: Penguin Books.

Friederici, A. D., Pfeifer, E. and Hahne, A. (1993) Event related brain potentials during natural speech processing: Effects of semantic, morphological and syntactic violations. *Cognitive Brain Research* **1**: 183–192.

Frith, U. (1997) Brain, mind and behaviour in dyslexia. In: Hulme, C. and Snowling, M. (Eds) *Dyslexia: Biology, Cognition and Intervention*, 1–19. London: Whurr Publishers.

Gabbard, C. LeBlanc, B. and Lowry, S. (1994) (2nd edn) *Physical Education for Children: Building the Foundation*. Upper Saddle River, NJ: Prentice Hall.

Gallagher, J. M. and Reid, D. K. (1981) *The Learning Theory of Piaget and Inhelder*. Belmont, CA: Brooks/Cole.

Gathercole, S. E. and Baddeley, A. D. (1993) *Working Memory and Language*. Hove, UK: Lawrence Erlbaum Associates.

Gee, J. P. (2005) *An Introduction to Discourse Analysis: Theory and Method*. London: Routledge.

Gehring, W. J. and Knight, R. T. (2000) Prefrontal–cingulate interactions in action monitoring. *Nature Neuroscience* **3**: 516–520.

Giedd, J. N., Blumenthal, J., Molloy, E. and Castellanos, F. X. (2001) Brain imaging of attention deficit/hyperactivity disorder. In: Wassertein, J., Wolf, L. E. and Lefever, F. F. (Eds) *Adult Attention Deficit Disorder: Brain Mechanisms and Life Outcomes, 931*, 33–49. New York: New York Academy of Sciences.

Geller, B., Reising, D., Leonard, H. L. *et al.* (1999) Critical review of tricyclic antidepressant use in children and adolescents. *Journal of the American Academy of Child and Adolescent Psychiatry* **38**: 513–516.

Geschwind, N. and Levitsky, W. (1968) Human brain: Left–right asymmetries of the temporal speech region. *Science* **161**: 186–187.

Gibbon, F. and Wood, S. (2003) Using electropalatography (EPG) to diagnose and treat articulation disorders associated with mild cerebral palsy: A case study. *Clinical Linguistics and Phonetics* **17**: 365–374.

Glendon, M. (1991) *Rights Talk: The Impoverishment of Political Discourse.* New York: The Free Press.

Goldberg, E. (2001) *The Executive Brain: Frontal Lobes and the Civilised Mind.* New York: Oxford University Press.

Goode, C. D., Johnsrude, I., Ashburner, J. *et al.* (2001) Cerebral asymmetry and the effects of sex and handedness on brain structure: A voxel-based morphometric analysis of 465 normal adult human brains. *NeuroImage* **14**: 685–700.

Goodley, D. (2001) 'Learning difficulties', the social model of disability and impairment: Challenging epistemologies. *Disability and Society* **16** (2): 207–231.

Goswami, U. (2004) Neuroscience, education and special education. *British Journal of Special Education* **31** (4): 175–183.

Goswami, U. (2008) *Cognitive Development: The Learning Brain.* New York, Hove: Psychology Press.

Goswami, U., Thompson, J., Richardson, U. *et al.* (2002) Amplitude envelope onsets and developmental dyslexia: A new hypothesis. *Proceedings of the National Academy of Sciences* **99** (16): 10911–10916.

Greenberg, L. S. and Leone-Pascual, J. (2001) A dialectical constructivist view of the creation of personal meaning. *Journal of Constructivist Psychology* **14**: 165–186.

Greenhill, L. (1998) Childhood ADHD: pharmacological treatments. In: Nathan, P. and Gorman, M. (Eds) *A Guide to Treatments that Work.* Oxford: Oxford University Press.

Greenspan, S. (2006) Functional concepts in mental retardation: Finding the natural essence of an artificial category. *Exceptionality* **14** (4): 205–224.

Groce, N. E. (1985) *Everybody Here Spoke Sign Language: Hereditary Deafness on Martha's Vineyard.* Harvard, MA: Harvard University Press.

Grosjean, F. (1980) Spoken word recognition processes and the gating paradigm. *Perception and Psychophysics* **28** (4): 267–283.

Gruber, O., Indefrey, P., Steinmetz, H. and Kleinschmidt, A. (2001) Dissociating neural correlates of cognitive components in mental calculation. *Cerebral Cortex* **11**: 350–359.

Grunwell, P. (1985) *PACS – Phonological Assessment of Child Speech.* Windsor: NFER-Nelson.

Guess, D., Siegel-Causey, E., Roberts, S. *et al.* (1990) Assessment and analysis of behavioural state and related variables among students with profoundly handicapping conditions. *Journal of the Association for Persons with Severe Handicaps* **15**: 211–230.

Gurman, A. S. and Messer, S. B. (Eds) (2005) *Essential Psychotherapies: Theory and Practice.* New York: Guilford Press.

Guyton, A. C. and Hall, J. E. (1997) (6th edn) *Human Physiology and Mechanisms of Disease*. New York, London: Elsevier Science.

Hale, J. B., Bertin, M. and Brown, L. (2004) Modelling frontal-subcortical circuits for ADHD subtype identification, unpublished manuscript.

Hale, J. B. and Fiorello, C. A. (2004) *School Neuropsychology: A Practitioners Handbook*. New York: Guilford Press.

Hardy, C. (2000) *Information and Communications Technology for All*. London: David Fulton Publishers.

Harris, B. (1979) Whatever happened to Little Albert? *American Psychologist* **34** (2): 151–160.

Hasselbring, T. S. and Williams Glaser, C. H. (2000) Use of computer technology to help students with special needs. *The Future of Children* **10** (2): 102–122.

Hasler, D., Drevets, W. C., Manji, H. K. and Charney, D. S. (2004) Discovering endophenotypes for major depression. *Neuropsychopharmacology* **29**: 1765–1781.

Hatcher, P. (2000) Sound links in reading and spelling with discrepancy defined dyslexics and children with moderate learning difficulties. *Reading and Writing: An Interdisciplinary Journal* **13**: 257–272.

Heller, K. W., Alberto, P. A., Forney, P. E. and Schwartzman, M. N. (1996) *Understanding Physical, Sensory and Health Impairments: Characteristics and Educational Implications*. Pacific Grove, CA: Brooks-Cole.

Henry, L. C. and Maclean, M. (2002) Working memory performance in children with and without intellectual disabilities. *American Journal on Mental Retardation* **107** (6): 421–432.

Hernandez, M. T., Sauerwein, H. C., de Guise, E. *et al.* (2001) Neuropsychology of frontal lobe epilepsy in children. In: Jambaqué, I., Lassonde, M. and Dulac, O. (Eds) *Neuropsychology of Childhood Epilepsy*, Advances in Behavioural Biology, 50. New York: Kluwer Academic/Plenum Publishers.

Hiscock, M. and Kinsbourne, M. (1982) Laterality and dyslexia: A critical view. *Annals of Dyslexia* **32**: 177–228.

Hodapp, R. (1998) *Development and disabilities: Intellectual, sensory, and motor impairments*. New York, NY: Cambridge University Press.

Hodges, L. (2000) Effective teaching and learning. In: Aitken, S., Buultjens, M. and Clark, C. *et al.* (Eds) *Teaching Children who Are Deafblind: Contact, Communication and Learning*. London: David Fulton Publishers.

Hoyt, M. F. (2003) Brief Psychotherapies. In: Gurman, A. S. and Messer, S. B. (Eds) *Essential Psychotherapies: Theory and Practice*. New York: Guilford Press.

Ingenmey, R. and Van Houten, R. (1991) Using time delay to promote spontaneous speech in an autistic child. *Journal of Applied Behaviour Analysis* **24**: 591–596.

Inhelder, B. (1968) The diagnosis of reasoning in the mentally retarded. Thesis. New York, University of Geneva (Le diagnostic du raisonnement chez les débiles mentaux, 1943).

Irlen, H. L. (1994) Scotopic sensitivity: Irlen syndrome hypothesis and explanation of the syndrome. *Journal of Behavioural Optometry* **5**: 65–66.

Isaacs, E. B., Edmunds, C. J., Lucas, A. and Gadian, D. G. (2001) Calculation difficulties in children with very low birth weight. *Brain* **124**: 1701–1707.

Jambaqué, I., Lassonde, M. and Dulac, O. (Eds) (2001) *Neuropsychology of Childhood Epilepsy*, Advances in Behavioural Biology, 50. New York: Kluwer Academic/Plenum Publishers.

Jan, J. (1993) Neurological causes of visual impairment and investigation. In: Fielder, A., Best, A. and Bax, M. C. O. (Eds) *The Management of Visual Impairment in Childhood*. London: Mackieth.

Janicak, P. G., Davis, J. M., Prescorn, S. H. and Ayd, F. J. (2001) (3rd edn) *Principles and Practice of Psychopharmacology*. Philadelphia, PA: Lippincott Williams & Wilkins.

Johnson, M. and Parkinson, G. (2002) *Epilepsy: A Practical Guide*. London: David Fulton Publishers.

Jones, P. (2005) *The Arts Therapies: A Revolution in Healthcare*. Hove: Brunner-Routledge.

Jordan, N. C. and Hanich, L. B. (2003) Characteristics of children with moderate mathematics deficiencies: A longitudinal perspective. *Learning Disabilities Research and Practice* **18** (4): 213–221.

Jordan, N. C., Hanich, L. B. and Kaplan, D. (2003) A longitudinal study of mathematical competencies in children with specific mathematics difficulties versus children with comorbid mathematics and reading difficulties. *Child Development* **74** (3): 834–850.

Jormanainen, I., Kärnä-Lyn, E., Lahti, L. *et al.* (2007) A framework for research on technology-enhanced special education. Seventh International Conference on Advanced Learning Technologies, Nigata, Japan.

Just, M. A., Newman, S. D., Keller, T. A., McEleney, A. and Carpenter, P. A. (2004) Imagery in Sentence Comprehension. An fMRI Study. *Neuroimage* **21**: 112–124.

Kail, R. (1994) A method for studying the generalized slowing hypothesis in children with specific language impairment. *Journal of Speech and Hearing Research* **37**: 418–421.

Kandel, E. R. (1998) A new intellectual framework for psychiatry. *American Journal of Psychiatry* **155** (4): 457–469.

Kandel, E. R., Schwartz, J. H. and Jessell, T. M. (2000) (4th edn) *Principles of Neural Science*. New York: McGraw-Hill.

Kanner, L. (1943) Autistic disturbances of affective contact. *Nervous Child* **2**: 217–250.

Kaplan, J.S. and Carter, J. (1995) (3rd edn) *Beyond Behavior Modification: A Cognitive-Behavioral Approach to Behavior Management in the School*. Austin, TX: Pro-Ed.

Karkou, V. (1999a) Art therapy in education: Findings from a nationwide survey in arts therapies. *Inscape* **4** (2): 62–70.

Karkou, V. (1999b) Who? Where? What? A brief description of DMT: Results from a Nationwide Study. *E-motion* **XI** (2): 5–10.

Karpov, Y. V. (2005) *The Neo-Vygotskian Approach to Child Development*. New York: Cambridge University Press.

Kazdin, A. E. (2001) (5th edn) *Behavior Modification in Applied Settings*. Pacific Grove, CA: Brooks-Cole.

Kazdin, A. E. (2003) Problem-solving skills training and parent management training for conduct disorder. In: Kazdin, A. E. and Weisz, T. R. (Eds) *Evidence Based Psychotherapies for Children and Adolescents*, 241–262. New York: Guilford Press.

Kazdin, A. E. and Wasser, G. (2000) Therapeutic changes in children, parents and families resulting from treatment of children with conduct problems. *Journal of the American Academy of Child and Adolescent Psychiatry* **39**: 414–420.

Kearns, G. L., Abdel-Rahman, S. M. and Alander, S. W. *et al.* (2003) Developmental pharmacology – drug disposition, action, and therapy in infants and children. *New England Journal of Medicine* **349**: 1157–1167.

Keenan, T. (1992) *An Introduction to Child Development*. London: Sage Publications.

Kellinghaus, C., Lüders, H. O. and Wyllie, E. (2006) Classification of seizures. In: Wyllie, E., Gupta, A. and Lachhwani, D. K. (Eds) *The Treatment of Epilepsy: Principles and Practice* (4th edn) 217–221. Philadelphia, PA: Lippincott Williams & Wilkins.

Kellogg, R. T. (1995) *Cognitive Psychology*. New York, London: Sage Publications.

Kelly, M. P. and Field, D. (1994) Reflections on the rejection of the bio-medical model in sociological discourse. *Medical Sociology News* **19**: 34–37.

Kendall, P. C., Aschenbrand, S. G. and Hudson, J. L. (2003) Child focused treatment of anxiety. In: Kazdin, A. E. and Weisz, T. R. (Eds) *Evidence Based Psychotherapies for Children and Adolescents*, 81–100. New York: Guilford Press.

Kennerley, S. W., Diedrichsen, J., Hazeltine, E. *et al.* (2002) Callosotomy patients exhibit temporal uncoupling during continuous bimanual movements. *Nature Neuroscience* **5**: 376–381.

King, N. J., Tonge, B. J., Heyne, D. *et al.* (1998) Cognitive-behavioural treatment of school refusing children: A controlled evaluation. *Journal of the American Academy of Child and Adolescent Psychiatry* **37**: 395–403.

King, N. J., Tonge, B. J., Heyne, D. *et al.* (2001) Cognitive-behavioural treatment of school refusing children: Maintenance of improvement at 3 to 5 year follow up. *Scandinavian Journal of Behaviour Therapy* **30**: 85–89.

King-de Baun, P. (1990) *Storytime: Stories, Symbols and Emergent Literacy Activities for Young Special Needs Children*. Park City, UT: Creative Communicating.

Kirigin, K. A. (1996) Teaching-family model of group home treatment of children with severe behaviour problems. In: Roberts, M. C. (Ed.) *Model Programs in Child and Family Mental Health*, 231–247. Mahwah, NJ: Erlbaum.

Klein, M. (1932) *The Psychoanalysis of Children*. London: Hogarth Press.

Klein, M. ([various dates]/ 1964) *Contributions to Psychoanalysis, 1921–1945*. New York: McGraw-Hill.

Klein, M. ([1957]/1975) *Envy and Gratitude*. New York: Delacorte Press.

Kliegman, R. M., Behrman, R. E., Jenson, H. B. and Stanton, B. F. (2007) (9th edn) *Nelson Textbook of Paediatrics*. Philadelphia, PA: Saunders Elsevier.

Koegel, L. K. and Koegel, R. L. (1995) Motivating communication in children with autism. In: Schopler, E. and Mezibov, G. (Eds) *Learning and Cognition in Autism: Current Issues in Autism*, 73–87. New York: Plenum Press.

Koenig, A. J. and Holbrook, M. C. (Eds) (2000) *Foundations of Education: Instructional Strategies for Teaching Children and Youth with Visual Impairments*, 2. New York: American Foundation for the Blind Press.

Kopera-Frye, K., Dahaene, S. and Streissguth, A. P. (1996) Impairments of number processing induced by prenatal alcohol exposure. *Neuropsychologia* **34**: 1187–1196.

Korkman, M., Kirk, U. and Kemp, S. (1998) *NEPSY: A Developmental Neuropsychological Assessment Manual*. San Antonio, TX: The Psychological Corporation.

Kumar, V., Abbas, A. K., Mitchell, R. and Fausto, N. (2005) (8th edn) *Robbins Basic Pathology*. New York, London: WB Saunders.

Kumar, P. and Clark, M. (Eds) (2005) (6th edn) *Clinical Medicine*. New York, London: WB Saunders.

Kundera, M. (1991) *Immortality*. London: Faber and Faber.

Kushlick, A. and Blunden, R. (1974) The epidemiology of mental subnormality. In: Clarke, A. M. and Clarke, A. D. B. (Eds) *Mental Deficiency* (3rd edn). London: Methuen.

Lacey, P. (1991) Managing the classroom environment. In: Tilstone, C. (Ed.) *Teaching Pupils with Severe Learning Difficulties*. London: David Fulton Publishers.

Ladefoged, P. (1993) (3rd edn) *A Course in Phonetics*. New York: Harcourt Brace.

Lancioni, G. E., O'Reilly, M. F., Oliva, D. *et al.* (2002) Multiple microswitches for multiple responses with children with profound disabilities. *Cognitive Behaviour Therapy* **31** (2): 81–87.

Langdon, D. W. and Warrington, E. K. (1997) The abstraction of numerical relations: A role for the right hemisphere in arithmetic? *Journal of the International Neuropsychological Society* **3**: 260–268.

Lathe, R. (2006) *Autism, Brain and Environment*. London, and Philadelphia, PA: Jessica Kingsley Publishers.

Leonard, L. B. and Deevy, P. (2006) Cognitive and linguistic issues in the study of children with specific language impairment. In: Traxler, M. and Gernsbacher, M. A. (Eds) *Handbook of Psycholinguistics* (2nd edn) 1143–1171. San Diego, CA: Academic Press.

Leonard, C. M., Lombardino, L. J., Mercado, L. N. *et al.* (1996) Cerebral asymmetry and cognitive development in children: A magnetic resonance imaging study. *Psychological Science* **7**: 89–95.

Larson, P.J. and Maag, J.W. (1998). Applying functional assessment in general educational classrooms: Issues and recommendations. *Remedial and Special Education* **19** (6): 338–349.

Levelt, W. J. M. (1989) *Speaking*. Cambridge, MA: MIT Press.

Lewis, A. and Norwich, B. (Eds) (2005) *Special Teaching for Special Children? Pedagogies for Iinclusion.* Maidenhead: UK Open University Press.

Lezak, M. D., Howieson, D. B. and Loring, D. W. (2004) (2nd edn) *Neuropsychological Assessment.* New York: Oxford University Press.

Lichter, D. G. and Cummings, J. L (Eds) (2001) *Frontal-Subcortical Circuits in Psychiatric and Neurological Disorders.* New York: Guilford press.

Light, G. J. and DeFries, J. C. (1995) Comorbidity of reading and mathematics disabilities: Genetic and environmental etiologies. *Journal of Learning Disabilities* **28**: 96–106.

Light, J. (1989) Towards a definition of communicative competence for individuals using augmentative and alternative communication systems. *Augmentative and Alternative Communication* **5**: 134–137.

Lissauer, T. and Clayden, G. (2007) (3rd edn) *Illustrated Textbook of Paediatrics.* London: Elsevier Science, Mosby.

Litow, L. and Pumroy, D. K. (1975) A brief review of classroom group-orientated contingencies. *Journal of Applied Behavioural Analysis* **3**: 341–347.

Lochman, J. E. and Wells, K. C. (1996) A social-cognitive intervention with aggressive children: Prevention effects and contextual implementation issues. In: Peters, R. E. and McMahon, R. J. (Eds) *Preventing Childhood Disorders, Substance Abuse and Delinquency,* 111–143. Thousand Oaks, CA: Sage Publications.

Lochman, J. E., Barry, T. D. and Pardini, D. A. (2003) Anger control training for aggressive youth. In: Kazdin, A. E. and Weisz, T. R. (Eds) *Evidence Based Psychotherapies for Children and Adolescents,* 263–281. New York: Guilford Press.

Loddenkemper, T., Lüders, H. O., Najm, I. M. and Wyllie, E. (2006) Classification of the epilepsies. In: Wyllie, E., Gupta, A. and Lachhwani, D. K. (Eds) *The Treatment of Epilepsy: Principles and Practice* (4th edn). Philadelphia, PA: Lippincott Williams & Wilkins.

Lovaas, O. I. (1987) Behavioural treatment and normal intellectual and educational functioning in autistic children. *Journal of Consulting and Clinical Psychology* **55**: 3–9.

Luxem, M. and Christopherson, E. (1994) Behavioural toilet training in early childhood: Research, practice and implications. *Journal of Developmental Behavioural Pediatrics* **15** (5): 370–378.

Lyons, J. (1995) *Linguistic Semantics: An Introduction.* Cambridge, Cambridge University Press.

Mackintosh, K. and Dissanayake, C. (2004) Annotation: The similarities and differences between autistic disorder and Asperger's disorder. *Journal of Child Psychology and Psychiatry* **45**: 421–434.

Macintyre, C. and Deponio, P. (2003) *Identifying and Supporting Children with Specific Learning Difficulties: Looking Beyond the Label to Assess the Whole Child.* New York: RoutledgeFalmer.

Mahoney, M. (1991) *Human Change Processes.* New York: Basic Books.

Magg, J. W. (2007) Behavioural theory and practice: Current and future issues. In: Florian, L. (Ed.) *The Sage Handbook of Special Education*. Thousand Oaks, CA; London.

March, J. S. (1999) Psychopharmacological management of paediatric obsessive-compulsive disorder (OCD). Paper presented at the 46th annual meeting of the American Academy of Child and Adolescent Psychiatry. Chicago.

Mar, H. M. and Sall, N. (1999) Profiles of the expressive communication skills of children and adolescents with severe cognitive disabilities. *Education and Training in Mental Retardation and Developmental Disabilities* **34** (1): 77–89.

Martin, D. and Miller, C. (2003) (2nd edn) *Speech and Language Difficulties in the Classroom*. London: David Fulton Publishers.

Mason, H., McCall, S., Arter, C. *et al.* (Eds) (1997) *Visual Impairment: Access to Education for Children and Young People*. London: David Fulton Publishers.

Mathews, P. H. (1991) (2nd edn) *Morphology*. Cambridge: Cambridge University Press.

Matson, J. L., Sevin, J. A., Box, M. L. and Francis, K. L. (1993) An evaluation of two methods for increasing self-initiated verbalisations in autistic children. *Journal of Applied Behaviour Analysis* **26**: 389–396.

Mayer, E., Martory, M. D., Pegna, A. J. *et al.* (1999) A pure case of Gertmann syndrome with a subangular lesion. *Brain* **122**: 1107–1120.

Mazzocco, M. M. M. (2001) Math learning disability and math LD subtypes: Evidence from studies of Turner syndrome, fragile X syndrome, and neurofibromatosis type 1. *Journal of Learning Disabilities* **34**: 520–533.

McClelland, J. L. and Elman, J. L. (1986) The TRACE model of speech recognition. *Cognitive Psychology* **18**: 1–86.

McClosky, M., Alminosa, D. and Sokol, S. M. (1991) Facts, rules and procedures in normal calculation: Evidence from multiple single-patient studies of impaired arithmetic fact retrieval. *Brain and Cognition* **17**: 154–203.

MacKay, G. (2002) The disappearance of disability? Thoughts on a changing culture. *British Journal of Special Education* **29**: 4.

McDonnell, J., Hardman, M. L., Hightower, J. *et al.* (1993) Impact of community based instruction on the development of adaptive behaviour of secondary level students with mental retardation. *American Journal on Mental Retardation* **97** (5): 575–584.

McInnes, J. M. and Treffry, J. A. (1982) *Deaf-Blind Infants and Children: A Developmental Guide*. Toronto, ON: University of Toronto Press.

McLeod, S. (2002) Articulation and phonology: Typical development of speech. http://members.tripod.com/Caroline_Bowen/acquisition.html.

McLeod, S., van Doorn, J. and Reed, V. (2001) Normal acquisition of consonant clusters. *American Journal of Speech Language Pathology* **10**: 99–110.

McPhee, S. J. and Ganong, W. F. (2006) (5th edn) *Pathophysiology of Disease: An Introduction to Clinical Medicine*. New York: Lange Medical Books, McGraw-Hill.

Meese, R. L. (2001) (2nd edn) *Teaching Learners with Mild Disabilities: Integrating Research and Practice*. Belmont, CA: Wadsworth-Thompson.

Meltzoff, J. and Kornreich, M. (1970) *Research in Psychotherapy*. New York: Atherton.

Menzies, R. G. and Clarke, J. C. (1993) A comparison of in vivo and vicarious exposure in the treatment of childhood water phobia. *Behaviour Research and Therapy* **31**: 9–15.

Middleton, F. A. and Strick, P. L. (2000) Basal ganglia output and cognition: Evidence from anatomical behavioural and clinical studies. *Brain and Cognition* **42**: 183–200.

Mildner, V. (2008) *The Cognitive Neuroscience of Communication*. New York: Lawrence Erlbaum Associates.

Millar, S. (1994) *Understanding and Representing Space: Theory and Evidence form Studies with Blind and Sighted Children*. Oxford: Clarendon Press.

Mezibov, G. and Howley, M. (2003) *Accessing the Curriculum for Pupils with Autistic Spectrum Disorders: Using the TEACCH Programme to Help Inclusion*. London: David Fulton Publishers.

Minick, N. J. (1987) *The Development of Vygotsky's Thought. An Introduction to Thinking and Speech*. New York: Plenum Press. (Edited and translated by Minick. Reprinted in Daniels, H. (Ed.) (2nd edn) *An Introduction to Vygotsky*. New York: Routledge, 33–57).

Mitchell, S. A. and Black, M. J. (1995) *Freud and Beyond: A History of Psychoanalytic Thought*. New York: Basic Books.

Mohan, H. (2005) (5th edn) *Textbook of Pathology*. Royal Tunbridge Wells: Anshan.

Morra, S., Gobbo, C., Marini, Z. and Sheese, R. (2007) *Cognitive Development: Neo-Piagetian Perspectives*. New York, Hove: Psychology Press.

Morton, J. (2004) *Understanding Developmental Disorders: A Causal Modelling Approach*. Oxford: Blackwell Publishing.

Munden, A. and Arcelus, J. (1999) *The AD/HD Handbook*. London: Jessica Kingsley.

Mundy, P. and Neale, A. (2001) Neural plasticity, joint attention and a transactional social-orienting of autism. In: Glidden, L. (Ed.) *International Review of Research in Mental Retardation. Autism 23*, 139–168. San Diego, CA: Academic Press.

Muratori, F., Picchi, L., Casella, C. *et al.* (2002) Efficacy of brief dynamic psychotherapy for children with emotional disorders. *Psychotherapy and Psychosomatics* **71**: 2838.

Nathan, L and Simpson, S (2001) Designing a literacy programme for a child with a history of speech difficulties. In: Stackhouse, J. and Wells, B. (Eds) *Children's Speech and Literacy Difficulties Book 2: Identification and Intervention*, 249–298. London: Wiley.

National Institute of Clinical Excellence (2000) *Guidance on the Use of Methylphenidate for ADHD*. London: NICE.

Nigg, J. (2006) *What Causes ADHD? Understanding What Goes Wrong and Why*. New York: Guilford Press.

Nigg, J. and Hinshaw, S. (1998) Parent personality traits and psychopathology associated with anti-social behaviours in childhood ADHD. *Journal of Child Psychology and Psychiatry* **39** (2): 145–159.

Nind, M. and Hewett, D. (2001) *A Practical Guide to Intensive Interaction*. Kidderminster: British Institute of Learning Difficulties.

Nordli, D. R., Kuroda, M. M. and Hirsh, I. J. (2001) The ontogeny of partial seizures in infants and young children. *Epilepsia* **2000** (42): 986–990.

Nozick, R. (1974) *Anarchy, State and Utopia*. Oxford: Blackwell.

Obler, L. K. and Gjerlow, K. (1999) *Language and the Brain*. Cambridge: Cambridge University Press.

Ojemann, G. (1983) Brain organization for language from the perspective of electrical stimulation mapping. *Behavioural and Brain Sciences* **6**: 189–230.

O'Leary, K. D. and Drabman, R. (1971) Token reinforcement programs in the classroom: A review. *Psychological Bulletin* **75**: 379–398.

Ollendick, T. H. and King, N. J. (1998) Empirically supported treatments for children with phobic and anxiety disorders. *Journal of Clinical Child Psychology* **27**: 156–167.

Oliver, M. (1996) *Understanding Disability: From Theory to Practice*. Basingstoke: Macmillan.

Oliver, M. (2004) The social model in action: If I had a hammer. In: Barnes, C. and Mercer, G. (Eds) *Implementing the Social Model of Disability: Theory and Research*. Leeds: The Disability Press.

Osborn, L. M., DeWitt, T. G., First, L. R. and Zenel, J. A (Eds) (2005) *Pediatrics*. Philadelphia, PA: Elsevier Science, Mosby

Ouvry, C. and Saunders, S. (2001) Pupils with profound and multiple learning difficulties. In: Carpenter, B., Ashdown, R. and Bovair, K. (Eds.) *Enabling Access: Effective Teaching and Learning for Pupils with Learning Difficulties*, 240–256. London: David Fulton Publishers.

Ozonoff, S. (1997) Components of executive function in autism and other disorders. In: Russell, J. (Ed.) *Autism as an Executive Disorder*. Oxford: Oxford University Press.

Pagliano, P. (2002) Using all the senses. In: Ashman, A. and Elkins, J. (Eds) *Educating Children with Diverse Abilities*. Sydney: Prentice Hall, Pearson Education.

Pantelemidou, V., Herman, R. and Thomas, J. (2003) Efficacy of speech intervention using electropalatography with a cochlear implant user. *Clinical Linguistics and Phonetics* **17**: 383–392.

Panter, S. (2001) Mathematics. In: Carpenter, B., Ashdown, R. and Bovair, K. (Eds) *Enabling Access: Effective Teaching and Learning for Pupils with Learning Difficulties* (2nd edn) 36–51. London: David Fulton Publishers.

Parsons, T. (1952) *The Social System*. New York: Free Press.

Pascoe, M., Stackhouse, J. and Wells, B. (2005) Phonological therapy within a psycholinguistics framework: Promoting change in a child with persisting speech difficulties. *International Journal of Language and Communication Disorders* **40**: 189–220.

Pascoe, M., Stackhouse, J. and Wells, B. (2006) *Children's Speech and Literacy Difficulties Book 3: Persisting Speech Difficulties in Children.* London: Wiley.

Paveley, S. (2002) Inclusion and the web: strategies for improving access. In: Abbott, C. (Ed.) *Special Educational Needs and the Internet: Issues for the Inclusive Classroom.* London: Routledge.

Pavlov, I. P. ([1926]/1960) *Conditioned Reflexes: An Investigation of the Physiological Activity of the Cerebral Cortex* (translation by G.V. Anrep). New York: Dover Publications.

Patterson, G. R. and Forgatch, M. S. (1995) Predicting future clinical adjustment from treatment outcome and process variables. *Psychological Assessment* **7**: 275–285.

Pease, L. (2000) Creating a communicating environment. In: Aitken, S., Buultjens, M. and Clark, C. *et al.* (Eds.) *Teaching Children who are Deafblind: Contact, Communication and Learning.* London: David Fulton Publishers.

Peppé, S. and McCann, J. (2003) Assessing intonation and prosody in children with atypical language development: The PEP-C test and the revised version. *Clinical Linguistics and Phonetics* **17** (4-5): 345–354.

Peppé, S., Maxim, J. and Wells, B. (2000) Prosodic variation in southern British English. *Language and Speech* **43** (3): 309–334.

Peterkin T. (2004) Feudal laird prepares for battle with islanders who want to buy him out. *The Daily Telegraph* Tuesday 1, June 2004.

Peters, R. S. (1966) *Ethics and Education.* London: Allen and Unwin.

Pfeiffer, S. I., Reddy, L. A., Kletzel, J. E. *et al.* (2000) The practitioners view of IQ testing and profile analysis. *School Psychology Quarterly* **15**: 376–385.

Piaget, J. and Inhelder, B. ([1966]/1969) *The Psychology of the Child* (translated from French by Helen Weaver). London: Routledge & Keegan Paul Ltd.

Piaget, J. (1970) Piaget's theory. In: Mussen, P. H. (Ed.) *Manual of Child Psychology,* London: Wiley.

Plomin, R. and McGuffin, P. (2003) Psychopathology in the post genomic era. *Annual Review of Psychology* **54**: 205–228.

Pollock, J., Waller, E. and Pollitt, R. (2004) (2nd edn) *Day-to-Day Dyslexia in the Classroom.* London: RoutledgeFalmer.

Popple, J. and Wellington, W. (2001) Working together: the psycholinguistic approach wthin a school setting. In: Stackhouse, J. and Wells, B. (Eds) *Children's Speech and Literacy Difficulties Book 2: Identification and Intervention,* 299–329. London: Wiley.

Power, D. and Leigh, G. (Eds) (2004) *Educating Deaf Students: Global Perspectives.* Washington, DC: Gallaudet University Press.

Prizant, B. M., Wetherby, A. M. and Rydell, P. J. (2000) Communication intervention issues for children with autism spectrum disorders. In: Prizant, B. M., Wetherby, A. M. (Eds) *Autism Spectrum Disorders: A Transactional Developmental Perspective,* 193–224. Baltimore, MD: Brookes.

Pryde, K. M. (2000) Sensorimotor functioning in developmental coordination disorder: A kinematic and psychometric analysis. Unpublished doctoral dissertation, University of Waterloo: Waterloo, Ontario, Canada.

Qualifications and Curriculum Authority (1999a) *Shared World – Different Experiences: Designing the Curriculum for Pupils who Are Deafblind*. London: QCA.

Qualifications and Curriculum Authority (1999b) *Qualifications and Curriculum Authority Review of the National Curriculum for England*. London: QCA, public consultation document.

Qualifications and Curriculum Authority (2001a) *Planning, Teaching and Assessing the Curriculum for Pupils with Learning Difficulties: English*. London: QCA.

Qualifications and Curriculum Authority (2001b) *Planning, Teaching and Assessing the Curriculum for Pupils with Learning Difficulties: Mathematics*. London: QCA.

Qualifications and Curriculum Authority (2001c) *Planning, Teaching and Assessing the Curriculum for Pupils with Learning Difficulties: Personal, Social and Health Education and Citizenship*. London: QCA.

Quinn, M. M., Kavale, K. A., Mathur, S. R. *et al.* (1999) A meta analysis of social skill interventions for students with emotional or behavioural disorders. *Journal of Emotional and Behavioural Disorders* 7: 54–64.

Rang, H. P., Dale, M. M., Ritter, J. M. and Flower, R. (2007) (6th edn) *Rang and Dales Pharmacology*. New York, London: Churchill Livingstone.

Rapoport, M. D., van Reekum, R. and Mayberg, H. (2000) The role of the cerebellum in cognition and behaviour. *Journal of Neuropsychiatry* 12: 193–198.

Rawls, J. (1971) *A Theory of Justice*. Cambridge, MA: Harvard University Press.

Reid, R. and Maag, J.W. (1998). Functional assessment: A method for developing classroom-based accommodations and interventions for children with ADHD. *Reading and Writing Quarterly* 14: 9–42.

Reinecke, M. A. and Freeman, A. (2003) Cognitive therapy. In: Gurman, A. S. and Messer, S. B. (Eds) *Essential Psychotherapies: Theory and Practice*. New York: Guilford Press.

Rice, M. L., Wexler, K. and Hershberger, S. (1998). Tense over time: The longitudinal course of tense acquisition in children with specific language impairment. *Journal of Speech, Language, and Hearing Research* 41: 1412–1431.

Riddle, M. A., Reeve, A. E., Yaryura-Tobias, J. A., Yang, H. M., Claghorn, J. L., Gaffney, G., Greist, J. H., Holland, D., McConville, B. J., Pigott, T. and Walkup, J. T. (2001). Fluvoxamine for children and adolescents with obsessive-compulsive disorder: A randomised, controlled, multicenter trail. *Journal of the American Academy of Child and Adolescent Psychiatry* 40: 222–229.

Rieber, R. W. and Carton, A. S. (Eds) ([various dates]/1993) *The Collected Works of L. S. Vygotsky Volume 2: The Fundamentals of Defectology (Abnormal Psychology and Learning Disabilities)* (translated from the Russian by J.E. Knox and C.B. Stevens). New York: Plenum Press.

Rinaldi, W. (2001) *Social Use of Language Programme*. Windsor: NFER-Nelson.

Rioux, M. and Bach, M. (Eds) (1994) *Disability is not Measles: New Research Paradigms in Disability*. New York: Roeher Institute.

Roy, E. A., Bottos, S., Pryde, K. and Dewey, D. (2004) Approaches to understanding the neurobehavioral mechanisms associated with motor impairment in children. In: Dewey, D. and Tupper, D. E. (Eds) *Developmental Disorders: A Neurological Perspective*. New York: Guilford Press.

Rourke, B. P. (2000) Neuropsychological and psychosocial subtyping: A review of investigations within the University of Windsor laboratory. *Canadian Psychology* **41**: 34–51.

Russell, B. ([1946]/1996) *History of Western Philosophy*. New York, London: Routledge.

Rutherford, R. B., Jr. and Nelson, C. M. (1982) Analysis of response contingent time-out literature with behaviourally disordered students in classroom settings. In: Rutherford, R.B., Jr. (Ed.) *Severe Behaviour Disorders of Children and Youth*, 5, 79–105. Reston, VA: Council for Children with Behavioural Disorders.

Rutherford, R. B. Jr. and Nelson, C. M. (1988) Generalisation and maintenance of treatment effects. In: Witt, J. C., Elliott, S. W. and Gresham, F. M. (Eds) *Handbook of Behaviour Therapy in Education*, 277–324. New York: Plenum Press.

Rutherford, R. B., Jr. and Polsgrove, L. J. (1981) Behavioural contracting with behaviourally disordered and delinquent children and youth: An analysis of the clinical and experimental literature. In: Rutherford, R. B. Jr., Prieto, A. G. and McGlothlin, J. E. (Eds) *Severe Behaviour Disorders of Children and Youth*, **4**, 49–69. Reston, VA: Council for Children with Behavioural Disorders.

Ryle, G. ([1949]/2000) *The Concept of Mind*. New York, London: Penguin Books.

Sacks, S. Z. and Wolffe, K. E (Eds) (2005) *Teaching Social Skills to Students with Visual Impairments: From Theory to Practice*. New York: American Foundation for the Blind Press.

Sage, R. and Sluckin, A. (2004) *Silent Children: Approaches to Selective Mutism*. Leicester: University of Leicester.

Sandler, A. D., Watson, T. E., Footo, M. *et al.* (1992) Neurodevelopmental study of writing disorders in middle childhood. *Journal of Developmental and Behavioural Paediatrics* **13**: 17–23.

Sapsted, D. (2004) TV is human right says tree row man. *The Daily Telegraph* 31 May 2004, News page 6, columns 6–7.

Sardegna, J., Shelly, S., Rutzen, A. R. and Steidl, S. M. (2002) (2nd edn) *The Encyclopaedia of Blindness and Vision Impairment*. New York: Facts on File Library of Health and Living.

Sarnat, H. B. and Flores-Sarnat, L. (2006) Human nervous system development and malformations. In Wyllie, E., Gupta, A. and Lachhwani, D. K. (Eds) *The Treatment of Epilepsy: Principles and Practice* (4th edn) 13–36. Philadelphia, PA: Lippincott Williams & Wilkins.

Savage, R. C. and Wolcott, G. (Eds.) (1995) *An educator's manual: What educators need to know about students with traumatic brain injury.* Washington, DC: Brain Injury Association.

Schaverien, J. (1995) Researching the esoteric: Art therapy research. In: Gilroy, A. and Lee, C. (Eds) *Art and Music Therapy Research.* London: Routledge.

Schoenbrodt, L. (Ed.) (2001) *Children with Traumatic Brain Injury: A Parent's Guide.* Bethesda, MD: Woodbine House.

Schopler, E. (1997) Implementation of TEACCH philosophy. In: Cohen, D. and Volkmar, F. (Eds) *Handbook of Autism and Pervasive Developmental Disorders* (2nd edn) 767–795. New York: Wiley.

Searle, J. R. (1969) *Speech Acts: An Essay on the Philosophy of Language.* Cambridge: Cambridge University Press.

Seifert, J., Scheuerpflug, P., Zillerssen, K. E. *et al.* (2003) Electrophysiological investigations of the effectiveness of methylphenidate in children with and without ADHD. *Journal of Neural Transmission* **110** (7): 821–828.

Sergent, J., Zuck, E., Lévesque, M. and MacDonald, B. (1992) Positron emission tomography study of letter and object processing: Empirical findings and methodological considerations. *Cerebral Cortex* **2**: 68–80.

Shakespeare, T. (2006) *Disability Rights and Wrongs.* London and New York: Routledge.

Shapleske, J., Russell, S. L. Woodruff, P. W. R. and David, A. S. (1999) The planum temporale: A systematic quantitative review of its structural, functional and clinical significance. *Brain Research* **29**: 26–49.

Shaywitz, B. A., Shaywitz, S. E., Pugh, K. R. *et al.* (2002) Disruption of posterior brain systems for reading in children with developmental dyslexia. *Biological Psychiatry* **52** (2): 101–110.

Shorter, E. (1997) *A History of Psychiatry: From the Era of the Asylum to the Age of Prozac.* New York: John Wiley & Sons.

Sigafoos, J., Arthur, M. and O'Reilly, M. (2003). *Challenging Behaviour and Developmental Disability.* London: Whurr Publishers.

Simpson, R. L. (2005) Evidence based practices and students with ASD. *Focus on Autism and Other Developmental Disabilities* **20** (3): 140–149.

Singer, J. (1999) Why can't you be normal for once in your life? From 'a problem with no name' to the emergence of a new category of difference. In: Corker, M. and French, S. (Eds) *Disability Discourse.* Buckingham: Open University Press.

Skinner, F. B. ([1953]/1965) *Science and Human Behaviour.* New York: The Free Press.

Skinner, B. F. (1957) *Verbal Behaviour.* New York: Appleton-Century-Crofts.

Skrtic, T. M. (1995a) The functionalist view of special education and disability: deconstructing the conventional knowledge tradition. In: Skrtic, T. M. (Ed.) *Disability and Democracy: Reconstructing (Special) Education for Post-Modernity.* New York: Teachers College Press.

Skrtic, T. M. (1995b) (Ed.) *Disability and Democracy: Reconstructing (Special) Education for Post-Modernity.* New York: Teachers College Press.

Slater, A. M., Morrison, V. and Rose, D. (1983) Perception of shape by the newborn baby. *British Journal of Developmental Psychology* **1**: 135–142.

Sleeter, C. E. (1995) Radical structural perspectives on the creation and use of learning disabilities. In: Skrtic, T. M. (Ed.) *Disability and Democracy: Reconstructing (Special) Education for Post-Modernity*. New York: Teachers College Press.

Smith, N. (1999) *Chomsky: Ideas and Ideals*. Cambridge: Cambridge University Press.

Smith, M. and Levack, N. (1997) *Teaching Students with Visual and Multiple Impairments: A Resource Guide*. Austin, TX: Texas School for the Blind and Visually Impaired. www.tsbvi.edu.

Snell, M. and Brown, F. (1997) (5th edn) *Instruction of Students with Severe Disabilities*. Upper Saddle River, NJ: Merill.

Soanes, C. and Stevenson, A. (Eds) (2003) (2nd edn) *Oxford Dictionary of English*. Oxford: Oxford University Press.

Stackhouse, J. (2001) Identifying children at risk for literacy problems. In: Stackhouse, J. and Wells, B. (Eds) *Children's Speech and Literacy Difficulties Book 2: Identification and Intervention*, 1–40. London: Wiley.

Stackhouse, J. and Wells, B. (1997) *Children's Speech and Literacy Difficulties Book 1: A Psycholinguistic Framework*. London: Wiley.

Stackhouse, J. and Wells, B. (Eds) (2001) *Children's Speech and Literacy Difficulties Book 2: Identification and Intervention*. London: Wiley.

Standring, S. (39th edn) (2005) *Grays Anatomy: The Anatomical Basis of Clinical Practice*. London: Elsevier Science, Churchill Livingstone.

Steinberg, A. G. and Knightly, C. A. (1997) Hearing: sounds and silences. In: Batshaw, M. L. (Ed.) *Children with Disabilities*. Sydney: Maclennan and Petty.

Stewart, D. A. and Kluwin, T. N. (2001) *Teaching Deaf and Hard of Hearing Students: Content, Strategies and Curriculum*. Boston, MA: Allyn and Bacon.

Stewart, E. and Ritter, K. (2001) Ethics of assessment. In: Beattie, R. G. (Ed.) *Ethics of Deaf Education*. San Diego, CA: Academic Press.

Strain, P. and Hoyson, M. (2000) The need for longitudinal, intensive social skill intervention: LEAP follow-up outcomes for children with autism. *Topics in Early Childhood Special Education* **20** (2): 116–122.

Strauss, C. C. and Last, C. G. (1993) Social and simple phobias in children. *Journal of Anxiety Disorders* **7**: 141–152.

Stright, A. D. and Supplee, L. H. (2002) Children's self-regulatory behaviours during teacher-directed, seat-work, and small-group instructional contexts. *Journal of Education Research* **95**: 235–245.

Swanson, H. L., Harris, K. R. and Graham, S. (Eds) (2003) *Handbook of Learning Disabilities*. New York: Guilford Press.

Swanson, J. M., Lerner, M. and Williams, L. (1995) More frequent diagnosis of ADHD. *New England Journal of Medicine* **333**: 944.

Talcott, J. B., Hansen, C., Willis-Owen, C. *et al.* (1998) Visual magnocellular impairment in adult developmental dyslexics. *Neuro-ophthalmology* **20**: 187–201.

Tallal, P. (2004) Improving language and literacy is a matter of time. *Nature Reviews Neuroscience* **5**: 721.

Tandon, N., Fox, P., Ingham, R. *et al.* (2000) TMS induced modulation of cerebral blood flow in stutters. www.apnet.com/www/journal/hbm2000/6161.html.

Tannock, R. (1998) ADHD: Advances in cognitive, neurobiological and genetic research. *Journal of Child Psychology and Psychiatry* **39** (1): 65–99.

Teasedale, G. and Jennet, B. (1974) Assessment of Coma and Impaired Consciousness: A Practical Scale. *Lancet* **2**: 81–84.

Tharp, R. (1993) Institutional and social context of educational practice and reform. In: Forman, A. E., Minick, N. and Stone, C. A. (Eds) *Contexts for Learning: Socio-Cultural Dynamics in Children's Development*. Oxford: Oxford University Press.

Thompson, N. (2001) (3rd edn) *Anti-Discriminatory Practice*. New York, Basingstoke UK: Palgrave.

Thorndyke, E. L. ([1911]/1965) *Animal Intelligence*. New York: Hafner Publishing.

Tomblin, J. B., Records, N., Buckwalter, P. *et al.* (1997) Prevalence of specific language impairment in Kindergarten children. *Journal of Speech, Language and Hearing Research* **40**: 1245–1260.

Tomlinson, S. (1995) The radical structuralist view of special education and disability: unpopular perspectives on their origins and development. In: Skrtic, T. M. (Ed.) *Disability and Democracy: Reconstructing (Special) Education for Post-modernity*. New York: Teachers College Press.

Thompson, G. (2003) *Supporting Children with Communication Disorders: A Handbook for Teachers and Teaching Assistants*. London: David Fulton Publishers.

Toren, P., Wolmer, L., Rosental, B. *et al.* (2000) Case series: Brief parent–child group therapy for childhood anxiety disorders using a manual based cognitive-behavioural technique. *Journal of the American Academy for Child and Adolescent Psychiatry* **39** (10): 1309–1312.

Traurig, H. H. (2003) The brain stem: An overview. In: Conn, P. M. (Ed.) *Neuroscience in Medicine* (2nd edn). Totowa, NJ: Humana Press.

Traxler, M. and Gernsbacher, M. A. (Eds) (2006) (2nd edn) *Handbook of Psycholinguistics*. San Diego, CA: Academic Press.

Turnbull, R., Turnbull, A., Shank, M. *et al.* (2002) (3rd edn) *Exceptional Lives: Special Education in Today's Schools*. Upper Saddle River, NJ: Merrill, Prentice Hall.

United States Department of Education (1999) Assistance to states for the education of children with disabilities program and the early intervention program for infants and toddlers with disabilities: Final regulations. *Federal Register* **64**: 48, CFR Parts 3000 and 303.

Vaidya, C. J., Austin, G., Kirkorian, G. *et al.* (1998) Selective effects of methylphenidate in attention deficit hyperactivity disorder: A functional magnetic resonance study. *Proceedings of the National Academy of Sciences USA* **95**: 14494–14499.

Valente, L. and Fontana, D. (1997) Assessing client progress in drama therapy. In: Jennings, S. (Ed.) *Dramatherapy: Theory and Practice, 3*. London: Routledge.

Vance, M. (1997) Christopher lumpship: developing phonological representations in a child with an auditory processing deficit. In: Chiat, S. W., Law, J. and Marshall, J. (Eds) *Language Disorders in Children and Adults*. London: Whurr Publishers.

Van der Lely, H. (1994) Canonical linking rules: Forward versus reverse thinking in normally developing and language impaired children. *Cognition* **51**: 29–72.

Vargha-Khadem, F., Gadian, D., Copp, A. and Mishkin, M. (2005) FOXP2 and the neuroanatomy of speech and language. *Nature Reviews Neuroscience* **6**: 131–138.

Vygotsky, L. S. ([original date unknown]/1993) The blind child. In: Rieber, R. W. and Carton, A. S. (Eds) *The Collected Works of L. S. Vygotsky Volume 2: The Fundamentals of Defectology (Abnormal Psychology and Learning Disabilities)* (translation by J.E. Knox and C.B. Stevens). New York: Plenum Press.

Vygotsky, L. S. ([1924]1993) The psychology and pedagogy of children's handicaps (originally published in *Questions of Education of the Blind, the Deaf-Mute and Mentally Retarded Children* edited by Vygotsky, 1929). In: Rieber, R. W. and Carton, A. S. (Eds) *The Collected Works of L. S. Vygotsky Volume 2: The Fundamentals of Defectology (Abnormal Psychology and Learning Disabilities)* (translation by J.E. Knox and C.B. Stevens). New York: Plenum Press.

Vygotsky, L. S. ([1925-1926]/1993) Principles of education for physically handicapped children (based on a report of the same title prepared for the Second Congress on the Social and Legal Protection of Minors, 1924). In: Rieber, R. W. and Carton, A. S. (Eds) *The Collected Works of L. S. Vygotsky Volume 2: The Fundamentals of Defectology (Abnormal Psychology and Learning Disabilities)* (translation by J.E. Knox and C.B. Stevens). New York: Plenum Press.

Vygotsky, L. S. ([1927]/1993) Defect and compensation (a version was published as 'Defect and Overcompensation' in *Retardation, Blindness and Deafness*, 1927). In: Rieber, R. W. and Carton, A. S. (Eds) *The Collected Works of L. S. Vygotsky Volume 2: The Fundamentals of Defectology (Abnormal Psychology and Learning Disabilities)* (translation by J.E. Knox and C.B. Stevens). New York: Plenum Press.

Vygotsky, L. S. ([1929]/1993) The Fundamental Problems of Defectology (Originally published in *Works of the Second Moscow University Volume 1*, Moscow, 1929). In: Rieber, R. W. and Carton, A. S. (Eds) *The Collected Works of L. S. Vygotsky Volume 2: The Fundamentals of Defectology (Abnormal Psychology and Learning Disabilities)* (translation by J.E. Knox and C.B. Stevens). New York: Plenum Press.

Vygotsky, L. S. ([1931]/1993) The collective as a factor in the development of the abnormal child (originally published in the journal *Questions of Defectology*, 1931, Nos. 1–2). In: Rieber R. W. and Carton A. S. (Eds) *The Collected Works of L. S. Vygotsky Volume 2: The Fundamentals of Defectology (Abnormal Psychology and Learning Disabilities)* (translation by J.E. Knox and C.B. Stevens). New York: Plenum Press.

Vygotsky, L. S. ([1934]/1962) *Thought and Language* (translated from Russian and edited by E Hanfmann and G Vakar, Massachusetts Institute of Technology). Cambridge, MA: MIT Press.

Vygotsky, L. S. ([1934]/1984) *Thought and Language* (translated from Russian and edited by A. Kozulin, Massachusetts Institute of Technology). Cambridge, MA: MIT Press.

Vygotsky, L. S. ([various dates]/1978) *Mind in Society: The Development of Higher Psychological Processes*. In: Cole, M., John-Steiner, V., Scribner, S. *et al.* (Eds) Cambridge, MA: Harvard University Press.

Walker, H. M. (1983) Application of response cost in school settings: Outcomes, issues and recommendations. *Exceptional Children Quarterly* 3 (4): 46–55.

Walker, J. A. and Crawley, S. B. (1983) Conceptual and methodological issues in studying the handicapped infant. In: Gray Garwood, S. and Fewell, R. R. (Eds) *Educating Handicapped Infants: Issues in development and Intervention*. Rockville, MD: Aspen Systems Corporation.

Walker, S. and Wicks, B. (2005) *Educating Children with Acquired Brain Injury*. London: David Fulton Publishers.

Ware, J. (2003) *Creating a Responsive Environment for People with Profound and Multiple Learning Difficulties*. London: David Fulton Publishers.

Ware, J. (2005) Profound and multiple learning difficulties. In: Lewis, A. and Norwich, B. (Eds) *Special Teaching for Special Children? Pedagogies for Inclusion*. Maidenhead: Open University Press.

Warnock, M. (2005) *Special Educational Needs: A New Look*. Impact No. 11 London: The Philosophy of Education Society of Great Britain.

Warnock, M. (2006) Preface. In: Farrell, M. *Celebrating the Special School*. London: David Fulton Publishers.

Watson, J. B. and Morgan, J. J. B. (1917) Emotional reactions and psychological experimentation. *American Journal of Psychology* 28: 163–174.

Watson, J. B. and Rayner, R. (1920) Conditioned emotional reactions. *Journal of Experimental Psychology* 3 (1): 1–14.

Weyandt, L. L. (2007) (2nd edn) *An ADHD Primer*. New York: Taylor & Francis.

Weber, M. (1972) Selections on education and politics. In: Cosin, B. (Ed.) *Education Structure and Society*. Harmondsworth: Penguin Books.

Webster-Stratton, C., and Reid, M. J. (2003) The Incredible Years Parents, Teachers and Children Training Series. In: Kazdin, A. E. and Weisz, J. R. (Eds.) *Evidence Based Psychotherapies for Children and Adolescents*, 224–240. New York: Guilford Press.

Wechsler, D. (2003) (4th edn) *Wechsler Intelligence Scale for Children*. San Antonio, TX: Psychological Corporation.

Weinberger, S. E. (1993) Recent advances in pulmonary medicine. *The New England Journal of Medicine* 328: 1389–1397.

Weismer, G. (2006) Speech disorders. In: Traxler, M. and Gernsbacher, M. A. (Eds) *Handbook of Psycholinguistics* (2nd edn) 93–124. San Diego, CA: Academic Press.

Weisz, J. R., Southam-Gerow, M. A., Gordis, E. B. and Connor-Smith, J. (2003) Primary and secondary control enhancement training for youth depression: Applying the deployment-focused model of treatment development and testing. In: Kazdin, A. E. and Weisz, T. R. (Eds) *Evidence Based Psychotherapies for Children and Adolescents*, 165–183. New York: Guilford Press.

Wells, G. (1985) *Language Development in the Preschool Years*. Cambridge: Cambridge University Press.

Wells, B. and Peppé, S. (2001) Intonation within a psycholinguistic framework. In: Stackhouse, J. and Wells, B. (Eds) *Children's Speech and Literacy Difficulties Book 2: Identification and Intervention*, 366–395. London: Wiley.

Wendell, S. (1996) *The Rejected Body: Feminist Philosophical Reflections on Disability*. New York: Routledge.

Wertsch, J. V. (1985) *Vygotsky and the Social Formation of Mind*. Cambridge, MA: Harvard University Press.

Westbrook, G. L. (2000) Seizures and epilepsy. In: Kandel, E. R., Schwartz, J. H. and Jessell, T. M. (Eds) *Principles of Neural Science* (4th edn), 910–935. New York: McGraw-Hill.

Westbury, C. (1998) Research strategies (psychological and psycholinguistic methods in neurolinguistics). In: Stemmer, B. and Whitaker, H. (Eds) *Handbook of Neurolinguistics*, 83–93. San Diego, CA: Academic Press.

Westermann, G., Mareschal, D., Johnson, M. H. *et al.* (2007) Neuroconstructivism. *Developmental Science* **10** (1): 75–83.

Westwood, P. (2000) *Numeracy and Learning Difficulties: Approaches to Teaching and Assessment*. London: David Fulton Publishers.

Westwood, P. (2003) (4th edn) *Commonsense Methods for Children with Special Educational Needs: Strategies for the Regular Classroom*. London: RoutledgeFalmer.

Whitaker, S. (1996) A review of DRO: The influence of the degree of intellectual disability and the frequency of the target behaviour. *Journal of Applied Research in Intellectual Disabilities* **9**: 61–79.

Whitney, P. (1998) *The Psychology of Language*. Boston, MA: Houghton Mifflin.

Winnicott, D. W. (1964) *The Maturational Process and the Facilitating Environment*. London: Hogarth Press.

Wilson, J. and Frederickson, N. (1995) Phonological awareness training: An evaluation. *Educational and Child Psychology* **12** (1): 68–79.

Wilson, B. M. and Proctor, A. (2000) Oral and written discourse in adolescents with closed head injury. *Brain and Cognition* **43**: 425–429.

Wilson, P. H. and McKenzie, B. E. (1998) Information processing deficits associated with developmental coordination disorder: A meta-analysis of research findings. *Journal of Child Psychology and Allied Disciplines* **39**: 829–840.

Wilson, P. (2005) Visuospatial, kinaesthetic, visuomotor integration, and visuoconstructional disorders: Implications for motor development. In: Dewey, D. and Tupper, D. E. (Eds) *Developmental Disorders: A Neurological Perspective*. New York: Guilford Press.

Wing, L. and Gould, J. (1979) Severe impairments of social interaction and assorted abnormalities in children: Epidemiology and classification. *Journal of Autism and Childhood Schizophrenia* **9**: 11–29.

Winnicott, D. W. (1958) *Through Paediatrics to Psychoanalysis*. London: Hogarth Press.

Winnicott, D. W. (1965) *The Maturational Process and the Facilitating Environment*. London: Hogarth Press.

Witelson, S. F. and Kigar, D. L. (1992) Sylvian fissure morphology and asymmetry in men and women: Bilateral difference in relation to handedness. *Journal of Comparative Neurology* **323**: 326–340.

Wittgenstein, L. (1918/1974) *Tractatus Logico-Philosophicus* (translation by D.F. Pears and B.F. McGuinness). New York: Routledge and Keegan Paul.

Wolf, M. (Ed.) (2001) *Dyslexia, Fluency, and the Brain*. Timonium, MD: York Press.

Wood, D. (1998) (2nd edn) *How Children Think and Learn*. Oxford: Blackwell Publishing.

Wong, B. Y. L. (1991) On cognitive process-based instruction: An introduction. *Journal of Learning Disabilities* **25**: 150–152, 172.

Woodward, J. and Ferretti, R. (2007) New machines and new agendas: The changing nature of special education technology research. In: Florian, L. (Ed.) *The Sage Handbook of Special Education*. London, Thousand Oaks, CA: Sage Publications.

Woolfenden, S. R., Williams, K. and Peat, J. K. (2003) Family and parenting interventions in children and adolescents with conduct disorder and delinquency aged 10–17, Cochrane review. In: *The Cochrane Library, 4*. Chichester: Wiley.

Wyllie, E., Gupta, A. and Lachhwani, D. K. (Eds) (4th edn) *The Treatment of Epilepsy: Principles and Practice*. Philadelphia, PA: Lippincott Williams & Wilkins.

Yeates, K. O., Ris, M. D. and Taylor, H. G. (2000) *Paediatric Neuropsychology: Research, Theory, and Practice*. New York: Guilford Press.

Ysseldyke, J. and Algozzine, B. (2006a) *The Legal Foundations of Special Education: A Practical Guide for Every Teacher*. Thousand Oaks, CA: Corwin Press.

Ysseldyke, J. and Algozzine, B. (2006b) *Public Policy, School Reform and Special Education: A Practical Guide for Every Teacher*. Thousand Oaks, CA: Corwin Press.

Zago, L., Presenti, M., Mellet, E. *et al.* (2001) Neural correlates of simple and complex mental calculation. *Neuroimage* **13**: 314–327.

Zeki, S. (1992) The visual image in mind and brain. *Scientific American* **267** (3): 69–76.

Index

ability training, 238–239
absence seizures, 91
academic achievement, 7, 35
accommodation, 172
adaptive behaviour, 140
adhocracy, of special education, 62
aetiology, 83
age-inappropriate telegraphic utterances, 31
aggressive behaviour, 90, 96
amputations, 26
amygdala, 112
anatomy, 82
Anger Coping Program, 244
anti-psychotic drugs, 89
anti-social personality disorder, 28
anxiety disorders, 28–29, 244
    cognitive-behavioural therapy, 144–145
Applied Behaviour Analysis model, 165
apraxia, 120
'a priori notion,' 71
Armstrong's study on learning difficulties, 68
articulatory buffer, 196
art software, 214
art therapy, 136–137
Asperger's syndrome, 33
assimilation, 172, 185
asthma, 26, 83, 89
    therapy, 84
astigmatism, 25
attentional processes, 155

attention deficit hyperactivity disorder (ADHD), 9, 26, 28–30, 40, 86, 110–111, 113, 161–162, 244
    classification of, 95
    diagnostic criteria, 95
    as a distinctive condition, 95
    use of medication for, 96–97
    validity and the credibility of, 95
attention/executive functions, 109
auditory sequential memory, 31
augmentative communication, 253
autism, 33, 67–68, 71–72, 112–113, 242
    observational learning and modelling, 164–167
autistic spectrum disorder, 246
automaticity, of ICT, 216
aversive stimulus, 152
axons, 104

barriers, notion of, 43–44
Bayley framework, 171
behavioural learning
    and ABC record, 157
    evaluation, 153–154
    Pavlov's classical conditioning, 150
    scope, 159–162
    Skinner's operant conditioning, 151–153
    Thorndyke's learning by trial and accidental success, 149–150
    Watson's conditioned emotional responses, 150–151

behaviour environment plan (BEP), 133–134
behaviour therapy, 238–239
biological impairment, 69
biological reductionism, 70
blindness, 24–25
body–mind dualism, 45
bone tuberculosis, 26
brain, 193–194
brittle bone syndrome, 88

cancer treatment, 84
cataract, 25
category mistakes, 45
cerebellum, 112, 116–117
cerebral hemispheres, 103–105
cerebral lobes, 103–105
cerebral palsy, 26
child cognitive development
    developmental milestones, 169–171
    fuller examples
        sensorimotor period and profound cognitive impairment, 178–188
    Piaget's theory, 171–174
        scope, 177–178
    relevance in special education, 174–176
    scope, 176–178
childhood absence epilepsy, 92
child's attachment, to the mother, 136
child–therapist relationships, 144
classroom organization, defined, 5
club foot, 26
clumsy child syndrome, 34
cochlear implants, 74
Code of Federal Regulations (CFR), 26, 75
cognitive access, to technology, 219
cognitive-behavioural interventions, 129, 140
cognitive-behavioural therapy (CBT), 112, 238, 240, 245

cognitive hypothesis-testing model, 121–123
cognitive impairment, 70–71
    mild, 23, 241, 248–251
    moderate to severe, 22–23, 241, 251–255
    profound, 21–22, 67, 243
        and sensorimotor period, 183–188
    and technology, 224–225
cognitive/neuronal architecture, 195
cognitive skills training, 238
cognitive structuring, 238
cognitive therapy, 138, 140–141
Commission on Classification and Terminology of the International League Against Epilepsy, 92
communicative disorder, 241, 245–246
community paediatrics, 84–85
compensation, of technology, 221
compensatory development, 175
conditioned emotional responses, 150–151
conditioned reflex factors, 150
conditioned reinforcers, 152
conditioned response, 150
conduct disorder, 27, 174
    cognitive-behavioural therapy, 143–144
    observational learning and modelling, 162–164
congenital anomaly, 26, 115
congenital heart disease, 83, 87–88
connections, 194
connotation, of a word, 41
consequence, 165
contextual knowledge, 87
contingency management, 237
cooperative learning, 239
Coping Power strategies, 244
corpus callosum, 103, 116
corresponding epilepsy syndromes, 92
cortical visual impairment, 25
counselling therapy, 239

critical thinking, 238–239
cultural learning, 171
cultural reductionism, 69–70
curriculum, defined, 4
cylindrical correction, 25
cystic fibrosis, 83

daily living activities, 35
deafblindness, 25–26, 87, 241
defectology, 61
delayed development, 175
developmental cognitive neurolinguistic
    framework, 192
developmental coordination disorder
    (DCD), 34, 67, 246
  deficit with, 118
  different causal levels, 117–119
  importance of motor and of non-motor
      factors in the aetiology of, 117–
      118
  role of cerebellum, 117
developmental delays, 34
Dewey's philosophy, of education,
    62
diabetes, 26
diabetes mellitus, 83
diagnosis, 83
differential reinforcement, 153–154
diffuse brain damage, 27
digit span, 114
direct instruction, 238
disability/disorder, types of, 3–4
discrete trial training/training (DTT),
    164, 246
discrimination, concept of
  equality of opportunity and a rights
      view of social justice, 50–51
  equality of opportunity and justice as
      fairness, 49–50
  top-down and bottom-up views of,
      51–52
  as treating people with undeserved
      contempt, 53

disruptive behaviour disorders, 27–28,
    67, 244
Division Treatment and Education of
    Autistic and related Communication
    handicapped Children (TEACCH),
    236
dominant hemisphere, 104
Down's syndrome, 83, 241
drama therapy, 136–137
DSM-IV-TR, 27–30, 33–35,
    208
Duchenne muscular dystrophy,
    84
'dyscalculia,' 36
dyslexia, 35, 115, 241
dyspraxia, 118, 202
dysthymic disorder, 29

economic reductionism, 70
education
  defined, 2
  implied change, 2
  'morally acceptable manner' element
      of, 2
  'worthwhile' in, 2
Education Act 1981, England,
    17–18
Education Act 1993, England, 18
Education for All Handicapped Children
    Act 1975, 15–16
elective mutism, 159
electroclinical syndromes, 92
electroencephalography (EEG), 92,
    106–107
elicited imitation strategy, 160
emotional security, 136
endophenotypes, 111
epilepsy, 9, 26
  causal factors, 91
  classifications, 91–93
  defined, 90
  with generalized tonic-clonic seizures
      on awakening, 92

epilepsy (*cont'd*)
  implications of classification for
      educators and others, 93–94
  reflex, 92
evidence-based practice, 242
exclusion, 42
expressive–receptive language disorder,
  31
extinction, 152

fairness, concept of, 42–43
feedback, 237
focal psychodynamic psychotherapy,
  136
foetal alcohol syndrome, 120
formal operations stage, 173–174
Foucault's philosophy, of education,
  62
foundations, of special education, 6–7
fractures, 26
frontal lobe, 103
functional family therapy, 130–131
functional limitations, 60
functional magnetic resonance imaging
  (fMRI), 107, 115
functional near-infrared spectroscopy
  (fNIRS), 107–108

Gang Resistance Education Training
  (GREAT), 244
gating, 197
general difference position, 6, 240–241
generalized anxiety disorders, 29
generalized reinforcement, 153
generalized seizure, 91
Gerstmann syndrome, 121
Glasgow Coma Scale, 98
goal-directed needs, 46–47
grammatical coding tasks, 193, 203–
  204
grammatical difficulties, 31–32
group difference position, 6

haemophilia, 26
haemophilia A, 84, 88
head injury, penetrating, 27
health care plan, 85
health impairments, 26, 247–248
  and technology, 225
hearing impairment, 26, 89
  categories, 24
  categorizations, 73
  and technology, 225–226
  in terms of frequency, 24
heart condition, 26
hereditary deafness, 73
hyperactivity, 30, 93
hypermetropia, 25

impulsivity, 30, 93
inattention, 30
inclusion, 41–42
Incredible Years Training Series,
  163
Individuals with Disabilities Education
  Act 1990, 16–17, 26, 220
inference and implication, 33
information and communications
  technology (ICT), 213. *see also*
  technology
  automaticity, 216
  capacity and range of, 216
  interactivity of, 217
  provisionality, 216
  sociability of, 217
injuries, causing TBI, 27
input processing, 199
instructing, 237
interactivity, of ICT, 217
interference, 197
International Classification of Epileptic
  Seizures (ICES), 91–92
*International Convention on the Rights of
  Persons with Disabilities,*
  55

International League Against Epilepsy Task Force on Classification and Terminology, 92
Internet, the, 214
intervention tasks, 200–201
intonation, 202

'justice as fairness' theory, 49
juvenile absence epilepsy, 92

labelling difficulty, 32
language, 193
  deficits, 35
  impairment, 241
law of effect, 149
lead poisoning, 26
learning difficulties, 241
  severe, 22
Learning Experiences–An Alternative Program for Pre-schoolers and Parents (LEAP), 65, 164–166
learning strategies, 239
left-handed people, 105
legal framework, of special education considerations in structure of
    identification and assessment, 19
  economic influences, 14
  England
    classifications, 18–19
    Education Act 1981, 17–18
    Education Act 1993, 18
    main legislation, 17
    Special Educational Needs and Disability Act 2001 (SENDA), 18–19
  political factors, 14
  social values and attitudes, 13–14
  terminology used, 20–21
  US laws
    designated disability codes, 20

Education for All Handicapped Children Act 1975, 15–16
  Individuals with Disabilities Education Act 1990, 16–17
  main legislation, 15
  No Child Left Behind Act 2001 and developments, 17
Lennox–Gastaut syndrome, 94
leukaemia, 26
lexical cohesion, 114
lexical representations, 198–200
limbic system, 112
limb straightening and lengthening, 86
linguistic categorization deficit, 30
linguistics, 192–193
logical development, 174
long-term memory, 195
Lovaas programme, 164

magical-phenominalist perception, of casuality, 187–188
mainstreaming, 42
mainstream schools, 68
major depressive disorder, 29, 111–112, 244
  cognitive-behavioural therapy, 145–146
  marital therapies, 128
Martha's Vineyard Sign Language, 73–74
mathematics disorder, 35–36, 40, 247
  and associated cognitive skills, 119–120
  co-occurrence of reading disorders, 119
  left and right cerebral hemisphere location, 120
  neural systems, 121
  number–symbol association and poor automaticity of mathematical facts, 119
  parietal areas, 120–121
  and technology, 226–227
  types of, 119–120
'medical model,' in special education, 60

medical perspectives and children with
disorders/disabilities
considerations relating to medical
approaches, 85–86
fuller examples and applications
ADHD, 94–97
epilepsy, 90–94
traumatic brain injury (TBI),
97–100
related professions, 85
relevance to special education,
81–89
scope, 89–90
mental-conduct concepts, 45
mental lexicon, 195
mental representations, 195
mental retardation
diagnostic criteria for, 22
moderate, 22
severe, 22
methylphenidate, 84, 86, 96, 161
milestones, 171
modelling, 237
morphology, 32, 192
mother's holding environment, 135
motivational processes, 156
motor impairment and technology,
229–231
motor planning, 200
motor program, 200
movement therapy, 136
multimedia CD-ROMs, 214, 216
multisensory deprivation, 26
multi-systemic therapy, 129
music therapy, 136
myelin sheath, 104
myoclonic seizures, 91
myopia, 25

needs, concept of
goal-directed, 46–47
lack of clarity of, 49
meeting of, 48

overidentification of supposed special
educational, 49
unconditional, 47–48
vs want, 45–46
negative connotation, 42
negative labelling, 67
nephritis, 26
neural imaging techniques
considerations, 108
electroencephalography, 106–107
functional magnetic resonance imaging
(fMRI), 107
functional near-infrared spectroscopy
(fNRIS), 107–108
neuroanatomy, 106
neuromotor impairment, 26
neurons, 104
Neuro Psycholgical assessment, 109–108,
122
neuropsychology, 105
assessment, 108–109
constraints, 110
fuller examples and applications
cognitive hypothesis-testing model,
121–123
developmental coordination
disorder (DCD), 117–119
mathematics disorder, 119–121
reading disorder and related deficits,
114–116
and psycholinguistics, 193
reading disorder and related deficits,
114–116
relevance in special education,
110–111
scope and types, 111–114
night blindness, 25
No Child Left Behind Act 2002, 9, 17,
242
nystagmus, 25

object permanence, 187
object relations theory, 135

observational learning and modelling
constituent processes of
attentional, 155
motivational, 156
production, 155–156
retention, 155
fuller examples
autism, 164–167
conduct disorder, 162–164
relevance in special education, 157–159
scope, 159–162
social learning theory and social
cognitive theory, 154–155
evaluation, 156
within social cognitive theory, 155–156
obsessive-compulsive behaviours, 90
obsessive-compulsive disorder, 29
occipital lobe, 104
occupational therapists, 85, 89
operant conditioning, 151–153
operational stages, 173
oppositional defiant disorder (ODD),
27
optodes, 107
oral reading, 34
Oregon Social Learning Center Program,
163
organizational flexibility, 88
orthopaedic impairment, 26, 89,
247
removing barriers
and aspects of the curriculum, 75
mobility and physical access issues,
76
organization of the school and the
classroom, 77
role of APE teacher, 75
therapy and care, 77
use of resources, 76
use of technology, 229–231
osteogenesis imperfecta, 88
output, of speech production, 196
output processing, 200

packaging and network building,
difficulty in, 32
paediatrics, 81–82
parietal lobe, 104, 120
partial seizure, 91–92
pathology, 82
Pavlov's classical conditioning, 150
pedagogy
defined, 4–5
examples, 237–239
fuller examples and applications
mild cognitive impairment, 248–251
moderate and severe cognitive
impairment, 251–255
nature of, 235–236
relevance in special education,
239–242
scope, 243–248
peer directed learning, 239
perceptual motor deficits, 35
perceptual reasoning, 108
peripheral auditory processing, 199
persisting speech difficulties (PSD)
case studies, 206–207
connected speech, 206
consonant clusters in single words, 205
segments in single words, 204–205
pervasive memory, 32
pharmacokinetics, 82
pharmacology, 82
phobias, 29, 160
phonemic code, 8
phonetic discrimination, 199
phonological awareness, 114, 193
phonological disorders, 30, 114
phonological memory, 114
phonological recognition, 199
photophobia, 89
physiology, 82
Piaget's theory, 171–174
scope, 177–178
pivotal response training, 165
planum, 106

play therapy, 137
poliomyelitis, 26
positive reinforcement, 152
positron emission tomography (PET),
    108, 116
post-traumatic amnesia, 98
pragmatic difficulties, 33
pragmatics, 193
precision teaching, 238–239
pre-operational stage, 173
presentation, 164
prevalence, 83
'Primary and Secondary Control
    Enhancement Training for youth
    depression' programme, 145
primary control, 145
priming, 197
principle of justice in acquisition, 51
problem-solving skills training (PSST),
    141, 163, 244
processing speed, 109
production processes, 155–156
profound cognitive impairment
    defined, 21
    description of pupils, 21–22
    diagnostic criteria, 21
    intelligence quotient (IQ), 21
    and mental retardation, 21
prognosis, 84
proprioception, 118–119
Prosodic Systems–Children (PEPS-C),
    203
provision, elements of, 4–5
provisionality, of ICT, 216
psychodynamic psychotherapy, 134
psycholinguistics
    aspects, 191–194
    definitions, 194–196
    fuller examples
        persisting speech difficulties,
            204–207
        speech language impairment,
            207–209

multidisciplinary nature of, 191–192
relevance in special education,
    198–202
research techniques in, 196–197
scope, 202–204
psychological constructivism, 139
psychostimulant drugs, 96–97
psychotherapy
    approaches
        cognitive-behavioural perspective,
            138–142
        psychodynamic perspectives,
            134–138
        system, 130–134
    essential, 128
    Freud's clinical work, 134
    fuller examples
        anxiety disorders, 144–145
        depressive disorders, 145–146
        disorders of conduct, 143–144
    Klein's clinical work, 134–135
    relevance in special education, 127–129
    Winnicott's theory, 135
punishment, 152

questioning, 237

Rancho Los Amigos Cognitive Scales,
    99
rational beliefs, 140
rational-emotive behavioural therapy,
    138, 140
'readiness,' idea of, 170
reading achievement, 34
reading disorders, 8, 34–35, 247
    co-occurrence with mathematical
        disorders, 119
    and technology, 226
remediation, 221
repetition tasks, 186–187, 197
resources, defined, 5
response, 165
    time, 196–197

retention processes, 155
retinitis pigmentosa, 25
rheumatic fever, 26
rhyme analogy strategies, 114
rights, concept of
    nature of, 53–54
    and special education, 54–56
role-play sessions, 161
routines, 186–187

school neuropsychologist, 105
school organization, defined, 5
school refusal, 160
Scottish Prison Officers Association, 56
secondary control, 146
segregation, 42
seizures, 9
self-talk, 142
semantic difficulties, 32, 203
semantics, 192–193
sensorimotor areas, impairment in, 23
sensorimotor cognition, 174
sensorimotor coordination, 186
sensori-motor functions, 109
sensorimotor intelligence, 181
sensorimotor period
    nature of, 179
    object, space, time and causality,
        181–182
    stages, 179–181
    symbolic function, 182–183
sensorimotor stage, 173
sensory impairment, 243
serotonin systems, 112
shaping behaviour, 151
shared understanding, of the context,
    33
short-sightedness, 25
short-term memory, 31
sickle cell anaemia, 26
Skinner's operant conditioning, 151–153
Skrtic's view, of special education, 62–63
sociability, of ICT, 217

sociable behaviour, 152
social cognitive theory, 154–155
    evaluation, 156
Social Foundations of Thought and Action
    (Bandura), 154
social learning theory, 154–155
    evaluation, 156
socially constructed phenomenon, 72
socially engendered psychoemotional
    problems, 69
social phobia, 29, 160
social view, of disability
    considerations in, 68–70
    debates on the positioning of
        individual factors and
        social/cultural factors, 60–62
    fuller examples and applications,
        72–73
    individual perspectives, 60
    optimistic structural-functionalist
        view, 63
    orthopaedic impairment, 75–77
    scope, 70–72
    social constructionist perspectives,
        64
    social creationist perspective, 64
    and special education, 65–67
    structural-functionalist view, 63
    understanding and responding to
        hearing impairment, 73–74
sound frequency, 24
sound–symbol correspondences, 8
speaker's intention, 33
special education
    aims, 8
    foundational areas, 260–264
        interrelationships between, 268–269
    implications, 264–267
    methods, 8–10
    progress and development, 259
    traditional special needs categories, 6
    United States Department of Education
        definition, 1

Special Educational Needs and Disability
   Act 2001, UK, 52
special educators, 87
specialist resources, 88
specific language impairment (SLI)
   expressive difficulties and receptive
      difficulties, 207–208
   extended optional infinitive account,
      208–209
   inconsistency in producing tense and
      agreement morphemes, 208
   processing limitations, 209
specific phobia, 29, 160
speech and language therapy, 5, 54
speech comprehension, 104
speech impairment, 241
   and technology, 231–232
speech/non-speech discrimination,
   199
speech sounds, 24
spreadsheets, 214
stage-related theory of cognitive,
   172–174
stuttering/stammering, 30–31
survival mechanism, 172
Sylvian fissure, 116
syntax, 192

talking mats, 253
task structuring, 238
Teaching Family Model, 162
technology
   aids, 214
   benefits to learner
      access, 218–220
      curriculum requirements, 217–218
      qualities, 216–217
   fuller examples and applications
      motor impairment, 229–231
      orthopaedic impairment, 229–231
      speech impairment, 231–232
      visual impairment, 227–229
   range of applications of, 222–227

relevance to special education,
   220–222
remediation and compensation, 221
use of, 213–215
temporal lobe, 104
terminology
   concept of discrimination
      equality of opportunity and a rights
         view of social justice, 50–51
      equality of opportunity and justice
         as fairness, 49–50
      top-down and bottom-up views of,
         51–52
      as treating people with undeserved
         contempt, 53
   concept of 'need'
      goal-directed, 46–47
      lack of clarity of, 49
      meeting of, 48
      overidentification of supposed
         special educational, 49
      unconditional, 47–48
      vs want, 45–46
   concept of rights
      nature of, 53–54
      and special education, 54–56
   definitions, 39–40
   related to special education, 40–41
   scope of
      conceptual analysis, 44–45
      connotation, 41–42
      underextended and overextended
         terms, 42–44
textured mat, 253
theory of attachment, 135–136
theory of mind, 112
Thorndyke's learning by trial and
   accidental success, 149–150
token economies, 153
tonic-clonic seizures, 91, 93
Tractatus Logico-Philosophicus
   (Wittgenstein), 44
traumatic brain injury (TBI), 27, 72, 248

assessments of the location and severity
    of, 98–99
causes, 97
medical information and, 97–98
rehabilitation, 99–100
and technology, 225
treatment, 84
tunnel vision, 25

ultra minimal state, 50
unconditional needs, 47–48
unique difference position, 6, 240–241
United States Individuals with
    Disabilities Education Act, 75

verbal comprehension, 108
visual impairment, 24–26, 70
    physical aids for, 70
    use of technology, 227–229
visuospatial processing, 109

Vygotsky's theory of learning, 171, 237
Vygotsky's view of psychology, 60–62
    neo-Vygotskian approaches, to child
        development, 61

wants, concept of, 45–46
Watson's conditioned emotional
    responses, 150–151
Wechsler Intelligence Scale for Children
    (WISC-IV), 108, 122
whole word recognition strategies, 114
word-finding difficulty, 203
word processing, 214
word reading disorders, 114
working memory, 109, 195
written expression, 113
    disorder of, 247

zone of proximal development (ZPD),
    237